THE NEW LABOUR CONSTITUTION

The New Labour government first elected in 1997 had a defining influence on the development of the modern UK constitution. This book combines legal and political perspectives to provide a unique assessment of the way in which this major programme of constitutional reform has changed the nature of the UK constitution. The chapters, written by leading experts in UK public law and politics, analyse the impact and legacy of the New Labour reform programme some twenty years on from the 1997 general election, and reveal the ways in which the UK constitution is now, to a significant extent, the 'New Labour constitution'.

The book takes a broad approach to exploring the legacy of the New Labour years for the UK constitution. The contributors evaluate a range of specific substantive reforms (including on human rights, devolution, freedom of information, and the judicial system), changes to the process and method of constitutional reform under New Labour, the impact on key institutions (such as the judiciary and Parliament), and a number of wider constitutional themes (including national security, administrative justice, and the relationship between the Labour Party and constitutionalism). The book also reflects on the future challenges for the constitution constructed by New Labour, and the prospects for further constitutional reform.

In bringing together this range of perspectives to reflect on the implications of the New Labour era of reform, this book offers a critical examination of a foundational period in the development of the contemporary UK constitution.

Volume 10 in the series Hart Studies in Constitutional Law

Hart Studies in Constitutional Law

Volume 1 The House of Lords 1911–2011: A Century of Non-Reform
Chris Ballinger

Volume 2 Parliament and the Law
Edited by Alexander Horne, Gavin Drewry and Dawn Oliver

Volume 3 Law in Politics, Politics in Law
Edited by David Feldman

Volume 4 Parliamentary Sovereignty in the UK Constitution
Michael Gordon

Volume 5 Parliament: Legislation and Accountability
Edited by Alexander Horne and Andrew Le Sueur

Volume 6 The Codes of the Constitution
Andrew Blick

Volume 7 Essays on the History of Parliamentary Procedure: In Honour of Thomas Erskine May
Edited by Paul Evans

Volume 8 Parliament and the Law
Edited by Alexander Horne and Gavin Drewry

Volume 9 Stretching the Constitution
Andrew Blick

Volume 10 The New Labour Constitution: Twenty Years On
Edited by Michael Gordon and Adam Tucker

The New Labour Constitution

Twenty Years On

Edited by
Michael Gordon
and
Adam Tucker

•HART•
OXFORD • LONDON • NEW YORK • NEW DELHI • SYDNEY

HART PUBLISHING

Bloomsbury Publishing Plc

Kemp House, Chawley Park, Cumnor Hill, Oxford, OX2 9PH, UK

1385 Broadway, New York, NY 10018, USA

29 Earlsfort Terrace, Dublin 2, Ireland

HART PUBLISHING, the Hart/Stag logo, BLOOMSBURY and the Diana logo are trademarks of Bloomsbury Publishing Plc

First published in Great Britain 2022

A catalogue record for this book is available from the British Library.

Library of Congress Cataloging-in-Publication Data

Names: Twenty Years On: Assessing the State and Legacy of New Labour's Constitution (Conference) (2017 : University of Liverpool) | Gordon, Michael (Michael J.), editor. | Tucker, Adam (Law teacher) editor.

Title: The New Labour Constitution : twenty years on / edited by Michael Gordon and Adam Tucker.

Description: Oxford ; New York : Hart, 2022. | Series: Hart studies in Constitutional Law ; volume 10 | Includes bibliographical references and index.

Identifiers: LCCN 2021053522 (print) | LCCN 2021053523 (ebook) | ISBN 9781509924646 (hardback) | ISBN 9781509957255 (paperback) | ISBN 9781509924660 (pdf) | ISBN 9781509924653 (Epub)

Subjects: LCSH: Constitutional law—Great Britain—Congresses. | Law reform—Great Britain—Congresses. | Labour Party (Great Britain)—Congresses. | Great Britain—Politics and government—1997–2007—Congresses.

Classification: LCC KD3989.A2 T84 2017 (print) | LCC KD3989.A2 (ebook) | DDC 342.41—dc23/eng/20211220

LC record available at https://lccn.loc.gov/2021053522

LC ebook record available at https://lccn.loc.gov/2021053523

Library of Congress Control Number: 2021053522

ISBN: HB: 978-1-50992-464-6
ePDF: 978-1-50992-466-0
ePub: 978-1-50992-465-3

Typeset by Compuscript Ltd, Shannon

Acknowledgements

THIS BOOK IS the result of a conference, 'Twenty Years On: Assessing the State and Legacy of New Labour's Constitution', held at the University of Liverpool in July 2017. We are very grateful to the British Academy and Leverhulme Trust for funding this event through their Small Grants scheme.

We are very grateful to all contributors, most of whom also presented papers at the original conference, for their support throughout this project. The global coronavirus pandemic slowed down the process of finalising the manuscript, and we really appreciate the perseverance and patience of all contributors in these challenging circumstances. Most of all, we thank them for their outstanding chapters.

We also thank our colleagues in the School of Law and Social Justice at the University of Liverpool for their help with the 2017 conference. In particular, the organisational support of Rachel Barrett and Natasha Graham was invaluable, and Eleanor Drywood, Stephanie Reynolds and Brian Thompson very kindly chaired panels during the event.

We are grateful to Kate Whetter, our editor at Hart Publishing, for her sustained support and encouragement during this project. We also thank Rosie Mearns and Linda Staniford for all their help in seeing the book through to publication.

Finally, we are extremely grateful to our families. Mike thanks Fiona and Sophie for their love, support, tolerance and advice. Adam thanks Ange, Ayla and Amber for love, patience and companionship.

Table of Contents

List of Contributors

Professor Rodney Brazier is Emeritus Professor of Constitutional Law at the University of Manchester.

Lord Falconer of Thoroton is a member of the House of Lords, and a former minister in the Labour government between 1997 and 2007, including holding office as Lord Chancellor and the first Secretary of State for Justice.

Professor Graham Gee is Professor of Public Law at the University of Sheffield.

Dr Arianna Giovannini is Reader in Local Politics and Public Policy at De Montfort University.

Professor Michael Gordon is Professor of Constitutional Law at the University of Liverpool.

Dr Richard Kirkham is a Senior Lecturer in Law at the University of Sheffield.

Dr Robert Knox is a Senior Lecturer in Law at the University of Liverpool.

Professor Roger Masterman is Professor of Constitutional Law at Durham University.

Dr Chris McCorkindale is a Senior Lecturer in Law at the University of Strathclyde.

Dr Paul Scott is a Senior Lecturer in Law at the University of Glasgow.

Dr Louise Thompson is a Senior Lecturer in Politics at the University of Manchester.

Dr Joe Tomlinson is a Senior Lecturer in Law at the University of York.

Dr Leah Trueblood is a Career Development Fellow at Worcester College, University of Oxford.

Dr Adam Tucker is a Senior Lecturer in Law at the University of Liverpool.

Dr Hélène Tyrrell is a Lecturer in Law at Newcastle University.

Dr Rumyana van Ark is a Researcher in Terrorism, Counter-Terrorism and Human Rights at TMC Asser Institute (University of Amsterdam), and a Senior Research Fellow and Coordinator at the International Centre for Counter-Terrorism, The Hague.

Dr Se-shauna Wheatle is an Associate Professor in Law at Durham University.

Dr Ben Worthy is a Senior Lecturer in Politics at Birkbeck College, University of London.

Table of Legislation

Table of Constitutional Legislation Enacted under New Labour Governments, 1997–2010

Prime Minister Tony Blair (1997–2007)

Referendums (Scotland and Wales) Act 1997
Greater London Authority (Referendum) Act 1998
Bank of England Act 1998
Data Protection Act 1998
Government of Wales Act 1998
Human Rights Act 1998
Regional Development Agencies Act 1998
Scotland Act 1998
Northern Ireland Act 1998
European Parliamentary Elections Act 1999
Local Government Act 1999
Greater London Authority Act 1999
House of Lords Act 1999
Representation of the People Act 2000
Terrorism Act 2000
Local Government Act 2000
Regulation of Investigatory Powers Act 2000
Freedom of Information Act 2000
Political Parties, Elections and Referendums Act 2000
Anti-terrorism, Crime and Security Act 2001
European Parliamentary Elections Act 2002
Local Government Act 2003
Courts Act 2003
Civil Contingencies Act 2004
Prevention of Terrorism Act 2005
Constitutional Reform Act 2005
Inquiries Act 2005
Terrorism Act 2006
Legislative and Regulatory Reform Act 2006
Government of Wales Act 2006
Northern Ireland (St Andrews Agreement) Act 2006
Identity Cards Act 2006

Prime Minister Gordon Brown (2007–10)

Tribunals, Courts and Enforcement Act 2007
European Union (Amendment) Act 2008
Counter-Terrorism Act 2008
Northern Ireland Act 2009
Political Parties and Elections Act 2009
Parliamentary Standards Act 2009
Equality Act 2010
Constitutional Reform and Governance Act 2010

The New Labour Constitution: Twenty Years On

Introduction

MICHAEL GORDON AND ADAM TUCKER

I. NEW LABOUR, MORE THAN 20 YEARS ON

THIS BOOK AIMS to analyse a crucial period in the modern development of the UK constitution. New Labour came to power in 1997 and retained office until 2010, winning three general elections under the leadership of Tony Blair before he was replaced as Prime Minister by his long-standing Chancellor, collaborator and antagonist Gordon Brown. After 18 years of Conservative rule, the election of New Labour was a key moment in UK political history. It was deliberately and self-consciously promoted as commencing an era of change in which (as Labour's original election anthem declared) 'Things Can Only Get Better'. It was unquestionably an eventful 13 years – spanning Cool Britannia, with Britpop celebrities attending drinks in Downing Street, to the world-shaking events of 9/11, followed by catastrophic wars in Iraq and Afghanistan, ending with a global financial crisis complemented by a domestic MPs' expenses scandal.

The very idea of 'New' Labour signalled that this would be an era of government which sought to break with tradition. It was a 'new' approach to Labour's left-wing values, but also an approach to government which sought the modernisation of the state, and 'new' answers to social, economic and political challenges. As the 1997 general election manifesto put it: 'We have modernised the Labour Party and we will modernise Britain.'[1] In this sense, New Labour had no lack of ambition – its strategy was nothing less than to 'reinvent Britain'.[2] This was an agenda which included the reinvention of the UK constitution, which had been planned and discussed in detail in opposition,[3] but this was simply one strand of a wider programme of political change. The number one

[1] *New Labour: Because Britain Deserves Better* (Labour Party, 1997).

[2] A Rawnsley, *Servants of the People: The Inside Story of New Labour* (Penguin, 2000) xiii.

[3] See, eg R Blackburn and R Plant, *Constitutional Reform: The Labour Government's Constitutional Reform Agenda* (Longman, 1999).

priority was 'education, education, education', but the New Labour government would also freeze income tax rates, be 'tough on crime and tough on the causes of crime', introduce a national minimum wage, give the Bank of England independent control of interest rates, cut NHS waiting lists, provide leadership in the EU (including through an abandoned pledge for a referendum on joining the single currency) and introduce a 'welfare-to-work programme' removing the 'option of life on full benefit'.

This agenda was characteristic of the 'Third Way' politics of New Labour. This approach sought to move 'beyond left and right', but not simply by adopting the outlook and substantive policies of the political centre ground.[4] Instead, the Third Way was intended to be a model of radical politics which conceived of change as an end in itself, and foregrounded the idea of modernisation in a way which was not inherently tied to a left (or right) wing set of values, in an attempt to make it more palatable to a wider political audience. While this generated considerable electoral success for New Labour, it also exposes one of the key potential gaps in its constitutional programme – the apparent absence of any overarching principles which provide coherence and structure to the broad package of measures which it proposed and/or delivered. The highly stylised and managerial approach to government which was consonant with the politics of the Third Way also ironically meant that New Labour was pursuing a 'new constitutional order' while simultaneously operating as a government based on a 'concentration of power' among a group of key individuals, and which was often accused of 'control-freakism'.[5]

Inevitably for a political dynasty of this nature and extent, the wider legacy of New Labour is deeply contested, both within and beyond the Labour Party itself. New Labour's time in office may now be seen as defined by the power struggles between Tony Blair and his eventual successor Gordon Brown; the rise of political 'spin'; the decision-making which led to war in Iraq in the face of major public protests; the political apathy which became fully evident in the 2005 election; or the state expenditure required to prop up the banking system in the financial crisis which dominated the final years of its period in government.

Yet despite this, New Labour's constitutional legacy has been viewed in largely positive terms. Some elements of it, most obviously the Human Rights Act 1998, have been consistently controversial. And it ended much more meekly than it began, with the stark ambition of Gordon Brown's *Governance of Britain* programme – announced with fanfare upon his appointment as Prime Minister in 2007 – primarily resulting in the miscellaneous and unspectacular changes grouped together in the Constitutional Reform and Governance Act 2010, enacted in the final days of the New Labour era. But for the most part – whether grudgingly, enthusiastically, pragmatically or unconsciously – the

[4] See A Giddens, *Beyond Left and Right* (Polity Press, 1994).
[5] Rawnsley (n 2) xiv, xvi, 18.

broad framework of the 'new constitutional order' constructed by New Labour appeared to be accepted by most political, constitutional and legal actors, academics, civil society organisations and the wider public. Indeed, it was striking that some of the key architects of the New Labour project were among the most outspoken critics of some of their reforms – Tony Blair, for example, came to lament aspects of the Human Rights Act 1998[6] and the 'dangerous' Freedom of Information Act 2000.[7]

It would be premature to believe the reforms introduced by New Labour will endure as a complete and resilient constitutional settlement for the UK. Brexit has demonstrated both that constitutional change of the most fundamental kind remains entirely possible and that a single event can quickly destabilise a relatively settled legal and political system. There is also currently a considerable degree of pushback against key components of the New Labour project under the government of Boris Johnson, including a review of the Human Rights Act, clashes between the devolution system and a new UK Internal Market Act 2020, legislation to reform judicial review and heavily rumoured plans to replace or reconfigure the UK Supreme Court. Nevertheless, the aim of this book is to analyse the events, reforms and processes which led to the point where the UK constitution became, in effect, the 'New Labour constitution'.

II. THE NEW LABOUR CONSTITUTION

The essays collected in this book explain and assess, in various ways and from various perspectives, what happened in New Labour's constitutional project: how different reforms were delivered, their operation and consequences, and their overall effects. We have described the product of this period of legal and political reform as producing 'the New Labour constitution'. But this is a claim in itself, attributing to New Labour the decisive role in authoring the current settlement. This clearly requires some justification, given the UK constitution long predates 1997, there has been no categorical shift from an uncodified to a codified constitutional model and New Labour's reform programme did not comprehensively alter every aspect of the pre-existing system. However, we think it is justified: the contemporary UK constitution is now defined by the programme of reform delivered by New Labour.

The idea that the UK constitution is in essence the 'New Labour constitution' is based on four fundamental constitutional shifts which the New Labour project effected, and which are exposed and analysed across the substantive chapters of this book. First, New Labour changed the substance of the UK constitution in a range of dramatic ways: from devolution to human rights legislation, from freedom of information to Lords reform, many of the core

[6] 'Revealed: Blair Attack on Human Rights Law' *The Observer* (14 May 2006).
[7] T Blair, *A Journey* (Random House, 2010).

features of the constitution were either created or fundamentally modernised by New Labour. Second, New Labour entrenched a new paradigm for the process by which the constitution is reformed – this was a proactive and deliberate approach to constitutional reform, in marked contrast with the reactive and minimalistic approach to constitutional change which dominated prior to 1997. Third, the New Labour programme has shifted attitudes to the constitution, which is now widely seen across the different political parties as a construct which can (and should) be actively reconfigured, while the legal and political system is now increasingly engaged with (not least by the judges) in more explicitly 'constitutional' terms. Fourth, New Labour's project created the basis for the current constitutional reaction – in that sense, the changes implemented by New Labour (in particular the Human Rights Act and the creation of a UK Supreme Court) are driving this next phase of constitutional reform (or constitutional reversal) in the UK.

This is a pretty remarkable set of impacts on the contemporary constitution, whatever view you take of the desirability of the actual outcomes of this period (especially given constitutional reform was just one of a number of agendas pursued by New Labour from 1997 onwards). New Labour's modernisation project was a decisive shift with the past, resulting in change of a considerable extent. Yet it is ultimately the cumulative impact which is really crucial to understanding the significance of the New Labour years: the combined effects on constitutional substance, process and attitudes, and the direct reaction now being generated. In combination, these factors explain why the UK constitution can be described as the New Labour constitution.

Further, arguably as a consequence of these cumulative impacts, the New Labour project has stimulated greater public consciousness of the constitution. In this sense, the idea of the 'New Labour constitution' captures more than just New Labour's active political influence over the reformed legal and political system. Instead, to describe our current settlement as the New Labour constitution also captures the more overt sense of 'The Constitution' which has, directly or indirectly, also emerged from this period. We have arguably seen a shift from the UK constitution being viewed as historic or traditional to a constitutional framework which is now, if not completely modern, then at least less archaic. This shift in constitutional consciousness also appears to have changed public expectations of the constitution. In the post-Labour era, the Brexit process has also arguably been a key driver of these changing ideas of UK constitutionalism. But equally, it is also worth considering how far the New Labour constitution provided the backdrop to the Brexit debates we have experienced, and whether it created some of the conditions which shaped the way the process unfolded.

For example, we can potentially trace a path to Brexit from New Labour's (unfulfilled) promise to hold a referendum on joining the single currency in the 1997 manifesto, via the European Parliamentary Elections Act 2002 and the European Union (Amendment) Act 2008, which created various requirements of statutory authorisation or parliamentary approval to ratify treaties or support decisions which expanded the EU's powers. The mechanisms in these Acts were then extended in the (post-Labour) European Union Act 2011, which established a series of 'referendum locks' to prevent further transfers of power or competence to the EU. And this Act led to the promise of an 'in/out' referendum, which ultimately produced the 2016 referendum and the decision to withdraw from the EU. Similarly, we can also see the very prominent role in the Brexit process of New Labour's Supreme Court in *Miller (No 1)*[8] and *Cherry/Miller (No 2)*,[9] as well as the many tensions and contradictions generated in the context of EU withdrawal as a result of the UK's devolution system.

But the expanded constitutional consciousness generated by New Labour's reform programme may also have affected the Brexit process in a further way. In a manner consistent with New Labour's 'Third Way' approach to politics, which aimed to transcend conventional left/right political categories, the reform project may have succeeded in rationalising the UK constitution, and making it appear autonomous while obscuring its core political nature. Ironically, this may have created false expectations (especially for Labour's 'remain' supporting membership) that a constitutional 'solution' to Brexit might be available to bypass highly politicised debates. Ultimately, the Brexit process, which was only concluded following a general election, instead demonstrates that – despite the New Labour reforms – the UK constitution remains deeply political.

Against this backdrop, there is a renewed importance to understanding the content and parameters of, as well as the tensions within, the New Labour constitution. That is the core aim of this book.

III. NATURE OF THE PROJECT

This book is derived from a conference held at the University of Liverpool in 2017, to mark 20 years since the election of New Labour to office.[10] The chapters in the book are primarily drawn from papers presented and discussed at that conference, which aimed to assess the state and legacy of the New Labour constitution. While the parameters of the project have not changed in the gap between the conference and publication of this book (separated, among other things, by the coronavirus pandemic), it is worth reflecting that the nature of New Labour's constitutional legacy has changed even during the lifespan of this project. In 2017, in the aftermath of the initial constitutional uncertainty generated by the unexpected national vote to withdraw from the EU, New Labour's reforms looked, in contrast, like they provided a relatively stable and resilient constitutional settlement for the UK. In the years since, this has become less clear, as different aspects of the New Labour constitution have been recontested (such as the Human Rights Act), come under fresh political pressure (such as the UK Supreme Court) and been rendered more vulnerable through the indirect

[8] *Miller v Secretary of State for Exiting the EU* [2017] UKSC 5.
[9] *Cherry v Advocate General for Scotland; Miller v Prime Minister* [2019] UKSC 41.
[10] Funded by the British Academy/Leverhulme Small Grants Scheme.

consequences of removing the internal domestic ties of EU law (in particular in the context of devolution). The New Labour constitution has gone from a relatively uncontested liberal framework to a more divisive structure which is to be pushed against.

This does not mean that prior ideas about the endurance or significance of the reforms of the New Labour era have been undone – there is much that remains to be seen in this respect. But it does, however, highlight vividly the tensions in the UK constitution: between the flexibility of a constitution which can in principle be easily changed and the implacability of a constitution which is organised around historic institutions and deeply embedded doctrines and traditions. This tension runs throughout the book, largely because it is an unresolved tension in the New Labour legacy, and in the UK constitution in general. While the New Labour project could never have provided a permanent constitutional settlement for the UK, given the inevitability of political contestation and future change, events since 2017 may paradoxically even more clearly demonstrate the fundamental status of New Labour's constitution. For if even in this period there is difficulty in breaking away from the constitutional model which primarily derives from New Labour, it suggests the changes made between 1997 and 2010 played a remarkable role in redefining the way we think about the UK constitution today.

The approach taken in this book is thematic rather than comprehensive. The chapters within it cover a range of issues from different perspectives – some are focused on specific reforms (sometimes from multiple perspectives), while others reflect on the reform process, assess the overall implications of this programme or place the reforms in wider political and historical context. The chapters are evaluative rather than aiming to offer an exhaustive description of events. This approach to the project, coupled with the scale of the New Labour reform programme and the practical constraints of any edited collection, means that inevitably there are some issues which have received less attention. That topics such as House of Lords reform[11] or (unfulfilled) UK-wide electoral reform[12] have not been covered in dedicated chapters does not mean we think they are unimportant. It is simply a reflection of choices made by us and the contributors, and may tell us something about which elements of the New Labour reform programme have been most controversial or have attracted most interest (rightly or wrongly) from constitutional, legal and political scholars. Equally, it may reflect other challenges – for example, the Good Friday Agreement was clearly a key achievement of New Labour's time in office, but it was much more than one element of a constitutional reform programme, and much more than just

[11] On which see, eg M Russell, *The Contemporary House of Lords: Westminster Bicameralism Revived* (Oxford University Press, 2013); C Ballinger, *The House of Lords 1911–2011: A Century of Non-Reform* (Hart Publishing, 2012).

[12] On which see, eg P Dunleavy and H Margetts, 'From Majoritarian to Pluralist Democracy? Electoral Reform in Britain since 1997' (2001) 13 *Journal of Theoretical Politics* 295; M Flinders and D Curry, 'Deliberative Democracy, Elite Politics and Electoral Reform' (2008) 29 *Policy Studies* 371.

New Labour's achievement. Rather it was an intensely complex political challenge, reliant for its success on the political parties in Northern Ireland and consecutive Irish governments, raising a 'distinct' set of constitutional issues.[13] In generally focusing on the common issues concerning devolution in Northern Ireland, Scotland and Wales we do not mean to disregard such differences, but in a context when the Northern Ireland Assembly was not sitting throughout most of the period in which this book was conceived and written, attempts to assess the impact of New Labour's intervention as part of a package of constitutional reform could have been superficial.

Ultimately, the scope and structure of the book can be as much a matter for debate as the content itself. We hope that its design is such that it provides new insights into the details and the overarching implications of the New Labour reform era, and the constitution which emerged from this period.

IV. OVERVIEW OF THE BOOK

This book brings together essays from a collection of leading academics working in public law and political studies. It begins, however, with a set of 'insider' reflections on the New Labour constitution from one of its key political architects, **Lord Falconer of Thoroton**. In his chapter, Lord Falconer assesses and defends the New Labour constitution as an integral part of a wider package of political, social and economic reform undertaken by the Blair and Brown governments. He concludes by arguing it is 'time for more', changing his previously adopted position and advocating the adoption of a written constitution. This, Lord Falconer argues, is necessary to preserve the fundamental constitutional settlement captured by the New Labour constitution which is now, in his assessment, under threat. He argues a written constitution would be 'the consequence of the retreat from progress' experienced in the years since New Labour.

Rodney Brazier next provides an overarching account of the causes and consequences of New Labour's constitutional reform programme. Brazier explains why Labour offered such an unprecedented and vast programme of constitutional reform to the electorate in 1997, and explores the programme's wider implications. He traces its roots to Labour's response to Thatcherism, and identifies the normalisation of proactive constitutional reform as one of the period's main legacies.

A number of chapters then analyse some of the main substantive reforms of the New Labour period and their constitutional consequences.

[13] C O'Cinneide, 'The UK's Post-Brexit "Constitutional Unsettlement"', *Verfassungsblog* (16 April 2021) https://verfassungsblog.de/the-uks-post-brexit-constitutional-unsettlement/: 'Northern Ireland was never successfully governed in line with this traditional model, and is inevitably going to remain constitutionally distinct.'

Hélène Tyrrell considers the apparent tension between the resilience of the Human Rights Act and its persistent (relative) unpopularity. She traces that unpopularity to deficiencies in the Act's conception and neglect rather than to substantive problems with its content or value. She criticises Labour for its role in the shift in the UK towards a culture where legislating to dilute individual rights has become not just thinkable, but a mainstream political position.

Se-shauna Wheatle draws attention to two unintended consequences of what she describes as New Labour's 'legislative constitutionalism', namely the rejuvenation of the tradition of common law constitutionalism and increased attention to and contestation of judicial comparativism. She argues that these aspects of the legacy of the New Labour constitution are capable of outliving the legislative interventions which prompted them, most notably the Human Rights Act, but on which they do not continue to depend.

Graham Gee assesses the process of standardising, depoliticising, formalising and pluralising the making of judicial policy under New Labour, through the creation of the UK Supreme Court, the Judicial Appointments Commission and the transformation of the role of Lord Chancellor. He reflects on the place of judicial policy in New Labour's wider constitutional project, which he argues was not systematic, contained inconsistencies, was dynamic and continuous, and contributed to tensions with the UK's arrangements. He draws attention to the important way in which this has established a new judicial policy community, while identifying some of the longer-term risks of these reforms and their connection with other changes to the authority of the judges.

Chris McCorkindale argues that – assessed on its own terms – devolution left a mixed legacy and has an uncertain future. He frames devolution as a fundamental feature (rather than a peculiarity at the fringes) of the contemporary constitution, charting how the scope of devolved powers has broadened and the degree of constitutional entrenchment has deepened since 1997. He argues that if devolution outlasts the challenges posed by independence movements, further reform at the centre of the state will be key to the survival of these settlements.

Arianna Giovannini pursues Hazell's characterisation of the issue of English devolution as the 'gaping hole' in the devolution settlements, analysing the pattern of division and uneven engagement with the English question under New Labour. She assesses subsequent developments as the Conservatives took ownership of the English devolution agenda, while arguing that the English question still stands unanswered. She concludes that the development of a clear strategy for devolution to England is vital to Labour's electoral mission to reconnect with its strongholds, particularly in the North, and hence return to government.

Ben Worthy explores the paradoxes of freedom of information legislation, applying this in particular to New Labour's Freedom of Information

Act 2000. He argues that this Act was becoming unpopular even as it was developed, but was passed nevertheless, only to subsequently be regretted by the very government which promoted it, and yet was never revisited or repealed. His chapter explores some competing explanations for this paradoxical entry in the New Labour project, arguing that the legacy of the Freedom of Information Act is as much about its perception as its concrete successes.

We then move to a series of chapters which focus on broader themes, concepts or features of the New Labour constitution.

Louise Thompson examines the legacy of the patchwork of internal reform to Parliament and its processes during the New Labour era, seeking to identify the vision which grounded this activity. While these reforms were generally branded as enhancing Parliament's opportunities to hold the government to account, she argues that many in fact had the opposite effect of enhancing the government's ability to exert its power over legislature. Still, she suggests, the cluster of reforms she examines nevertheless had the consequence of waking up a dormant House of Commons.

Roger Masterman focuses on the place of the judiciary in the New Labour constitution, and in particular the impact of the Human Rights Act and the establishment of a 'federal' jurisdiction in the new UK Supreme Court. He examines the extent to which these potentially transformative changes are better understood as being in continuity with more general developments going back to (at least) the 1960s. He argues that the New Labour reforms to the judiciary were consistent with more long-standing features, trends and principles in UK constitutionalism. This was not, he therefore suggests, a radical redrawing of judicial power, but an explicit demarcation of the judicial function within the UK constitution.

Paul Scott argues that there existed during the New Labour era a secret national security constitution. He shows how the avoidance of accountability and scrutiny was achieved through a combination of the exploitation of gaps in investigatory powers legislation and the employment of strategies to secure basic legality without publicity. He argues that this shows the limits of the rhetoric of modernisation and rationalisation which accompanied the New Labour constitution, and leaves a position of uncertainty about fidelity to the rule of law in the UK constitution.

Rumyana van Ark focuses on what she characterises as New Labour's 'legislative fever' in the area of counterterrorism, developing a critique which shows that this entrenched a regrettable dichotomy between 'their rights' and 'our security'. She argues that the upshot of this was to produce a hollowing out of certain individual rights in this context, analysing the issues of indefinite detention of terror suspects, control orders and the expanding use of closed material proceedings. She suggests that this legislated erosion of rights was exacerbated by the fact that it was structured to take place within and according to the constraints of the rule of law.

Joe Tomlinson and Richard Kirkham turn their attention to the range of reforms to and innovations in administrative justice initiated by New Labour. They develop the standard narrative of this period, which is of a 'rise' under New Labour, followed by a 'fall' from 2010 in the coherence and political commitment to administrative justice. They go beyond this by drawing attention to underexamined elements of the story, including reform to judicial leadership roles, the focus on 'users', the work of oversight bodies, and the interaction with devolution, which, they argue, contribute to an important and influential legacy.

Leah Trueblood develops a critique of New Labour's decisions about when, and when not, to hold referendums. She shows that the use of referendums presents a microcosm of New Labour's constitutional project overall – radical in some ways, conservative in others – and analyses whether a convention regarding the use of referendums might exist. She argues that an inconsistent approach to this issue exacerbated pre-existing confusion about the role of referendums in the UK constitution, the legacy of which is that New Labour laid the groundwork for the unprincipled use of this decision-making device by more recent governments.

Rob Knox explores the historical genesis of the New Labour constitution, situating it in a broader account of change to the relationship between the labour movement, capitalism and the British state. He identifies in the New Labour constitution a radical shift away from the left's historical anti-juridical constitutionalism to an 'impeccably liberal' set of constitutional policies, arguing that this internalised and reconstituted (rather than challenged) the neoliberal model of the capitalist state introduced under the Conservatives, and offers an explanation of the uneven nature of Labour's reform programme. He argues that there is a need to understand the constitutional sphere as extending beyond high politics, and, among other things, to reconceive the role of local government and the labour movement in the UK constitution.

In **our own contribution**, which closes the collection, we bring together some of the threads which run throughout the preceding chapters. We analyse the distinctive elements of the New Labour constitution: the process, the substance and the legacy of the reform project. We then try to connect the legacy of the New Labour constitution with the prospects for future Labour constitutional reform. We argue that the New Labour experience shows there is a need to revisit some fundamental questions about the nature of Labour constitutionalism, and explore how the values of democracy, equality and accountability might provide a compelling justification for a range of distinctively Labour constitutional improvements worth pursuing in future.

1

Labour's Constitutional Changes 1997–2010: Time for More

LORD FALCONER OF THOROTON

I. INTRODUCTION

LABOUR VERY SIGNIFICANTLY changed the constitution of the UK between 1997 and 2010. There was an overarching drive to those changes – to bring government much closer to the people, and to shift the balance of power much more towards the citizen and away from the executive. We believed it would promote more connected government and better-quality government. And it did.

Devolution gave Scotland and Wales direct power over huge swathes of domestic policy, and the Good Friday Agreement installed a government in Northern Ireland which could and did bring peace. The Human Rights Act gave the citizen enforceable protections, in the UK courts, for their human rights. The Freedom of Information Act exposed the executive to much more profound scrutiny: real scrutiny so often comes from seeing the documents which break through a government refusing to give any information about how they came to a decision. The Constitutional Reform Act 2005 created a Supreme Court as the final court of appeal for the UK, made it properly visible to the public, ensured an impartial method of judicial appointments, and removed the chief judge of England and Wales from the Cabinet. The Equalities Act provided widespread protection for the citizen against a whole range of discriminations. The removal of the hereditary peers from the Lords transformed the second chamber from being a deeply Conservative, largely irrelevant legislative chamber to an effective reviser of legislation. The Regional Development Agencies drove strategic change for the regions of England. And the introduction of mayors in our major cities has provided new dynamic leadership for the crucially important city-regions which drive economic growth.

The list is long and significant. These changes have affected our constitution hugely and in irreversible ways, but they remain in many aspects contested. For example, the Human Rights Act provokes opposition from sections of the community who believe it has tilted the balance too much in favour of the unmeritorious citizen and too far away from the state, and devolution is blamed by some for the strength of the independence movement in Scotland and by others for not going far enough. The Freedom of Information Act is said to restrict too much the executive's ability to have open discussions internally, and the Supreme Court, it is said, has strayed too much into the area of politics.

These details do show a very stark dividing line on the constitution now. The current government is strongly against continuing the process of bringing government closer to and empowering the people. Brexit aimed to do that. Taking back control is a good description for many of the constitutional changes Labour delivered. And the power and aptness of that message is shown by the electoral success of Brexit. Having taken back control from Brussels, the real battle now is about how much control the executive should cede from itself to the devolved institutions, to the regions, to Parliament and to the individual.

Against this backdrop, this chapter reflects on the key achievements of the Labour reform programme, as well as the constitutional priorities for the future. This piece is written in a pure personal capacity and does not reflect current Labour Party policy.

Labour's constitutional reforms need to be understood in the context of the wider package of social, economic and political change delivered by that Labour government. The constitutional reform package was, like these other reforms, driven by 18 years of Thatcherism and Conservative constitutional neglect.

The direction of travel of the Labour reforms were right. There needs to be more constitutional change now, to prevent an 'elective dictatorship' deciding everything from Westminster[1] – to ensure that the underlying principle of taking back control does not get hijacked by a government determined to concentrate power as much as possible on the elected Westminster government to the detriment of the nations and regions, and of individuals.

The financial crisis, the constitutional strains of Brexit, the response to the coronavirus pandemic and the election in December 2019 of a Conservative majority government led by Boris Johnson willing to govern in a blinkered majoritarian way have left the whole of our constitutional settlement exposed. The government attacks on the judiciary, the optional nature of the rule of law, the subversion of the independent role of the law officers, the refusal to accept the impartiality of the civil service, the breakdown of trust between the UK government and the devolved governments, the decrease in support for the Union throughout the whole of the UK, the disrespect for the Ministerial Code, the disregard by the executive for the Commons, and the failure of Parliament

[1] See Lord Hailsham, *The Dilemma of Democracy: Diagnosis and Prescription* (Collins, 1978).

and the executive to provide a solution to the Brexit issue until the 2019 general election have all left the constitution looking in need of change – to better connect the people to the government, to provide effective government, to preserve the Union between Scotland and Wales and the rest of the UK, to ensure the continued success of the Good Friday Agreement, and to provide appropriate checks and balances on the executive.

II. KEY FEATURES OF LABOUR'S CONSTITUTIONAL CHANGES

A. Constitutional Modernisation

The constitutional reforms implemented by Labour were the product of 18 years of constitutional conservatism on the part of the preceding Conservative governments. A number of weaknesses had been ignored, or developed, or increased in that time: first, a profound sense of resentment in Scotland and to a lesser extent in Wales about the distance of Westminster from those it governed; second – although I do not say this was the fault of the Conservatives' lack of constitutional change – violence and sectarianism in Northern Ireland; and third, the failure of the constitution to catch up with the desire for individual empowerment which was reflected around the world in the strengthening of individual rights. The Labour government's constitutional changes reflected this latter point in, among other things, the Human Rights Act 1998, the Freedom of Information Act 2000 and the Equality Act 2010, all of which embedded enforceable individual rights.

Although there are similarities between devolution in Scotland and Wales and the model of devolution in Northern Ireland, they are dealing with different problems. In Scotland and Wales, the issue was less discrimination against a particular community within the nation than a sense of disconnect between the drivers of the Westminster government and the concerns of Scotland and Wales. The aim of devolution was to bring the government closer to the people in Scotland and Wales. This has been successful. Devolution is irreversible. Without it, alienation would have grown hugely. But the cultural and political divides between England and the other nations have grown not because of devolution, but for a variety of other factors. The question now is what further change is required.

B. Is Parliamentary Sovereignty Still Accepted as the Key to UK Democracy?

The reform programme was designed to retain parliamentary sovereignty, in particular in relation to human rights and devolution. Brexit was driven by a desire to take back control from the EU, but it has introduced into the constitutional debate question marks over parliamentary sovereignty. And there are now a range of questions about parliamentary sovereignty, going beyond Brexit, which affect our constitutional debate. To what extent should a referendum trump whatever Parliament might want? Should the devolution settlements have greater entrenchment than simply a piece of primary legislation? And to what extent do our checks and balances, in particular the rule of law, the impartiality of the civil service, and human rights, require greater protection than random Acts of Parliament vulnerable to a big Commons majority?

The first of these three questions has, constitutionally, been resolved by the first *Miller* case in the Supreme Court which made clear the Brexit referendum did not trump parliamentary sovereignty.[2] That a majority had voted for Brexit in the 2016 referendum did not obviate the need for Parliament to decide and pass legislation to determine whether we left, and on what terms.

The Supreme Court may have determined the constitutional question. But Brexit raised brutally the sense amongst many in the electorate of a disconnect between judges and politicians on the one hand and the people on the other.

These pressures are reflected in all three of the big questions on parliamentary sovereignty raised in this section. And they need addressing if our constitution is to prove durable in the long term. It may be that our fundamental constitutional values – the protection of minority views, the rule of law, the primacy of the electorate, the rejection of majoritarianism – need to be protected by a written constitution.

III. THE CONSEQUENCES OF LABOUR'S REFORMS

A. The Constitution as Driver and Framer of Politics

The modernised constitution has become controversial. In particular, it now frames the political debate in Scotland.

The creation of the Scottish Parliament sought to address the disconnect between the wishes of the Scottish people and the UK government by, in effect, giving very substantial control over domestic policy, although not economic policy, to the Scottish people. And over 20 years that has been a success. But the thing which accelerated support for that devolution, namely Thatcher's government, which was very out of tune with Scotland, has re-emerged in the current UK government, which is culturally out of tune with Scottish sensibilities and with a majority of the Scottish electorate on Brexit. One can debate which comes first – the cultural divide or the difference of view on Brexit. Whichever it is, the two together fuel the argument for independence. Polling support for independence grew, but, from the beginning of 2021, it now appears to be falling back, and for some time (up until November 2021 when this chapter was

[2] *R (Miller) v Secretary of State for Exiting the European Union* [2017] UKSC 5.

finalised) there has been a consistent lead for the union.[3] The polling is in the context of no imminent referendum – the views expressed to pollsters demonstrate much anger, but not a settled choice.

The effect of Labour's devolution settlement was demonstrated by the result in the 2014 referendum, where there was a 10 per cent lead for the Union. This was a big lead when the government of the day in Scotland was using everything it possibly could to campaign against it, and there was a Conservative government at Westminster.

The new facts of a UK government, culturally deaf to Scottish sensibilities, and Brexit mean we must readdress the question of what the relationship is between the UK and Scotland, but also readdress the relationship between the Scottish Labour Party and the UK Labour Party.

A party whose membership is only in Scotland, and whose only concern is Scotland has a huge advantage over Great British national parties whose concerns are the whole of the United Kingdom, a UK in which a substantial majority of parliamentary seats are in England. But the fact that the SNP are best placed to press Scottish issues, and may most easily argue only they are exclusively concerned about Scotland, does not mean a majority of the Scots, by voting SNP, want independence. I suspect the contrary. A party which has engagement on both sides of the border can deliver best for Scotland, meaning in practice a Labour Party in power in Westminster and Holyrood is the best combination for Scotland, but one where there is a much higher degree of independence for the Scottish Labour Party from its English and Welsh Labour Party partners.

I do not believe a second referendum would be lost by those who support the union. But equally, I do not think there should be a second referendum now or in the foreseeable future. The constant focus on constitutional issues reduces both political stability and improvement in public services. The constitution is a big dividing line in Scottish politics. The big question is how to bring constitutional debate to an end and turn the focus to other issues. It is difficult to see that switch in focus occurring without further constitutional change.

It may be that the next stage in the constitutional process is a more federal constitution which embeds sovereignty on some issues in the Scottish Parliament under the terms of a written constitution which can be construed by the Supreme Court and cannot be changed simply by an Act of the UK Parliament, as is the current position. As with the EU, it may be that a position should be evolved where if the UK Parliament sought by primary legislation to legislate in a way which was contrary to the devolution settlement, the Supreme Court of the UK could strike that legislation down. The significance of that change would be to provide constitutional protection to

[3] J Curtice, 'Why Has Nationalist Support Fallen?' *What Scotland Thinks* (19 March 2021) https://whatscotlandthinks.org/2021/03/why-has-nationalist-support-fallen/.

the devolution settlement which it currently lacks – there are in practice no constitutional inhibitions on the UK Parliament passing primary legislation affecting Scotland which encroaches on devolved areas, to any degree the UK Parliament chooses.

Working out how that constitutional evolution since 1998 might be captured in further reform designed to embed devolution will be very significant in future attempts to sustain the Union.

IV. THE VULNERABILITY OF THE CONSTITUTION

A. Constitution in Crisis

Despite the success of the 1997–2010 reform programme, which has had a positive impact on the constitution, we currently have a constitution in crisis.

There are two main threads to the crisis: first, the preservation of the UK because of the real threat of Scottish independence and the government's weakened commitment to the rule of law; and secondly, abandonment of checks and balances by the government.

B. Preservation of the Union and the Rule of Law

I set out the position in Scotland above. The Good Friday Agreement is also in play because of the extent to which it has been regarded as secondary to achieving Brexit, and the changes to the relationship between the British mainland and Northern Ireland effected to facilitate Brexit. To leave the Single Market meant the EU would insist there had to be compliance with the rules of the Single Market and the Customs Union either by a hard border within the island of Ireland or by checks on goods coming from Great Britain to Northern Ireland. Agreement has been reached on a border through the North Sea, although the longevity of these arrangements is uncertain in light of the UK government's continuing resistance to them.

Before the deal was agreed there was an impasse, and in prioritising a hard Brexit, the UK government put the UK in a situation where the status of Northern Ireland and the stability of the open border between the North and the Republic of Ireland was threatened. The current inability of the EU and the UK to reach a stable landing on the position of Northern Ireland, despite having negotiated the Northern Ireland Protocol less than two years ago, raises big questions over the constitutional position of Northern Ireland. The clash between the desire to preserve the integrity of the Single Market and yet have no border between Great Britain and Northern Ireland, and the desire to preserve the key principle of the Good Friday Agreement of an open border between North and South, remains unresolved. For there to be integrity over the Single Market arrangements means there have to be some checks on goods coming into Ireland, either at the border with the North which offends the GFA, or between GB and NI, which offends the integration of NI into the UK. A compromise is required. It exists in the protocol. It has to be made to work. How it affects, in the long term, support for the border within Northern Ireland remains to be seen.

The future of Northern Ireland and its constitutional position will therefore inevitably be influenced by the ability of the EU and the UK to make the Northern Ireland Protocol work in a way which preserves the constitutional status quo.

The referendum vote for Brexit, and then the delivery of Brexit, initially delayed by the politicians but then delivered after the 2019 election, has rocked the constitution. The unwritten constitution, dependent for success on the acceptance of loosely defined convention, has been massively unsettled by that delay. The split between Parliament and the electorate over what to do about Brexit, and the range of constitutional steps taken to delay Brexit, undermined confidence in the constitution. The constitution is now associated by some with standing in the way of what they would see as true democratic delivery of change. The Good Friday Agreement, the rule of law and the Supreme Court were each characterised as obstructing the change the government said the referendum required. Whilst the Brexit debate is over, the extent to which there need to be changes to the constitution to reflect but also to restrain a government which sees itself in a new relationship with the people, Parliament and other constitutional institutions remains unresolved.

The Internal Market Bill as introduced in September 2020 revealed the willingness of the government to treat the rule of law and its international commitments as optional, by proposing 'notwithstanding' clauses which would have set aside obligations included in the Withdrawal Agreement with the EU. While a settlement was reached and those clauses were withdrawn, it demonstrates that constitutional fundamentals have shifted. Law used to be the big constraint; it would appear to be very much less so now. The office holders in government who you would have expected to stand out against the magnitude of that shift – the Lord Chancellor, the Attorney General, the Advocate General and the Solicitor General – have, with the honourable exception of the Advocate General, failed to challenge the idea of using a statute to override the international legal obligations to which this very government agreed. The Lord Chancellor, the Attorney General and the Solicitor General not only remained in place, but described attacks on the Internal Market Bill, in the words of the Attorney General, as 'unpatriotic'.[4]

[4] See 'Labour "Unpatriotic" for Opposing Breach of International Law, Government Claims' *The Independent* (24 September 2020) www.independent.co.uk/news/uk/politics/brexit-labour-unpatriotic-international-law-legislation-b572820.html.

And there are increasing indications that the judiciary, keen not to become the enemies of the people, are more deferential than previously in their decision-making on challenges to the executive. The judges are in the UK constitution the key protector of the rule of law. They have their eye much more on Downing Street these days than they used to. Of course their fundamental commitment to judicial independence remains intact and the Inns of Court echo with strong and sincere judicial proclamations of separation from the executive. But the 'wiser' judges recognise the judicial ship needs steadying – the heat has to be taken out of the relationship between judges and ministers.

In *SC, CB and 8 children*, the Supreme Court recently rejected a claim which sought a ruling that the two child limit on child tax credits offended human rights protection because it discriminated against women. There was little dispute it did discriminate against women because there were so many more single women responsible for bringing up two plus children than single men. But the Supreme Court wouldn't entertain the claim. Once Parliament had decided on the limit, that was that they said.

This represents a massive retrenchment from cases like the Belmarsh decision[5] where the court led by Lord Bingham (no radical) declared primary legislation to fight terrorism in the wake of 9/11 in breach of human rights. Just as in the Belmarsh cases, in the two child tax credit case pressure groups had supported the claims. In the tax credit case Lord Reed described these pressure groups in terms reflecting the Conservative party 2019 manifesto which complained of litigation being used to carry on politics by other means:

> In practice, challenges to legislation on the ground of discrimination have become increasingly common in the United Kingdom. They are usually brought by campaigning organisations which lobbied unsuccessfully against the measure when it was being considered in Parliament, and then act as solicitors for persons affected by the legislation, or otherwise support legal challenges brought in their names, as a means of continuing their campaign.[6]

These words were written by the judge who co-wrote the prorogation decision. The departure of his co-author Baroness Hale might explain some of the new found judicial deference. But steadying the ship by choosing their battles might well be a contributor.

C. Abandonment of Checks and Balances

The government are keen to take on checkers and balancers beyond the judges. In New Broadcasting House, BBC bosses are desperately slapping down

[5] *A and others v Secretary of State for the Home Department* [2004] UKHL 56.
[6] *R (SC, CB and 8 children) v Secretary of State for Work and Pensions* [2021] UKSC 26, [162].

broadcasters who appear over-hostile to the government. Emily Maitlis was reprimanded by the BBC for saying the country was 'shocked' that the government could not see that Dominic Cummings had broken the rules with his Barnard Castle eye test journey during the coronavirus restrictions, a view so universally held that probably only those then working in Downing Street disagreed with it, and probably not even a majority of them. The *Guardian*'s media correspondent Jim Waterson has reported that the Director General of the BBC will be 'acutely aware of how Downing Street will view any appointment of a new political editor to replace Laura Kuenssberg.' And the Sunday Times reported a Secretary of State's 'fury' at a BBC Radio 4 Today programme presenter telling the PM to stop talking on the Today programme, telling allies 'he had cost the BBC millions.' All this amounts to more pressure to reduce criticism of the government.

In the last year, six permanent Secretaries have been sacked or resigned, including the heads of the home and foreign civil service.The Home Secretary has emerged unscathed from being found guilty of bullying civil servants, in breach of the Ministerial Code. The consequence of making that finding was that the Independent Adviser to the PM on the Ministerial Code had to resign. Making it clear there is a price to pay if a ministerial view is resisted reduces resistance.Whether it be judges, civil servants or the BBC, they are more wary before embarking on a disagreement with ministers. The threat to these institutions caused by rightly resisting ministers in a particular case must now be weighed against the importance of resisting in that case. Sometimes truth, justice or the right advice will be sacrificed to avoiding a dangerous fuss.

This inevitably reduces the independence and the strength of the checkers and balances. And with that reduction the quality of government declines.

We are moving towards a majoritarian government, one governing explicitly for the plurality who elected it, and not being significantly constrained by law from favouring that one part of the nation only. Aiming to remove or ignore the checks and balances, the government seeks to limit the power of the law, the BBC or the civil service to restrain the government, whether by the Human Rights Act or by judicial review, or by media pressure, and pursue policies which, for example, allow it to dispense public money in a way which favours constituencies already in Tory hands or targeted by them.

This attitude is the driver of the Johnson government's constitutional agenda. It is the reason why the Human Rights Act is seen as a shackle, and not a protection. And it is also why the Supreme Court, far from ensuring individual freedom, is viewed as a means of preventing the government from doing what it conceives as necessary in order to deliver the change that very many people in the country want.

The coronavirus pandemic which began in 2020 has exacerbated this trend, and allowed the government to govern by decree. The public have accepted that. It is not an issue. They want health protection. They are understandably and rightly much more worried by the immediate threat than the possibility of abuse.

But a year of decrees where persuasion is not so necessary gives the government a taste for it. And whilst I am sure we will revert to normal legislating outside the context of the public health crisis, governments are notoriously poor at changing their style.

The current constitutional tension arises from the checks and balances having been used to try to thwart Brexit, and so now many of those who supported Brexit, from the Prime Minsiter outwards, want to neuter those checks and balances. The solution lies in preserving and entrenching those checks and balances, but also ensuring that where the people have spoken with clarity either in a referendum or a general election the constitution cannot be used to thwart that democratic instruction.

V. FUTURE CONSTITUTIONAL REFORM

Against this backdrop, what should a future constitutional reform programme look like?

A. Preserving Constitutional Values

The key constitutional values under attack are the Union, the idea that a government should govern for the whole country and the rule of law. Of course, the current government accepts the most basic constraints, such as that it can only change the law by legislation. But it is a government with a big Commons majority justifying much of what it does by the will of the people expressed in the 2016 referendum and the 2019 general election – and it is not accepting many other constraints. There needs to be much greater agreement and protection for the constraints. It must be crystal clear what the rule of law restrains our government from doing, and it needs to entrench the right of Scotland, Wales and Northern Ireland to a significant degree of self-government. It needs to give the regions of England much greater control over public expenditure and infrastructure decisions. And it needs to provide much better protection against a government that abuses its position.

For the Prime Minister, Boris Johnson, and the (then) Attorney General, Geoffrey Cox, both to say on the subject of the prorogation decision in *Miller (No 2)*[7] that the judges have become too politicised and the politicians would need some process to review the appointment of the most senior judges is an indication they are no longer accepting the separation between politics and the judges. They are accusing the judges of having become too

[7] *Cherry v Advocate General for Scotland; Miller v Prime Minister* [2019] UKSC 41.

involved in politics. That is not true. But to ensure the government does not legislate to allow the government of the day to pick judges on the basis of their political positions, the appointment on legal merit principle needs to be entrenched. It is perfectly legitimate and very common for an administration to say 'I don't like the decision, so I'll legislate to change it'. That is acceptable, and happens frequently. However, what is not acceptable is to say that the judges have constitutionally overstepped the mark so the government is going to change the constitutional position of the judges by having more parliamentary involvement in the selection of judges, which is what the Attorney General suggested, and also, as is now happening, trying to restrict the ability of the judges to interfere through judicial review of what the government does, both by primary legislation and public attacks.[8] If these values are in play, a way should be found to entrench them. The pursuit of greater power to oust judicial review is a sinister development.

There also needs to be much greater clarity about the effect of a referendum vote, and the circumstances in which a government can continue in office when its flagship policies have been defeated.

The defeat of the May government's Brexit deal in the Commons in 2019 should have led to a general election.That deal was the main purpose of the government. The Commons' rejection of that deal signalled their loss of confidence in the May administration.Our parliamentary system depends on the government retaining the confidence of the Commons. It justifies the government controlling the Commons' agenda and being able to thwart legislation being considered which wrests executive control from ministers. But the rigidity of the Fixed-term Parliament Act 2011 allowed the May government to stay in office without the confidence of the Commons. And the consequence was parliamentary stalemate and an ensuing reduction in public confidence in Parliament.

The Fixed-term Parliaments Act will shortly be repealed and there will be an explicit return to the pre-Act constitution. The Dissoluton and Calling of Parliament Bill repealing the FTPA does not spell out what the pre-Act constitution involved. In outline it can be summarised as follows: where the government loses a vote of confidence in the Commons it has to resign, or there has to be a general election, or a new government which can command the confidence of the Commons without a general election; a loss of confidence occurs where the government is defeated on an issue central to the government's programme or its performance as a government; the opposition can move a motion which explicitly asserts the House has no confidence in the government, which the Commons will debate as a matter of priority, or the government can designate a vote on a particular issue as a vote of confidence; defeats of the government on particular policy issues, for example on

[8] See the report of the Independent Review of Administrative Law (2021) https://www.gov.uk/government/consultations/judicial-review-reform.

amendments to Bills or on opposition day motions, are generally not regarded as votes of confidence.

Leaving the circumstances in which a government has to resign to a contested view of the historical precedents or non-binding 'Dissolution Principles' may not be the safest constitutional course. Again this may be an area where a written constitution could spell out the principles whilst allowing an appropriate degree of flexibility.

B. Future of Labour Constitutional Reform – Devolution, Democracy and the Elected Dictatorship

The challenge for the future is therefore profound.

First, there needs to be a fundamental rethink of the relationship with Scotland that will preserve the Union, but give Scotland much greater autonomy and greater entrenchment of self-government than it has at the moment. And that constitutional change is not just about the nature of the relationship between Scotland and England; it is also about the nature of the Scottish Labour Party's relationship with the UK Labour Party, and similarly with all the major parties.

Second, Labour should be on the side of much greater autonomy in the English regions. The English regions need to have the ability to make their own decisions about infrastrucuture, spending, public services and priorities. The governance of the regions needs to much more strongly reflect the views of those who live in the regions. They need to have much more control of their own destiny. They need to be valued and recognised as having an entitlement to their own layer of government close to them. The House of Lords should become an elected body where the nations and regions come together to revise legislation and hold the government of the UK to account.

Third, there needs to be much greater protection of the whole of the public from authoritarian government. The elective dictatorship is the way this government governs. And our constitutional arrangements are not proving up to stopping them. The human rights settlement should be defended in its current form. It is supported by many people, of course, but I do not feel that it is embedded in our constitutional consciousness in the way that, for example, parliamentary democracy is. And I would equally strongly defend the current arrangements for the separation of powers, because where we are strong as a country is that our law is regarded as being delivered by judges who are not liberal, not conservative, but are just applying the law. These two elements of our constitution do not need surgery, they need defending and entrenching.

Fourth, the ways in which the Commons can bring a government down need to be reconsidered and the principles set down.

C. Written Constitution

So much of this suggests the need for a written constitution in the UK to entrench the rights of the nations and regions, to preserve the Union and to protect individuals against an elected dictatorship. Until the events of the last decade, I had always been opposed to a written constitution. Significant constitutional change has been possible speedily from the beginning of the process to the end, which has been important when there has been political stagnation. It is what allowed the Labour governments to introduce such a broad package of constitutional reform relatively quickly. In contrast, in the USA, with its written constitution, the Equal Rights Amendment, for example, has taken many, many years. And the US Constitution was used over a long period of time to be a dampener on reform because the judges were essentially conservative.

In addition, the consequence of a written constitution is that it has the power by some mechanism or other to trump parliamentary sovereignty. That mechanism will inevitably involve judges, whether by declaring Acts of Parliament unconstitutional, and then leaving it to Parliament to take necessary remedial steps over a specified period, or striking the Act down. That inevitably draws judges more into politics. But is there a better way of protecting human rights and the basic freedoms that currently exist? I cannot see one, and view, for example, the proposals to allow greater success for the ouster of judicial review clauses as a further sign that the restraints on the government are weakening, and in consequence so is the protection the rule of law provides against bad government.[9]

So my desire now for a written constitution is in order to preserve what I believe to be the fundamental values in our constitution which are under challenge. In the face of the current crisis, anything else would not really be an adequate response. Labour did look at this issue towards the end of its time in government. When he succeeded Tony Blair to become Prime Minister, Gordon Brown looked at the idea of a concordat or a written set of arrangements between Parliament and the government, and codification of the prerogative and a number of other things which might have created a more formal constitution. Gordon was keen, I think, to reflect our constitutional values in some legally binding document. But it never came to fruition because, unless it is a written constitution, what does such a document amount to?

We might know what these values are in a political sense, but if you expressed that we are a country that is in favour of democracy, justice, the rule of law, solidarity, a legitimate concern for the environment – or, more widely, for social,

[9] See the government proposals in the *Judicial Review Reform Consultation* (CP 408, March 2021) https://assets.publishing.service.gov.uk/government/uploads/system/uploads/attachment_data/file/975301/judicial-review-reform-consultation-document.pdf.

economic, climate and cultural justice – what is the impact of that in legal or constitutional terms? Those very general principles, to the extent that they come up and are relevant in practical contexts, will already be taken into account by our judges.

I believe the time is ripe for a written constitution. I recognise that it will never happen under this majoritarian government. It involves those on the progressive end of politics defending more conservative values. It is the consequence of the retreat from progress.

Before there could be a written constitution, there would need to be, as Labour acknowledge, a process genuinely engaging the public, ending in a constitutional convention. And it would need to be a *truly* engaging process, including people's assemblies and citizens' juries. It would seek to produce a document which reflected the values of the whole country. Although the 'remain/leave' divide no longer animates as it did, both sides in that epic cultural and political divide must feel it is their constitution. I believe this is possible. Both sides felt and feel the most profound emotional connection to the UK. A written constitution must reflect that shared patriotic ownership.

VI. CONCLUSION

Between 1997 and 2010, the Labour government overhauled our constitution to bring it closer to the people – to increase the people's control over those who governed them. Those changes have served the country well. The events of the last decade mean it is time for a further overhaul. The financial, Brexit and coronavirus crises throw a very profound light on where further work is now required. History shows it is only Labour who ever deliver those profound structural changes to the constitution. We need to get to work again, just as we did in the long march to 1997.

2

Britain's New Labour Constitution: Causes and Consequences

RODNEY BRAZIER

THE FIRST OF May 1997 was beautifully warm and sunny. On that May Day, the Labour Party, which had been in opposition for 17 years, swept to power with a landslide majority of 179 seats. As the party's election campaign song had it, it seemed that 'Things Can Only Get Better'. The New Labour government was to remain in office for the following 13 years. One of the many things that New Labour wanted to make better was, of course, the British constitution. Indeed, its manifesto, *New Labour: Because Britain Deserves Better*,[1] devoted 34 paragraphs to the party's constitutional enterprise. It was a very long shopping list. The main items on it were to remove the hereditary peers, and to set up a Joint Committee of Parliament to examine radical House of Lords reform;[2] to modernise the House of Commons; to establish a commission on voting systems, and to hold a referendum on any suggested change;[3] to pass a Freedom of Information Act; to hold referendums in Scotland and Wales so as to endorse a new Scottish Parliament and Welsh Assembly; to continue the peace process in Northern Ireland begun by John Major; to establish a Mayor of London and an Assembly; to hold referendums in the English regions about whether to set up elected Regional Assemblies; and to incorporate the European Convention on Human Rights into domestic law.[4] It is slightly odd to recall that New Labour thought fit to guarantee explicitly just one part of the constitution that would be immune from change. As the manifesto put it, 'We have no plans to abolish the monarchy'.

[1] Labour Party, 1997.

[2] In the event, 92 were saved from exclusion (House of Lords Act 1999, s 2), and the investigation was conducted by a Royal Commission chaired by Lord Wakeham: *Report of the Royal Commission on Reform of the House of Lords* (Cm 4534, 2000).

[3] Lord Jenkins chaired a commission, which finished its work within a year: *Report of the Independent Commission on the Voting System* (Cm 4090, 1998). The promised referendum was never held.

[4] See generally R Blackburn and R Plant (eds), *Constitutional Reform: The Labour Government's Constitutional Reform Agenda* (Longman, 1999).

In this chapter, I have two aims. First, I want to explain why New Labour had constructed such a vast programme of constitutional reform. Never in the history of the constitution was so much constitutional reform offered to British voters by a major party at a single general election.[5] Secondly, I want to explain several general consequences of Labour's constitution-making.

I. CAUSES

A. Why Did New Labour Constitution-Make?

Depending on your politics, 1997 was either an *annus mirabilis* or an *annus terribilis*. In any event there was a marked and major change in British electioneering in that year. Before then, the political parties had had very little, if anything, to say in their manifestos about constitutional change. Indeed, with a few exceptions, the parties that were likely to form a government had been content to leave the constitution alone. Normally, changes had been made only as necessary to meet some irresistible force.[6] The Parliament Act 1911 was one example of that; votes for some women in 1918 was another; various constitutions for Ireland, or Northern Ireland, were yet others. Governments, and the opposition party, generally adopted a reactive approach. They preferred to let sleeping constitutional dogs lie, unless one woke up and did something unpleasant. Until the 1980s, party manifestos were usually – though not always[7] – silent about the constitution. New Labour's 1997 manifesto therefore marked a dramatic change with the past. The obvious question is: *why* did New Labour offer this constitutional cornucopia? I suggest that there were two causes. They can be expressed in very personal terms. One was Margaret Thatcher, and the other was John Smith.

Like its predecessors, the Thatcher government of 1979–90 was able to implement its radical and consensus-breaking policies free, in the main, from significant constitutional checks and balances.[8] It was in that context that an

[5] R Brazier, *Constitutional Reform*, 3rd edn (Oxford University Press, 2008) ch 3; R Brazier, 'New Labour, New Constitution?' (1998) 49 *Northern Ireland Legal Quarterly* 1.

[6] Brazier, *Constitutional Reform*, 3rd edn (2008) ch 2.

[7] The main exceptions were the Liberals' 1910 promise to assert the power of the Commons over the Lords; Labour's 1966 commitment to Lords reform; Labour's October 1974 commitments to Scottish and Welsh devolution; and Mrs Thatcher's 1983 promise to abolish the Greater London Council and the metropolitan county councils (to which bodies voters had the irritating habit of returning Labour majorities). In 1982, Mrs Thatcher thought that there was nothing to do to improve the constitution: M Thatcher, *The Downing Street Years* (HarperCollins, 1993) 282.

[8] During and just after that period, a number of books were published which grappled with contemporary constitutional problems and possible reforms. They included K Ewing and C Gearty, *Freedom under Thatcher* (Oxford University Press, 1991); J Jowell and D Oliver, *The Changing Constitution* (Oxford University Press, 1985); P McAuslan and J F McEldowney (eds), *Law, Legitimacy and the Constitution* (Sweet & Maxwell, 1985); D Oliver, *Government in the United Kingdom* (Oxford University Press, 1991); R Brazier, *Constitutional Reform* (Oxford University Press, 1991).

impotent Labour opposition – appalled by Thatcherite economic and social changes – undertook in the 1980s a root-and-branch review of all its policies. If Labour had no other reason to do this, then its defeat at Mrs Thatcher's hands in three consecutive elections, in 1979, 1983 and 1987, would have provided a painful and irresistible spur. Two years after the last of those defeats, Labour published a fresh statement of revised policies, in the paper 'Meet the Challenge: Make the Change'.[9] In it, Labour embraced constitutional reform, having more or less ignored it for over 80 years. In effect, 10 years of Thatcherism had forced Labour to change its stance. I will not go into the details of that paper.[10] Suffice to say that from 1989 Labour wanted reforms to extend democracy and human rights. But the party clung to the first-past-the-post voting system for the House of Commons. And it rejected the incorporation of the European Convention on Human Rights: Labour still distrusted the judiciary, which it continued to believe was anti-labour.[11]

With the political matricide of Mrs Thatcher by her party in 1990 and the succession to the premiership of a less confrontational and less ideologically driven John Major, it might have been understandable if the momentum had gone out of Labour's push for constitutional change. Labour-supporting people might have thought that they would have less to fear from the new Conservative government; perhaps constitutional reform would seem less important to them. Labour had seven years, from 1990 to 1997, if it wished to ditch or adapt any of its constitutional policies that might prove inconvenient for a Labour government. But *au contraire*: not only, during the 1990s, did New Labour keep the party's constitutional plans, it gave some of them a more radical edge. I suggest that, in significant part, this was driven by John Smith.

Labour lost consecutive general election number four in 1992. Neil Kinnock resigned as Labour leader. John Smith was elected by Labour's electoral college in his place. Among other things, Mr Smith was a lawyer, indeed a QC. He was one of a rapidly expanding band of people – from non-Conservative politicians, lawyers, academics, senior judges and many others – who were persuaded of the need for the UK to incorporate the European Convention. Under John Smith's leadership, that became Labour policy. As a Scot, he also had a deep personal commitment to devolution, and wanted a powerful Scottish Parliament to be established. He had been an early advocate of devolution. Back in 1976, the new Prime Minister, James Callaghan, had appointed him as a junior minister under Michael Foot, the Lord President of the Council. Mr Foot was in charge of the government's devolution plans. Both men 'were keen advocates of devolution'.[12] Alas for them, the Scots and Welsh rejected the Callaghan government's

[9] Labour Party, 1989.

[10] See Brazier, *Constitutional Reform*, 3rd edn (n 5) 26–28.

[11] As famously explained by JAG Griffith, *The Politics of the Judiciary*, 5th edn (Fontana Press, 2010).

[12] M Stuart, *John Smith: A Life* (Politico's Publishing Ltd, 2005) 79.

devolution models at referendums in 1979.[13] A vote of no confidence in the minority Labour government was carried by one vote, and that government was put out of its misery by the voters. But Mr Smith was to say that, for him, 'in a personal sense [devolution] is very much unfinished business'.[14]

After Neil Kinnock's resignation in 1992, Mr Smith won the leadership. His platform, 'New Paths to Victory', had included a section on constitutional reform. He proposed the incorporation of the European Convention into domestic law – which Labour had until then consistently opposed – an elected second chamber, a Freedom of Information Act, devolution to Scotland, Wales and the English regions, and fixed-term Parliaments.[15] Note that this was *five years before* Tony Blair became leader, and before the term 'New Labour' entered political discourse. But the one thing that Mr Smith did not want to change was the first-past-the-post (FPTP) voting system. The Labour Party commissioned the Plant Report, which was published a year after his election.[16] The Report suggested that the alternative vote, or perhaps an additional member system, might be better than FPTP, but the Plant Working Party was itself divided on the matter, and John Smith was content to leave the issue aside. A year or so into his leadership, the Labour Party published a revised statement of its constitutional reform policies, *A New Agenda for Democracy*.[17] It incorporated all of John Smith's constitutional ideas into official party policy.

If John Smith had not died suddenly of a heart attack in May 1994, he would have become Prime Minister in 1997 rather than Tony Blair. It is worth noting that while John Smith was Labour leader the party was led by someone who was personally committed to constitutional reform. Tony Blair, Peter Mandelson and the other New Labour apparatchiks persuaded the party to ditch voter-repellent policies and to offer more appealing ones. But they decided to keep the party's policy of major reform of the British constitution, and indeed added to it. Moreover, they did so despite the adage that there are no votes in constitutional reform. They were supported in this by the Liberal Democrats. Both parties were totally opposed in all this by the Conservatives, who rejected every one of Labour's constitutional reform proposals. They had not come very far from the Duke of Wellington's judgement in the nineteenth century that the British constitution was perfect. Indeed, during the 1992 election, John Major warned that devolution would lead to the break-up of the Union between England and Scotland. (Those words were to carry more weight when the Scottish National Party subsequently gained ground, and only lost some after the Scottish independence referendum in 2014.) In 1997,

[13] Welsh voters crushed the proposal. In Scotland, the supermajority required for a valid 'Yes' vote was not met – a provision that the minority government had not wanted to be in the legislation.

[14] Stuart, *John Smith* (2005) 293.

[15] ibid 232–33.

[16] *Report of the Working Party on Electoral Systems* (Labour Party, 1993).

[17] Labour Party, 1993.

while Labour was still in opposition, it had set up a Joint Consultative Committee on Constitutional Reform with the Liberal Democrats. Through it, the two parties drew together many – but not all – of their respective and similar constitutional plans.[18] In part, this initiative was based on the possibility that they might cooperate in the 1997 Parliament, perhaps even by forming a Labour–Liberal Democrat coalition. That was certainly what Paddy Ashdown believed,[19] and Tony Blair was still talking about coalition even when it was clear that Labour had a landslide majority. (Only after leaving office did he say that any formal cooperation with the Liberal Democrats would not, in fact, have worked because he thought that they would not have supported several tough decisions that would need to be taken in government. And, more importantly, he found that such a move was opposed by senior party colleagues when the time came to form his government.[20])

In one important respect, Labour's 1997 general election manifesto went further than John Smith's vision. If your party loses four consecutive general elections, it is natural to question the voting system. After 1992, many in the Labour Party thought that it was somehow skewed towards the right. Many others questioned its suitability for the UK at the end of the twentieth century. So Labour committed itself to appoint an independent commission to find a different method of electing MPs, and to put the new system to the people in a referendum.[21] On the other hand, New Labour's 1997 manifesto left out two matters which had been trailed in *A New Agenda for Democracy*. There was no mention in the manifesto of the creation of an independent judicial appointments commission to advise on the appointment of judges, or of any review of royal prerogative powers.

The very first Bill introduced into the 1997 Parliament was the Referendums (Scotland and Wales) Bill. One reason for the priority given to that measure was to underline New Labour's determination to carry out its constitutional reforms. Other constitutional Bills followed. But one change was not pursued in the first session of the new Parliament: Lords reform. The government announced that a reform Bill would be introduced in the second session. I think that one reason for that postponement was so that the treatment of Labour's whole initial legislative programme by the Conservative-dominated House of Lords could be taken into account when a Lords reform Bill was drafted. The prospect of that

[18] *Report of the Joint Consultative Committee on Constitutional Reform* (Labour Party and the Liberal Democrats, 1997).

[19] P Ashdown, *A Fortunate Life* (Aurum, 2010) 295–302; P Ashdown, *The Ashdown Diaries*, vol 2 (Allen Lane, 2001) 1–24.

[20] T Blair, *A Journey*, paperback edn (Arrow, 2011) 119, 120, 122. At least Liberal Democrat parliamentarians were appointed to a Cabinet Joint Consultative Committee on Constitutional Reform in equal numbers with Labour Ministers, until Charles Kennedy pulled the plug on it in 2001 on the ground that it had outlived its usefulness.

[21] At that time, the only precedent for such a vote was the 1975 referendum on continued membership of the European Economic Community.

Bill was held as a sword of Damocles over the House of Lords, to remind them that major change was coming.

B. Making it Up: Reform by Press Release

Manifestos obviously cannot give an exhaustive list of all the policies and things that will be done by a party in office. Just like anyone else, governments have fresh ideas as time goes on and they must also react to events. While voters should be told at a general election what a party will do in the following five years if it wins, manifestos cannot be completely comprehensive. In Labour's case, one new policy would amount to a fundamental constitutional change. Yet it had not featured in its manifestos; events did not demand that it be introduced; and there had been no planning for it. That lack of careful preparation was quickly exposed.

In a Cabinet reshuffle in 2003, the Prime Minister announced through a Number 10 press release to an unsuspecting world that he intended to abolish the office of Lord Chancellor and to set up a new Department for Constitutional Affairs, headed by a Secretary of State; to create a Supreme Court; and to establish an independent Judicial Appointments Commission. There had been no public, or other, consultation about this – not even with the senior judiciary.[22] An office that can be traced back to 1066 – over 900 years of constitutional history – was apparently to be expunged by a prime ministerial fiat issued on photocopies from Downing Street. Every Lord Chancellor, bar one, had been a peer.[23] In the 2003 reshuffle, Lord Irvine of Lairg was dropped and replaced as Lord Chancellor by Lord Falconer, who was also named as the new Secretary of State. It was easy enough to create the new Department, and to appoint the new Secretary of State. That was done under the royal prerogative. But otherwise there was a period of confusion, until the better-informed in government got to work on the other changes. What should have been obvious then became clear: legislation was needed. The Constitutional Reform Bill was drafted, and referred to a select committee.[24] It passed into law in 2005. Of course, the constitutionally unsatisfactory nature of the office of Lord Chancellor had been talked about for years.[25] That living denial of the separation of powers was to be cured by New Labour. (When Gordon Brown succeeded Tony Blair in 2007, an MP became Lord Chancellor for the first time. Jack Straw, a barrister, was to

[22] In his memoirs, Jack Straw records that the judges felt insulted, and, he adds, 'with good reason'. J Straw, *Last Man Standing*, paperback edn (Macmillan, 2012) 501.

[23] Sir Thomas More, Lord Chancellor from 1529 to 1532.

[24] Select Committee on the Constitutional Reform Bill, *Constitutional Reform Bill* (HL 125, 2003–04).

[25] See, eg D Woodhouse, *The Office of Lord Chancellor* (Hart Publishing, 2001).

be followed by Ken Clarke, QC. Four non-lawyers succeeded them.[26] Then, in 2017, Mrs Theresa May appointed David Gauke to be Lord Chancellor, the first solicitor to hold the post.[27]) Whatever the merits of these changes – and they are many, despite the very poor quality of two of those appointees – this was no way to do constitutional reform. Mr Blair was honest enough to acknowledge that after he had retired.[28] But that did not stop him repeating the mistake in 2007 when, in his last reshuffle, and with equal lack of preparation, he merged the Department for Constitutional Affairs and parts of the Home Office into the new Ministry of Justice.[29] Some people never learn.

Why did Mr Blair make this major constitutional change at all? In his memoirs, he said that Lord Irvine had to go because the Prime Minister and the Home Secretary, David Blunkett, wanted to get 'some modernity into the very old fashioned way the criminal justice system worked',[30] which necessarily implies that Lord Irvine did not support radical changes to that system. But Mr Blair's purpose of having a Lord Chancellor sitting in the House of Commons was met icily by Lord Irvine. He said to Mr Blair (quite fairly) 'You've replaced one peer with another!'[31] Perhaps the Prime Minister thought that he could make Lord Irvine's sacking more palatable to him by wrapping it up in a general Cabinet reshuffle. If so, the tactic was no more successful than Harold Macmillan's had been in 1962, when, wishing to get rid of his Chancellor of the Exchequer, he wrapped up Selwyn Lloyd's sacking from the post in a huge reshuffle, the night of the long knives, in which a third of the Cabinet was sacked. Irvine was no more mollified than Lloyd had been.

C. Be Careful What You Wish For

It was Gordon Brown's burning, and entirely honourable, ambition to lead the Labour Party. He stood aside to allow his friend Tony Blair to take over in 1994 after John Smith's death.[32] But Mr Brown remained determined to get the keys to Number 10 as soon as possible.[33] He had to make do with being Chancellor

[26] Chris Grayling, Michael Gove, Liz Truss and David Lidington.

[27] In the nine years from 2010 to 2019 there were six Lord Chancellors. That is a record, and an undesirable one.

[28] Blair, *A Journey* (2011) 631.

[29] Mr Straw has written of 'the outrageous, casual way in which the decision to establish a new Ministry of Justice was announced': Straw, *Last Man Standing* (2012) 549.

[30] Blair (n 20). He acknowledged that the way in which the 2003 changes were carried out was 'bumpy and chaotic'.

[31] For a robust defence by him of the old-style of Lord Chancellor, see Lord Irvine of Lairg (ed), *Human Rights, Constitutional Law and the Development of the English Legal System: Selected Essays* (Hart Publishing, 2003) 204–08.

[32] There remain different versions of what exactly happened, even after both former Prime Ministers have published their memoirs. See Blair (n 20) 39–40, 50–54, 61–74; G Brown, *My Life, Our Times* (Random House, 2017) ch 4.

[33] That well-known phrase is inaccurate. There is no external lock in the door of Number 10, which can only be opened from the inside.

for 10 years, and was probably the most powerful Chancellor ever. In 2007, Tony Blair stood down. Mr Brown was elected, unopposed, in the electoral college to succeed him.

The title of the definitive biography of Gordon Brown could be *The Unhappy Prime Minister*. The common criticism is that, having had more than a decade to prepare for the premiership, he did not know what to do with it when it was his. But there was one major exception to that curious state of things. He had been privately preparing a very ambitious programme of constitutional reform. The first meeting of his Cabinet discussed the matter and approved his plans.[34] In essence, he wanted Britain's democracy to be 'strengthened by an extensive devolution of power from the executive to Parliament and the people … "Power to the people" was the theme.'[35] And his very first Commons speech as Prime Minister was not, say, on any economic matter. Rather, to my personal delight, it was on constitutional reform.[36] His predecessor had been indifferent to it.[37] Mr Brown, however, brought to constitutional reform the passion of a zealot. His Lord Chancellor, Jack Straw, began to publish what became a stream of papers for consultation. The first, and most ambitious, was entitled *The Governance of Britain*.[38] Topics in that paper included the possible transfer of many royal prerogative powers to Parliament, including those governing the deployment of the armed forces overseas, the ratification of treaties and the dissolution of Parliament. The Prime Minister's patronage powers might be modified. House of Lords reform would take place through cross-party talks. The long-promised review of voting systems would be published, possibly with a suggested change from FPTP. In the medium term, there would be published a 'Statement of British Values' (in my view a near-hopeless enterprise), and there could be a new, British, Bill of Rights. Work would even be done on a codified UK Constitution.[39] Further papers appeared on a number of those subjects. However, very little progress was made on any of them, no doubt in significant part because the government had to deal with the economic emergency following the 2007–08 banking crash.

Let tribute be paid to that work. At the very least, the published work has an educational value.[40] How far we have come since the leaders of the major

[34] Brown, *My Life, Our Times* (2017) 205.

[35] ibid 207.

[36] 462 HC Debs 815–20 (3 July 2007).

[37] Save for continuing the Northern Ireland peace process, begun by John Major, and which he carried on passionately and with great success. (I briefly met Mr Blair socially three months into his premiership. When I answered his question about what I did for a living, did his eyes glaze over ever so slightly?).

[38] Cm 7170 (2007).

[39] Indeed, in 2010, oddly after Parliament had been dissolved for the election, I was invited to join a government committee to do such work. The offer died with the Brown government.

[40] *The Governance of Britain* (Cm 7170, 2007); *The Governance of Britain: Constitutional Renewal* (Cm 7342, 2008); *An Elected Second Chamber: Further Reform of the House of Lords* (Cm 7438, 2008); *Rights and Responsibilities: Developing our Constitutional Framework* (Cm 7577, 2009).

parties and Prime Ministers ignored constitutional matters! But what constitutional changes did the Brown government actually *achieve*? One was not in its plans. The Parliamentary Standards Act 2009 was a knee-jerk reaction to the MPs' expenses scandal. (MPs are still paying the price for that disgraceful saga. In an opinion poll about public trust in the professions, published late in 2016, estate agents actually *increased* their standing, to 35 per cent. At the very bottom, though – even below journalists (of all people) – came politicians, at 15 per cent.) But the Brown government's ambitious Draft Constitutional Renewal Bill did appear, and was referred to a Joint Committee.[41] (I was its Specialist Adviser. Significant time was spent debating whether the word 'Renewal' should be replaced. It was. It became the Constitutional Reform and Governance Bill.) But by time the measure went to Parliament, Mr Brown's period in office before he had to face the voters had almost run out. In the 'wash up',[42] most of the provisions of the Bill were dropped, leaving three significant changes: the civil service was put on to a statutory, in place of the prerogative, basis; the most important treaties would require approval by Parliament before they could be ratified; and the '30-year rule' was reduced to 20 years.[43] As well as those two statutes, an important piece of codification was begun. Mr Brown directed that a document be produced, which we now know as the *Cabinet Manual*.[44] The Cabinet Office worked flat out to draft one chapter ahead of the others. This was because the 2010 general election was then in sight, and a hung Parliament was predicted. After consultations,[45] the draft chapter on elections and government formation was published, and its statement of the relevant rules, conventions, practices and so on were broadly followed when Labour lost the election. The full *Cabinet Manual* was published the following year, and is an important constitutional source for us all. Let us give Gordon Brown the credit for kick-starting it. Rather oddly, in his memoirs he does not make any mention of his part in the creation of the document – which could not have been written without his consent. Indeed, when he analyses the events following the election of the 2010 hung Parliament, he concludes (presumably in that particular context, but the wording is much broader) that 'it is clear that the current *Cabinet Manual* is inadequate, an unacceptable halfway house between an unwritten constitution and a constitutional document'.[46] Separately, his Lord Chancellor was also able to publish, for the first time, an exhaustive official statement of all the royal prerogative powers.[47] That is a useful document.

[41] Joint Select Committee on the Draft Constitutional Renewal Bill, Report (HC 551, 2007–08).

[42] The few weeks before an election during which government Bills are hurried through Parliament into law, omitting contentious parts to minimise opposition.

[43] Constitutional Reform and Governance Act 2010, ss 1–25 and Sch 4.

[44] Cabinet Office, 2011.

[45] They included a meeting chaired by the Secretary of the Cabinet and including civil servants, the Queen's Private Secretary and academics (of whom I was one).

[46] Brown (n 32) 386.

[47] *The Governance of Britain: Review of the Executive Royal Prerogative Powers: Final Report* (2010).

But for my money, the *Cabinet Manual* is by far the most significant constitutional document from the Brown government.

And so Gordon Brown resigned just three years after achieving his life's ambition. In constitutional terms, measured against his predecessor's record, his government produced little. What an irony that is. On my count, the Blair government oversaw the enactment of 17 statutes that can fairly be described as wholly or partly constitutional. Despite Mr Brown's passion, his government produced just two.[48] Why did he not achieve more? One reason is, of course, that his government was hit by the great financial emergency, caused not least by those running the big banks lending money they did not actually have to people who would find it impossible to pay back. Even I must concede that fighting potential economic collapse is rather more important than constitutional reform. But that programme also suffered from what has been described as Gordon Brown's chronic indecision as Prime Minister.[49] More specifically, Jack Straw has written that the Constitutional Reform and Governance Bill got 'caught up in the sort of interdepartmental wrangling that only a prime minister could resolve. But Gordon [in 2010] was too exhausted, too weakened by then.'[50]

II. CONSEQUENCES

I turn now to the long-term effects of the 1997 Labour government's constitution-making. I think that there are four main ones.

A. The Ravens Did Not Leave the Tower of London

Legend has it that if the ravens leave the Tower of London, where they strut about in the open air, Britain will fall. (To guard against such an awful omen, spare ravens are kept securely in reserve.) As everyone is supposed to know, the ancient British constitution has developed, step by step, to meet

[48] The Parliamentary Standards Act 2009 and the Constitutional Reform and Governance Act 2010. In contrast, if we exclude counterterrorism legislation (which is not to deny such legislation is constitutional in effect), there were some 17 major statutes on constitutional matters enacted under the governments of Tony Blair: Referendums (Scotland and Wales) Act 1997; Scotland Act 1998; Government of Wales Act 1998; Northern Ireland Act 1998; Regional Development Agencies Act 1998; Human Rights Act 1998; European Parliamentary Elections Act 1999; House of Lords Act 1999; Greater London Authority Act 1999; Regulation of Investigatory Powers Act 2000; Political Parties, Elections and Referendums Act 2000; Freedom of Information Act 2000; European Parliamentary Elections Act 2002; Civil Contingencies Act 2004; Constitutional Reform Act 2005; Government of Wales Act 2006; Identity Cards Act 2006 (since repealed).

[49] S Richards, *Whatever It Takes* (Fourth Estate, 2010) 274.

[50] Straw (n 22) 542.

changing circumstances. As a result, it has become an interwoven web of rules and practices. Unbelievable as it may seem today, even as late as 1997 the argument was still being made that any unpicking of one part of the constitution would start to unravel other parts. That conclusion was used to argue against any significant changes. New Labour proved that this romantic picture and dire warning were baseless. It showed that constitutional change *is* possible without the roof of the constitutional architecture falling in. Of course, we can all argue about the merits of this or that reform that has taken place since 1997. But today no one uses that old defence of the constitutional status quo. By making massive changes during 13 years – the blink of an eye in constitutional history – Labour proved that reform of parts of the British constitution is entirely possible. Today, reformers can go straight to the arguments about the merits of any particular suggested reform.

B. Much More of the Constitution is in Statute

Given that there is no codified constitution in the UK, the use of the word 'constitutional' draws few boundaries. The Constitution Committee of the House of Lords has explained the difficulties in arriving at a satisfactory definition.[51] Indeed, if you approach the British constitution past the sign marked 'Human Rights', you see a vast terrain, for it is easy to say that many laws are touched by this or that issue of human rights, which can thereby attract the adjective of constitutional. Anyway, the reforming 1997 Labour government caused much extra work for Parliamentary Counsel, not least in drafting constitutional Bills. The 19 statutes that in whole or significant part could be termed 'constitutional' add substantially to British statute law concerning the constitution. There was much more statute law about the constitution in place after Labour lost office in 2010. This is not, of course, to imply that this amounted to an attempt at codification; those Acts merely set out new rules and arrangements. Although the corpus of law is greater, the UK was no nearer to having a codified constitution in 2010 than she had been in 1997. True, if a comprehensive codification exercise were to be embarked on in future, it would be somewhat easier than it would have been before. Thus, the section of a new constitution of the UK protecting rights could (note, I do not say should) be filled in with the essence of the Human Rights Act. Similarly, that Constitution could set out the balances of constitutional power between the national and devolved governments and legislatures as lifted from the devolution legislation. But that would be about it. The massive report *A New Magna Carta?*[52] underlines that any constitutional

[51] Indeed, it accepted that its own working definition was far from perfect, but that it would 'do for our purposes'. Select Committee on the Constitution, *Reviewing the Constitution* (HL 11, 2000–01) para 20.

[52] Political and Constitutional Reform Committee, 2nd Report (HC 463, 2014–15).

codification exercise would be a huge task. Parliamentary Counsel yet unborn would find marginal assistance, if handed such a task, in New Labour's legislative efforts.

That statutory incontinence raises several questions. First, was an appropriate methodology adopted before those constitutional Bills were sent to Parliament? I think not. The rules under which a state is governed are of a different – I would say superior – status from all other rules in the state. As such, they should be arrived at in a special way, rather than through ordinary legislation passed in the usual way. Ideally, constitutional reform should proceed so far as possible across the parties. But there should in any case be public consultations, and pre-legislative scrutiny in Parliament.[53] This is not only my view; it is the considered opinion of the Constitution Committee of the House of Lords, which reported on the matter at the end of the time in office of the Blair government.[54] In its opinion, constitutional change is 'qualitatively different from other legislation',[55] which requires 'a significant period of public debate' on every proposed major constitutional reform.[56] In the absence of any accepted special process for constitutional legislation, the Committee noted that many disadvantages result.[57] These include the ability of a government to mould the UK's constitution with few restraints;[58] the rush which sometimes accompanies constitutional changes, sometimes for no sound reason; and the adoption of individual changes without considering them in the context of the whole constitution. There was precious little of any of that under Tony Blair. By contrast, today's Labour Party says it would approach constitutional reform very differently. In its 2017 general election manifesto, it pledged to create a Constitutional Convention. It would examine and advise on reform of the British constitution.[59] Although the proposal lacks detail, if it were ever acted on it would add a procedural mechanism which might mark a distinct move away from New Labour's 1997 shopping list approach to constitutional change.

Secondly, was there an underlying constitutional theory, or theories, which linked together some or all of these new laws? I can identify none. There were clichés aplenty, particularly 'modernisation' (as if that somehow automatically justified change), and also 'extending democracy' (who could oppose that?). Rather, each statute was passed to address some perceived constitutional problem as identified by the Labour Party – or, in Sir Robert Peel's famous words, to bring about 'the correction of proved abuses'.[60] In political terms, there is

[53] For a development of this argument see Brazier, *Constitutional Reform*, 3rd edn (n 5) ch 2.
[54] *The Process of Constitutional Change* (HL 177, 2010–11).
[55] ibid para 26.
[56] ibid para 46.
[57] ibid para 51.
[58] ibid para 23.
[59] *For the Many, Not the Few* (Labour Party, 2017) 102.
[60] The Tamworth manifesto (1834).

nothing wrong with that. Working out such a theoretical framework would take time that politicians do not have – or, more to the point, that they will not make the time for. And perhaps a search for such theories would be fruitless, certainly not without taking a considered view of the whole British constitution. Possibly constitutional reform will never be based on such theoretical considerations. Now, if all that is too abstract, there is a linked, and severely practical, problem: what consideration was given by the Labour government to how, and to what extent, reform X would impact on areas Y and Z? For instance, how would Lords reform affect the status of the House of Commons? (In the event, that question was moot, given that Labour's plans screeched to a halt once phase one of the Lords reform – getting rid of most hereditary peers – had been achieved.) New Labour wanted, through a shopping list of reforms, to take the nation to an unidentified constitutional destination. That is not an ideal approach to constitutional reform.

C. A Rush to Join the Bandwagon

The Liberal Democrats, and their predecessors in title the Liberal Party,[61] can justifiably claim to be the first party to have proposed wide and radical constitutional reform in the UK. They have schemed their schemes for decades. But they did so without support from Conservatives or Labour, who were constitutionally conservative. The Liberals had the will, but lacked the means; the two parties of government had the means, but had no inclination. John Smith and New Labour, however, started a bandwagon rolling. And by 1997 all the smaller parties – the SNP, Plaid Cymru, the Greens, even UKIP – had leapt on it as well. They have all offered their versions of new, or revised, UK constitutions. Even the Conservative Party after 1997 joined – well, perhaps trotted behind – the reformist bandwagon. It tried to outflank the Labour government on one point by advocating, from early in this century, and before Labour,[62] the creation of a new wholly or partly elected second chamber. And constitutional reform has featured in Conservative election manifestos ever since.

We are all reformers now, and no sensible person would take the rather snooty view that only what the Conservatives and Labour want is worth thinking about. If anyone does, he or she must have been asleep since the 2010 general election. The unique selling point of FPTP – that, despite its unfairness and unrepresentativeness, it always produces strong and stable majority governments – is now less persuasive. Two hung Parliaments were returned

[61] I will not trace the creation of the SDP, then the SDP/Liberal Alliance, and the morphing of it in 1988 into the Liberal Democrats.

[62] At that time, the Labour government was content to do little to implement the recommendations of the Wakeham Commission (on which see n 4).

at the last four general elections, in 2010 and in 2017. Moreover, the critical power that a small party can sometimes exert has been vividly shown by Mrs May deciding that she had to do a deal with the 10 Democratic Unionist MPs after the (for her) disastrous early election which she engineered in 2017.[63] I am not thinking of the DUP's price of over £1 billion that the Chancellor had to find from somewhere (where?) to go to Northern Ireland, but of that party's veto of one part of the draft stage one Brexit agreement with the EU, and the revised wording which it obtained in it about the Irish border. Small parties can have an effect on constitutional policy – for what is Brexit but the greatest constitutional change for 45 years?

Today, there is wide agreement between the parties on a number of future constitutional reforms. As to Parliament, all the political parties agree that the Lords should be replaced by a wholly or partly elected second chamber, although for the time being the Conservatives have removed Lords reform from their agenda.[64] All the parties, except for the Conservatives and Labour, want FPTP to be replaced – although there is disagreement about the preferred replacement.[65] Four parties, including Her Majesty's Opposition, assert that the voting age should be reduced to 16.[66] A new Bill of Rights, more comprehensive than, but building on, the Human Rights Act, should be adopted, and, some say, entrenched.[67] Three parties, including Labour, want the mechanics of constitutional reform to be changed by setting up a Constitutional Convention, although those parties do not envisage the same terms of reference.[68] (May I interpose that – at last – the methodology of constitutional reform is being seriously considered? I have been arguing for over 30 years that it should.) Naturally, the three nationalist parties maintain their fundamental aspirations, although Plaid Cymru seems to blow hot and cold over independence: currently it is an 'ambition'. All the parties have supported greater powers to the devolved authorities in Scotland and Wales, and the Conservatives have introduced elected regional mayors in England. And most radical of all, the Liberal Democrats look towards a constitutional heaven in which there is a federal, codified UK constitution.

That is quite a list. And how utterly different it is from the political prospectuses that were offered to Britain before John Smith and then New Labour

[63] *Confidence and Supply Agreement between the Conservative and Unionist Party and the Democratic Unionist Party* (Prime Minister's Office, updated 14 December 2017). What would Conservative Prime Ministers such as Churchill, Macmillan and Thatcher have thought of that?

[64] 'comprehensive [Lords] reform is not a priority': *Forward, Together* (Conservative Party, 2017) 43.

[65] The single transferable vote for the Liberal Democrats and for the SNP (under whose aegis it has been adopted for local government elections in Scotland); the additional member system for the Greens; and some form of proportional representation for UKIP. There was no mention of reform of the voting system in Labour's 2017 manifesto.

[66] Labour, the Liberal Democrats, the Greens and the SNP.

[67] Entrenchment is the ideal for the Liberal Democrats.

[68] Labour, the Liberal Democrats and the Greens.

embraced constitutional reform as mainstream party policy. Would the other parties have seen the light but for the 1997 Labour landslide? That is a matter of judgement and opinion, and would involve a counterfactual examination that I am not going to conduct. In any case, anyone who did so would have to make allowance for reactive reform forced on the government of the day. I cannot resist reference to David Cameron's self-inflicted wound of his 2013 promise of the Brexit referendum. This was his answer to the euroscepticism of many in his party, and as a way of defusing the electoral threat then posed by UKIP. His reaction to those forces, made on the generally held assumption that voters would want to stay in the EU, proved to be a personal disaster which has launched the UK into an uncertain world.

D. Parts of the British Constitution have been Entrenched

Of course, the British constitution is not legally entrenched. Yet, for political reasons, parts of it enjoy the trappings of entrenchment. New Labour's changes remain intact, despite the Conservatives, who opposed all of them, being the major party in government since 2010. The Coalition, then Mr Cameron's short-lived Conservative government, then Mrs May's government and now Boris Johnson's administration have all had the legal and political power to amend or repeal any of Labour's constitutional statutes. But they have not. Why not? Inertia must play a part. Why go through all the trouble of changing this or that bit of the constitution when the changes have not caused the heavens to fall? And certain parts are entrenched by the popular will as expressed through referendums. Thus, the Scottish Parliament and the Welsh Parliament are safe. Indeed, on the face of the statute book, they are safer still now that post-Scottish referendum statutes have declared them to be 'a permanent part of the United Kingdom's constitutional arrangements'.[69] Moreover, what party is going to go to the voters with cries of 'Return the hereditaries, repeal freedom of information, strip Parliament of rights over sending the forces overseas, and over ratifying treaties!' That just would not sound right. And for the five years of the 2010 Coalition government, the Liberal Democrats acted as a constitutional restraint on the Conservative Party. Overall, however, nothing of substance has been altered in New Labour's constitutional Acts, other than to enhance them. Indeed, even though the Human Rights Act has been on the Conservatives' death row since its birth, it is still alive, and has survived Conservative governments since 2010.[70]

[69] Scotland Act 2016, s 1; Wales Act 2017, s 1.

[70] That stay was promised in their manifesto at the 2017 general election: *Forward, Together* (Conservative Party, 2017) 37. On the resilience of the HRA, see H Tyrrell, ch 3 of this volume.

III. BRIEF REFLECTIONS

For better or worse – and that depends on the judgements of individuals – the British constitution was fashioned during the 10 years from 1997 largely according to the wishes of Tony Blair's government. That government only failed to deliver three of its constitutional promises. There was no referendum on voting reform, surely not because the existing system suddenly looked much better when it delivered power to the Labour Party after 18 years in opposition and repeatedly confirmed it in office. There was no stage two of Lords reform. And now we know why. In his memoirs, Mr Blair said that the idea of an elected second chamber was 'mad', and 'all in all I was against it'.[71] And no elected regional assemblies were created for England. The North East referendum result put paid to that.[72]

The place of the 1997 Labour government in constitutional history is assured. Most of its constitution-making is solidly cemented as part of Britain's constitutional structures. Before that famous day in May 1997, the UK, to take the main examples, was a unitary state, with only local councils having limited powers to decide local matters. Centuries-old divisions within one part of that kingdom made Northern Ireland very difficult, and occasionally more or less impossible, to govern. British citizens had no code of positive rights. They could not, even through journalists and historians, get hold of official information often until three decades had passed. Governments could make treaties without Parliament's approval being automatically required. Legislators at Westminster were the sole arbiters of their own standards, however high or low they might be. For centuries, this undoubted Western liberal democracy had a parliamentary chamber most of whose members owed their presence to the death of a relative who had sat in it at the time of that demise. And that House contained a living denial of the separation of powers, a peer who could also sit as a judge (and, moreover, who appointed the judiciary), was Speaker of that chamber and was a cabinet minister who came and went with the government of the day. The highest court in the country was technically a committee of that House, albeit consisting of peers appointed for the purpose with the required legal qualifications to sit on it. All that, and more, the Labour Party was pledged to address,[73] and did so in office.

Given all that has happened politically in the UK and around the world over the past few years, the making of forecasts should now be confined to the rash and to those who are paid to make them. But, foolish though it may be, I make one prediction: even though the political parties nowadays all have constitutional

[71] Blair (n 20) 649–50.

[72] It was rejected by a crushing 78% to 22%. Voting was done by post only: 48% returned their ballot papers. The North East referendum is discussed in more detail in L Trueblood, ch 14 of this volume, s IIIC; A Giovannini, ch 7 of this volume.

[73] Although not, as noted, the changes made by the Constitutional Reform Act 2005.

agendas, it is very unlikely that we will see a repeat of the breadth and scale of what flowed in constitutional terms after the 1997 general election. What might be seen as unfinished business might well remain unfinished. The search for an elected second chamber has defeated Liberal and Labour governments since 1910, and the current Upper House, expressed to be 'interim' after the passage of the House of Lords Act 1999, might one day be transformed into an elected chamber. But, given the history of Lords reform, I doubt it. The way that MPs are elected might be changed, but the Conservatives are wedded to FPTP, and Labour has not had a consistent reform policy. The Human Rights Act might be altered, but repeal is unlikely, given that an alternative text has eluded the Conservative Party. Further devolution is probable, although not of the magnitude of Labour's settlement to the nations and regions of the UK. Perhaps – who knows? – there might be codification of the whole constitution, although, given the difficulties again, I rather doubt that. Broadly speaking, therefore, although there are items of further constitutional change on the to-do lists of political parties, those enumerations collectively fall well short of what turned out to be New Labour's British constitution.

3

The Human Rights Act 1998: Two Decades Swimming Upstream

HÉLÈNE TYRRELL[1]

I. INTRODUCTION

THE HUMAN RIGHTS Act 1998 (HRA) was a cornerstone of New Labour's constitutional reforms. By incorporating elements of the European Convention on Human Rights (ECHR) into domestic law, the HRA represented a voluntary surrender of government power and contributed to a significant rebalancing of the relationship between the individual and the state. Yet, two decades on, the HRA has excited such opposition that the electoral majority is courted with promises of its repeal. This chapter traces the contours of hostility towards the HRA, focusing on three themes: (i) New Labour's own internal struggle over individual rights protections; (ii) the foreignness of the HRA; and (iii) complaints about judicial empowerment. All three themes evidence significant hostility towards the Human Rights Act, but it is argued that the unpopularity of the Act says more about its conception and neglect than it does about its value in the constitutional order. That the Act has survived a strong adverse tide is testament to its substance. By incorporating the ECHR into domestic law, the HRA has forced successive governments to protect unpopular minorities and to justify decisions by reference to convention rights. The Act has also cemented the importance of human rights protections in the constitutional landscape.

II. THE UNLOVED NEW LABOUR FLAGSHIP: INTERNAL STRUGGLE AND POLITICAL FILICIDE

The HRA was the flagship New Labour project. It was a crucial component in a suite of constitution reform, together designed to 'renew faith in politics'

[1] I am grateful to Conall Mallory and Colin Murray for helpful comments on an earlier draft of this chapter. All errors and omissions remain my own.

and herald an era of democratic renewal.[2] But as a discrete policy initiative, the human rights agenda had a mixed history within the Labour Party.[3]

Human rights legislation had been on and off Labour's legislative wish list for nearly half a century – promises around the protection of individual rights and personal liberties can be found as far back as the 1945 manifesto.[4] It was the post-war Labour government that ratified the ECHR in 1951 and it was under Harold Wilson's premiership that the UK accepted the right of individual petition in 1966.[5] Yet the Labour Party was never unanimous on the prospect of incorporating the same instrument into UK law. The proposal to incorporate the ECHR was actually a creature of the Society of Conservative Lawyers in 1976.[6] When the Labour Party first proposed incorporation of the ECHR in the same year, the National Executive Committee refused to recognise the paper as official policy. Scepticism was mainly political: some of the Labour Party feared the possibility that individual rights could be used to frustrate collectivism and were suspicious of judicial involvement on questions of civil liberties – particularly the prospect of courts playing a central part in controversial political issues.[7]

It was not until the late 1980s that the Labour Party was ready to focus on the constitutional virtues of rights reform, setting out to market themselves as the would-be government that 'accepts the responsibilities of power as well as exercising the rights of power'.[8] In fact, the Labour Party's 1990s Policy Review outlined an explicit commitment to stronger protections for individual rights than had so far been mooted: a simple 'Bill of Rights' would not adequately provide 'the protection which [the Party] regard[ed] as necessary'.[9] Given the impossibility of entrenchment in a system of parliamentary sovereignty, the worry was that – on its own – a Bill of Rights could too easily be 'repealed by a government with no concern for individual liberty';[10] a more 'dependable and more permanent constitutional change [was] necessary'.[11] To that end, the

[2] *New Labour, New Life for Britain* (Labour Party, 1996).

[3] KD Ewing and CA Gearty, *Democracy or a Bill of Rights* (Society of Labour Lawyers, 1991).

[4] *Let Us Face the Future* (Labour Party, 1945).

[5] E Bates, *The Evolution of the European Convention on Human Rights: From Its Inception to the Creation of a Permanent Court of Human Rights* (Oxford University Press, 2010); G Marston, 'The United Kingdom's Part in the Preparation of the European Convention on Human Rights, 1950' (1993) 42 *ICLQ* 796; Lord Lester of Herne Hill, 'UK Acceptance of the Strasbourg Jurisdiction: What Really Went on in Whitehall in 1965' [1997] *PL* 237; KD Ewing, 'The Human Rights Act and Parliamentary Democracy' (1999) 62 *MLR* 79, 80; AWB Simpson, *Human Rights and the End of Empire* (Oxford University Press, 2001).

[6] *Another Bill of Rights? A Report by the Committee of the Society of Conservative Lawyers* (CPC, 1976).

[7] JAG Griffith, *Politics of the Judiciary*, 5th edn (Fontana, 1997) 297–301; Ewing, 'The Human Rights Act' (1999) 98; F Klug, *A Magna Carta for Humanity: Homing in on Human Rights* (Routledge, 2015) 246.

[8] *Meet the Challenge. Make the Change: Final Report of Labour's Policy Review for the 1990* (Labour Party, 1989) 8.

[9] ibid 55.

[10] ibid.

[11] ibid.

Policy Review announced a complementary suite of reforms that would include a 'right to know' and reform of the House of Lords. In fact, a stated objective of the latter was that it would make way for an Upper House empowered (through composition and constitutional function) to 'protect and preserve the rights which we incorporate in law'.[12] The second chamber would acquire new 'powers to delay measures affecting fundamental rights for the whole life of a Parliament', which would allow the 'electorate to determine whether or not the government which proposes such measures should remain in office'.[13] At that point, the prospect of an electorate returning a government to power on the basis of *diluting* human rights protections was difficult to imagine.

This commitment to human rights was reinforced after the 1992 election defeat, when the Party's new leader, John Smith, declared his support for an Act that could incorporate the ECHR.[14] At the 1993 Labour Party conference, the commitment seemed to be to an Act that would incorporate but also go further than the ECHR.[15] The policy survived Smith's untimely death in 1994, when Tony Blair honoured the pledge as part of his New Labour project, but it had been stripped back to an Act which would merely provide domestic redress for international treaty obligations. The 1996 Labour Party manifesto promised an instrument to give 'citizens … statutory rights to enforce their [Convention] rights in the UK courts'.[16] Some human rights advocates complained that this sort of rights instrument was too narrow and too timid: 'a new, home-grown, British Bill of Rights would have looked rather different'.[17] The then Lord Chancellor was nevertheless 'convinced' that incorporating the ECHR would deliver 'a modern reconciliation' of the 'tension between the democratic right of the majority to exercise political power and the democratic need of individuals and minorities to have their human rights secured'.[18] Moreover, the incorporation of the ECHR would be one part of a constitutional rights framework. The HRA would 'establish a floor, not a ceiling, for human rights' since Parliament would 'remain free to enhance these rights, for example by a Freedom of Information Act'.[19]

More significant than making Convention rights enforceable in domestic courts was the ambition to divide responsibility for the protection of human

[12] ibid 55–56; the broader package included inter alia a 'right to know' initiative, detailed at 59.

[13] ibid.

[14] J Smith, 'A Citizen's Democracy' (Charter 88, 1 March 1993).

[15] Klug, *A Magna Carta for all Humanity* (2015) 245.

[16] *New Labour, New Life for Britain* (1996).

[17] S Kentridge QC, 'The Incorporation of the European Convention on Human Rights' in University of Cambridge Centre for Public Law (ed), *Constitutional Reform in the United Kingdom: Practice and Principles* (Hart Publishing, 1998) 69.

[18] HL Deb 3 November 1997, vol 582, col 1234.

[19] ibid; the contemporaneous strength of the ECHR had already been made evident through the devolution settlements. The Scottish and Welsh devolution settlements each limited the exercise of devolved power to prevent inconsistency with the ECHR. The ECHR was also incorporated as a provision into the Belfast Good Friday Agreement of 10 April 1998.

rights between the institutions of government, developing 'a culture of awareness of human rights'.[20] During the legislative stages, and prior to its coming into force, the HRA was described as the start of a 'new constitutional chapter for Britain',[21] the 'beginning of a written constitution for Britain',[22] 'a defining moment in the life of our constitution'[23] and 'unquestionably the most significant formal redistribution of political power in this country since 1911'.[24] But such large-scale constitutional change also carried a risk of rejection. As the Labour Party had recognised at the start of the 1990s:

> Change can come as an uncontrolled tide that buffets individuals, communities and countries that are not ready to cope with its flow. Change can be imposed … [o]r change can be prepared for, guided, controlled, its costs and its benefits shared throughout the community.[25]

In these respects, the HRA was given less attention than contemporaneous constitutional reforms. The Scotland Act 1998, the Government of Wales Act 1998 and the Northern Ireland Act 1998 were implemented after endorsement by referendums,[26] while the HRA received royal assent on 9 November 1998 without specific political endorsement beyond the election of a new government with a manifesto commitment to address the protection of human rights.[27] Nor was the HRA subject to extensive consultation. While human rights instruments in other jurisdictions had been implemented after extensive periods of consultation,[28] the White Paper, *Rights Brought Home*, was published within six months of New Labour's general election victory and the HRA received royal assent just over a year later.[29]

The absence of significant consultation or particular effort to promote a climate of support for the legislation was despite the fact that the Labour government were cognisant of human rights scepticism when the Human Rights Bill was introduced. In particular, the tension between protecting the national

[20] HL Deb 3 November 1997, vol 582, col 1228.

[21] 'Rule of Judges' *The Economist* (24 August 2000) www.economist.com/leaders/2000/08/24/rule-of-judges.

[22] ibid.

[23] HL Deb 3 November 1997, vol 582, col 1234 (Lord Kingsland).

[24] ibid; Ewing (n 5) 79.

[25] *Meet the Challenge. Make the Change* (1989) 6.

[26] On the connection between referendums and building legitimacy in the New Labour constitution, see L Trueblood, ch 14 of this volume, s IIIA.

[27] C Harvey, 'Taking the Next Step? Achieving Another Bill of Rights' [2011] *European Human Rights Law Review* 24, 28.

[28] R Penner, 'The Canadian Experience with the Charter of Rights: Are There Lessons for the United Kingdom?' [1996] *PL* 104; A Smith, 'The Drafting Process of a Bill of Rights for Northern Ireland' [2004] *PL* 526. The Australian governments later followed a more substantial consultation programme in respect of their human rights legislation, 'involv[ing] high levels of public engagement, and produc[ing] strong community support in favour of legislative reform': A Williams and G Williams, 'The British Bill of Rights Debate: Lessons from Australia' [2016] *PL* 471, 474.

[29] M Amos, 'Problems with the Human Rights Act 1998 and How to Remedy Them: Is a Bill of Rights the Answer?' (2009) 72 *MLR* 883, 903.

interest versus the rights of unpopular claimants had been a feature of political discourse well before the HRA landed on the legislative programme, both within the Labour Party itself and more broadly.[30] On several occasions, the Strasbourg Court had protected the rights of suspected terrorists over efforts to protect national security.[31] One of the most controversial was a decision against the UK in which the Strasbourg Court held that members of the IRA had suffered a breach of their Article 2 ECHR rights when shot by the Special Air Service.[32] In another, it was held that Article 3 ECHR prevented a state from deporting any individual (regardless of the security risks) to any country where they would face a real risk of torture, or inhuman or degrading treatment.[33] As others have pointed out, this created a serious restriction on the ability of the state to deport, amongst others, suspected terrorists.[34] Cultivating a 'culture of awareness of human rights' would prove difficult and, when the HRA finally came into force on 2 October 2000, it was drawn into a near-immediate adverse tide of press and political hostility.[35] While heralding the 'landmark human rights law',[36] the BBC reported the concerns held by some members of the Conservative Party that the Act was likely to 'place the courts in confrontation with Parliament' and be 'a mechanism for all sorts of nonsense', including 'frivolous legal actions and allow convicted killers and rapists to challenge the banning of conjugal rights and the removal of the vote'.[37]

The government of the day did very little to defend their legislative achievement. At best, the Labour government was 'ambivalent' towards the HRA.[38] At worst, it was tempted into blaming its own legislation for obstructing efforts to deport terrorists, or preventing the administration from taking a robust approach to immigration, crime and punishment. A little over two years into the life of the HRA, the ECHR was factored into a High Court judgment upholding

[30] A McColgan, 'Lessons from the Past: Northern Ireland Terrorism Now and Then, and the Human Rights Act' in T Campbell, K Ewing and A Tomkins (eds), *The Legal Protection of Human Rights: Sceptical Essays* (Oxford University Press, 2011); J Straw, *Aspects of Law Reform. An Insider's Perspective* (Cambridge University Press, 2013) 28.

[31] *Ireland v United Kingdom* [1978] 2 EHRR 25; *Brogan v United Kingdom* [1988] 11 EHRR 117; *Brannigan and McBride v United Kingdom* [1993] 17 EHRR 539.

[32] *McCann v United Kingdom* [1995] 21 EHRR 97.

[33] *Chahal v United Kingdom* [1996] 23 EHRR 413.

[34] Lord Dyson, *Justice Continuity and Change* (Hart Publishing, 2018) 137; C Gearty, *On Fantasy Island* (Oxford University Press, 2016).

[35] Members of the Human Rights Task Force reportedly shared 'one abiding concern that the HRA should not be "demonized" or allowed to flounder' but were restricted in both mandate and resources: J Croft, 'Whitehall and the Human Rights Act 1998' [2001] *European Human Rights Law Review* 392. For a (sceptical) account of the early efforts to promote the HRA or provide leadership around the purported culture of human rights awareness, see, eg J Wadham, 'The Human Rights Act, One Year On' [2001] *European Human Rights Law Review* 620, 627.

[36] 'Landmark Human Rights Law Enforced' (*BBC News*, 2 October 2012) http://news.bbc.co.uk/1/hi/uk/951753.stm.

[37] ibid, quoting then Shadow Home Secretary Ann Widdecombe.

[38] Lord Dyson, *Justice Continuity and Change* (2018) 199.

the right of six asylum-seekers to receive support from the National Asylum Support Service (an agency of the Home Office).[39] Sections of the press took it as an invitation to condemn the unelected judges and their 'zeal to interpret European legislation' for 'usurping the role of Parliament'.[40] David Blunkett (then Home Secretary) made no effort to defend the operation of the HRA, preferring the political opportunity to sympathise with the public mood and condemn the judgment: Blunkett was 'fed up with having to deal with a situation where Parliament debates issues and judges overturn them'.[41] The *Chahal* principle (preventing deportation of individuals to countries where they would face a real risk of torture, or inhuman and degrading treatment) and decisions flowing from it apparently led former Home Secretary, John Reid, to 'regret that his government had ever introduced the HRA'.[42]

Prime Minister Tony Blair did not do much better. Faced with immigration difficulties, Blair announced on the radio that he was thinking about reviewing the UK's obligations under the ECHR if other measures to reduce application numbers did not work.[43] The 2005 terror attack in London prompted Blair to announce a willingness to amend the HRA 'in respect of the interpretation of the European Convention on Human Rights' if there arose any 'legal obstacles' to deporting Islamic extremists.[44] A year later, the High Court handed down a judgment which overturned the Home Secretary's decision not to grant discretionary leave to enter the UK to the nine Afghan nationals who had arrived after hijacking an aircraft to escape the Taliban regime.[45] Blair declared the situation to be an 'abuse of justice' and an 'abuse of common sense', while the Home Secretary reportedly gave a statement declaring that 'decisions ... which appear inexplicable or bizarre to the general public ... only reinforces the perception that the system is not working to protect ... ordinary decent, hard-working citizens in this country'.[46] Around this time, the press reported that Blair had ordered a review of 'whether primary legislation is needed to address the issue of court rulings which overrule the government in a way that is inconsistent

[39] *R (Q) v Secretary of State for the Home Department* [2003] EWHC 195 Admin.

[40] *Daily Mail* (20 February 2003); A Bradley, 'Judicial Independence Under Attack' [2003] *PL* 397, 401.

[41] 'Blunkett to Fight Extradition Ruling' (*BBC News*, 20 February 2003) http://news.bbc.co.uk/1/hi/uk/2779343.stm.

[42] Lord Dyson (n 34) 204, citing from an interview in the *News of the World* (16 September 2007). Similar sentiments were reported later, see, eg B Carlin, 'John Reid Calls for Human Rights Law Reform' *The Telegraph* (17 September 2007) www.telegraph.co.uk/news/uknews/1563347/John-Reid-calls-for-human-rights-law-reform.html.

[43] BBC Breakfast with Frost, Interview with Tony Blair, 26 January 2003, available at http://news.bbc.co.uk/1/hi/programmes/breakfast_with_frost/2695903.stm.

[44] George Jones, 'Blair to curb human rights in war on terror', *The Telegraph* (6 August 2005) www.telegraph.co.uk/news/uknews/1495605/Blair-to-curb-human-rights-in-war-on-terror.html.

[45] *R (S) v Secretary of State for the Home Department* [2006] EWHC 1111 (Admin), appealed in *S v Secretary of State for the Home Dept* [2006] EWCA Civ 1157.

[46] 'Government Appeal over Hijackers' *BBC News* http://news.bbc.co.uk/1/hi/uk_politics/4760873.stm.

with other EU countries' interpretation of the European Convention on Human Rights'.[47] Blair reinforced this message during Prime Minister's Questions (PMQs) a few days later: 'we will make sure that our human rights legislation does not get in the way of common-sense legislation to protect our country'.[48] Just over a month after Blair's statement at PMQs, David Cameron (then Leader of the Opposition) proposed a replacement instrument on the basis that the HRA could not 'strike a commonsense balance between civil liberties and the protection of public security'.[49]

The antiterrorism context, in particular, fed a perception that the HRA tipped the balance against the police and security services.[50] And it was a perception that the Labour government of the day nurtured rather than deflected. The HRA was a neat vehicle for blame – a convenient scapegoat for unrelated administrative failings within government.[51] The Joint Committee on Human Rights was damning in its report:[52]

> We must … draw to Parliament's attention the extent to which the Government itself was responsible for creating the public impression that in relation to each of [three contentious judgments] it was either the Human Rights Act itself or misinterpretations of that Act by officials which caused the problems. In each case, very senior ministers, from the Prime Minister down, made assertions that the Human Rights Act, or judges or officials interpreting it, were responsible for certain unpopular events when … in each case these assertions were unfounded. Moreover, when those assertions were demonstrated to be unfounded, there was no acknowledgment of the error, or withdrawal of the comment, or any other attempt to inform the public of the mistake … [P]ublic misunderstandings of the effect of the Act will continue so long as very senior ministers fail to retract unfortunate comments already made and continue to make unfounded assertions about the Act and to use it as a scapegoat for administrative failings in their departments.[53]

Alongside hostility from sections of the media, the Committee warned that 'unless efforts are made to address it, there is a real risk that the Human Rights Act, and indeed the very language of human rights, will become permanently discredited in the eyes of the public'.[54] But the floodgates were already open. Even when, under Gordon Brown's leadership, the government claimed that it

[47] eg N Temko and J Doward, 'Revealed: Blair Attack on Human Rights Law' *The Observer* (14 May 2006) www.theguardian.com/politics/2006/may/14/humanrights.ukcrime.

[48] HC Deb 17 May 2006, vol 446, col 990.

[49] D Cameron, 'Balancing Freedom and Security – A Modern British Bill of Rights' *The Guardian* (26 June 2006) www.theguardian.com/politics/2006/jun/26/conservatives.constitution.

[50] C Gearty, 'Terrorists Threats, Antiterrorism and the Case Against' in Frederick Cowell (ed), *Critically Examining the Case Against the Human Rights Act* (Routlege 2017) 131.

[51] Joint Committee on Human Rights, *The Human Rights Act: The DCA and Home Office Reviews* (2005–06, HL 278, HC 1716) [40]; Lord Dyson (n 34).

[52] Joint Committee on Human Rights, *The Human Rights Act* (2005–06).

[53] ibid [41].

[54] ibid [72].

was 'proud to have introduced the Human Rights Act', it suggested that the Act needed to be subsumed or supplemented by a new 'Bill of Rights and Responsibilities'.[55] Internal disagreements around human rights might also have contributed to more surprising aspects of constitutional reform. When the architect of the HRA 1998, Lord Irvine, was sidelined through the Constitutional Reform Act 2005, there was some speculation that it was the result of internal squabbles over ministerial reactions when human rights judgments had gone against the will of the executive.[56] Although Labour never actually altered the HRA or the relationship with the ECHR, the party's internal incoherence on the subject of human rights had set in motion a narrative that would gradually undermine public confidence in their legislative achievement and the rights that it protects.

Few issues could have set New Labour up for an own goal better than the saga surrounding the (dis)enfranchisement of prisoners. Protocol 1, Article 3 ECHR provides for 'free elections … under conditions which will ensure the free expression of the opinion of the people in the choice of the legislature', but UK prisoners were denied the vote by the Representation of the People Act 1983 as amended by the Representation of the People Act 1985.[57] The blanket ban affected all convicted prisoners, 'irrespective of the length of their sentence and irrespective of the nature or gravity of their offence and their individual circumstances'.[58] In *Hirst v UK (No 2)*, the Grand Chamber found such 'a general, automatic and indiscriminate' ban to fall outside the margin of appreciation so as to constitute a breach of Convention rights.[59] But enfranchising prisoners was not thought to be politically savvy.[60] Rather than comply with the judgment, the Labour government of the day embarked on a programme of deliberate procrastination. Jack Straw admitted that he had spent three years in his post as Justice Secretary 'ensuring that the government took no decision in response to [the

[55] Ministry of Justice, *Rights and Responsibilities: Developing our Constitutional Framework* (Cmd 7577, 2009) 10; P Eleftheriadis, 'On Rights and Responsibilities' [2010] *PL* 33; A Le Sueur, 'Gordon Brown's Constitutional Settlement' [2008] *PL* 21.

[56] See eg HL Deb 12 February 2004, vol 656, col 1278 (Lord Ackner): 'If one goes back and asks, '"What is the genesis out of which these proposals have arisen?" … we can probably start with the unconstitutional and inexcusable behaviour of the Home Secretary in attacking the decision … that under the human rights legislation … a politician was not entitled to play any part in the decision of how long a person convicted of murder should stay in prison … That gave rise to a strong attack by the Home Secretary on the judiciary … [The] Lord Chancellor appeared before a Select Committee and [said] that it is wrong for the Government to cheer when they get a decision in their favour but when the decision is adverse then to attack the judiciary. That was said in public and no one had any doubt that he was directing his criticism towards the Home Secretary.'

[57] Representation of the People Act 1983, s 3.

[58] *Hirst v United Kingdon (No 2)* (2005) ECHR 681 [82].

[59] ibid.

[60] Joint Committee on Human Rights, *Monitoring the Government's Response to Court Judgments Finding Breaches of Human Rights*, Sixteenth Report of 2006–07 (HC 728) [77]: 'the Government would be taking a generally unpopular course if it were to enfranchise even a small proportion of the prison population'.

Hirst] judgment, kick[ing] the issue into touch, first with one inconclusive public consultation, then with a second'.[61]

When the Conservative Party arrived in office, it was easy to follow this lead. It was not long before the Prime Minister, David Cameron, proclaimed that the thought of giving prisoners the vote made him 'feel physically ill'.[62] Of course, the political reaction overplayed the judgment in *Hirst*. The Strasbourg Court had not suggested that a ban on prisoner voting was a violation of the Convention per se; it was the blanket nature of the ban that was problematic – especially as there had been no evidence of parliamentary engagement with the issue.[63] Nevertheless, this was an opportunity to take a public stand against an unpopular foreign judgment and it was a portrayal that sections of the media were happy to propagate.[64] Still reeling from losses to press freedom,[65] *Hirst* was an opportunity for the media to turn up the volume on anti-HRA sentiment,[66] 'monstering' the ECHR and the associated HRA in its wake.[67] The Iraq litigations ramped up the anti-Strasbourg sentiment still further. In *Al Saadoon*, the European Court of Human Rights found that the UK government had violated the Article 3 rights of two Iraqis who had been accused of murdering two British soldiers.[68] The prospect of human rights legislation protecting those that had killed 'our boys' was a powerful narrative. So grew a second strand of hostility towards the HRA, condemning the influence of the European Court of Human Rights and painting the HRA as a conduit for importing foreign norms.

[61] J Straw, *Last Man Standing* (Macmillan, 2012).

[62] HC Deb 3 November 2010, vol 517, col 921.

[63] *Hirst v UK (No 2)* (n 58) [84]; C Murray, 'A Perfect Storm: Parliament and Prisoner Disenfranchisement' (2013) 66 *Parliamentary Affairs* 511, 523; T Lewis, '"Difficult and Slippery Terrain": Hansard, Human Rights and *Hirst v UK*' [2006] *PL* 209, 212.

[64] Joint Committee of Human Rights, *Enforcing Human Rights*, Tenth Report of Session 2017–19 (2018) [141]; in an analysis of human rights 'frames', Counterpoint UK et al found that 80% of the media discourse about human rights was negative: 'Building Bridges: Connecting with Values to Reframe and Build Support for Human Rights' https://counterpoint.uk.com/wp-content/uploads/2018/04/Building-Bridges.pdf, 19.

[65] eg *Campbell v MGN Ltd* [2004] UKHL 22, [2004] AC 457; P Dacre, 'The Threat to Our Press' *The Guardian* (10 November 2008) www.theguardian.com/media/2008/nov/10/paul-dacre-press-threats; R Clayton and H Tomlinson, *Privacy and Freedom of Expression*, 2nd edn (Oxford University Press, 2010).

[66] L Gies, *Mediating Human Rights: Media, Culture and the Human Rights Act* (Routledge, 2014) 4.

[67] A Wagner, 'The Monstering of the Human Rights Act' (keynote address, Human Rights in the UK Media: Representation and Reality, University of Liverpool, 28–29 September 2014) https://adam1cor.files.wordpress.com/2014/09/the-monstering-of-human-rights-adam-wagner-2014.pdf; C Murray, 'Monstering Strasbourg over Prisoner Voting Rights' in E Drywood, M Farrell and E Hughes (eds), *Human Rights in the Media: Fear and Fetish* (Routledge, 2019); D McNulty, N Watson and G Philo, 'Human Rights and Prisoners' Rights: The British Press and the Shaping of Public Debate' (2014) 53 *Howard Journal of Criminal Justice* 360, 374; P Mason, 'Misinformation, Myth and Distortion: How the Press Construct Imprisonment in Britain' (2007) 8 *Journalism Studies* 481.

[68] *Al Saadoon and Mufdhi v The United Kingdom* 61498/08 [2010] ECHR 282.

III. FOREIGNNESS: THE IMPORT AND OWNERSHIP NARRATIVE

Perceptions of national ownership had long been a strong undercurrent in the HRA story. When the Labour government published the HRA white paper, *Rights Brought Home*, it had sought to emphasise the role that the UK had played in drafting the ECHR.[69] The HRA would be repatriating rights 'originally developed with major help from the United Kingdom Government [but which were] no longer actually seen as British rights'.[70] Therein lay an important admission: however 'British' the Convention might have been in conception, in the public mindset the instrument had since been associated with a foreign legal framework. Still worse, it was a *European* legal framework. Membership of the EU was already viewed as invasive in some quarters and the risk of incorporating the Convention was that rights would be seen as another European import.[71] It was not long before that risk materialised – being told to amend the law on prisoner voting was not quite as objectionable as the fact that 'a foreign court' had barked the order.[72]

Antagonism was rooted in control and framed as a concern about the impact of the HRA and the associated pan-European human rights institutions on the UK's 'sovereignty'. While often conflated with the domestic concept of 'parliamentary sovereignty' (an internal construct, regulating the relationship between the domestic legislature and domestic courts),[73] objections to the HRA and the jurisdiction of the Strasbourg Court were really an appeal to 'national sovereignty' (the notion that a sovereign state is the ultimate authority over its domestic legal system and legislative scheme). As Tucker has explained elsewhere, this is a 'moral–political concept' that features prominently in international legal doctrines.[74] It is also a point on which international human rights regimes require compromise and obvious long before to the enactment of the HRA.[75] Strasbourg judgments like *Hirst* and *Al Saadoon* would have imposed an international obligation on the UK with or without a domestic human rights law.

[69] Home Office, *Rights Brought Home: The Human Rights Bill* (Cmd 3872, 1997) [1.2].

[70] ibid.

[71] Lord Denning famously described European Union as an incoming tide, 'flow[ing] into the estuaries and up the rivers': *HP Bulmer Ltd v J Bollinger SA* [1974] Ch 401, 418.

[72] David Cameron declared that prisoner voting was a matter for Parliament, 'not a foreign court': HC Deb 23 May 2012, vol 545, col 1127; Michael Pinto-Duschinsky, *Bringing Rights Home: Making Human Rights Compatible with Parliamentary Democracy in the UK* (Policy Exchange, 2011).

[73] AV Dicey, *Introduction to the Study of the Law of the Constitution*, 10th edn (Macmillan, 1961) 39–40; for an alternative argument about a 'modern concept of sovereignty', see M Loughlin and S Tierney, 'The Shibboleth of Sovereignty' (2018) 81 *MLR* 989.

[74] A Tucker, 'Taking Sovereignty Seriously' in Cowell, *Critically Examining the Case Against the Human Rights Act* (2017) 105.

[75] eg Art 1 ECHR is entitled 'Obligation to Respect Human Rights' and provides that high contracting parties 'shall secure to everyone within their jurisdiction the rights and freedoms defined in Section I of this Convention'. Art 46(1) ECHR provides that a state is bound to abide by decisions of the Strasbourg Court to which it was a party; Bates, *The Evolution of the European Convention on Human Rights* (2010) 77 ff; A Horne and H Tyrrell, 'Sovereignty, Privilege and the European Convention on Human Rights' in A Horne and A Le Sueur (eds), *Parliament: Legislation and Accountability* (Hart Publishing, 2016).

Nevertheless, by the early 2010s, the HRA had become 'a lightning rod for populist anger',[76] inextricably linked with protecting the rights of the undeserving. When in post at the Home Office, Theresa May regularly reaffirmed her commitment to scrapping the HRA and leaving the ECHR. Rather than protecting the individual against the state, the Human Rights Act prevented the deportation of terror suspects on the basis that they would face a real risk of ill treatment sufficient to infringe *their* rights under Article 3.[77] May blamed 'real problems with our human rights laws' and the 'crazy interpretation of [those] laws' for the delay in the deportation of Abu Qatada.[78] Branded a 'Villain's Charter',[79] the HRA made it hard to safeguard law-abiding citizens while protecting the rights of, among others, sex offenders,[80] welfare claimants[81] or failed asylum seekers.[82] Numerous myths continued to grow around the HRA,[83] including the infamous tale (in May's 2011 Conservative Party Conference speech) of an illegal immigrant who had used the HRA to resist deportation on the basis that he had a pet cat.[84]

The momentum gathered pace without much intervention from the Labour Party, who seemed indifferent to attacks on their legislative achievement. Introducing his Human Rights Act 1998 (Repeal and Substitution) Bill to the House of Commons for a second reading, Charlie Elphicke MP (Conservative) explained that he was doing so because 'a new human rights settlement [was] needed to restore trust and confidence in human rights'.[85] More interesting

[76] F Cowell, 'Defining and Understanding the Case against the Human Rights Act' in Cowell (n 50) 3.

[77] *Naseer & Ors v Secretary of State for the Home Department* [2010] UKSIAC 77/2009 (18 May 2010).

[78] HC Deb 8 July 2013, vol 566, col 24. The theme continued through to May's 2017 electoral campaign. See, eg R Mason and V Dodd, 'May: I'll Rip Up Human Rights Laws that Impede New Terror Legislation' *The Guardian* (6 June 2017) www.theguardian.com/politics/2017/jun/06/theresa-may-rip-up-human-rights-laws-impede-new-terror-legislation?CMP=share_btn_tw.

[79] Wadham, 'The Human Rights Act, One Year On' (2001) 627.

[80] *R (F) v Secretary of State for the Home Department* [2010] UKSC 17, [2011] AC 331.

[81] L Lammasniemi, 'Welfare, Anti-austerity and Gender' in Cowell (n 50).

[82] Lord Wilson, 'Our Human Rights: A Joint Effort', The Howard J Trienens Lecture (Northwestern University Law School, Chicago, 25 September 2018) 9, www.supremecourt.uk/docs/speech-180925.pdf.

[83] See generally D Mead, '"You Couldn't Make It Up": Some Narratives of the Media's Coverage of Human Rights' in K Ziegler, E Wicks and L Hodson (eds), *The UK and European Human Rights: A Strained Relationship* (Hart Publishing, 2015); Liberty, 'Human Rights Act FactCheck' www.libertyhumanrights.org.uk/human-rights-act-factcheck; Rights Info, '14 Worst Human Rights Myths' https://rightsinfo.org/infographics/the-14-worst-human-rights-myths/.

[84] Theresa May, speech to the 2011 Conservative Party Conference (4 October 2011) www.politics.co.uk/comment-analysis/2011/10/04/theresa-may-speech-in-full. The 'catgate' myth was roundly criticised but retained force in some quarters: see, eg D Campbell, '"Catgate" and the Challenge to Parliamentary Sovereignty in Immigration Law' [2015] *PL* 426; D Campbell, Letter (2018) 40(18) *London Review of Books*, in response to S Sedley, 'Review of M Duranti, *The Conservative Human Rights Revolution: European Identity, Transnational Politics and the Origins of the European Convention* (Oxford University Press, 2017)' (2018) 40(6) *London Review of Books* 19 www.lrb.co.uk/v40/n16/stephen-sedley/be-careful-what-you-wish-for.

[85] HC Deb 1 March 2013, vol 559, col 574.

than what was said in that debate is what was not; Labour Party members were conspicuous by their absence. Conservative members joked that Liberal Democrat Party members might have been delayed by the celebration (or recovery after it) of a successful by-election in Eastleigh, but the Labour Party members had no particular excuse. Mr Elphicke was quick to pick up the point: 'Considering that [the Labour Party] made this massive change to the British constitution … is it not amazing that they have not turned up to defend it?'[86] The second reading debate had begun at 9:46 am, but it was not until after lunch that a Labour MP, Mr Andy Slaughter, arrived to 'address [Mr Elphicke's] request for the Opposition's views on the issue under discussion'.[87] Endearing himself to those that had spoken before him, Mr Slaughter commented that, while Mr Elphicke had produced a very impressive Bill, in listening to his speech he thought that his Article 3 rights might have been affected. Of course he quickly elaborated that this was not a result of the foregoing argument or oratory, but because he 'felt that we had been here before'. Indeed, the HRA had, only a few months before, sustained a near identical attack by way of a 10-minute rule Bill (which was defeated by 196 votes to 72).[88] Mr Slaughter finally gave a more explicit defence of the HRA in the dying minutes of the debate but, aside from a fleeting contribution from the Liberal Democrat benches,[89] both he and his defence stood alone. The only other member of the Labour Party that appears on the transcript (Mr Mark Hendrick) rose with a point of order about the length of speeches, such that his attendance could more appropriately be attributed to the anticipation of another legislative debate.[90] The Bill was never likely to be enacted, but the debate showcase the Labour Party's ambivalence towards attacks on its legislative achievement. Perhaps, given the Party's long-standing issue with the legal protection of human rights, ambivalence was the best outcome that one could expect. Still, the Party's own internal incoherence on the subject of human rights had become an effective gag in respect to any meaningful defence of the Act or its achievements. As Elliott pointed out in a blog post at the time, the Bill provided 'a (depressing) reflection of the direction in which thinking about human rights is developing within certain parts of the political spectrum'.[91]

[86] ibid col 615.

[87] ibid col 618.

[88] The Human Rights Act 1998 (Repeal) Bill was introduced by Mr Richard Bacon on 4 December 2012: HC Deb 4 December 2012, vol 554, col 728.

[89] Mr Martin Horwood stood to 'reassure the hon. Gentleman of the Liberal Democrats' support for the Human Rights Act' HC Deb 1 March 2013, vol 559, col 623.

[90] HC Deb 1 March 2013, vol 559, col 635.

[91] M Elliott, 'Human Rights Act 1998 (Repeal and Substitution) Bill: Going Nowhere, but a Sign of Things to Come?' *Public Law for Everyone* (28 February 2013) https://publiclawforeveryone.com/2013/02/28/human-rights-act-1998-repeal-and-substitution-bill-going-nowhere-but-a-sign-of-things-to-come.

By the mid-2010s, the political momentum had swung so far against the HRA (and the associated international regime) that repealing domestic human rights law had become a selling point. The Conservative Party thought it politically prudent to publish a document outlining 'proposals for changing Britain's human rights laws', denouncing the 'mission creep' of the Strasbourg Court.[92] There was a 'mounting concern' about the Strasbourg Court's alleged capacity 'to overrule decisions of our democratically elected Parliament and overturn the UK courts' careful applications of Convention rights'.[93] The long-running prisoner-voting saga was to be taken as evidence that the Strasbourg Court was stretching its mandate, 'setting itself up as a supreme court for Europe with an ever-widening remit'.[94] That court's 'living instrument' doctrine was a 'judicial coup' and 'a naked usurpation, by a judicial body, of the legislative power that properly belongs to democratically elected law makers'.[95] Much of the criticism of the HRA therefore had little to do with its operation and more to do with its relationship to an international court.[96] It is an 'alien intrusion',[97] transferring power to foreign judges in a foreign court. As Baroness Hale put it: 'Some Parliamentarians and commentators are concerned about the perceived threat to Parliamentary sovereignty … Many are concerned about what they see as the imperialism of the Strasbourg court … Some critics are simply hostile to anything European'.[98]

Parallel debates around membership of the EU probably added force to that tide. A growing unease about such membership fed a general anti-European sentiment, and it was easy to drag the HRA into the war on 'Europe'. In fact, it has been argued that the early noise around the prisoner voting judgment was really

[92] Conservative Party, *Protecting Human Rights in the UK: The Conservatives' Proposals for Changing Britain's Human Rights Laws* https://s3.amazonaws.com/s3.documentcloud.org/documents/1308198/protecting-human-rights-in-the-uk.pdf.

[93] ibid.

[94] HC Deb 10 February 2011, col 502; D Davis, 'Britain Must Defy the European Court of Human Rights on Prisoner Voting as Strasbourg is Exceeding its Authority' in S Flogaitis et al (eds), *The European Convention on Human Rights and its Discontents: Turning Criticism into Strength* (Edward Elgar, 2013).

[95] D Raab, *Strasbourg in the Dock: Prisoner Voting, Human Rights & the Case for Democracy* (Civitas, 2011) 9; J Goldsworthy, 'Losing Faith in Democracy: Why Judicial Supremacy Is Rising and What To Do About It', Launch of Policy Exchange Judicial Power Project (9 March 2015) 5–6; Lord Hoffmann, 'The Universality of Human Rights', Judicial Studies Board Annual Lecture (19 March 2009), subsequently published at (2009) 125 *LQR* 416. *cf* Dominic Grieve, speech to the BPP Law School on Parliament and the judiciary (25 October 2012). Grieve stressed that the UK Parliament had not been made 'subservient to the Strasbourg Court'.

[96] Other elements of the critique include concerns around democratic legitimacy, institutional balance, parliamentary sovereignty and the powers of the courts: Amos, 'Problems with the Human Rights Act 1998' (2009); Cowell (n 50).

[97] Gearty, *On Fantasy Island* (2016) 3.

[98] Baroness Hale, 'What's the Point of Human Rights?' (Warwick University, 28 November 2013) 20, www.supremecourt.uk/docs/speech-131128.pdf.

> the route in for fresh critique of the European Court of Human Rights at a time when Eurosceptics … could not have imagined themselves taking on their true enemy – Brussels – and so were content to settle for smaller Strasbourg fry.[99]

It did not help that numerous press reports conflated the ECHR with EU law. For example, when a convicted murderer successfully claimed that his deportation would be a contravention of his right to family life,[100] press reports focused on human rights arguments, ignoring the fact that the judgment had actually centred on issues of EU freedom of movement law.[101] Such reports cultivated a much more generalised hostility towards 'Europe', and referendum slogans like 'taking back control' fitted well with the earlier antagonism around the influence of a European court.

It is not surprising that appeals to the notion of ownership became a prominent feature of arguments for repealing the HRA.[102] The 2015 Conservative Party manifesto focused on 'break[ing] the formal link between British courts and the European Court of Human Rights'.[103] A Conservative government would 'introduce a *British* Bill of Rights which [would] restore common sense on the application of human rights in the UK' (emphasis added).[104] Labour presented no particular defence. The Party devoted relatively little space to the issue in its 2015 manifesto, stating simply that a Labour government would 'stand up for citizens' individual rights, protecting the Human Rights Act and reforming rather than walking away from the European Court of Human Rights'.[105] Perhaps a more robust defence of the HRA was made awkward by the fact that some of the Conservative Party campaign echoed the language of the Labour Party's own proposals for 'Bill of Rights and Responsibilities' under Gordon Brown.[106]

When in post as Lord Chancellor, Elizabeth Truss painted a Bill of Rights as part of a national story: 'We have a strong record, as a country, of human rights, dating back to Magna Carta, and the British Bill of Rights is going to be

[99] C Gearty, 'States of Denial. What the Search for a UK Bill of Rights Tells Us about Human Rights Protection Today' [2018] *European Human Rights Law Review* 415, 420.

[100] Cowell, 'Defining and Understanding' (n 76) 12; eg M Tran, 'Court Rejects Challenge over Chinamo Deportation Ruling' *The Guardian* (31 October 2007) www.theguardian.com/uk/2007/oct/31/humanrights.immigrationpolicy.

[101] A Wagner, 'Failure to Deport Philip Lawrence Killer Was Not About Human Rights' (*UK Human Rights Blog*, 29 November 2010) https://ukhumanrightsblog.com/2010/11/29/failure-to-deport-philip-lawrence-killer-was-not-about-human-rights/.

[102] C Murray, 'The Magna Carta's Tainted Legacy' in Cowell (n 50) 43.

[103] *A Strong Leadership, a Clear Economic Plan and a Brighter More Secure Future* (Conservative Party, 2015) 60.

[104] ibid.

[105] *Britain Can Be Better* (Labour Party, 2015) 67. The Liberal Democrats went furthest, writing that 'the Human Rights Act will remain' and that a Liberal Democrat government would 'take appropriate action to comply with decisions of UK courts and the European Court of Human Rights': *Stronger Economy, Fairer Society, Opportunity for Everyone* (Liberal Democrat Party, 2015) 14 and 114.

[106] *Rights and Responsibilities: Developing our Constitutional Framework*, n 55.

the next step in enshrining those rights in our laws.'[107] Combined with an objection to the 'foreign', Cameron's rationale for introducing a British Bill of Rights was that the UK needed a 'home-grown' instrument that 'enables people to feel they have ownership of their rights'.[108] Unlike 'Labour's human rights laws',[109] a new Bill of Rights would, Cameron argued, 'promote active citizenship and … forge a renewed sense of national cohesion making a lasting contribution to the general wellbeing of our country'.[110] A key feature of a British Bill of Rights would thus be to distance the UK legal system from international human rights law.[111] The focus had turned to asserting the primacy of domestic rights and domestic law, 're-emphasising the national'.[112] This was a clear theme of the 2010 Conservative Party election manifesto pledge to replace the Human Rights Act with a British Bill of Rights, although (since the Liberal Democrats had fought the same election on a promise to protect the Human Rights Act) plans were delayed by the Coalition. The Coalition Agreement compromised by creating a Commission to investigate the prospect of a British Bill of Rights,[113] which reported that the majority of Commissioners favoured a UK Bill of Rights because 'many people feel alienated from a system they regard as "European" rather than British'.[114] The public had no 'ownership' and this was 'the most powerful argument for a new constitutional instrument'.[115]

Ownership is important. The closing paragraphs of the 1996 Labour Party manifesto acknowledged a 'sharp division between those who believe the way to cope with global change is for nations to retreat into isolationism and protectionism, and those who believe in internationalism and engagement'.[116] It was envisaged that 'Britain could once again be at the centre of international decision-making instead of at its margins'.[117] In adopting an internationalist outlook, perhaps New Labour underestimated the electorate's preoccupation with national identity. 'Rights Brought Home' might not have been the best slogan. To bring rights 'home' meant that they had to be brought from somewhere else.

[107] HC Deb 6 September 2016, vol 614, col 186.
[108] Cameron, 'Balancing Freedom and Security' (2006).
[109] Conservative Party Manifesto 2015 (n 103) 60.
[110] Cameron (n 49).
[111] Klug (n 7) 250.
[112] R Masterman and S Wheatle, 'A Common Law Resurgence in Rights Protection' (2015) 1 *European Human Rights Law Review* 57, 61.
[113] R Hazell and B Yong (eds), *The Politics of the Coalition* (Hart Publishing, 2016).
[114] Commission on Human Rights, *A UK Bill of Rights? The Choice Before Us* (18 December 2012) www.webarchive.nationalarchives.gov.uk/20130206065653/www.justice.gov.uk/downloads/about/cbr/uk-bill-rights-vol-1.pdf.
[115] ibid. A recent study by Counterpoint UK confirmed a very low level of public ownership in respect of human rights: 'Everyone has human rights' made up only 1% of the discourse in the UK: Counterpoint UK et al, 'Building Bridges: Connecting with Values to Reframe and Build Support for Human Rights' 19, http://counterpoint.uk.com/wp-content/uploads/2016/06/Building-Bridges.pdf.
[116] *New Labour, New Life for Britain* (n 2).
[117] ibid.

IV. JUDICIAL EMPOWERMENT

The third persistent theme of hostility towards the HRA is concern about judicial empowerment. While it had long been evident that an Act of Parliament will prevail even in the event of a breach of international law,[118] the HRA gave judges new rules of statutory interpretation and a central role in remedying incompatibilities with the Convention. In doing so, it has been argued that the HRA 'impose[d] on our judges a radical new set of responsibilities in way that would otherwise have been thought highly improper'.[119]

In particular, the HRA places judges under a duty to read legislation compatibly with the Convention 'so far as it is possible' under section 3.[120] When that is not possible, courts are asked to make a declaration of incompatibility under section 4.[121] The correct balance between these two provisions was a matter for debate even in the early years of the HRA. While some commentators argued that meaningful protection of Convention rights required courts to use the interpretative duty in section 3 as often as possible,[122] others were less keen to downplay the section 4 power or to see it as a measure of last resort: judicial reluctance to use the section 4 power was based on the erroneous assumption that a declaration of incompatibility would enable courts to force a change in the law.[123] Section 4 makes clear that a declaration of incompatibility 'does not affect the validity, continuing operation or enforcement of the provision in respect of which it is given'.[124] In fact, because a declaration of incompatibility is non-binding, the European Court of Human Rights has not seen it as an effective remedy.[125] Despite some suggestion to the contrary,[126] there is no legal obligation on the government to take remedial action or on Parliament to accept any remedial measures the government may propose. In November 2018, the Ministry of Justice reported that there had been just 40 declarations of incompatibility made under the HRA. Of these, 10 were overturned on appeal and two were subject to appeal, while 19 had been remedied by primary legislation, secondary legislation, or remedial order under section 10 HRA. Four

[118] *Cheney v Conn* [1968] 1 All ER 779, 782; *R v Lyons* [2002] UKHL 44, [2003] 1 AC 976, [28].

[119] Richard Ekins and Graham Gee, written evidence from Policy Exchange's Judicial Power Project (HRA0033) (1 October 2018) [6], http://data.parliament.uk/writtenevidence/committeeevidence.svc/evidencedocument/human-rights-committee/twenty-years-of-the-human-rights-act/written/90593.html.

[120] Human Rights Act 1998, s 3(1).

[121] ibid s 4(2).

[122] G Phillipson, '(Mis)representing Section 3 of the Human Rights Act 1998' (2003) 119 *LQR* 183, 187.

[123] F Klug, 'Judicial Deference under the Human Rights Act 1998' [2003] *European Human Rights Law Review* 125, 131.

[124] Human Rights Act 1998, s 4(6)(a).

[125] *Burden and Burden v United Kingdom* App no 13378/05 (12 December 2006) [37]; Amos (n 29) 892.

[126] Ekins and Gee (n 119).

were intended to be addressed by remedial order and one would be addressed by administrative measures. Four were reported to be 'under consideration'.[127] The section 10 remedial power enables but does not require a minister to 'make such amendments to the legislation as he considers necessary to remove [an] incompatibility'.[128] That Parliament can ignore a declaration of compatibility is obvious from the fact that the declaration in respect of prisoner voting was not addressed until October 2017, when the *Sunday Times* reported on government plans to allow prisoners on day release (and serving a sentence of less than a year) to vote.[129]

The HRA did not grant primacy to human rights, or to the document containing those rights.[130] The most that could be said is that the HRA gives 'different degrees of relative authority to the legislature and the courts'.[131] As Young has explained:

> Section 3 tips the balance of power in favour of the court. The court is able to provide a remedy that protects rights. The legislature needs to enact legislation that is incapable of being interpreted in the manned wished by the courts it is to modify this judicial decision. Section 4 tips the balance of power in favour of the legislature. Rights are not protected unless and until the legislature chooses to act to modify the legislation declared incompatible with Convention rights, or enact different legislation in order to protect Convention rights.[132]

Striking the correct balance might require assessments of institutional competence (whether the matter is predominantly one for the courts or the legislature), but, in either case, the legislature has the final word.

The HRA also preserved the possibility of passing incompatible legislation. While section 19 requires ministers to make a declaration about the compatibility of new legislation, the duty can be discharged by making a statement to the effect that, 'although [the minister] is unable to make a statement of compatibility, the government nevertheless wishes the House to proceed with the Bill'.[133] The statement of compatibility is not binding on Parliament, has no particular authority in court[134] and the absence of a statement of compatibility does not

[127] Ministry of Justice, written evidence to the Joint Committee on Human Rights (HRA0017) http://data.parliament.uk/writtenevidence/committeeevidence.svc/evidencedocument/human-rights-committee/twenty-years-of-the-human-rights-act/written/89723.html.

[128] Human Rights Act 1998, s 10(2).

[129] T Shipman, 'Prisoners Gain Vote in Human Rights U-Turn' *Sunday Times* (29 October 2018) www.thetimes.co.uk/article/prisoners-gain-vote-in-human-rights-uturn-fwsvkmfqg. The marginal extension of the franchise was accepted by the Council of Europe in November 2018.

[130] AL Young, *Parliamentary Sovereignty and the Human Rights Act* (Hart Publishing, 2009) 129.

[131] ibid 131.

[132] ibid.

[133] Human Rights Act 1998, s 19(1)(b); such a statement was made in respect of the Communications Act 2003.

[134] *R v A (No 2)* [2001] UKHL 25, [2002] 1 AC 45, 75: s 19 statements 'are no more than expressions of opinion by the minister. They are not binding on the court, nor do they have any persuasive authority' (Lord Hope).

affect the validity of enacted primary legislation. Finally, section 6 makes clear that the duty for public authorities to act compatibly with Convention rights does not apply if 'as a result of one or more provisions of primary legislation, the authority could not have acted differently'.[135]

These provisions have made a significant impact on the protection of human rights in the domestic order. Even those that draw on UK's 'long and enviable' pre-HRA record of human rights protection are bound to admit that it was 'inevitably imperfect'.[136] There has been a reduction in the number of judgments against the UK at Strasbourg since the introduction of the HRA, falling from an annual average of 18 judgments against the UK from 1999 to 2009 to seven from 2010 to 2017.[137] The 'rate of defeat' (the number of applications against the UK that result in adverse judgment) is also falling. Donald's evidence to the Joint Committee on Human Rights was that from 1999 to 2017, less than 1.5 per cent of applications against the UK resulted in adverse judgment. For 2010–17, the rate of defeat was less than 0.7 per cent.[138]

The success of the legislative craftsmanship is also made evident by the fact that it is very difficult to come up with a convincing alternative to the HRA. Some of this might be explained on the basis of timing: withdrawal from the EU was an obvious diversion. Preoccupied with Brexit politics, the 2017 Conservative Party manifesto promised a period of relative quiet on the HRA front, admitting of no intention to withdraw from the ECHR for the duration of the new Parliament.[139] There was, it seemed, 'no energy to continue hostilities with what was after all always for them only a proxy enemy'.[140] The government would fight one battle with 'Europe' at a time. Even when the timing had seemed right, there were no unifying suggestions and no parliamentary appetite for change. The Commission to investigate the prospect of a British Bill of Rights' terms of reference did not make any mention of repealing the Human

[135] Human Rights Act 1998, s 6(2)(a).

[136] Ekins and Gee (n 119).

[137] Alice Donald, written evidence to the Joint Committee on Human Rights inquiry (HRA0021) http://data.parliament.uk/writtenevidence/committeeevidence.svc/evidencedocument/human-rights-committee/twenty-years-of-the-human-rights-act/written/89787.html; Merris Amos, written evidence to the Joint Committee on Human Rights inquiry (HRA0019) http://data.parliament.uk/writtenevidence/committeeevidence.svc/evidencedocument/human-rights-committee/twenty-years-of-the-human-rights-act/written/89739.html.

[138] Donald (ibid); European Court of Human Rights, *Violations by Article and by State* http://echr.coe.int/Pages/home.aspx?p=reports; A Donald and P Leach, *Parliaments and the European Court of Human Rights* (Oxford University Press, 2016); A Horne and V Miller, 'Parliamentary Sovereignty and the European Convention on Human Rights' (*House of Commons Library Blog*, 6 November 2014) https://commonslibrary.parliament.uk/parliament-and-elections/parliament/parliamentary-sovereignty-and-the-european-convention-on-human-rights/; for further details, see European Court of Human Rights Annual Reports, www.echr.coe.int/Pages/home.aspx?p=court/annualreports&c.

[139] *Forward, Together. Our Plan for a Strong Britain and a Prosperous Future* (Conservative and Unionist Party Manifesto 2017) 37.

[140] Gearty, 'States of Denial' (2018) 420.

Rights Act, focusing (per the Coalition Agreement) on investigating 'the creation of a UK Bill of Rights that incorporates and builds on all our obligations under the European Convention on Human Rights'.[141] The minister tasked with the brief of HRA repeal also struggled to make clear the necessity for replacing the Human Rights Act with a British Bill of Rights.[142] In fact, Gove's evidence to the House of Lords' European Union Committee suggested that the 'British Bill of Rights' seemed to have become 'a far less ambitious proposal than the one outlined in the Conservative Party manifesto'. The proposals 'did not appear to depart significantly from the Human Rights Act' and the Committee were left 'unsure why a British Bill of Rights was really necessary'.[143]

V. CONCLUSIONS

In the same year that the HRA came into force, Klug wrote that '[b]ills of rights have a reputation for longevity':

> No government is keen to be seen repealing them, even if they are introduced without any special protective measures, as is the case with this one. Even if – after an initial burst of energy – the UK's Bill of Rights should lie low for ten or twenty years or more, this would not last. As long as human rights advocates do not give up on it, then it is safe to say that it will get up and bite one day.

With the benefit of hindsight, we know that there *are* conditions under which governments may become keen to be seen as repealing Bills of Rights. In fact, as others have written, it is 'hard to find any direct parallels in British legal history of a statute exciting such high levels of opposition'.[144]

Much of the damage was done in house. Not even the party that introduced it was able to love the Act unequivocally. Press and politicians (including members of the New Labour government) came to blame the Act for administrative failings or for making the work of government unreasonable difficult – especially in the context of the fight against crime and counterterrorism. But it was the institutional influence of the European Court of Human Rights that caused particular febrility.[145] In time, antagonism over the unpopular judgments of a foreign court was allowed to bleed into a general perception of the HRA as a conduit for European control and judicial empowerment. Much of this could have been predicted, but most went undefended.

Yet the Act endures. It may yet be supplanted, but the fact that the narrative has generally been of replacement rather than repeal demonstrates that *some*

[141] HM Government, *The Coalition: Our Programme for Government* (2010) 11.

[142] European Union Committee, *The UK, the EU and a British Bill of Rights* (2015–16, HL 139) [45].

[143] ibid [46].

[144] Cowell, 'Defining and Understanding' (n 76) 3.

[145] Straw, *Aspects of Law Reform* (2013) 30.

conception of human rights has been embedded as part of the constitutional landscape. At the very least, it indicates the importance of human rights instruments in legitimising government action.[146] Even Charlie Elphicke MP, introducing his Human Rights Act 1998 (Repeal and Substitution) Bill to the House of Commons for its Second Reading, explained that he was doing so: 'because human rights are important. Human rights matter …'[147] Proposing a new human rights settlement was simply 'needed to restore trust and confidence in human rights – a settlement that works for Britain'.[148]

Through no particular effort of the New Labour government and often in spite of that effort, the Human Rights Act has contributed to continued stability in the new constitutional order:[149] the Act has 'an obvious claim to be recognised as [part] of a constitutional framework … even if the process is occurring in an untidy and unpredictable way, with changing winds of public opinion and all sorts of political cross-currents and undercurrents'.[150] In fact, hostility towards the HRA amongst those on whom it imposes obligations could be seen as a sign of its success: New Labour's legislative achievement was in creating a human rights instrument that could withstand an adverse tide. Nevertheless, given the popular scepticism about the HRA, an alternative Bill of Rights might only be a matter of time. What that might look like is another debate, but it will at least be an opportunity to learn from experience. One option might be to build legitimacy through public engagement and endorsement prior to the implementation of any new Bill of Rights. Even that would require careful scaffolding. The Brexit experience makes it hard to imagine much enthusiasm for a referendum and, given the climate of hostility to human rights, it will be difficult to create the conditions for meaningful debate. Whatever the approach, internal coherence within the governing party would be a useful start. A significant effort would also be required to create and promote a climate of respect for human rights more generally. A Bill of Rights should not feel like an imposition on those it is protects. In that respect at least, it is the very last kind of legislation that should need to swim upstream.

[146] ibid 29.

[147] HC Deb 1 March 2013, vol 559, col 574.

[148] ibid col 574.

[149] The HRA was explicitly given as an example of a 'constitutional statute' when Lord Justice Laws coined the term in *Thoburn v Sunderland City Council* [2002] EWHC 195 (Admin), [2003] QB 151, [62]. Lord Walker put it alongside the European Communities Act 1972 as 'one of two statutes which … must be recognised as instruments of special constitutional importance': R Walker, 'The New Supreme Court and the Other Changes in the Justice System' (2006) 6 *Legal Information Management* 292, 295.

[150] Walker (ibid) 295.

4

The Unintended Consequences of Legislative Constitutionalism: The Common Law Constitution and Judicial Comparativism

SE-SHAUNA WHEATLE [1]

I. INTRODUCTION

THE GENERAL TENOR and effect of New Labour's reforms were of legislative constitutionalism – the development of the constitution through a series of legislative enactments with Parliament making direct and explicit contributions to the content of the UK constitution. This legislative constitutional direction has had the knock-on effect of increased judicialisation in the sense of broadened and heightened judicial power. The expanded functions of the judiciary, emanating especially from the Human Rights Act 1998 (HRA), have been understandably subject to intense debate and scrutiny, as these functions seemed to require a recalibration of accepted constitutional relationships and power distribution. This chapter focuses, however, on the extent to which this judicialisation has been channelled through common law constitutionalism. Common law constitutionalism has been indirectly encouraged by the centrality of the judicial branch to the navigation of new constitutional powers and obligations, and the reconciliation of these constitutional innovations with mainstays of the constitution. The courts are also at the centre of a further indirect consequence of New Labour's reforms – increased attention to comparative engagement in the courts. By enhancing the external influence on, and the external outlook of, UK constitutional law, the reforms also shed more light and inspire greater reflection on the role of foreign law in

[1] I am grateful to Michael Gordon, Ruth Houghton, Roger Masterman and Adam Tucker for comments on earlier drafts.

UK courts. This chapter therefore identifies two (largely, I contend, unintended) consequences of the New Labour reforms from 1997 onwards: a rejuvenated common law constitution and attention to, and contestation over, judicial comparativism in the UK. The primary focus of this chapter is the impact of the HRA. It was not widely foreseen that constitutional legislation to make rights under the European Convention on Human Rights domestically enforceable would usher in enhanced common law constitutionalism and a broader judicial comparativism beyond engagement with the European Court of Human Rights. In what follows, I discuss the factors that nonetheless contributed to a revitalisation of common law constitutionalist reasoning and enhanced attention to engagement with foreign law.

Part II of the chapter addresses the growth of legislative constitutionalism, which indirectly fuelled the unintended consequences claimed herein. In part III, I discuss increased engagement with judicial comparativism, exploring whether available foreign legal materials extend beyond the European continent. Part IV then addresses the second unintended consequence in the form of the revival of common law constitutionalism. It is then argued in part V that the constitutional complexities triggered by legislative constitutionalism have the potential to outlive the legislation itself. The potential staying power of the New Labour reforms accordingly lies, at least in part, in the unintended consequences occasioned by those reforms.

II. LEGISLATIVE CONSTITUTIONALISM

The constitutional reforms ushered in by Prime Ministers Tony Blair and Gordon Brown from 1997 to 2010 represented an embrace of legislative constitutionalism. Legislative constitutionalism is partly a question of form, speaking to constitutional *enactment* (as opposed to exclusive reliance on unwritten norms or judicial action) as well as *piecemeal* introduction of constitutional norms (as opposed to promulgation of a comprehensive, or nearly comprehensive, constitutional code). However, legislative constitutionalism is also a matter of substance, a normative posture on the source of the constitution, its norms and their enforcement. As a substantive statement, it represents a normative stance regarding institutional responsibility for protection of fundamental constitutional precepts, articulating responsibility on the part of the legislature as well as the courts. It signals that the legislature plays a role and has an important voice in setting the terms of the ongoing constitutional settlement. The constitution is, accordingly, a function of the respective and interactive work of legislature and judiciary, rather than a function of the courts speaking for the constitution and to Parliament.

Conceptually, legislative constitutionalism is to be distinguished from political constitutionalism and legal constitutionalism; it is agnostic about whether political or legal mechanisms ought to dominate the constitutional landscape. The concept of legislative constitutionalism also differs from Stephen Gardbaum's influential 'new commonwealth model of constitutionalism'.[2] Legislative constitutionalism does bear some affinity with, and is undoubtedly influenced by, Gardbaum's model; it picks up on his idea of a claim to political responsibility for constitutional norms, especially rights.[3] In Gardbaum's model, this responsibility is manifested in the ability of the legislative organ to overturn judicial constitutional rights interpretation as well as in political scrutiny of Bills during the legislative process. Legislative constitutionalism as used in this chapter differs from Gardbaum's model by isolating statutes enacting constitutional norms; it does not extend to a constitution enacted in codified form with the force of constituent power. In that sense, it is narrower than Gardbaum's model, and is meant to capture the constitutional fuzziness of constitutional statutes enacted in a piecemeal fashion, without the lofty, comprehensive and deliberate objectives of constitutional codes. It is the constitutional fuzziness of legislative constitutionalism that has spurred the types of consequences discussed in this chapter.

Perhaps nowhere is the lack of lofty goals more evident than in the HRA. Lacking a preamble, lacking any exhortatory statements about the deeper values embedded in the Act or the contribution it seeks to make to British society, at first glance, one would be forgiven for seeing the Act as quite distinct from comparable Bills of Rights enshrined in codified constitutions.[4] By contrast, the Canadian Charter of Rights and Freedoms 1982 declares its assumption that 'Canada is founded upon principles that recognise the supremacy of God and the rule of law', and even the relatively modest New Zealand Bill of Rights Act 1990 declares itself to be 'an Act to affirm, protect, and promote human rights and fundamental freedoms in New Zealand'. The UK Act is more staid and technical, declaring an intention to 'give further effect to rights and freedoms guaranteed under the European Convention on Human Rights [ECHR]'. The tentativeness underlying the HRA has fed uncertainty about the foreign or domestic status of the rights it incorporated and the extent to which the Act is part of a global web of rights commitment and rights enforcement. This uncertainty surrounds much of the discourse and practice regarding the use of foreign law in human rights reasoning in the UK post-HRA. Enhanced attention to the use of foreign law is discussed in the following section, as the first unintended consequence of the New Labour reforms.

[2] S Gardbuam, *The New Commonwealth Model of Constitutionalism: Theory and Practice* (Cambridge University Press, 2013).

[3] See also J Hiebert, 'Parliament and the Human Rights Act: Can the JCHR Help Facilitate a Culture of Rights?' (2006) 4 *International Journal of Constitutional Law* 1, 3–5.

[4] F Klug, 'A Bill of Rights: Do We Need One or Do We Already Have One?' [2007] *PL* 701.

III. JUDICIAL COMPARATIVISM

With the reforms of 1997 – particularly the HRA – there has been an increasingly externalised orientation of UK constitutionalism, which has spurred debate over how far afield constitutional actors should look for inspiration and interpretative aids. Unlike the US Supreme Court and US constitutional discourse,[5] in the UK the focus of the dispute is not the legitimacy of engagement in judicial comparativism. Rather, the British debate largely addresses which jurisdictions ought to take centre stage as comparators. Early signs of the contestation over appropriate comparators or appropriate foreign references were evident in the drafting of the HRA. Central to the legislative debate on clause 2 of the HRA – which ultimately required that, in determining issues arising in connection with ECHR rights, UK courts 'must take into account' Strasbourg jurisprudence – was a dispute over the acceptable influence of foreign judgments on UK courts. Questions arising in relation to this clause addressed whether the Act should encourage domestic courts to refer to a wide range of foreign law and whether courts should be bound by, or merely bound to refer to, Strasbourg judgments. In House of Lords debates, Lord Kingsland raised the question whether a requirement to merely 'take into account' Strasbourg judgments would cast the judges adrift and leave them free to 'go in whatever direction they wish'.[6] The divide over the breadth of comparativism permitted or prudent under the HRA then found its way into early litigation under the statute, where in *Brown v Stott*, while Lords Bingham and Hope found Canadian case law on self-incrimination helpful, Lord Hope warned that care must be taken 'to ensure that the analysis by the Canadian courts proceeds upon the same principles as those which have been developed by the European Commission and the European Court'.[7] Interestingly, the concern was not about foreign references overawing domestic law and domestic will, but rather the fear that non-European forces would dominate over Strasbourg's influence.

The increased externalisation of UK constitutional law was made more complex in the case of the Human Rights Act because this externalisation was conflicted – and remains unsettled – in several ways. Primarily, there was and remains ambivalence about the nature of the HRA, whether it functions as a domestic Bill of Rights or the incorporation of (the majority of) the ECHR. The inconclusiveness about the domestic status of the rights under the HRA is weaved through Lady Hale's explanation that:

> The Human Rights Act 1998 gives effect to the Convention rights in our domestic law. To that extent they are domestic rights for which domestic remedies are

[5] See, eg, R Bader Ginsburg, 'Looking beyond Our Borders: The Value of a Comparative Perspective in Constitutional Adjudication' (2004) 22 *Yale Law & Policy Review* 329; A Scalia, 'Keynote Address: Foreign Legal Authority in the Federal Courts' (2004) 98 *Proceedings of the Annual Meeting (American Society of International Law)* 305.

[6] HL Deb 18 November 1997, vol 583, col 512.

[7] *Brown v Stott* [2003] 1 AC 681 (UKHL) 74.

> prescribed: *Re McKerr* [2004] UKHL 12, [2004] 1WLR 807. But the rights are those defined in the Convention, the correct interpretation of which lies ultimately with Strasbourg: *R (Ullah) v Special Adjudicator* [2004] UKHL 26, [2004] 2 AC 323, para 20.[8]

That this ambivalence persists is represented in the judgment in January 2017 in *R (Minton Morrill Solicitors) v Lord Chancellor*[9] rejecting the argument that the ECHR is 'domestic law' for the purposes of legal aid under the Access to Justice Act 1999. Mr Justice Kerr explained that:

> The judges who have spoken of the HRA *incorporating* into our domestic law the Convention rights referred to in it, used that language, in my judgment, as no more than a convenient shorthand to describe the enactment in domestic law of rights expressed in words that mirror those of the articles of the European Convention that are referred to in section 1 of the HRA and reproduced in schedule 1 to that Act.
>
> The fact that the domestic law Convention rights are expressed in the same words as those that appear in the articles of the Convention which are reproduced in schedule 1, does not mean that the content of the domestic Convention rights enacted by the HRA is necessarily identical to the content of the rights expressed in the same words as applied by the ECtHR [European Court of Human Rights].[10]

Further, in terms that elucidated the distinction between the European Communities Act of 1972 and the Blair reforms regarding the UK's relationship with Europe, it was explained that:

> The nature of EU law rights in our domestic law is completely different from that of Convention rights in the domestic law of England and Wales. The former are part of domestic law because of a statutory cession of sovereignty to a source of law outside the United Kingdom. The HRA, by contrast, is a domestic statute that does not cede any ground to an external legislature.[11]

Thus, the court was not swayed by the claimant solicitors' reference to Lord Neuberger's position in *Miller v Secretary of State for Exiting the EU* that the ECA 1972 was 'the "conduit pipe" by which EU law is introduced into UK domestic law', the effect of which 'is to constitute EU law an independent and overriding source of domestic law'.[12] At least some of Justice Kerr's views that the HRA creates domestic rights that may mirror, but are distinct from, ECHR rights sit uncomfortably with Lady Hale's position that 'the rights are those defined in the Convention'. The implication of the view in *Morrill* that the ECHR does not become domestic law by virtue of the HRA should be that the HRA is indeed a domestic rights instrument enacting domestic rights,

[8] *Animal Defenders International v Secretary of State for Culture, Media and Sport* [2008] UKHL 15 [53] (Lady Hale).
[9] [2017] EWHC 612 (Admin).
[10] *Minton Morrill* (n 8) [27]–[28].
[11] ibid [31] (Mr Justice Kerr).
[12] *R (Miller) v Secretary of State for Exiting the European Union* [2017] UKSC 5 [65].

rather than just a tool – or, to use the now popular term, 'conduit pipe' – for the ECHR. However, the correct conceptualisation of the rights under the HRA appears to remain unsettled.

The unresolved question whether the HRA guarantees domestic or international rights underlies to some extent the difficulties in interpreting section 2 of the Act. While the section confers an interpretative role on the Strasbourg Court, it does not prescribe the interpretative weight of Strasbourg in HRA decisions. There is, accordingly, a menu of options arising from the section 2 duty:

> s 2(1) creates a significant judicial discretionary power to apply Strasbourg jurisprudence directly, to take it 'into account' but fail to apply it, or to come to a decision somewhere between the two extremes by either applying (or being influenced by) the Convention jurisprudence to a greater or lesser degree.[13]

The extent to which UK courts maintain freedom of action – being free to depart from Strasbourg judgments – is correctly perceived as an indicator of the Act's nature as either a domestic Bill of Rights or as merely incorporative of European rights norms.[14] While courts initially adopted a mirror principle – taking a strict approach to using and following Strasbourg jurisprudence – that approach has given way to greater flexibility and willingness to depart from the ECtHR if the latter has ruled without sufficient appreciation of domestic law or if the subject matter is thought to fall within the UK's margin of appreciation.[15] As was acknowledged in 2018 in the UK Supreme Court, 'in more recent cases, a departure from the mirror principle can be detected'.[16] Lord Hoffmann in *R v Lyons*, for instance, allowed for departure from ECtHR decisions and dialogue between Strasbourg and domestic courts:

> It is obviously highly desirable that there should be no divergence between domestic and ECtHR jurisprudence but section 2(1) says only that the courts must 'take into account' the decisions of the ECtHR. If, for example, an English court considers that the ECtHR has misunderstood or been misinformed about some aspect of English law, it may wish to give a judgment which invites the ECtHR to reconsider the question: compare *Z v United Kingdom* (2001) 10 BHRC 384. There is room for dialogue on such matters.[17]

These themes were reinforced in the *Horncastle* judgment, in which Lord Phillips maintained:

> The requirement to 'take into account' the Strasbourg jurisprudence will normally result in this Court applying principles that are clearly established by the Strasbourg

[13] R Masterman, 'Aspiration or Foundation? The Status of the Strasbourg Jurisprudence and the "Convention Rights" in Domestic Law' in H Fenwick, G Phillipson and R Masterman (eds) *Judicial Reasoning under the Human Rights Act* (Cambridge University Press, 2011) 62.

[14] ibid.

[15] M Amos, *Human Rights Law* (Bloomsbury, 2014) 21–22.

[16] *D v Commissioner of Police of the Metropolis* (*Worboys case*) [2018] UKSC 11 [77] (Lord Kerr).

[17] *R v Lyons* [2002] UKHL 44 [46].

> Court. There will, however, be rare occasions where this court has concerns as to whether a decision of the Strasbourg Court sufficiently appreciates or accommodates particular aspects of our domestic process. In such circumstances it is open to this court to decline to follow the Strasbourg decision, giving reasons for adopting this course. This is likely to give the Strasbourg Court the opportunity to reconsider the particular aspect of the decision that is in issue, so that there takes place what may prove to be a valuable dialogue between this court and the Strasbourg Court.[18]

In *Moohan*, a modification of the mirror principle was recognised, Lord Wilson declaring that:

> where there is no directly relevant decision of the ECtHR with which it would be possible (even if appropriate) to keep pace, we can and must do more. We must determine for ourselves the existence or otherwise of an alleged Convention right.[19]

This approach of heightened independence and flexibility was endorsed in the Supreme Court by Lord Kerr in *D v Commissioner of Police of the Metropolis*:

> Reticence by the courts of the UK to decide whether a Convention right has been violated would be an abnegation of our statutory obligation under section 6 of HRA. This section makes it unlawful for a public authority, including a court, to act in a way which is incompatible with a Convention right.[20]

Uncertainty about the role and identity of the Human Rights Act is seen not only between the lines of case law, but also in wider social science assessment of the impact of the HRA. Francesca Klug's claim that 'the Act has never been sufficiently "owned" by British people as "their" Bill of Rights' was reinforced by the Bill of Rights Commission Report in 2012. While the Commission failed to deliver a clear conclusion on the overall question of whether the UK should adopt a British Bill of Rights, the majority were of the view that 'there is a lack of public understanding and "ownership" of the Human Rights Act'.[21] The lack of ownership has been attributed to limited public consultation prior to the passage of the HRA, inaccurate and sensational tabloid reports about judicial decisions under the Act, the Act's success in restraining government action, especially antiterrorism measures,[22] antipathy towards human rights and 'skepticism about the universalist nature of human rights'.[23] Moreover, the absence of popular embrace of the HRA is unsurprising in light of political machinations surrounding the Act. The Conservative Party pejoratively referred to the Act as 'Labour's Human Rights Act' and positioned ECHR rights as an impediment to

[18] *R v Horncastle* [2009] UKSC 14 [11].
[19] *Moohan v Lord Advocate* [2014] UKSC 67 [105] (Lord Wilson).
[20] *Worboys case* (n 16) [78].
[21] Commission on a Bill of Rights, 'A UK Bill of Rights? The Choice Before Us' (December 2012) [80].
[22] Klug, 'A Bill of Rights' (2007) 713–14.
[23] M Elliott, 'A Damp Squib in the Long Grass: The Report of the Commission on a Bill of Rights' [2013] *European Human Rights Law Review* 137, 140–41.

antiterrorism efforts while the Act was described by some sections of the media as a 'criminals' charter'.[24]

A further complexity in the externalisation of the HRA that contributes to the contours of judicial comparativism is the conceptual ambivalence about whether 'rights' protections enacted through the HRA connect the statute to global rights traditions or, alternatively, speak exclusively to the European rights tradition as expressed in the ECHR. Some clues to resolving this second issue can be gleaned from responses to the first question, since if the HRA is not strictly an incorporation of the ECHR, there is scope for a broader conceptualisation of the place, purpose and relevant material for interpreting the statute. While the Act itself does not furnish an answer to this question, the history of both the HRA and the ECHR provide support for the perception of the Act as part of a global rights project. The text of the HRA is centrally concerned with the Convention, the long title starting with the phrase 'An Act to give further effect to rights and freedoms guaranteed under the European Convention on Human Rights'. The 'Rights Brought Home' White Paper, however, included a preface by the Prime Minister claiming that the Human Rights Bill 'will enhance the awareness of human rights in our society. And it stands alongside our decision to put the promotion of human rights at the forefront of our foreign policy.'[25] This framing of the Bill beckons beyond Europe and speaks to wider human rights aspirations.

Beyond the framing of the HRA, further potential for comparativism is encapsulated in the view that human rights measures in any constitutional democracy are part of a common rights enterprise. The common rights enterprise position has both substantive and institutional dimensions, speaking to both a belief in common human rights values and judicial perception of the courts' role in the interpretation and enforcement of rights. The claim of a common rights enterprise has been advanced by Waldron in defence and encouragement of judicial comparativism in rights cases, arguing that 'when we think about fundamental rights we understand that the courts of various countries are engaged in what is more or less the same enterprise'.[26]

The common rights enterprise discourse is sometimes envisioned as a commonality of rights conceptions or objectives. This, I would argue, is too narrow a view of the commonality of human rights. Shared beliefs in the public

[24] See, eg Conservative Party, *Protecting Human Rights in the UK: The Conservatives' Proposals for Changing Britain's Human Rights Laws* (October 2014) 4; K McDonald, 'Theresa May Has Lied about Human Rights Before and She's Lying Now, Warns Nick Clegg' (7 June 2017) https://inews.co.uk/news/politics/theresa-may-lied-human-rights-shes-lying-now-nick-clegg-warns/; 'Human Rights Is a Charter for Criminals and Parasites Our Anger Is No Longer Enough' *Daily Mail* (15 July 2012) https://www.dailymail.co.uk/debate/article-2173666/Human-rights-charter-criminals-parasites-anger-longer-enough.html.

[25] Home Office, *Rights Brought Home: The Human Rights Bill* (Cm 3782, 1997) Preface.

[26] J Waldron, 'Universalism or the Integrity of a Common Enterprise?' (2016) Public Law & Legal Theory Research Paper Series Working Paper No 16-48, 10.

good of human rights do not rely on shared beliefs in the correct conceptions of these rights. Courts can and do engage with each other on rights issues across conceptual divides, and indeed such comparative engagement can serve to expose those divides, and sharpen and cement domestic rights positions. Consistency or uniformity are not necessarily the foundation or objective of the common enterprise. The objective is to reason about the core values of human rights principles to achieve the maximum fulfilment of those principles in accordance with the legal, social and political environment of the jurisdiction in question.[27] Since uniformity is not the goal, 'Foreign judgments can even be referred to for the main purpose of demonstrating why they should not be followed'.[28] UK case law on freedom of expression provided evidence of reference to foreign law to distinguish the existing and preferred domestic approach. Lady Hale explained in *Animal Defenders International v Culture Secretary* why a different legislative and judicial approach to freedom of expression in political advertising is adopted in the UK when compared to the law of the USA:

> There was an elephant in the committee room, always there but never mentioned, when we heard this case. It was the dominance of advertising, not only in elections but also in the formation of political opinion, in the United States of America. Enormous sums are spent, and therefore have to be raised, at election times: it is estimated that the disputed 2000 elections for President and Congress cost as much as US$3 billion. Attempts to regulate campaign spending are struck down in the name of the First Amendment: 'Congress shall make no law … abridging the freedom of speech, or of the press': see particularly Buckley v Valco, 424 US 1 (1976). A fortiori there is no limit to the amount that pressure groups can spend on getting their message across in the most powerful and pervasive media available.
>
> In the United Kingdom, and elsewhere in Europe, we do not want our government or its policies to be decided by the highest spenders. Our democracy is based upon more than one person one vote. It is based on the view that each person has equal value.
>
> …
>
> So this case is not just about permissible restrictions on freedom of expression. It is about striking the right balance between the two most important components of a democracy: freedom of expression and voter equality.[29]

The common enterprise view rests in part on the idea of a special nature of human rights norms, an idea reinforced by judicial comparative practice. It has been found that in the UK Supreme Court 'reference to foreign jurisprudence is generally more likely in human rights cases'.[30] Tyrrell's groundbreaking study

[27] S Fredman, 'Foreign Fads or Fashions? The Role of Comparativism in Human Rights Law' [2015] *ICLQ* 631, 634.

[28] ibid.

[29] [2008] UKHL 15 [47]–[49].

[30] H Tyrrell, *Human Rights in the UK and the Influence of Foreign Jurisprudence* (Hart Publishing, 2018) 77. In Tyrrell's study, 'foreign jurisprudence' does not include judgments of the European Court of Human Rights or the Judicial Committee of the Privy Council.

of the use of foreign jurisprudence in the first eight years of the UK Supreme Court found that while 26 per cent of non-human rights cases explicitly cited foreign jurisprudence, in relation to human rights cases that refer to foreign jurisprudence the proportion rises to 38 per cent. A higher incidence of the use of foreign case law in human rights jurisprudence is not unique to the UK, and mirrors similar observations on the use of comparative material in human rights case law. Groppi and Ponthoreau noted 'citations of foreign case law prevail … in human rights decisions, whereas they appear less frequently in institutional decisions'.[31] This therefore prompts the oft-posed question among comparativists of whether there is something special about human rights issues that makes judges more likely to consult foreign law. Special characteristics of human rights law that have been posited include human rights universalism, 'awareness of a common enterprise',[32] the proliferation of international human rights instruments, and the desire and commitment to treat like cases alike.[33] Slaughter, speaking to judicial self-conception in relation to human rights, has offered that:

> courts of some subset of countries may see their primary function as the protection of individual rights against the government. From this perspective, it is not surprising that one of the most active areas of transjudicial communication outside the European Community is among courts specifically charged with the interpretation and application of international instruments concerning human rights.[34]

Even in the limitation of rights, there is a distinctiveness about human rights as 'many bills of rights allow States to limit rights only when necessary in a democratic society, suggesting that there are common values in democratic societies'.[35] Common values in both the scope of rights and their limitation can be seen to encourage communication across jurisdictions.

The observed trends towards judicial comparativism on rights issues suggest that rights enactments will most likely lead to engagement with foreign law. Accordingly, whilst unintended, increased attention to comparativism would likely follow from any legislative rights effort. The likelihood of resulting comparativism may stoke fears that enacting rights legislation almost inevitably undermines domestic political preferences. However, the mere fact of inter-jurisdictional engagement does not dictate the impact of foreign law on domestic rights resolutions. The extent to which domestic preferences are displaced by foreign material depends on the ways in which the court refers to foreign law. Uses of foreign law have been categorised as ranging from soft uses – in which

[31] T Groppi and M-C Ponthoreau, *The Use of Foreign Precedents by Constitutional Judges* (Hart Publishing, 2013) 416.

[32] A-M Slaughter, 'A Typology of Transjudicial Communication' (1994) 29 *University of Richmond Law Review* 99, 128; Tyrrell, *Human Rights in the UK* (2018) 139.

[33] Waldron, 'Human Rights: Universalism' (2016) 13.

[34] Slaughter, 'Typology' (1994) 128.

[35] Fredman, 'Foreign Fads or Fashions' (2015) 631, 633.

foreign law does not influence the court's final resolution – to hard uses – whereby foreign law has an impact on the court's reasoning.[36] Further, as noted above, foreign law can be cited to distinguish local circumstances and reinforce a commitment to a contrary domestic approach. Moreover, if courts engage with foreign law as a means of fulfilling the legislatively assigned task of determining whether rights have been violated, they remain within the bounds of the powers and duties which political actors have conferred on the judiciary. The reality is that this interpretative task is increasingly recognised as an exercise that traverses jurisdictional boundaries. Yet, drafting preferences and textual language can have an influence, as reflected in the specific mandate in section 2 of the HRA to take account of ECtHR decisions. This requirement would influence the extent to which courts look beyond Strasbourg in making decisions under the Act; this issue is discussed in the following section.

IV. BEYOND STRASBOURG?

UK courts have shown openness towards looking beyond the shores of Europe in their rights reasoning. There are ebbs and flows in references to non-ECtHR foreign law, and judgments evince a marked preference for common law jurisdictions. Initially, after the HRA was passed and entered into force, there were references to a wide swathe of foreign law in order to grapple with the new rights regime.[37] Much of this comparativism could be seen in the court's effort to unpack and apply the woolly doctrine of proportionality. Judges considered both ECtHR and common law countries' jurisprudence on the doctrine but preferred the Canadian formulation of the test (expressed in *Oakes v R*[38]) and the Privy Council's framing (expressed in *De Freitas v Permanent Secretary of Ministry of Agriculture*[39]) to Strasbourg's framing. British judges have praised the clarity of the Canadian formulation of the proportionality test, and expressed preference for this structure over that of Strasbourg. The Canadian test was described as being more closely aligned with common law sensibilities. Speaking in *Bank Mellat*, Lord Reed maintained:

> The approach to proportionality adopted in our domestic case law under the Human Rights Act has not generally mirrored that of the Strasbourg court. In accordance with the analytical approach to legal reasoning characteristic of the common law, a more clearly structured approach has generally been adopted, derived from case law under Commonwealth constitutions and Bills of Rights, including in particular the Canadian Charter of Fundamental Rights and Freedoms of 1982.[40]

[36] C Saunders, 'The Use and Misuse of Comparative Constitutional Law' (2006) 13 *Indiana Journal of Global Studies* 37, 50.

[37] See, eg *Attorney General's Reference (No 2 of 2001)* [2003] UKHL 68 [2004] 2 AC 72.

[38] [1986] 1 SCR 103.

[39] [1999] 1 AC 69.

[40] *Bank Mellat v Her Majesty's Treasury (No. 2)* [2013] UKSC 38 [72] (Lord Reed).

While Lord Reed spoke in dissent, Lord Sumption also invoked the *Oakes* requirements in the majority judgment, referring to the Privy Council structure as 'the classic formulation of the test'.[41]

Over time, however, foreign law references came to concentrate on the ECtHR. Lord Justice Toulson therefore bemoaned the practice that had developed of the courts citing 'Strasbourg decisions in abundance' while 'the citation of decisions of senior courts in other common law jurisdictions is now less common'. Noting that he 'regret[s] the imbalance', he admonished that:

> The development of the common law did not come to an end on the passing of the Human Rights Act. It is in vigorous health and flourishing in many parts of the world which share a common legal tradition. This case provides a good example of the benefit which can be gained from knowledge of the development of the common law elsewhere.[42]

The reasons for the trend observed by Toulson LJ are unclear. It is possible that the statutory mandate to take account of Strasbourg judgments – originally interpreted rigidly as an instruction to hew closely to the European Court – led advocates and courts to concentrate on Strasbourg cases. The section 2 requirement would thereby have indirectly limited explicit engagement with other foreign judgments.

Nonetheless, there are now indications that the proportion of ECtHR jurisprudence to more general rights jurisprudence may be rebalanced. This rebalancing is foreshadowed by the Court of Appeal in *R (Guardian News & Media Ltd) v City of Westminster Magistrates' Court*, where the appellate court overruled the courts below to hold that a judge had the power to allow The Guardian to inspect and take copies of documents which had been provided to the judge and referred to in argument but had not been read out in court. In delivering judgment, Toulson LJ considered statements of Canadian, South African, New Zealand and American courts on the principle of open justice. Toulson LJ was explicit that:

> I base my decision on the common law principles of open justice. In reaching it I am fortified by the common theme of the judgments in other common law countries to which I have referred. Collectively they are strong persuasive authority.[43]

Lord Reed adopted this approach in *A v BBC*, saying that the principle of open justice can

> develop having regard to the approach adopted in other common law countries, some of which have constitutional texts containing guarantees comparable to the Convention rights, while in others the approach adopted reflects the courts' view of the requirements of justice.[44]

[41] ibid [20].
[42] *R (Guardian News and Media Ltd) v City of Westminster Magistrates' Court* [2012] EWCA Civ 420, [2013] QB 618 [88].
[43] ibid [88].
[44] *A v BBC* [2014] UKSC 25 [41].

On Lord Reed's account, the incorporation of Convention rights ought not to stymie interaction with non-Strasbourg courts; it may sow the seeds for further dialogue through similarities in constitutional rights.

The resurgence of common law in the UK Supreme Court (examined in further detail below) also opens the door for further non-ECtHR comparativism. Reliance on the common law principle of open justice in *A v BBC* was accompanied by consideration of the transnational development of the common law.[45] The course of constitutional jurisprudence 'in the common law world demonstrates transnational judicial dialogue in developing common law constitutional norms'.[46] Accordingly, by tapping into common law norms and methods, British courts thereby access a transnational web of material.

V. COMMON LAW CONSTITUTIONALISM

A second consequence of the HRA which merits attention is that of accelerated common law constitutionalism. Much has been made – including by Roger Masterman and myself – of the revival of common law rights in the wake of the recent Eurosceptic tide in the UK.[47] This chapter contends that common law acceleration has also been evident in other, perhaps less obvious, ways as a result of constitutional reforms, including the HRA. There has been growing recognition of constitutionalism in the wake of the New Labour reforms. The reforms themselves were seen as ushering in renewed attention to the UK's constitutional arrangements. The legislative constitutionalism that typified the reforms contributed to a larger constitutional awareness. In addition to drawing renewed attention to the features of the constitution, the reform package fuelled two forms of constitutional responses: accommodation and defensiveness. Accommodation involved reflection on the constitutional implications of the reforms, their relationship to prevailing constitutional norms and the need for adaptations to the constitution to accommodate or respond to the new laws. The growing constitutionalism occasioned by New Labour's reforms can also been said to include a defensive strain, meant to buttress domestic constitutionalism against external legal power. Sir Stephen Sedley has maintained, in this vein, that:

> The jurisprudential impulse towards constitutionalism may at one level be a response to a growing sense, now publicly shared by a number of senior judges, that the UK's political and legal sovereignty has been compromised or surrendered to supranational courts and institutions.[48]

[45] ibid.

[46] S Wheatle, 'Bounded Cosmopolitanism and a Constitutional Common Law' (2014) 11 *Journal of Comparative Law* 235, 247.

[47] R Masterman and S Wheatle, 'A Common Law Resurgence in Rights Protection?' [2015] *European Human Rights Law Review* 57.

[48] S Sedley, *Lions under the Throne: Essays on the History of Public Law* (Cambridge University Press, 2015) 118.

Common law constitutionalism emerged as a crucial feature of this renewed constitutionalism. The courts – largely as a result of powers conferred by relevant statutes – have been central to resolution of constitutional issues arising from the new legislation. In sum, the acceleration of common law constitutionalism was precipitated by the need to interpret the new statutes, reconcile new and existing norms, and plug holes in the rights framework.

Firstly, the introduction of the HRA impelled courts to devise or revise interpretative principles and rules for a new spate of legislation, legislation that was distinctive not only in quantity but also quality. Thus, section 3 of the HRA, though itself conferring a strong interpretative power, also required judicial construction to determine when interpretation consistent with the ECHR could be legitimately undertaken. The benchmark for consistent ECHR interpretation specified in section 3 is merely what is 'possible'. By leaving it to the courts to determine what is constitutionally possible, the Act vested substantial power in the judiciary. The Act therefore required judicial activity in applying or even adapting the content of constitutional doctrines and principles, such as separation of powers, deference and related norms, in order to determine the constitutional limits of the section 3 power.[49] Further, consistent interpretation has sometimes been achieved using familiar techniques of reading in and reading down, techniques which could potentially outlive the HRA. Specifically, reading in and reading down, which have become more common tools and more common in judicial vocabulary, and strong uses of which have been seen under the HRA, can also operate pursuant to the common law principle of legality.[50] These techniques, fortified as they have been under the HRA, are therefore relevant beyond the textual confines of the HRA.

Section 4 of the HRA, though only empowering courts to make declarations of incompatibility, not invalidity, in relation to Acts of Parliament, nonetheless raised questions about the assumed boundaries of judicial legitimacy and competence. The statute itself invites space for debate over these boundaries by using the phrasing that the court 'may' – rather than must – make a declaration of incompatibility upon finding an incompatibility. For this reason, *Nicklinson* saw the Supreme Court grapple with the institutional propriety of determining whether a right had been violated as well as the institutional propriety of making a declaration of incompatibility upon finding a rights violation.[51] The factors which influenced the former question included the gravity of the alleged rights violation, the strength or otherwise of the arguments in support of government policy, the similarity of the issues courts have addressed under

[49] See generally A Kavanagh, *Constitutional Review under the UK Human Rights Act* (Cambridge University Press, 2009); A Young, *Parliamentary Sovereignty and the Human Rights Act* (Hart Publishing, 2008).

[50] *Federal Steam Navigation Co Ltd v Department of Trade and Industry* [1974] 1 WLR 505 (UKHL) 524; Kavanagh (ibid) 102.

[51] *R (Nicklinson) v Ministry of Justice* [2014] UKSC 38.

common law and the strength of the rational connection between the aim and effect of the challenged government policy.[52] The factors that influenced whether it was institutionally appropriate to make the declaration occupy the ground of well-trodden disputes over the line between political and legal decision-making. Two factors related to the nature of the issue and its resolution. The issue of assisted dying law and policy in *Nicklinson* was said to be 'difficult, controversial and sensitive ... with moral and religious dimensions',[53] while its resolution was seen as complex, requiring 'anxious consideration' from the legislature. On the institutional side of the matter, Lord Neuberger took account of the reality that Parliament was currently 'actively considering the issue' and that the courts 'only thirteen years ago' indicated to Parliament that a declaration of incompatibility on the issue would have been inappropriate.[54]

Alongside construction of the new legislation and securing internal consistency of such legislation, there was an effort to reconcile new legislative initiatives, powers and objectives with existing constitutional precepts. Thus, the principle of legality was used as a method of understanding the nature and impact of the section 3 power.[55] The boundaries of both the interpretative power under section 3 and the declarative power under section 4 have been understood by reference to long-standing principles of the rule of law, parliamentary supremacy and separation of powers. Moreover, our understanding of the content and normative force of these principles has been refined by reference to reform legislation, including the HRA.[56] The separation of powers, for instance, has been further instrumentalised in interpreting the demand for an independent and impartial tribunal under Article 6 of the ECHR.[57]

Further, constitutional developments of the twentieth century, which led to the explicit judicial recognition of constitutional norms of special status, now necessitate determination of the rules for resolving tensions between competing fundamental norms. It was the potential conflict of statutory constitutional norms that led Lords Neuberger and Mance in *R (HS2 Action Alliance Ltd) v Secretary of State for Transport* to advance constitutional knowledge and the constitutional (un)settlement of the UK by clarifying that not all constitutional statutes are equal.[58] The inequality of constitutional statutes is the logical conclusion of the Lords' view that it is arguable 'that there may be fundamental

[52] ibid [110].

[53] ibid [115].

[54] ibid.

[55] *R v Secretary of State for the Home Department, ex parte Simms* [2000] 2 AC 115, 131 (Lord Hoffmann).

[56] See, eg *Thoburn v Sunderland City Council* [2003] QB 151; *R (Jackson) v Attorney General* [2006] 1 AC 262; R Masterman and JEK Murkens, 'Skirting Supremacy and Subordination: The Constitutional Authority of the United Kingdom Supreme Court' [2013] *PL* 800.

[57] *R (Anderson) v Secretary of State for the Home Department* [2003] 1 AC 837.

[58] *R (HS2 Action Alliance Ltd) v Secretary of State for Transport* [2014] UKSC 3.

principles, whether contained in other constitutional instruments or recognised at common law, of which Parliament when it enacted the European Communities Act 1972 [ECA 1972] did not either contemplate or authorise the abrogation'.[59] Thus, while it is the ECA 1972 that has come closest to challenging the principle of parliamentary supremacy, it does not automatically trump other constitutional norms, including norms derived under other constitutional statutes. While the potential conflict might arise from legislation, there is every indication that the resolution will fall to courts, as the interpreters and arbiters of law: 'it is for United Kingdom law and courts to determine'.[60] The *HS2* judgment therefore stands as a marker of the centrality of the judicial role in constructing the new constitutional edifice of the UK through the interpretation of constitutional legislation. Under the increasingly textured rules governing the interpretation of constitutional legislation, under which implied repeal is displaced, this judicial role is heightened. Moreover, in grappling with the complexification of the constitutional landscape, courts have come to engage in more constitutionalist reasoning, including the layering of norms, the articulation of fundamental rules and principles, and the assessment of state actions against those rules and principles. These interpretative developments must form part of our understanding of the increased judicialisation emerging from New Labour's reforms.

A spotlight has also been shone on areas in which common law constitutional requirements filled the gaps of, or clarified, constitutional and human rights legislation. Human rights legislation triggers renewed attention to rights and impetus to safeguard rights, and, by leading to a higher incidence of rights litigation, creates opportunities to scrutinise the common law terrain for applicable norms where legislation falls short. Sometimes those common law norms are not immediately apparent; as Lord Toulson explained in a 2014 speech: 'The common law is our habitat. It is like the water in which we swim. We are not always as conscious as we should be of what is to be found in it'.[61] In such cases where the common law's breadth and capabilities are not easily visible, human rights legislation may open the door by triggering claims in the courts, while the common law carries the case over the threshold. A perfect example is the *Al Rawi* case, in which the government made a claim to use closed material proceedings in civil litigation where the use of closed material proceedings had not been authorised by statute. The HRA and the ECHR as interpreted by the Strasbourg Court did not provide a clear answer to the question, but the court was able to conclude that it was not open to judges under the common law to order closed material proceedings. Lord Dyson observed:

> The basic rule is that (subject to certain established and limited exceptions) the court cannot exercise its power to regulate its own procedures in such a way as will deny

[59] ibid [207].
[60] ibid.
[61] Lord Toulson, 'International Influence on the Common Law' (11 November 2014).

> parties their fundamental common law right to participate in the proceedings in accordance with the common law principles of natural justice and open justice.[62]

Finally, common law rights and principles also come to the rescue by providing clarity where Strasbourg jurisprudence is opaque and unsettled. In this way, the common law principle of, and right to, open justice aided the courts in *Guardian News Media* and *Kennedy* on the issues of journalists' claims to inspect documents presented in court and to obtain disclosure from public charities.[63] The notion of the common law supplying clarity where the ECHR and ECtHR lack it is surprising considering that one of the benefits of the ECHR system over common law rights is a catalogue of rights from which constitutional actors and citizens can draw. However, rights are, of course, delineated in a very general way in any rights instrument and their content must be further revealed through, inter alia, judicial decisions. That inherent generality and the need for judicial clarification have been critical to increasing judicialisation and common law reasoning.

VI. ENDURING JUDICIAL POWER AND CHANGING CULTURE

Among the benefits that the Labour government thought would accrue from 'bringing rights home' were that:

> the rights will be brought much more fully into the jurisprudence of the courts throughout the United Kingdom, and their interpretation will thus be far more subtly and powerfully woven into our law. And there will be another distinct benefit. British judges will be enabled to make a distinctively British contribution to the development of the jurisprudence of human rights in Europe.[64]

Of course, there are impending threats to the Human Rights Act; the Act's impact has been criticised by members of the very Labour Party that introduced it[65] and, more importantly, the Conservative Party has pledged to review the Act with a view towards repeal. More recently, the Conservative government has launched an independent review of the Human Rights Act to consider the operation and impact of the HRA and report whether there should be amendments to the Act. The review centres on the judicial role, with the terms of reference directing the panel to scrutinise the relationship between domestic courts and the ECtHR and to examine whether the HRA's impact on the branches of government risks 'over-judicialising' public administration.[66]

[62] *Al Rawi v Security Service* [2011] UKSC 34 [22].

[63] *Guardian News* (n 42); *Kennedy v Charity Commission* [2014] UKSC 20.

[64] *Rights Brought Home* (n 25) [1.14].

[65] 'Jack Straw Plans to "Rebalance" Human Rights Act' *The Guardian* (8 December 2008) https://www.theguardian.com/politics/2008/dec/08/human-rights-act-straw.

[66] 'Independent Human Rights Act Review: Terms of Reference' https://assets.publishing.service.gov.uk/government/uploads/system/uploads/attachment_data/file/953347/human-rights-review-tor.pdf.

However, the effect of the constitutional changes occasioned by the HRA cannot be so easily erased. Firstly, as Lord Neuberger has explained, 'the introduction of the Convention into UK law has been a breath of fresh air for the judiciary, the legal profession and legal academics. It has … made us more questioning about our accepted ideas and assumptions.'[67] Indeed, such reflection and introspection is part of the most basic and lasting effect of engagement with foreign law. Secondly, the assertiveness that has manifested in the judiciary, especially through interpretative techniques such as strong presumptions of constitutionality accompanied by reading in and reading down legislation, is unlikely to disappear. Judicial assertiveness through constitutional interpretation is pronounced in the Supreme Court's interpretation of section 53 of the Freedom of Information Act 2000 (FOIA) in *R (Evans) v Attorney General*. The Upper Tribunal decided that communications between the Prince of Wales and government ministers should be disclosed under the FOIA, but the Attorney General overrode this decision. Despite section 53 of the Act conferring authority on the Attorney General to override a disclosure notice if there are 'reasonable grounds' for concluding that the Act did not require disclosure, the Supreme Court held that, applying the principle of legality, clearer statutory words were needed to authorise override of an Upper Tribunal decision.[68] While the case arose from the terms of the FOIA, the disclosure and the restriction of the Attorney General's powers were a consequence of common law interpretation.

The assertive approach being adopted by courts is fundamentally methodological and institutional, and therefore has less dependence on statute; it can be seen as an evolution of common law methods, and it might prove difficult to disaggregate common law methods from methods developed under section 3 of the HRA. For instance, Lord Hoffmann's approximation of section 3 of the HRA with the principle of legality in *ex p Simms*, while underestimating the transformative power of section 3, nonetheless touches upon the core connection between legislative and common law rights interpretation.[69]

Moreover, the methodological advances made in the wake of legislative constitutionalism might survive due to path dependence. Path dependence (in the sense that legal decisions and outcomes are shaped by the historical sequence of legal developments) also points to some retention of the interpretative approach developed under the Human Rights Act. There is a likelihood that judicial experience with broader, more creative interpretative experiences will inhibit relinquishment of such powers, particularly if there is (as there likely will be) some vagueness, ambiguity or level of indeterminacy in any new interpretation provisions enacted under a new statute. Path dependence is to an extent an

[67] Lord Neuberger, 'The Role of Judges in Human Rights Jurisprudence: A Comparison of the Australian and UK Experience' (8 August 2014) [31].

[68] *R (Evans) v Attorney General* [2015] UKSC 21 [56]–[58].

[69] *Simms* (n 55) 132.

inbuilt component of the common law method.[70] Rule builds upon rule, case upon case; though there are qualifications and reversals, common law development is typified by a steady progress of rules and principles, with each rule and principle premised on existing norms. Essentially, the argument here is that 'the tone has been set' and that if there is some limited scope within any new Bill of Rights for consistent interpretation of rights, similar conflicts about the boundary between legislation and adjudication will arise and the courts might be similarly activated to jealously guard their power to regulate rights against governmental and potentially parliamentary interference.

Beyond the formidable judicial powers that have resulted from the constitutional reforms of the New Labour era, judicial and constitutional culture have changed. *Jackson* and *HS2* stand as evidence of statute providing the impetus for judicial strides in untested waters and judicial (common law) regulation of parliamentary enactments and governmental objectives. Thus, in *Jackson*, legislative reforms were raised by Lord Steyn and Lady Hale to explain and justify the transformation of the constitutional landscape and distribution of constitutional power. Rejecting the notion that the UK possesses an 'uncontrolled constitution', Lord Steyn argued that the 'European Convention on Human Rights as incorporated into our law by the Human Rights Act, 1998, created a new legal order'.[71] He concluded that 'The classic account given by Dicey of the doctrine of the supremacy of Parliament, pure and absolute as it was, can now be seen to be out of place in the modern United Kingdom.'[72] Moreover, while accepting that parliamentary supremacy remains 'the *general* principle of our constitution', it was deemed 'a construct of the common law' which therefore leaves open the possibility 'that circumstances could arise where the courts may have to qualify a principle established on a different hypothesis of constitutionalism'.[73] Lord Hope then followed that line of thought regarding the evolution of the principle of parliamentary sovereignty, maintaining that 'Our constitution is dominated by the sovereignty of Parliament. But Parliamentary sovereignty is no longer, if it ever was, absolute'.[74] Though acknowledging that most of the qualifications on parliamentary sovereignty were introduced by Parliament itself, these statutes were seen as affecting the constitution in a broader sense and, significantly, the court's function in enforcing the norms of the constitution. Consequently, both the ECA 1972 and the HRA gave rise to new interpretative obligations on the court and raised the constitutional and political profile of the judiciary. A similar line of reasoning can be observed in *R (Privacy International) v Investigatory Powers Tribunal*.[75] The Supreme Court

[70] See O Hathaway, 'Path Dependence in the Law: The Course and Pattern of Legal Change in a Common Law System' (2001) 86 *Iowa Law Review* 101.
[71] *Jackson* (n 56) [102] (Lord Steyn).
[72] ibid.
[73] ibid.
[74] ibid [104].
[75] [2019] UKSC 22.

restrictively interpreted the ouster clause in section 67(8) of the Regulation of Investigatory Powers Act 2000, concluding that the clause did not exclude judicial review.[76] Lord Carnwath invoked the combination of statutory recognition of the rule of law in section 1 of the Constitutional Reform Act 2005 and judicial recognition of such statutes as constitutional statutes to justify the view that it is within the judicial province to determine the content and limits of the rule of law.[77]

The legislative reforms, placed alongside the traditional Diceyan view of the constitutional centrality of ordinary law developed by the courts, have provided strong support for increased judicial involvement in constitutional formulation and enforcement. Further, the rule of law, which Lord Hope has described as the 'ultimate controlling factor on which our constitution is based',[78] was seen as being reinforced by the HRA. The HRA can in that sense be perceived as a contribution to the modernisation of the rule of law, with the protection of the individual from arbitrary government becoming embedded in the modern rule of law.[79] Lord Hope thereby gave voice to an evolution of both the rule of law and parliamentary supremacy, both of which were said to lie within the definitional and regulatory sphere of the courts. The extent of judicial involvement in the definition and protection of Parliament's constitutional role was laid bare in the Supreme Court's conclusion in *Miller, Cherry* that the decision to advise the Monarch to prorogue Parliament 'will be unlawful if the prorogation has the effect of frustrating or preventing, without reasonable justification', the constitutional principles of parliamentary sovereignty and parliamentary accountability.[80] On this understanding, the court does not merely play a passive role in respecting parliamentary supremacy by recognising the superior status of legislation, but also actively protects supremacy by preventing prerogative powers from encroaching on the power and functions of Parliament. Further, the denomination of parliamentary accountability as a constitutional principle subject to judicial enforcement – rather than solely a political constitutional convention – expands the scope of judicial supervision over the respective roles of Parliament and the executive.

The forces unleashed by legislative constitutionalism – particularly common law constitutionalism – may heighten fears that legal constitutionalist practices and judicial power have displaced the political role.[81] As partial political

[76] ibid [145], [147].

[77] ibid [120]–[121].

[78] *Jackson* (n 56) [107].

[79] ibid [107]. Since Dicey also inveighed against arbitrary government, Lord Hope's description of this idea as part of the modern rule of law raises the question whether the modern rule of law conceives of arbitrariness or the tools of protection in more expansive terms than Dicey.

[80] *R (Miller) v Prime Minister, Cherry v Advocate General for Scotland* [2019] UKSC 41 [50].

[81] Such fears are partly reflected in the Terms of Reference of the Independent Review of Administrative Law, launched in July 2020: 'Independent Review of Administrative Law' https://assets.publishing.service.gov.uk/government/uploads/system/uploads/attachment_data/file/915624/independent-review-admin-law-terms-of-reference.pdf.

responsibility for constitutional norms is a central pillar of legislative constitutionalism, the displacement of the political role could be tantamount to the displacement of the very project of legislative constitutionalism. However, while the rise of common law constitutionalism and the evolution of constitutional culture have increased the power of the judiciary, they have not supplanted the role of political actors. Instead, there is growing collaboration among political and legal actors in defining and upholding the precepts of the constitution. A collaborative vision of constitutional relationships is outlined in the judgment of Lord Reed on the common law right of access to justice in *R (UNISON) v Lord Chancellor*:

> Parliament exists primarily in order to make laws for society in this country. Democratic procedures exist primarily in order to ensure that the Parliament which makes laws includes Members of Parliament who are chosen by the people of this country and are accountable to them. Courts exist in order to ensure that the laws made by Parliament, and the common law created by the courts themselves, are applied and enforced. That role includes ensuring that the executive branch of government carries out its functions in accordance with the law. In order for the courts to perform that role, people must in principle have unimpeded access to them.[82]

The strong defence of common law rights in *UNISON* – through the Supreme Court requiring express and clear statutory language to undermine access to justice – was accordingly part of a collaborative constitutional enterprise.[83] A collaborative framework similarly permeates the Supreme Court's presumptions in favour of judicial supervision in *Evans* and *Privacy International*. Parliament was seen as responsible for prescribing in legislation the limits of powers granted to executive bodies or functionaries, and the courts, in retaining supervisory jurisdiction over the grantees of power, were upholding the rule of law.[84] So understood, common law constitutionalism and the changing constitutional culture have not uprooted legislative constitutionalism; they exist alongside each other and contribute to productive collaboration among the organs of state.

VII. CONCLUSION

The key to the lasting influence of the New Labour constitutional reforms is that their impact on constitutional methods and the institutions of state – especially the judiciary – has the potential to outlive substantive amendments. The legislative changes ushered in by the successive Blair and Brown governments have transformed the normative structure of the constitution and triggered evolution

[82] *R (Unison) v Lord Chancellor* [2017] UKSC 51 [68] (Lord Reed).

[83] A Bogg, 'The Common Law Constitution at Work: *R (on the application of UNISON) v Lord Chancellor*' (2018) 81 *MLR* 509, 514.

[84] *Privacy International* (n 75) [120]–[121].

in the interactions of political and legal actors. Common law constitutionalism has been encouraged in part by the need to fashion or develop rules of interpretation applicable to new constitutional legislation. Moreover, the discourse on constitutional norms, their content and application became more urgent and assumed new relevance in attempts to accommodate the reforms within existing rules and principles. Accordingly, the common law constitution has been rejuvenated in part by a need to maintain the coherence of the legal system. The renewed activation of the common law cannot simply be undone. The added content and weight given to constitutional norms and principles within the last 30 years lie within the common law – within the province of judges – and has the potential to persist beyond statutory reversals.

Alongside its increased internal complexification, the UK constitution has become more externalised in the wake of the series of constitutional reforms. The Human Rights Act and the ECHR rights it guarantees form a bridge between the domestic and the international. As a result of the introduction of a catalogue of rights justiciable within UK courts, there is now a budding connection between British rights protection and the near-global spread of constitutional rights. While ambivalence about the status of the Human Rights Act persists, British courts have become more engaged in exchanges with Strasbourg and the common law world on rights issues. The resurgence of the common law will likely contribute to continued judicial comparativism in UK courts and further embed the UK within a broader rights enterprise. The advance of common law constitutionalism and judicial comparativism, while unintended effects of New Labour's reforms, may prove to fuel much of the resilience of the constitutional refurbishment of the Blair and Brown years.

5

Judicial Policy and New Labour's Constitutional Project

GRAHAM GEE

I. INTRODUCTION

BETWEEN 1997 AND 2010, New Labour pursued a project of constitutional reform that in one way or another touched much of the governing apparatus of the UK. The judicial system was not immune from New Labour's reforming zeal. The various judicial reforms pursued by New Labour helped to recalibrate relationships not only between judges, politicians and civil servants, but also between the judges themselves. But more than this, these reforms helped to create a new, more formal, inclusive and dynamic regulatory space in which policy relating to the judicial system is made. In this chapter I want to assess New Labour's reforms to the leadership, management, funding and selection of the judiciary: a bundle of issues that I label 'judicial policy'. My focus is primarily on judicial policy in England and Wales, although in places I touch on changes to the governance of the UK's apex court. Assessments of New Labour's judicial policy – its motivations, methodologies and significance – are few and far between,[1] and so far as I am aware there has been no sustained analysis of these judicial reforms in terms of and by reference to New Labour's wider constitutional project.[2] There has been very little attempt, in other words, to consider the extent to which New Labour's reforms to judicial policy coheres with that larger project. In this chapter I seek to remedy this.

[1] Exceptions include S Shetreet and S Turenne, *Judges on Trial: The Independence and Accountability of the English Judiciary*, 2nd edn (Hart Publishing, 2013); G Gee, R Hazell, K Malleson and P O'Brien, *The Politics of Judicial Independence in the UK's Changing Constitution* (Cambridge University Press, 2015).

[2] There are edited collections on New Labour's constitutional reforms that include chapters on judicial policy – but these tend to involve discrete assessments of the judicial reforms without assessing those reforms in terms of and by reference to New Labour's wider constitutional project. See, eg L Blom-Cooper, 'Government and Judiciary' in A Seldon and D Kavanagh (eds), *The Blair Effect 2001–2005* (Cambridge University Press, 2005) 233; K Malleson, 'Judicial Reform: The Emergence of the Third Branch of Government' in A McDonald (ed), *Reinventing Britain: Constitutional Change under New Labour* (Politico's, 2007) 133.

I begin in part II by outlining the main features of the New Labour constitutional project. Caution is required when describing New Labour's various reforms as a 'project'. Some question whether there are sufficient shared rationales and methodologies running across these reforms to justify such a programmatic label. As I see it, it is possible to talk meaningfully of a 'constitutional project', insofar as a willingness to envisage a more plural, formal, rational, rights-based and multi-tiered constitutional framework formed a prominent part of the New Labour agenda throughout their time in office. This constitutional project represented an important way in which Labour portrayed itself as 'new', and for better or worse ranks amongst its most important legacies. In part III, I turn to one part of that constitutional project, namely New Labour's reforms in the judicial sphere. The focus of those reforms was the Constitutional Reform Act 2005, which created a UK Supreme Court, introduced new methods of appointing judges in England and Wales, and recast the role and responsibilities of the ancient office of Lord Chancellor. Each of those reforms is important and interesting, but most relevant for present purposes is the way that the reform of the office of Lord Chancellor created the space for a new approach to how judicial policy would be designed, implemented and overseen. Prior to these reforms, judicial policy emerged from a largely closed, informal and insular system centralised around the Lord Chancellor, where change tended to be gradual and policy outcomes were typically fairly stable. I explain in part IV how, largely as a result of these reforms, judicial policy is now forged through a more open, formal, inclusive and in some ways accountable system, with multiple actors on a more differentiated institutional landscape involved in making and scrutinising judicial policy. On this new approach to judicial policy, change is continuous, and the agenda is dynamic. Despite this, some of the policy outcomes have been disappointing. In part V, I close by considering the extent to which the new approach to judicial policy coheres with New Labour's larger constitutional project.

II. NEW LABOUR'S CONSTITUTIONAL PROJECT

I begin with a thumbnail sketch of several of the main features of New Labour's constitutional project.[3] The starting point is to acknowledge the sheer volume of reforms within this project. Few would deny that the constitutional reforms introduced between 1997 and 2010 are among the most important legacies of

[3] This is not the place to provide a detailed account of each of the reforms. Useful summaries of the various reforms, including snapshots at different points in time during New Labour's period in power, can be found in R Blackburn and R Plant (eds), *Constitutional Reform: The Labour Government's Constitutional Reform Agenda* (Longmans, 1999); FN Forman, *Constitutional Change in the United Kingdom* (Routledge, 2002); McDonald, *Reinventing Britain* (2007); M Flinders, *Democratic Drift: Majoritarian Modification and Democratic Anomie in the UK* (Oxford University Press, 2010); V Bogdanor, *The New British Constitution* (Hart Publishing, 2009).

New Labour. True, there is an important debate about whether the reforms amount to a radical remaking of the constitutional fabric of the UK. However, most would accept that the volume of constitutional reforms within a short period of time was 'unprecedented'.[4] After all, the reforms touched most (admittedly not all) parts of the constitution. Amongst other things, the reforms: (i) granted operational independence over monetary policy to the Bank of England; (ii) introduced new schemes of devolution in Northern Ireland, Scotland, Wales and London; (iii) incorporated into domestic law most of the provisions of the European Convention on Human Rights, and thus heralded a new approach to their domestic legal protection; (iv) revised the composition of the House of Lords by providing for the removal of most hereditary peers from the upper chamber of the Westminster Parliament; (v) provided for various forms of proportional representation for elections to the European Parliament and the devolved legislatures; (vi) enacted a scheme providing the public with rights to access information held by public bodies; (vii) required local authorities to introduce management structures, with the possibility of directly elected mayors; (viii) enacted a scheme requiring the registration of political parties, with new rules on donations and campaign expenditure, with an Electoral Commission created to oversee elections; (ix) created a UK Supreme Court, introduced a new system for judicial appointments in England and Wales centred around an independent body and remodelled the role of the Lord Chancellor; (x) provided a statutory basis for the Civil Service Code; (xi) put the rules on parliamentary scrutiny of treaty ratification on a statutory footing; and (xii) made increasing use of referendums to determine constitutional questions. All told, this is 'a formidable list'.[5]

Stepping back from the specific contents of this list, and at the risk of painting with a broad brush, I want to suggest that there were four overarching features of New Labour's constitutional project. First, the project was not systematic, insofar as the reforms neither unfolded according to a single, clear and fixed blueprint nor followed consistent methodologies. Several of the reforms were the product of long years of careful planning and consultation with stakeholders, and received popular endorsement through inclusion in an election manifesto and/or endorsement in a referendum – but others were not. Some of the reforms had distinct lineages that had been shaped by different personalities and distinct political imperatives that stretched back to the very origins of the labour movement itself.[6] But others had little foretelling in the

[4] For examples of commentary that characterise the volume of New Labour's reforms as 'unprecedented', see Bogdanor, *The New British Constitution* (2009) 4; M Finn and A Seldon, 'Constitutional Reform Since 1997: The Historians' Perspective' in M Qvortrup (ed), *The British Constitution: Continuity and Change* (Hart Publishing, 2013) 17, 18.

[5] Bogdanor (n 3) 4.

[6] M Evans, 'Studying the New Constitutionalism: Bringing Political Science Back In' (2001) 3 *British Journal of Politics and International Relations* 413, 422. See also M Evans, *Constitution-Making and the Labour Party* (Palgrave Macmillan, 2003).

prior policy positions of the Labour Party, while other reforms were shaped by entirely different considerations, such as the peace process in Northern Ireland. It is true that certain common themes traversed the reforms (decentralisation, transparency and enhanced legal protection of rights) and most of the reforms were framed within the familiar patterns of parliamentary sovereignty, representative democracy and the 'Westminster model'. But while the reforms were loosely coherent in the sense of sharing the same background understanding of the constitution,[7] there was no unifying rationale to explain why this or that part of the constitution was reformed but not others.[8] Moreover, very little effort was made to articulate such a rationale beyond vacuous references to the need to 'modernise', with only limited evidence that much thought had been given to the possible knock-on effects of reform.[9] Indeed, a chief characteristic for at least long stretches of New Labour's constitutional project was the lack of a coherent vision at the centre of government. Not helping matters was that responsibility for the various reforms was scattered across ministerial departments in Whitehall prior to the creation of the Department of Constitutional Affairs in 2003 (and even after that, responsibility for devolution was divided across multiple territorial departments of state). In short, there was a 'deafening silence about the rationale, implications and ultimate goal of the changes set in train' throughout the New Labour era,[10] with 'plenty of change but no overall strategy'.[11]

Second, and as a partial product of this, there were inconsistencies, contradictions and gaps within this constitutional project. In a very real sense New Labour's project was 'bi-constitutional'.[12] More plural, consensual governing arrangements were introduced subnationally through the partial and asymmetric devolution of power, but the highly centralised governing tradition at the national level was largely preserved, notwithstanding some changes to the national political and legal architecture. For all of the talk of the need to modernise the constitution, reforms at the national level with real potential to disrupt the power-hoarding tradition were rejected, notably electoral reform, save for a brief flirtation in the dying days of Gordon Brown's government with a possible referendum on whether to adopt the alternative vote for elections to

[7] On this loose coherence, see M Bevir, 'Socialism and Democracy: New Labour and the Constitution' (2007) 3 *Observatoire de la Société Britannique* 21.

[8] Or what Matthew Flinders has termed 'constitutional anomie': Flinders, *Democratic Drift* (2010) 4.

[9] For an attempt to articulating the guiding principles of New Labour's constitutional project by one of the architects of some of the reforms, see J Straw, 'New Labour, Constitutional Change and Representative Democracy' (2010) 63 *Parliamentary Affairs* 356, 359–60. For brief discussions of New Labour's reforms as an expression of 'egalitarian ambitions', see Lord Falconer, 'Foreword' in McDonald (n 2) v; Lord Falconer, ch 1 in this volume.

[10] D Marquand, *Populism or Pluralism? New Labour and the Constitution* (Mishcon Lecture, University College London, 1999).

[11] R Johnson '(Review) Democratic Drift: Majoritarian Modification and Democratic Anomie in the United Kingdom' (2011) 64 *Parliamentary Affairs* 370, 370.

[12] M Flinders, 'Majoritarian Democracy in Britain: New Labour and the Constitution' (2005) 28 *West European Politics* 61.

Westminster.[13] Intensifying this was an elitist and centralist statecraft squarely in line with 'the British political tradition',[14] with Blair increasing the strategic role of the Cabinet Office and many ministers tightening executive powers of control and patronage.[15] Some reforms barely made it onto the agenda at all, such as the need to further democratise local government. Other reforms were aborted early on, for example the proposal for an elected regional assembly in the North East, which voters decisively rejected in a referendum in 2004.[16] Related to this, the question of how to govern England and the English regions was a 'gaping hole'[17] in this constitutional project. Other reforms were initiated, but left unfinished, with the attempt to refashion the House of Lords into a more representative, more democratic second chamber the standout example. In all of this there was a patchwork quality to this constitutional project.

Third, despite, or perhaps to some extent because of, these gaps and inconsistencies, New Labour's constitutional project was dynamic and continuous, 'unleash[ing] powerful forces' that created 'new challenges and tensions'.[18] The project was characterised by spill-over effects and unintended consequences, and ultimately seemed to generate a momentum of its own.[19] For the purposes of exposition, the various reforms can be broken down into three more or less distinct waves (1997–2000; 2003–05; and 2007–10), with several reforms in the second and third waves the result of forces that had been unleashed in the first. Many of New Labour's reforms involved the creation of institutional fora, where new policy centres were superimposed upon existing ones. These new policy centres provided politicians, interest groups, trade unions and corporate entities with new institutional platforms through which to agitate for further reform. At the same time, reforms that formalised and rationalised the traditional constitution highlighted the anomalies, peculiarities and imbalances that remained, in turn creating pressure for yet more reform. In this, New Labour's constitutional project became 'a continuous process with no finite boundaries'.[20] But New Labour never seemed to fully grasp the forces that their

[13] M Flinders, 'Conserving the Constitution? The Conservative Party and Democratic Renewal' (2009) 80 *Political Quarterly* 248, 248–49.

[14] For an excellent discussion of the 'British political tradition', see M Hall, D Marsh and E Vines, 'A Changing Democracy: Contemporary Challenges to the British Political Tradition' (2018) 39 *Policy Studies* 365.

[15] See generally P Dunleavy, H Margetts, T Smith and S Weird, 'Constitutional Reform, New Labour in Power and Public Trust in Government' (2001) 54 *Parliamentary Affairs* 405.

[16] See L Trueblood, ch 14 in this volume, s IIIC; A Giovannini, ch 7 in this volume.

[17] R Hazell, 'The English Question' (2006) 36 *Publius* 37, 38.

[18] R. Hazell, 'The Continuing Dynamism of Constitutional Reform' (2007) 56 *Parliamentary Affairs* 3, 18.

[19] That the reforms might develop a momentum of their own had been anticipated by some commentators from the outset. See, eg A Barnett, *This Time: Our Constitutional Revolution* (Vintage, 1997).

[20] Writing in the early years of the New Labour period in office, and speaking of constitutional reform more generally, Foley noted that 'constitutional innovation may initially consist of discrete legislative measures, but reform is a continuous process with no finite boundaries': M Foley, *The Politics of the British Constitution* (Manchester University Press, 1999) 276.

reforms released, a matter not helped by the lack of a coherent strategic vision at the very heart of the New Labour governments. This was perhaps most evident in the devolutionary context. Here, New Labour struggled to recognise that newly institutionalised subnational political communities might lead not only to divergent policy agendas, but to questions about the ultimate source and location of political authority, which in turn might encourage the public to shift their allegiance from the national political system to the subnational political system. In the same vein, New Labour seemed to struggle to grasp the potential for the devolutionary dynamics unleashed by their reforms to upend the traditional, centralised political and legal order. For example, while Scottish devolution can be read as a relatively limited response to the need for greater self-government within the Union state, consistent with traditional precepts such as parliamentary sovereignty, it could also be read through a nationalist lens as a response to declining popular allegiance to the national political community and an assertion of the sovereignty of the Scottish people.[21]

Finally, and building on this prior point, New Labour's project has helped to render explicit, and also in very real ways contributed to, tensions within the UK's constitutional arrangements. There is a debate about whether New Labour's reforms are aptly characterised as radical. For some, their cumulative consequence was to fashion something akin to a 'new' constitution,[22] but for others the reforms fell very far short of a radical remaking of the constitutional fabric, and indeed on this view many of the reforms were as much about continuity as change. Such debates are interesting and not easily resolved, since 'Radical breaks and turning points are always hard to discern at the time'.[23] There is also a sense in which these debates are perhaps beside the point, insofar as it is clear that New Labour's constitutional project contributed to the unsettling of the constitution. This project presents a paradox, inasmuch as several of the reforms within it seem relatively stable in the sense of being unlikely to be reversed,[24] yet their combined effect has been to contribute to the unsettling of the UK's traditional constitution. To be clear, New Labour's project is not the cause of the current constitutional flux, or at least not its primary cause, and indeed the project itself is perhaps best seen as at least a partial product of constitutional instability that was brewing throughout the latter half of the twentieth century. There may also be several respects in which this project staved off instability that might otherwise have boiled over at some point in the last

[21] For an important discussion, see A McHarg, 'The Constitutional Case for Independence' in A McHarg, T Mullen, A Page and N Walker (eds), *The Scottish Independence Referendum: Constitutional and Political Implications* (Oxford University Press, 2016) 101, 108.

[22] See, eg Bogdanor (n 3).

[23] A Gamble, 'The Constitutional Revolution in the United Kingdom' (2006) 36 *Publius* 19, 19.

[24] See Straw's assessment that most of the reforms introduced as part of New Labour's constitutional project seem unlikely to be reserved, with the Human Rights Act the one exception to this: Straw, 'New Labour, Constitutional Change and Representative Democracy' (2010).

20 years. But it is difficult to avoid the conclusion that New Labour's project has both revealed and reinforced a constitutional rupturing within the UK. It has done so, above all, by crystallising new policy centres that function as alternative sites of political legitimacy from which political actors can promote practices, principles and – ultimately – divergent constitutional visions and political identities not easily reconciled with the Westminster model within which New Labour's constitutional project was formulated.

III. NEW LABOUR AND JUDICIAL POLICY

I return to reflect on New Labour's constitutional project later in this chapter, but for now I want to outline their main judicial reforms. The centrepiece of New Labour's judicial reforms was the Constitutional Reform Act 2005 (CRA), which instituted three main changes. First, it provided for the creation of a UK Supreme Court, which ultimately commenced its work in 2009, replacing the Appellate Committee of the House of Lords as the UK's top court. Second, it introduced new methods for appointing judges in England and Wales centred around an independent body known as the Judicial Appointments Commission (JAC). Third, it refashioned the job of Lord Chancellor, transferring its role as the constitutional head of the judiciary in England and Wales to the Lord Chief Justice (LCJ) and hiving off many judiciary-related functions to arm's-length bodies, such as the JAC, or to new bodies created in response to the 2003 changes (for example, the Judicial Office, which comprises civil servants who support the LCJ and other senior judges in discharging their leadership and management responsibilities). Augmenting this were important changes to the machinery of government. The Lord Chancellor's Department was replaced by the Department of Constitutional Affairs in 2003, which was itself replaced just four years later by the Ministry of Justice. An additional piece of the jigsaw were changes in the governance of the Court Service. In 2008, the Court Service in England and Wales evolved from an 'executive model' (where court administration was the Lord Chancellor's responsibility, with minister and officials deciding the level and allocation of resources) to a 'partnership' model (where court administration is seen as a shared responsibility between the Lord Chancellor and the LCJ, with senior judges possessing a much stronger voice in decision-making, including in helping to set the Court Service's budgets and objectives). In all of this, the CRA marked neither the beginning nor the end of New Labour's judicial reforms, but it crystallised a basic dynamic whereby the Lord Chancellor's day-to-day involvement in managing, funding and selecting judges substantially shrank, with this offset by greater judicial responsibility for their own governance. In this way, the CRA's significance is less in its institutional innovations, such as creating the Supreme Court and the JAC, and more in carving out a new regulatory sphere in which judicial policy is designed, implemented and monitored.

The background to some of New Labour's judicial reforms was emblematic of the chaotic and ad hoc approach that often characterised constitutional reform under New Labour. The proposals that culminated in the CRA were announced on 12 June 2003 in a press briefing at the back end of a ministerial reshuffle. This 'constitutional reform by press release'[25] must rank as a particular low point in New Labour's guardianship of the constitution. Downing Street had devised the proposals over several weeks, but there had been no scrutiny by a cabinet subcommittee as might have been expected for such significant constitutional reforms, and the proposals were not even discussed at the cabinet meeting held in the hours immediately before the reshuffle itself. The proposals had not featured in the Labour Party's 2001 election manifesto. Nor was there prior consultation with senior judges, or any other stakeholders in the justice system for that matter – although a formal consultation process, sustained negotiation between the Lord Chancellor and LCJ about how to implement the proposals and prolonged parliamentary scrutiny followed between 2003 and 2005, with the government's initial policy of wholly abolishing the office of Lord Chancellor abandoned in favour of pruning its judiciary-related functions and recasting it along the lines of a conventional ministerial job.[26] Initial failure to consult also characterised the creation of the Ministry of Justice in 2007. As in 2003, senior judges were taken by surprise by the news that the Blair government intended to replace the Department of Constitutional Affairs with a new Ministry of Justice, with the LCJ only learning of the development in a newspaper report. The most generous interpretation of this is that the Blair government 'failed to learn the crucial lessons from the way changes to the Lord Chancellor's office were announced and subsequently effected between 2003 and 2005'.[27] A less generous interpretation is that the failure to consult on reforms to the judicial system in 2003 and 2007 was a 'feature not a bug' of New Labour's approach to reforming the justice system. After all, the Blair government had learned in 2001 just how effective senior judges could be at stymieing change, when a plan to reconfigure departments, where responsibility for the Court Service would have moved from the Lord Chancellor's Department to a department run by the then Home Secretary David Blunkett, unravelled in the face of opposition from senior judges and Lord Irvine, the then Lord Chancellor.

Reforming the role of the Lord Chancellor, and the character of the ministerial department led by that office, was the main motivation for Blair's

[25] A Le Sueur, 'From Appellate Committee to Supreme Court: A Narrative' in L Blom-Cooper, B Dickson and G Drewry (eds), *The Judicial House of Lords 1876–2009* (Oxford University Press, 2009) 64, 68.

[26] For an account of the events following the announcement of the reforms in June 2003, including the immediate difficulties that the government faced with its plan to abolish the office of Lord Chancellor, see Lord Windlesham, 'The Constitutional Reform Act 2005: Ministers, Judges and Constitutional Change – Part 1' [2005] *PL* 806.

[27] House of Commons Constitutional Affairs Committee, *The Creation of the Ministry of* Justice, Sixth Report 2006–07 (HC 466, 17 July 2007) 11.

government to pursue the 2003 reforms. So, whilst the creation of a Supreme Court and the introduction of new ways of selecting judges might have been the most eye-catching elements of the reform package, it was the remodelling of the role of the Lord Chancellor that helps to explain why these judicial reforms were pursued by New Labour in the first place. To grasp the reasons for this, it is necessary to consider the changing nature and functions of the office of Lord Chancellor and the associated ministerial department. In its late-twentieth-century guise, the office mixed executive, legislative and judicial responsibilities. The Lord Chancellor was a cabinet minister in charge of a large and growing ministerial department, bound by collective responsibility and accountable to the Westminster Parliament for the efficient and effective administration of the justice system. The Lord Chancellor also presided over the upper chamber at Westminster and was entitled to speak on behalf of the government in legislative debates. Rounding out a trinity of roles was the Lord Chancellor's status as head of the judiciary in England and Wales, with the office holder entitled to sit as a judge in the Appellate Committee of the House of Lords. A golden thread running throughout these functions was a customary duty on the Lord Chancellor to defend judicial independence at the very heart of the government, with the office holder viewed as a bridge between the legal and political worlds who could operate as the senior judiciary's representative in the Cabinet and the Cabinet's representative in the senior judiciary.[28] Facilitating this role as a bridge between these two worlds was the office holder's legal and political profile, since Prime Ministers typically appointed as Lord Chancellor either a party politician towards the twilight of their career who had substantial legal experience or a prominent barrister who shared the political sympathies of the government of the day. By convention, Lord Chancellors sat in the House of Lords, rather than the House of Commons. One product of the blended political and legal responsibilities attached to the office, together with the professional profiles of its occupants, was that Lord Chancellors tended to be 'policy minimalists', exhibiting limited policy leadership, mostly legitimating existing policies and sometimes successfully serving as a channel for senior judges to frustrate attempts by ministers to introduce new policies on the administration of justice.[29]

As for the department headed by the Lord Chancellor, it functioned as a very small private office until the 1970s, one that tended to be largely insulated from the pressures that shaped ministerial behaviour throughout Whitehall.[30]

[28] For one office holder's account of this customary duty to defend judicial independence, see Lord Hailsham, 'The Office of Lord Chancellor and the Separation of Powers' (1989) 8 *Civil Justice Quarterly* 308.

[29] I borrow this language of 'policy minimalists' from Headey's typology of British cabinet ministers: B Headey, *British Cabinet Ministers: The Role of Politicians in Executive Office* (Allen & Unwin, 1974) 56. For an application of this terminology to the changing nature and responsibilities of the office of Lord Chancellors, see G Gee 'What Are Lord Chancellors For?' [2014] *PL* 11.

[30] See generally R Stevens, *The Independence of the Judiciary: The View from the Lord Chancellor's Office* (Oxford University Press, 1993); D Woodhouse, *The Office of Lord Chancellor* (Hart Publishing, 2001) 39–65.

This office was staffed by a handful of legally qualified officials, with their work focused on the judiciary and courts. Traditionally, its culture was narrow, legalistic and protective of judicial interests and settled ways of doing things in the justice system. Indeed, at times, Lord Chancellors and their officials seemed little more than lobbyists for judges. From the 1970s onwards, the Lord Chancellor's role expanded, acquiring additional responsibilities, such as for the administration of the courts in 1972, legal aid in 1988 and human rights and freedom of information from 2001. In this way, the Lord Chancellor's office had evolved over three decades from a small private office with a limited policy remit into a large and resource-hungry department, staffed by thousands of civil servants, with an expanding policy portfolio and subject to the same public management pressures of value-for-money, efficiency, effectiveness and accountability as any other Whitehall department. The departmental culture also began to evolve from its traditional legalistic character towards a more conventional policy-focused, executive mindset. In other words, by the turn of the century, the Lord Chancellor's Department had evolved from a 'single subject department' (with a narrow and stable policy portfolio that mostly involved technical issues with low political salience) to a 'fragmented department' (with a much wider policy portfolio comprising multiple more or less unconnected issues, each with fairly high degrees of political salience).[31] Yet, even after it had evolved into a large ministerial department, the Lord Chancellor's Department stood apart from the rest of Whitehall in several respects: for example, its work was exempt from routine scrutiny by a select committee until 1990, and the first non-lawyer was appointed as its permanent secretary only in 1998.[32]

By 2003, despite the changes that had occurred over the previous 30 years, there was a growing consensus inside Downing Street that Lord Chancellors still led an 'antiquated'[33] department, with 'priorities that didn't coincide with those of the government' (as Blair himself would subsequently put it).[34] The concern inside Downing Street was that Lord Chancellors and civil servants in the Department were insufficiently focused on delivering the government's policy objectives. Here, the concern was not on judicial policy per se; that is, it was not on policy relating to the funding, management, leadership and appointment of the judiciary, which tended to have very low electoral salience. The concern was instead chiefly with the working of the criminal justice system, a matter with very high electoral salience. Outside of government, by contrast, the concern for some judges and lawyers was that the Lord Chancellor and officials

[31] Headey, *British Cabinet Ministers* (1974) 155.

[32] As Lord Browne-Wilkinson put it, when head of the Chancery Division, the Lord Chancellor's Department was 'wholly different from any other department of State': N Browne-Wilkinson, 'The Independence of the Judiciary in the 1980s' [1988] *PL* 44, 48.

[33] J Powell, *The New Machiavelli: How to Wield Power in the Modern World* (Vintage, 2010) 153.

[34] T Blair, *The Journey* (Hutchinson, 2010) 632.

in the Department were excessively focused on the pursuit of government policy.[35] On this view, over 30 years or so, Lord Chancellors and civil servants in the Department had become overly focused on the search for efficiency in the administration of justice – and, as a result, had grown inattentive to the duty to defend judicial independence at the centre of government.[36] These differing assessments were emblematic of the growing gulf between the political and legal domains, a gulf that could no longer be papered over by the overlapping roles of the Lord Chancellor. To be sure, the political imperative of aligning the Lord Chancellor and Department more closely to the delivery of government policy, especially in the politically contentious context of criminal justice, was not the only factor motivating the 2003 reforms. A contributing factor was a personality clash between Irvine and Blunkett, the then Lord Chancellor and Home Secretary respectively. Vindicating a stricter notion of the separation of powers in light of the increasing scope and intensity of judicial review, and especially an enlarged judicial role in politically sensitive disputes following the enactment of the Human Rights Act 1998, also provided a conceivable principle-based rationale for reform. But, above all, it was a political concern to better coordinate the delivery of government policy that drove the reforms. In a similar vein, it was concerns about coordinating criminal justice policy that led the Blair government to reconfigure the Department of Constitutional Affairs into a Ministry of Justice in 2007. This saw the criminal justice functions of the Home Office and its agencies (including the Prison Service and Probation Service) transfer to the new Ministry, thus enabling the Home Office to concentrate on counterterrorism. The efficient delivery of government policy is plainly of constitutional significance – but the reforms in 2003 and (to a lesser extent) 2007 were examples of changes to the machinery of government being used to propel larger, constitutionally significant reforms to the judicial system, rather than featuring as one part of a more considered approach to those larger reforms.

IV. A NEW APPROACH TO JUDICIAL POLICY

Policy was the driving force behind both the 2003 and 2007 reforms. But it was policy in a broad sense of reconfiguring ministerial departments in Whitehall in order to deliver the government's objectives, especially in the electorally important context of criminal justice. Judicial policy – that is to say, policy relating to the funding, leadership, management and appointment of judges – was peripheral. Nevertheless, the reforms helped to crystallise a new regulatory space in which judicial policy is fashioned. Prior to 2003, the approach

[35] Gee, 'What Are Lord Chancellors For?' (2014) 19.

[36] See generally D Woodhouse, 'The Office of Lord Chancellor: Time to Abandon the Judicial Role – The Rest Will Follow' (2002) 22 *Legal Studies* 128.

to judicial policy was, for the most part, informal, insular and secretive.[37] It was also heavily centralised around the Lord Chancellor and a fairly small number of officials in the Department. The Lord Chancellor's executive responsibilities included ministerial responsibility for the administration of justice, which in turn encompassed: the running of the Court Service; determining the pay, pensions and conditions of judicial service; and making and advising on judicial appointments. At the same time the Lord Chancellor's functions as head of the judiciary included the training and welfare of judges.[38] This represented a very considerable concentration of power in the hands of Lord Chancellors and their officials. Statute performed only a limited role in guiding how the Lord Chancellor should discharge these various functions, with non-legal conventions often more important, as illustrated by the conventional requirement that the Lord Chancellor consult via 'secret soundings' with senior judges about the names of the candidates under consideration for appointment as a judge. That Lord Chancellors were ministers ensured some measure of political accountability for judicial policy, but this was undercut by the fact that Lord Chancellors were always peers, sitting in the unelected House of Lords. Not only was there little attempt to map a clear separation of powers between the judicial and political spheres, the fused functions in the office of Lord Chancellor had in fact been viewed as reflecting and reinforcing a set of values largely shared by ministers, officials and judges. These shared values helped to ensure, amongst other things, that the settled ways of managing the judicial system were seldom disturbed, and thus policy change tended to be slow and incremental. They also helped to ensure broad agreement about the proper scope of and limits on the judicial role within the UK's traditional constitution.

Today, the making, implementing and monitoring of judicial policy is a much more formal, open and collaborative enterprise, with this largely a product of the regulatory space that was carved out by New Labour's reforms. More particularly, I want to suggest that New Labour's reforms helped to standardise, depoliticise, formalise and pluralise the making of judicial policy. There are also new and multiple accountabilities within a regime defined by a more dynamic policy agenda.

At the heart of New Labour's reforms were their attempts to *standardise* the office of Lord Chancellor. The job of Lord Chancellor is now, in almost all respects, a standard ministerial office, and one that since 2007 is twinned with that of the Secretary of State for Justice, with Prime Ministers appointing the same person to these two separate but related offices. Before 2003, the role of Lord Chancellor was generally regarded as a prestigious final posting prior

[37] This section draws on the analysis developed in G Gee, 'Judicial Policy in England and Wales' in R Devlin and A Dodek (eds), *Regulating Judges: Beyond Independence and Accountability* (Cheltenham, Edward Elgar, 2016) 145, 146–49.

[38] See generally D Oliver, 'The Lord Chancellor as Head of the Judiciary' in Blom-Cooper et al, *The Judicial House of Lords 1876–2009* (2009) 97.

to retirement for an esteemed lawyer or politician, and at state occasions the office ranked in precedence even above the Prime Minister. In several respects, the office was above ordinary politics, insofar as its occupants were peers, at the twilight of their careers and normally with no interest in jockeying for promotion. Today, the Lord Chancellor is a deflated job, lacking its former prestige and now well down the ministerial pecking order. No longer is the Lord Chancellor required to be a lawyer or a peer, or towards the end of their career. It is true that, under the CRA, the Prime Minister may only appoint as Lord Chancellor someone who is, in the Prime Minister's view, 'qualified by experience'.[39] In reality, however, this provision is drafted so widely that Prime Ministers can appoint 'jobbing politicians' to this role. This has led some (and especially some lawyers and judges) to question whether Lord Chancellors can effectively discharge their now statutory duty to have regard to the need to defend judicial independence, especially in light of the fallout of the High Court's judgment in the Article 50 litigation in 2016 and the Enemies of the People furore.[40]

The broad thrust of New Labour's reforms were to *depoliticise* judicial policy, in the sense of shifting responsibility for the making and implementation of that policy away from ministers to new arenas and new decision-makers.[41] The CRA limited the day-to-day involvement of the Lord Chancellor in the making and exercise of judicial policy, and instead enlarged the LCJ's responsibility for the governance of the judiciary. Today, the LCJ is the constitutional head of the judiciary in England and Wales,[42] and is responsible for judicial welfare, training and deployment. The Lord Chancellor no longer serves the role as a vital hinge between the judiciary and the Cabinet, with the LCJ now responsible for representing the views of the judiciary to the government and Parliament.[43] Lord Chancellors continue to exercise an extensive range of responsibilities relating to the judiciary, but are much less involved than their pre-2003 predecessors in the nitty gritty of everyday decision-making on matters relating to the judicial system and have much less contact with senior judges

[39] Constitutional Reform Act 2005, s 2.

[40] See Constitutional Reform Act 2005, s 3. On the fallout to the High Court's judgment in *Miller v Secretary of State for Exiting the EU* [2016] EWHC 2768 (Admin), see generally J Rozenberg, *Enemies of the People: How Judges Shape Society* (Bristol University Press, 2020) 27–48. For insightful critiques of what this episode suggests about the remodelled office of Lord Chancellor, see P O'Brien, ''Enemies of the People': Judges, the Media and the Mythic Lord Chancellor' [2017] *PL* (Nov Suppl) 135; P Daly, 'Judicial Independence and Accountability in the British Constitution' [2019] *European Yearbook of Constitutional Law* 143. But *cf* G Gee, 'Lawyers, Lord Chancellors and Some Common Mistakes about Judicial Independence' in D Galligan (ed), *The Courts – Friend or Foe?* (Hart Publishing, forthcoming).

[41] For a discussion of depoliticisation as arena-shifting, where the involvement of representative political institutions is reduced, as applied to judicial selection in England and Wales, see G Gee, 'The Persistent Politics of Judicial Selection: A Comparative Analysis' in A Seibert-Fohr (ed), *Judicial Independence in Transition* (Springer, 2010) 139–45.

[42] Constitutional Reform Act 2005, s 7(1).

[43] ibid s 7(2).

as a result. Most of the responsibilities that are now exercisable by the Lord Chancellor are systemic in nature, and some can only be exercised either concurrently with, or after consulting, the LCJ. For example, Lord Chancellors must ensure that there is an efficient and effective court system, including by providing necessary resources and accounting to the UK Parliament for their efficient and proper use.[44] They also continue: to determine the framework for the organisation of the court system, including deciding the total number of judges after consulting the LCJ; to determine the pay, pensions and conditions of judicial service, taking into account the recommendations of the Senior Salaries Review Body; to determine (with the LCJ) the aims of the Court Service, and to strive to agree its budget with the LCJ; and to exercise a shared responsibility (with the LCJ) for complaints, supported by the Judicial Conduct and Investigations Office (JCIO), and accounting to Parliament for the working of the complaints system as a whole. All told, these judiciary-related functions, while still extensive, are a pale imitation of those discharged by Lord Chancellors prior to 2003. The dynamic of depoliticisation is most evident in judicial appointments, where the CRA replaced a highly informal, secretive system based around the Lord Chancellor's almost unfettered discretion with a formal system based around the JAC, where the Lord Chancellor is responsible for the judicial appointments system as a whole, but has no decision-making role in respect of 95 per cent of selections, and little more than a nominal role in the remaining 5 per cent.

New Labour's reforms have helped to *formalise* roles, responsibilities and relationships within the judicial system and, in this way, to map more formal divisions of power between ministers, judges, officials and new institutional actors. The CRA gives expression to a more formal account of the separation of powers, for example by relocating the UK's top judges away from the judicial House of Lords to their own building in the new Supreme Court on the other side of Parliament Square. Detailed statutory provisions now govern most aspects of the Court's administration, with its day-to-day running shaped by the business-like culture of Whitehall rather than the informal, old-world culture of Westminster that had governed the working of the Appellate Committee of the House of Lords.[45] Similarly, by making the LCJ the formal head of the judiciary, the CRA both formalised and expanded the already powerful role of LCJ. Statute now confers a range of responsibilities on the LCJ, although in practice the LCJ delegates functions to other senior judges, such as the Senior Presiding Judge (SPJ). For example, the LCJ is formally responsible for judicial deployment, but in practice delegates this to the SPJ, who in turn delegates everyday

[44] Courts Act 2003, s 1.

[45] See generally G Drewry, 'The UK Supreme Court: A Fine New Vintage or Just a Smart New Label on a Duty Old Bottle?' (2011) 3 *International Journal for Court Administration* 20; G Gee, 'The Financial and Administrative Independence of the UK Supreme Court: Five Years On' (2015) 21 *European Journal of Current Legal Issues* https://webjcli.org/index.php/webjcli/article/view/408/519.

decision-making to presiding judges and resident judges. Concerns about the performance of individual judges can now be raised up a management structure. A particular concern is the length of time that different court centres take to dispose of cases, with this management structure enabling a more proactive approach to monitoring performance and identifying and addressing problems. This underscores an important if indirect consequence of New Labour's reforms: the emergence of clearer leadership within the judiciary.[46] So, the formalisation of the LCJ's role is just part of a larger change within which the judiciary has evolved into a more centralised, hierarchical and professional institution, with more clearly articulated expectations on how judges should discharge their responsibilities in order to ensure the consistent and timely administration of justice throughout the court system.

The *pluralisation* of the institutional landscape was an additional important feature of the approach to judicial policy that crystallised partly as a result of New Labour's reforms. As noted above, prior to the CRA, the making and implementation of judicial policy was heavily centralised around the office of Lord Chancellor. Today, the institutional landscape is much more differentiated. Some familiar actors have expanded roles (eg the LCJ, and the Court Service), while others have a much diminished, albeit still important, input into judicial policy (eg the Lord Chancellor and officials in the Ministry of Justice). There are also new actors discharging new and important roles, notably the JAC, JCIO and the Judicial Appointments and Conduct Ombudsman (JACO). Through bodies such as the JAC, JACO, JCIO and the board of the Court Service, lay people are also now involved in decisions that were previously the exclusive preserve of politicians, judges and civil servants. Since the CRA, the UK Parliament has also taken much more interest in judicial policy, with senior judges now routinely giving evidence to select committees,[47] although parliamentary interest in judicial matters remains sporadic, operating more like a spotlight that can illuminate issues of concern rather than a constant and ever reliable monitoring mechanism. The pluralisation of the institutional landscape goes hand in hand with the formalisation of roles and responsibilities, insofar as there is greater need for a more formal map of the divisions of power between all of the different actors who are involved in the making, implementing and monitoring of judicial policy. It bears emphasising that within this pluralised and formalised landscape, informal factors remain important since one counter-intuitive consequence of insisting on a more formal separation of powers is to require senior judges to interact with a much wider range of actors. The judiciary no longer relies on the Lord Chancellor to be its conduit with the outside world, with the LCJ now managing relations with, among others, ministers in

[46] For a discussion of the formalisation of a judicial management structure, see Gee, 'Judicial Policy in England and Wales' (2016) 151.

[47] See generally R Hazell and P O'Brien, 'Meaningful Dialogue: Judicial Engagement with Parliamentary Committees at Westminster' [2015] *PL* 54.

the UK government, Welsh ministers, the UK Parliament, the Welsh Parliament, the Supreme Court and bodies such as the JAC and JCIO. That there are now many more interactions for senior judges such as the LCJ to manage also means that more scope exists for informal social factors to come to the fore, such as the personalities of individual officeholders.[48]

There are multiple accountabilities within this new approach to judicial policy. As noted earlier, despite the changes to the office, the Lord Chancellor retains an overarching responsibility for the proper and efficient working of the justice system as a whole and must account to the UK Parliament for this. However, the Lord Chancellor no longer has close involvement in most of the day-to-day decisions affecting the judiciary and the courts, which might in turn lead some to doubt the value of the overarching systemic responsibilities attached to that office and to wonder whether there is now an 'accountability gap'. However, the ministerial responsibility of the Lord Chancellor does not stand in isolation: there is now a complex web of statutory duties on different actors such as the JAC and the Chief Executive of the Supreme Court to provide Parliament with annual reports and accounts.[49] Indeed, one of the defining features of the new approach to judicial policy is that much of the business of the judicial system that was previously transacted behind closed doors is now out in the open and publicly accessible through annual reports, accounts, mission statements, annual statistics, audit reports and so forth. More generally, the revamped approach to judicial policy has encouraged (and, to some degree, required) the senior judiciary to be more outward looking, with a more proactive approach to engaging with the media, the public and parliamentary committees. This is perhaps most evident in respect of the Supreme Court, which has an outward-facing and user-friendly approach, with a website, live streaming of hearings, public outreach work and press releases accompanying judgments.[50] In short, and as a consequence of the greater stress on judicial self-governance, senior judges are much more conscious of the need to offer an account of their stewardship of the justice system.

This new approach has been characterised by a dynamic policy agenda, defined by ongoing change but with arguably mixed policy outcomes. Prior to the CRA, judicial policy tended to be relatively stable, with Lord Chancellors

[48] The continued (and perhaps increased) importance of informal factors within a more formal judicial system was a central finding of Gee et al, *The Politics of Judicial Independence* (2015). For a discussion of how informal social forces influenced the early years of the administration and leadership of the Supreme Court, see Gee, 'The Financial and Administrative Independence of the UK Supreme Court' (2015).

[49] Constitutional Reform Act 2005, s 54 (Annual report and accounts of the Supreme Court) and para 31 of Sch 12 (Annual report and accounts of the JAC).

[50] See generally R Cornes, 'Gains (and Dangers of Losses) in Translation: The Leadership Function in the United Kingdom's Supreme Court, Parameters and Prospects' [2011] *PL* 509; R Cornes, 'A Constitutional Disaster in the Making? The Communications Challenge Facing the United Kingdom's Supreme Court' [2013] *PL* 266.

tending to be policy minimalists, who mostly administered the status quo, supported by a departmental culture that favoured only incremental change. Today, judicial policy is much more open, inclusive and dynamic. The new approach recognises that the design and delivery of judicial policy requires input from multiple actors, no one of which possesses all of the resources, information and expertise that are necessary to make intelligent policy choices.[51] A more densely populated landscape also means that there are more actors to agitate for reform, although this can also present a coordination challenge insofar as the Lord Chancellor is no longer the singular central figure who can determine policy. The policy agenda is much wider today than prior to 2003, with issues such as the diversity, performance, appraisal, workloads and well-being of judges receiving overdue attention. Emblematic is judicial appointments, which is an area of judicial policy that has been characterised by ongoing change. This is an area that has been marked by numerous reviews (under the auspices of the Ministry of Justice, by select committees, by the JAC itself and by outside think tanks), with significant legislative change in the Crime and Courts Act 2013 that updated the 2005 statutory scheme in important ways.[52] Many actors are now charged with coordinating and monitoring this aspect of judicial policy, including the LCJ, Lord Chancellor, JAC, JACO, Judicial Diversity Forum, Judicial Diversity Taskforce and Judicial Diversity Committee of the Judges' Council. There have been tensions between some of these actors, although many of these have been productive insofar as they encouraged changes that mean that today the judicial appointment process is quicker and cheaper than when the JAC began its work in 2006. However, some are very disappointed about the policy outcomes, insofar as much less progress has been made on diversifying the judiciary than might have been expected (and especially in terms of the number of black, Asian and minority ethnic applicants being appointed as judges, the number of solicitors recruited and the number of women reaching the highest echelons of the court system).[53] Similarly, the potential for and importance of judicial appraisal is increasingly recognised by actors involved in judicial policy, but there is still no comprehensive system of judicial appraisal.

V. JUDICIAL POLICY AND THE NEW LABOUR CONSTITUTIONAL PROJECT

By now, it should be clear that New Labour's reforms helped to carve out a very different approach to judicial policy. In this part, I want to consider how their judicial reforms relate to the rest of New Labour's constitutional project.

[51] Gee (n 37) 153.

[52] P O'Brien, 'Changes to Judicial Appointments in the Crime Courts Act 2013' [2014] *PL* 179.

[53] See G Gee and E Rackley, 'Introduction: Diversity and the JAC's First Ten Years' in G Gee and E Rackley (eds), *Debating Judicial Appointments in an Age of Diversity* (Routledge, 2018) 1.

The starting point is to acknowledge that there are echoes of that larger project within New Labour's judicial reforms. For a start, just as New Labour's 13 years in power saw an unprecedented amount of reform to the constitution as a whole, so too can it be claimed that the Blair and Brown governments oversaw an unprecedented amount of reform to the judiciary and courts within a short period of time. There had been other important shake-ups of the judicial system of course, for example the Courts Act 1971 introduced unified court administration. But no recent governments can claim to have made such extensive changes to the judicial system. After all, the New Labour governments oversaw: the creation of a new top court; new ways of appointing judges; new arrangements that promoted judicial self-governance; new arrangements providing for a partnership model of court administration; and two sets of changes to the ministerial department with primary responsibility for the administration of justice. It is true that these reforms mixed continuity and change, as did New Labour's wider project. For example, the Supreme Court was a new institution in a new building with a new administrative infrastructure, but the overall appellate jurisdiction in the UK remained the same. It is also true that many of the reforms instituted by the CRA built on changes already underway. For example, there had been various tweaks to the judicial appointment process in the previous 10 years that, in retrospect, can now be seen to hint at growing recognition of the need to formalise the appointments process. Similarly, the role of Lord Chancellor and the character of the department had been evolving since the 1970s.

In one sense, New Labour's judicial reforms may seem peripheral to the rest of their constitutional project. The details of how judges are selected, funded, managed and led have low electoral salience, and generate little interest amongst the public at large. But, in another sense, New Labour's judicial reforms were prompted in part by earlier reforms to the domestic regime for rights protection and the introduction of the devolution schemes, both of which created new species of legal questions that could come before the courts relating to the exercise of public power. This in turn heightened the importance of ensuring that adequate arrangements are in place to ensure the independence of the judiciary, both individually and collectively. In other words, by catapulting the courts into choppy political waters, the Human Rights Act and devolution issues litigation led more people to question the long-term sustainability of an approach to judicial policy that was centred around the overlapping roles of the Lord Chancellor. So, as with other elements to New Labour's project, the judicial reforms pursued from 2003 onwards can be said to have been partially prompted by earlier reforms. Similarly, reforms to judicial appointments in Scotland and Northern Ireland that were modelled around independent selection bodies increased the pressure for reform in England and Wales. In other words, creating the Judicial Appointments Board for Scotland and the Northern Ireland Judicial Appointments Commission rendered anomalous an approach to appointments in England and Wales that was based on almost untrammelled ministerial discretion. But as with a number of other limbs to New Labour's constitutional project, there was no principled method of reforming the judicial system, and indeed one might even surmise that not consulting with key stakeholders such as senior judges in 2003 and 2007 was a deliberate decision to sidestep possible roadblocks to reform. This criticism is relevant, but risks seeming somewhat churlish, given that New Labour's judicial reforms involved, in the final analysis, the executive limiting its own role in an area of public policy. In this, there are echoes of other parts of New Labour's constitutional project, which involved the imposition of limits on executive power. However, as with the Human Rights Act, which came to be a source of frustration for some ministers, including the Prime Minister and successive Home Secretaries, so too did a New Labour Lord Chancellor (Jack Straw) come to feel that the CRA may have gone too far in limiting ministerial involvement in judicial appointments.[54]

Just as New Labour purported to modernise parts of the traditional constitution along rational lines, eschewing the pragmatic approaches that distinguished parts of our governing apparatus, so too might New Labour's judicial reforms be said to vindicate more standard, rational and modern accounts of judicial independence and the separation of powers. Even though the initial driver for the 2003 judicial reforms was the desire in Blair's Downing Street for more effective delivery of criminal justice policy, several of the reforms seem informed by a collective account of judicial independence within a more rational, formal and modern separation of powers. In the UK, stress was traditionally placed by policy-makers on an 'individual' notion of judicial independence: that is to say, the ability of individual judges to resolve disputes impartially, according to the relevant law, and free from any improper pressure.[55] Weight had therefore been placed on issues such as security of tenure and adequate remuneration for individual judges. There tended to be much less stress on a 'collective' notion of judicial independence: that is, those institutional arrangements necessary to ensure that the judiciary as a branch of government is free, and is also seen to be free, from improper pressure, especially pressures emanating from the political branches of government. So, for example, the overlapping responsibilities of the Lord Chancellor and the concentration of power in the hands of someone appointed by and dismissible at the whim of the Prime Minister had tended not to raise red flags. However, by the turn of the century, the relative lack of attention paid to collective independence had arguably become untenable, given that the courts were increasingly called upon to hold those exercising political power to account on legal grounds for legal wrongs. The CRA, and the reforms to the model of court service that followed it, can be said to emphasise the collective

[54] See J Straw, *Aspects of Law Reform: An Insider's Perspective* (Cambridge University Press, 2013) 51–77. See also G Gee, 'Rethinking the Lord Chancellor's Role in Judicial Appointments' (2017) 20 *Legal Ethics* 4.

[55] See generally R Stevens, 'A Loss of Innocence? Judicial Independence and the Separation of Powers' (1999) 19 *OJLS* 365.

independence of the judiciary as a whole. Parts of New Labour's wider constitutional project reflected a more open, transparent and inclusive approach to public life, and something similar can once again be said for the more plural and differentiated institutional judicial landscape that flowed from the 2003 reforms, with a much wider range of actors now involved in the design, implementation and oversight of judicial policy. As I noted earlier, a common criticism levelled against the New Labour constitutional project was that it lacked a compelling narrative that could explain the rationale and content of 13 years of constitutional reform. The same is less true for New Labour's judicial reforms, where a stress on a more rational and modern account of judicial independence and separation of powers featured in governmental justifications for the reforms,[56] albeit in the years since 2003 these rationales for reform were more often articulated by senior judges than leading politicians. Indeed, it was arguably senior judges who had a clearer vision of the future directions of judicial policy than ministers and officials.

One of the hallmarks of New Labour's constitutional project was the creation of new (or the remaking of established) policy communities. A similar dynamic was evident in the judicial sphere, where New Labour's reforms recrafted the policy community responsible for judicial policy. Some actors remained the same, albeit exercising new responsibilities, for example the enlarged role for the LCJ and the much-diluted role for the Lord Chancellor. New actors entered the scene, either as a result of statute (the JAC and JCIO, for example) or in response to the reforms (for example, the growing interest of the House of Lords Select Committee on the Constitution and the House of Commons Justice Select Committee). More provision was also made for the involvement of lay people, with the JAC notably having a lay chair and more lay members than judicial members. As I suggested above, these changes have led to a more dynamic and broader policy agenda, with important topics such as judicial diversity, appraisal and well-being now receiving serious sustained consideration for perhaps the first time, albeit with only limited evidence of much policy progress. In other parts of New Labour's project, new policy communities were superimposed on existing communities, leading not only to policy divergence, but also to questions about the ultimate location of political authority. There has been no equivalent issue within the judicial sphere, where by and large most judges, lawyers, politicians and officials seem broadly content with the shape of the new policy community, and in particular with the dynamic whereby the senior judiciary has assumed greater responsibility for their own governance, with the day-to-day involvement of the Lord Chancellor substantially reduced. The political opposition that accompanied these reforms in 2003 quickly died away. True, relations

[56] See, eg Department for Constitutional Affairs, *Constitutional Reform: A New Way of Appointing Judges* (CP10/03) July 2003.

have been occasionally fraught between ministers, officials and senior judges, notably in 2010–11, when relations deteriorated between the Supreme Court and Ministry of Justice over financial and administrative matters, and between the Ministry and the JAC in the last couple of years of the New Labour era.[57] But for the most part, the new policy community responsible for judicial policy has forged constructive relationships.

At one very important level, then, there has been broad acceptance of this new approach to judicial policy. At another level, however, there is still some worry about its long-term effects. More particularly, there is reason to worry that the dynamic of growing judicial self-governance and diluted ministerial responsibility may have gone too far, with judges today enjoying too much responsibility for their own governance, leading to an accountability gap and to an unbalanced approach to judicial policy. This critique is most applicable to judicial appointments, where some argue that, despite a central role for the JAC in recommending candidates for judicial office, senior judges now enjoy too much influence over judicial appointments, given their involvement at almost all stages of the selection process.[58] More generally, it can be suggested that today the greater threat to the stability of judicial policy is not inappropriate ministerial interference with decision-making, but rather ministerial indifference. The risk is that ministers might become disinterested in judicial policy, and over time fail to recognise the need to allocate sufficient resources to the court system. Related to this are concerns that hiving off functions (and civil servants) from central government to new bodies such as the JAC and the Judicial Office has led to the atrophying of constitutional understanding inside the Ministry of Justice and the Cabinet Office, with some judges worried that even senior officials sometimes now display much less appreciation of the importance of judicial independence and the rule of law. All that said, the new judicial policy community seems relatively stable, at least for the time being, with very little prospect of significant backsliding on the structural reforms introduced by the CRA. Also of note is the fact that the new approach to judicial policy was stress-tested during the age of austerity and – despite the occasional spikes in tensions between ministers and judges mentioned above – the various actors in the refashioned policy community were able to arrive at budget allocations with which they could live.[59]

[57] G Gee, 'Guarding the Guardians: The Chief Executive of the UK Supreme Court' [2013] *PL* 538.

[58] See A Paterson, 'Power and Judicial Appointment: Squaring the Impossible Circle' in Gee and Rackley, *Debating Judicial Appointments* (2018) 32; G Gee, 'Judging the JAC: How Much Judicial Influence Over Judicial Appointments Is Too Much?' in Gee and Rackley (ibid) 152; E Delaney, 'Searching for Constitutional Meaning in Institutional Design: The Debate over Judicial Appointments in the United Kingdom' (2016) 14 *International Journal of Constitutional Law* 752.

[59] Gee et al (n 1).

VI. CONCLUSION

New Labour's constitutional project ranks amongst the important legacies of the Blair and Brown years. With the notable exception of the Human Rights Act and putting the relationship between devolution and the rise of separatist sentiment to one side, many of the reforms that comprised that project now seem to be settled parts of the constitutional landscape. Certainly, this seems true of New Labour's judicial reforms. There are concerns about aspects of those reforms, and further tweaks and changes have been implemented since 2003, especially to the appointments system, but few clamour for substantial modification of the new architecture of the justice system. There is, in other words, broad acceptance of the post-CRA settlement, with widespread recognition that New Labour's reforms strengthened judicial independence and accountability.[60] There are many echoes of New Labour's wider constitutional project within their judicial reforms (including: the lack of a clear, principled methodology for reform; the interrelationship between different reforms pursued at different points during New Labour's period in power; a stress on more formal, rational, plural and modern approaches to governance; and the creation of a new policy community). But there are also differences, including a clear narrative relating to the collective independence of the judiciary within a mature separation of powers that explains many of the judicial reforms pursued by New Labour.

Though New Labour's judicial reforms seem stable and settled, there are questions about whether New Labour (and, for that matter, subsequent governments) have given sufficient thought to how shared understandings and values can flourish within a more formal separation of powers. Here, relevant values include a shared commitment to judicial independence and the rule of law within a democratic system of self-government. Relevant shared understandings include about the proper role of and limit on judicial role, and equally a recognition of the need for elected politicians to be able to pursue new directions in public policy within the limits of the law. The rules, structures, processes and practices of the justice system must help politicians to develop a clear grasp of the importance of judicial independence and the rule of law, and more particularly to recognise how decision-making by independent judges can help to realise socially, economically and politically desirable outcomes. Those same rules, structures, processes and practices must also help judges to develop a clear grasp of the proper limits on the judicial role, and the proper place of political decision-making within a democratic polity committed to self-government. More than 15 years on from the CRA, it is far from clear whether the current settlement will help to nurture and sustain those shared values and understandings over the long term. Given the growing concern amongst some politicians

[60] R Hazell, 'Judicial Independence and Accountability in the UK Are Both Stronger Following the Constitutional Reform Act 2005' [2015] *PL* 198.

about the constitutional role of the courts, domestic and European, and in light of rising fears about the prospect of populist backlashes against the courts and the rule of law, it may be that New Labour's judicial reforms have yet to be really tested. A final verdict on New Labour's judicial reforms may need to wait for the constitutional stress-testing that is likely to be a dominant feature of political life in the UK for the next few years.

6

Devolution: A New Fundamental Principle of the UK Constitution

CHRIS McCORKINDALE

I. INTRODUCTION

In an event that marked its twentieth anniversary, Tony Blair – the Prime Minister whose government delivered legislative devolution to Scotland and Wales (and who returned legislative devolution to Northern Ireland) – revealed what he believed to have been the twofold purpose of those reforms. The first, *principled* purpose was 'to bring about a new settlement' whereby 'decision making was brought closer to the people who felt a strong sense of identity'; the second, *political* purpose was 'to ward off the bigger threat of secession'.[1] Of course, these purposes are indelibly linked. First, because the 'threat' of secession, more pronounced in Scotland, albeit latent in Wales, is on one reading a manifestation of the desire to bring decision-making closer to those who share a sense of (national) identity. Second, the prospect of secession has been a significant driver of the broadening scope and deepening entrenchment of devolution during its first 20 years. To these, we might add a third, *constitutional* purpose of devolution: to bring about radical (in Blair's words, 'necessary')[2] change to the territorial distribution of power in the UK whilst at the same time preserving the indivisible sovereignty of the Crown-in-Parliament.

Whilst some of the analysis applies generally across Scotland, Wales and Northern Ireland, the focus of this chapter – reflecting the approach taken to devolution by the Kilbrandon Commission and the lockstep evolution of devolution in the two countries from that moment to the present day – will be on Scotland and Wales. I will argue that, measured against the purposes of

[1] T Blair, 'Devolution, Brexit and the Future of the Union' (speech at the Institute for Government, London, 24 April 2019) www.instituteforgovernment.org.uk/sites/default/files/publications/tony-blair_0.pdf.

[2] ibid 3.

devolution identified by Blair, the legacy of these reforms is mixed and its future uncertain. Nationalism, as it was for the failed attempts to deliver devolution in Scotland and Wales 20 years prior to the New Labour reforms (part II), continues to be a major catalyst for the broadening scope of devolved powers (part III), as well as of their deepening constitutional entrenchment (part IV). Indeed, as we look to the next 20 years (part V), the prospect of secession by Scotland, and of greater political and legal autonomy for Wales, looms large. Even if the UK is to withstand those challenges, however, it is unlikely to do so without further reform at its core to nourish and sustain this new fundamental principle of our constitution (conclusion).

II. TWENTY YEARS PRIOR: LEGACIES FOR NEW LABOUR

Devolution in response to nationalism has a long (still unfolding) history. It was the surprise election in Wales of the first Plaid Cymru MP, Gwynfor Evans, in the Carmarthen by-election in 1966, followed by the election of the SNP candidate Winnie Ewing in the Hamilton by-election a year later, that revived the Home Rule debate and that caused another Labour Prime Minister, James Callaghan, to reach for devolution as the solution to the possible break-up of the UK.

Provoked by these nationalist gains in what previously had been thought of as Labour strongholds, in 1969 a Royal Commission on the Constitution (the Kilbrandon Commission) was established by Harold Wilson's Labour government to 'examine the present functions of the central legislature and government in relation to the several countries, nations and regions of the United Kingdom' and to consider 'whether any changes are desirable in those functions or otherwise in present constitutional and economic relationships'.[3] The Commission reported in 1973 and, whilst it was unable to agree to a singularly coherent position, both the report and the unsuccessful attempt at devolution that followed left significant legacies for New Labour's efforts to reform the territorial constitution.

The positive legacies of this period were at least fourfold. First, Kilbrandon rejected both separatism (the transfer of sovereignty to the nations over all matters) and federalism (sovereignty divided between the nations and the centre) as solutions to those grievances in Scotland and Wales that, albeit 'coloured by feelings of national identity',[4] related to the concentration, as well as to the unrepresentative and unresponsive nature, of executive and legislative power in London. In the case of the former, it was said that the political will for separation was lacking.[5] In the case of the latter, the report concluded that the

[3] Kilbrandon Commission, *Report of the Royal Commission on the Constitution 1969–1973* (1973).

[4] A Page, *Constitutional Law of Scotland* (W Green, 2015) 22.

[5] Kilbrandon Commission (n 3) para 497.

UK would be unlikely to adapt to federal arrangements. The major obstacles included the need for wider constitutional reforms – 'a written constitution, a special procedure for changing it and a constitutional court to interpret it'[6] – that had not formed part of the UK's constitutional tradition; that federalism would be unlikely to find general acceptance;[7] and that the dominant position of England, in terms of 'political importance and wealth', would be 'so unbalanced as to be unworkable'.[8] Instead, the report set the path of reform towards devolution – in which significant (though asymmetrical) powers are exercised at the substate level but where full sovereignty is retained at the centre[9] – in order to 'counter over-centralisation … to … strengthen democracy [and to respond to] national feeling in Scotland and Wales'.[10]

The Commission's report was published to little fanfare. As one MP said, the Commission was established only 'to get the Labour Government over the difficulty of what to say about nationalist victories at by-elections', and by the time of its publication 'the Nationalists [were no longer] a serious proposition'.[11] However, a second burst of nationalism put the question of devolution back on the agenda. In February 1974, the SNP won seven seats on 22 per cent of the Scottish vote and Plaid won two seats (including its first win in a general election), and in October 1974 the SNP won 11 seats on 30 per cent of the Scottish vote and Plaid won three seats. With a wafer-thin majority, the return of nationalists as 'a serious proposition' caused Wilson to revive the report and to take measures that would lead, ultimately, to the Scotland and Wales Acts of 1978. In line with the majority view of the Commission, those Acts provided for a directly elected executive Assembly for Wales with fairly strong powers to develop distinct Welsh approach across a range of policy areas, broadly in line with those that fell within the remit of the Welsh Office, and for a directly elected legislative assembly for Scotland, from which would be drawn an executive headed by a First Secretary. The new Assembly would have been established according to a conferred powers model of devolution, with the power to make primary legislation (to be known as 'Measures') in a broad range of areas specified in a schedule to the 1978 Act. What explained the different models recommended by the majority of the Commission was twofold: first, the perception that the demand for devolution was much stronger in Scotland than it had been in Wales; and second, that Scotland's distinct legal system – protected expressly in the Acts of Union and culturally by a strand of legal nationalism that has been resistant to assimilation – called for a legislature empowered to make laws for Scotland.

[6] ibid para 527.
[7] ibid.
[8] ibid para 539.
[9] ibid para 1106.
[10] ibid para 1102.
[11] HC Deb 31 October 1973, vol 863, cols 163–75.

The second legacy of the period was the turn to referendums as the means of 'unlocking' devolution. In order for the first legislative response to the Commission's report, the (combined) Scotland and Wales Bill 1976, to proceed to a second reading, the government was forced to concede to hold a post-enactment referendum in order to placate influential devolution sceptics on its own side. That Bill was defeated on a guillotine motion. However, when the (now separate) Scotland and Wales Bills returned to Parliament, not only was a commitment to hold post-legislative referendums retained, but an amendment by the Labour MP and devolution sceptic, George Cunningham, created an additional hurdle: a duty on the relevant Secretary of State to repeal the legislation where it appeared to them that less than 40 per cent *of those entitled to vote* had voted 'yes' to devolution.[12] In Wales, that amendment was not determinative: the referendum was lost decisively, with just 20.26 per cent of those voting doing so in favour of devolution and 79.74 per cent voting against. In Scotland, on the other hand, the Cunningham amendment was fatal. Whilst a majority (51.62 per cent) *of those voting* did so in support of devolution, on a 63.7 per cent turnout that amounted to just 32.9 per cent *of those entitled to vote*, so both Acts were repealed. Vernon Bogdanor has said that Cunningham's amendment might be 'the most significant backbench initiative in British politics'.[13] Not only did it deprive Scotland of an Assembly for which a majority had voted, but the failure to deliver devolution caused the SNP and the Liberals to withdraw their support for the minority Labour government and caused the Conservatives, led by Margaret Thatcher, to put down and win a vote of no confidence. The rest is history.

Third, the report identified principles that ought to underpin devolution. One such principle was that reform of the territorial constitution should not challenge the 'essential political and economic unity of the United Kingdom', which was held to be 'a long-established fact … [that] ought to be preserved'.[14] It followed that '[the UK] Parliament must continue to represent all parts of the United Kingdom and retain overriding power'.[15] Nevertheless, that unity would be stronger and not weaker for respecting in its governmental arrangements the 'considerable diversity [within the UK], based on differences of history, tradition and culture'.[16] Another principle was that reform should strengthen the fundamental principles of democratic representation, control and accountability whilst respecting individual liberty.[17] In addition, it was said, reform of the territorial distribution of power within the UK must be of general acceptance to the people and 'cannot be imposed against [their] will … with any real hope of success'.[18]

[12] Scotland Act 1978, s 85; Wales Act 1978, s 80.
[13] V Bogdanor, 'The 40 Percent Rule' (1980) 33 *Parliamentary Affairs* 249.
[14] Kilbrandon Commission (n 3) para 417.
[15] ibid.
[16] ibid.
[17] ibid para 418.
[18] ibid para 497.

Finally, that only the report's recommendations for Scotland and Wales were distilled and acted upon, with England left untouched and Northern Ireland treated separately, spoke both to the unique conditions under which the latter operates and to two particular features of devolution to the Celtic nations as against devolution to England: first, that devolution is on one level about *minority* protection for nations within the Union; and second, that the devolution of power *to* those nations is qualitatively different from – and therefore could (indeed, ought to) be delivered in a distinct process from – devolution *within* a nation (to the English regions).

We see, then, the positive legacy of the period in the case made for asymmetrical devolution; the emergence of the referendum as the vehicle through which the devolution debate should be conducted and the outcome decided upon; (for better or for worse) the case that devolution in Scotland and in Wales could be given effect to in a process that is distinct from and therefore not contingent upon reforms in England and in Northern Ireland; and the articulation of the principles – unity strengthened by diversity; democracy and individual liberty; popular legitimacy – that should guide such reform. There were, however, important lessons here which New Labour heeded about how not to 'do' devolution. Here, I highlight two. First, the sense of injustice in Scotland that arose from the failure to cross Cunningham's referendum threshold in large part turned future governments – including Blair's in relation to devolution – away from the use of any form of referendum super-majority or special amendment procedure, even where (as with various subsequent devolution referendums, and also in relation to the Scottish independence referendum in 2014 and the Brexit referendum in 2016) the outcome might lead to significant constitutional change. Second, future devolution referendums in Scotland and Wales would be held on a *pre*-legislative basis – a vote on the *principle* of devolution as set out in a White Paper rather than a *post*-legislative referendum on a pre-determined *form* of devolution as set out in statute – in order that parliamentary opposition to detailed devolution Bills might be controlled and contained by the prior expression of a clear popular mandate.

III. DELIVERING ON DEVOLUTION: NEW LABOUR'S LEGACY

A. The 1998 Settlement

The 1979 referendum defeats dealt a blow to proponents of devolution. However, it was an indirect consequence of those failures – 18 years of Conservative rule and the stranglehold of Thatcherism – that reignited the cause. For Scotland and Wales, their constitutional position throughout the 1980s and early 1990s was a precarious one. The 1987 general election had brought about a 'doomsday scenario' whereby Conservative victory across the UK stood in stark contrast to the party's showing in those nations. The Conservative Party had won the election convincingly, with 42.2 per cent of the share of votes giving them 376 seats in the Commons – a majority of 101. However, they had won just

24 per cent of the vote in Scotland and 29.5 per cent in Wales, giving them 10 of 72 seats in the former and eight of 38 seats in the latter. By contrast, Labour had won 42.4 per cent of the Scottish vote and 50 Scottish seats, and 45.1 per cent of the Welsh vote and 24 Welsh seats. If these results reflected a broader trend in Scottish and Welsh politics – the rejection of Thatcherism[19] – it was a trend that barely registered at a constitutional level: the Scottish and Welsh Offices, their Secretaries of State and the policies that they pursued would be Conservative.[20] Nations comprised of large public sectors, and in need of state intervention to maintain the competitiveness of their heavy industries, were vulnerable under a government that sought the contraction of the public sector and that refused to prop up struggling industries.

For Scotland, the repudiation of Thatcherism was tied with a more positive, constitutive moment. The Scottish Constitutional Convention, launched in 1989 and encompassing the Labour Party, the Liberal Democrats, the Green Party, trade unions, local authorities, churches and a number of others across a broad range of civic bodies, emerged as a direct and extra-parliamentary response to Scotland's constitutional predicament – one where legislation came to be seen as an oppressive tool of the government over the people: 'an abuse of parliamentary sovereignty and therefore a violation of the unwritten norms of the constitution'.[21] Reacting to this, the Scottish Constitutional Convention asserted the sovereignty of the Scottish people – a claim given currency by Scotland's Claim of Right 1988.[22]

The Claim of Right set out the case for a new constitutional settlement. In the negative sense, it 'described a situation in which [the constitutional status quo was] no longer being honoured; in which the wishes of the massive majority of the Scottish electorate are being disregarded'. In the positive sense, the Claim reaffirmed Scotland's right to self-determination: the right 'to articulate its own demands and grievances, rather than have them articulated for it by a Government utterly unrepresentative of the Scots'.[23] In that respect, it concluded with the call for a Convention to draw up the framework for a Scottish Assembly, and to mobilise Scottish public opinion behind the scheme.

Duly established, the Convention set to work. Despite the various interests present, the group was able to achieve substantial consensus in the face of disagreement: on the policy areas which should be devolved; on the tax-raising

[19] J Mitchell, 'From National Identity to Nationalism, 1945–99' in HT Dickinson and M Lynch (eds), *The Challenge to Westminster: Sovereignty, Devolution and Independence* (Tuckwell Press, 2000) 154, 160.

[20] House of Commons, Public Information Fact Sheet No 47, *General Election Results, 11 June 1987*, www.parliament.uk/documents/commons-information-office/m11.pdf.

[21] M Keating, 'Managing the Multinational State: Constitutional Settlement in the United Kingdom' in TC Salmon and M Keating (eds), *The Dynamics of Decentralization: Canadian Federalism and British Devolution* (McGill-Queen's University Press, 2001).

[22] OD Edwards (ed), *A Claim of Right for Scotland* (Polygon, 1989).

[23] ibid.

powers which the Parliament should enjoy (powers to vary income tax (3p in the £1), but no power to control corporation tax); on the Parliament's relationship with the EU, and with the European Convention on Human Rights; on gender equality; on the models of openness and consultation to be adopted; on the number of seats in the chamber; and on the issue where there was most disagreement to be overcome – the electoral system to be adopted.[24] Beyond the impressive work done by the Convention, there are two points worth stressing here as they relate to devolution in Scotland and Wales.

First, whilst the Conservative Party's general election win in 1992 knocked the stuffing out of the Convention,[25] when the devolution project was kick-started by New Labour, the will of the Scottish people as expressed by the Convention was paramount. In their 1997 general election manifesto, New Labour committed to create a Parliament 'firmly based on the agreement reached in the Scottish Constitutional Convention',[26] whilst the new government opposed a number of legislative amendments on the basis that they departed from the Convention's detail and vision.[27]

It was on this basis that support for devolution was mobilised – with 74.29 per cent of a 60.18 per cent turnout voting yes to devolution and 63.48 per cent also voting yes to the devolution of that limited (and, as it would transpire, unused) income tax power. What was delivered in the Scotland Act 1998 was therefore an altogether more impressive form of devolution than that on offer in the 1978 Act: a reserved powers model of devolution, with a degree of fiscal power but with extensive and deep-cut legislative competence over 'the majority of domestic policy';[28] a political model of devolution that rejected the Westminster style in favour of a 'new politics' built on power-sharing (between the executive, legislature and citizens), accessibility and participation, and equal opportunity;[29] and a settlement given form by an Act of the Crown-in-Parliament but given substance by Scottish civil society and endorsed by the people of Scotland.

Second, the absence of an equivalent exercise in constitution building in Wales had two limiting effects on the model of devolution adopted there. On the one hand, where the Convention had mobilised public opinion behind the new settlement in Scotland, attitudes to devolution in Wales remained somewhat

[24] See B Taylor, *The Scottish Parliament* (Polygon, 1999). For the final report of the convention, containing the details of the agreed framework, see *Scotland's Parliament, Scotland's Right* (Convention of Scottish Local Authorities, 1995).

[25] J Mitchell, *Strategies for Self-Government: The Campaign for a Scottish Parliament* (Polygon, 1996) 287–90.

[26] 'New Labour – Because Britain Deserves Better', 1997 general election manifesto, http://labourparty.org.uk/manifestos/1997/1997-labour-manifesto.shtml.

[27] B Hadfield, 'The United Kingdom as a Territorial State' in V Bogdanor (ed), *The British Constitution in the Twentieth Century* (Oxford University Press, 2004) 623.

[28] Calman Commission, *Serving Scotland Better: Scotland and the United Kingdom in the 21st Century* (2009) para 2.7.

[29] Set out in the report of the Consultative Steering Group, *Shaping Scotland's Parliament* (1999).

tepid. Devolution eventually won the support of just 50.3 per cent voters in the 1997 referendum on a 50.22 per cent turnout. On the other hand, where the Convention had established a plan for devolution in Scotland drawn by a broad spectrum of civil society, no such blueprint existed in Wales. Instead, Blair later admitted that his government 'steamrollered' devolution in Wales on the back of prior commitments and on the coattails of much stronger support for the contemporaneous devolution of power to Scotland and Northern Ireland.[30] For sure, the strong sense of cultural nationalism in Wales was reflected in the commitment in section 47 of the Government of Wales Act 1998 to treat the Welsh and English languages equally, so far as it was practicable to do so. Yet the ambivalence of the people of Wales towards indigenous political institutions was reflected in the limited form of executive-only devolution that took effect in 1999: an unintelligibly complex, conferred powers model of devolution; an Assembly that functioned as a single corporate body without separate executive and legislative functions nor, therefore, the accountability of the former to the latter; and subject to a limited transfer of some (but by no means all) competences in defined devolved fields. If, then, devolution, for Blair, was a response to political nationalism and the provision of meaningful self-government, it is little wonder that the Welsh settlement struggled from the start to assert its legitimacy.[31] The rapid evolution of that settlement began with the de facto separation of executive and legislative functions in 2002, but took shape with the passage by the UK Parliament of a further devolution act. The Government of Wales Act 2006, which gave effect to the main body of recommendations made by the Richard Commission – established by the then First Minister, Rhodri Morgan, to examine the powers and electoral arrangements of the Assembly – put the separation of executive and legislative functions onto a legislative footing.[32] More significantly, the 2006 Act marked a two-step change in the Assembly's legislative powers. First, granting to the Assembly the power to pass Assembly Measures, which were to be treated as primary legislation but which retained an unsatisfactory gatekeeping role for the UK Parliament who would trigger those powers one by one with the passage of a Legislative Competence Order. Second, the 2006 Act allowed the people of Wales to unlock, via a referendum, primary law-making powers in the form of Assembly Acts in devolved fields, without the need for approval by the UK Parliament.[33] On 3 March 2011, 63.49 per cent of a 35.63 per cent referendum turnout voted to do so.

New Labour's Secretary of State for Wales in 1999, Paul Murphy, might have captured the mood of the party when he said that he was 'convinced most people in Wales don't want the kind of Parliament they have in Scotland', but by 5 May

[30] 'Tony Blair: I Steamrollered Devolution for Wales' *BBC News* (11 September 2017).

[31] For the definitive overview, see R Rawlings, *Delineating Wales: Constitutional, Legal and Administrative Aspects of National Devolution* (University of Wales Press, 2003).

[32] Government of Wales Act 2006, Parts 1 (on the Senedd) and 2 (on the Welsh Government).

[33] Ibid, ss 103–09.

2011, when the Assembly assumed those primary law-making powers, it was Morgan's prediction – that devolution would grow 'in status and authority with the full-hearted consent and support of the people of Wales' – that rang true.[34]

B. (D)evolution: Twenty Years On

'Devolution,' as Ron Davies famously said, 'is a process and not an event.'[35] So it has proved. The most significant dynamic that has driven that process in Scotland has been the rise of the SNP as a (indeed, for the moment, it seems *the*) party of government, first forming a minority government in 2007 (repeated in 2016) and, somewhat remarkably, winning a majority of seats in the Scottish Parliament in 2011. Most recently, in 2021 the SNP fell just short of a majority but entered into a cooperation agreement with the Scottish Greens according to which the latter would receive two junior ministerial posts in exchange for their support across a negotiated set of areas of agreement (as well as, in other areas, agreement to differ).[36]

The result of the 2007 election sparked two distinct discussions about Scotland's constitutional future. On the one hand, the Scottish Government – unable to find majority support for independence within the Scottish Parliament – initiated its National Conversation, a public consultation exercise on Scotland's constitutional future, which included the publication of a draft independence referendum Bill. The response, by an opposition coalition of Labour, Conservative and Liberal Democrats in the Scottish Parliament and with the support of the UK government, was to establish a commission, chaired by Sir Kenneth Calman, that would review the 1998 devolution settlement and 'recommend any changes … that would enable the Scottish Parliament to serve the people of Scotland better, improve the financial accountability of the Scottish Parliament, and continue to secure the position of Scotland within the United Kingdom'.[37] The Commission, across its interim (December 2008) and final (June 2009) reports, took the position that devolution had been a 'real success' that 'works well in practice' and 'is in general popular with the Scottish people', and restated the strength and value of Scotland's place within the UK.[38] It nevertheless made a number of recommendations as to how the devolution settlement might be improved, most (but not all) of which were given form by the Scotland Act 2012.

[34] Murphy and Morgan quoted in House of Commons Library Briefing Paper 08318, 'A Process, Not an Event: Devolution in Wales, 1998–2018' (11 July 2018) 13.

[35] R Davies, *Devolution: A Process Not an Event* (Institute of Welsh Affairs, 1999).

[36] Scottish Government and Scottish Green Party Parliamentary Group: draft Cooperation Agreement (20 August 2021) www.gov.scot/publications/scottish-government-and-scottish-green-party-cooperation-agreement/.

[37] Calman Commission, *Serving Scotland Better* (2009).

[38] ibid para 14.

The 2012 Act made some (relatively) modest adjustments to the legislative competence of the Scottish Parliament (eg the regulation of airguns; the administration of elections; drink-drive limits; national speed limits) and some symbolic (eg the change of nomenclature from Scottish Executive to Scottish Government) and substantive (eg the introduction of 'compatibility issues' in relation to the compatibility of criminal trials with the European Convention on Human Rights and EU law) institutional changes. More significantly, it initiated a (still ongoing) paradigm shift towards greater fiscal responsibility. In what the then Secretary of State for Scotland, Michael Moore, described as being 'the largest ever transfer of financial powers to Scotland since the creation of the UK',[39] the 2012 Act: (i) replaced the limited power of the Scottish Parliament to vary the UK rate of income tax with a duty to set a distinct Scottish Rate of Income Tax; (ii) devolved a number of other tax powers (Stamp Duty Land Tax and Landfill Tax); and (iii) created significant new borrowing powers for capital projects and to mitigate the volatility of tax receipts. Despite the historical significance that Moore attached to the 2012 Act reforms and the adoption of a distinct referendum question in 1997 to confer much more modest tax-varying powers upon the new Parliament, the use of a referendum to mandate the new fiscal settlement appears not to have been seriously considered.

The 2012 Act had not yet been passed when further nationalist gains rapidly accelerated the devolution process. The historic election in 2011 of an SNP (and, therefore, of the first pro-independence) majority in the Scottish Parliament probably did not reflect any great desire for independence. Polls at the time seemed to indicate a drop in support for independence (to around 23 per cent) at a time when the SNP's electoral success (and Labour's corresponding failure) seemed to be driven by perceptions of leadership, of competence and of which party was best able to stand up for Scotland's interests within the Union.[40] Nevertheless, with parliamentary support for an independence referendum now secured, it was to that question – should Scotland be an independent country – that the national conversation quickly turned. Debate about the legal basis for a referendum[41] was (perhaps, given the stakes, surprisingly) quickly put to bed when, in October 2012, the Scottish and UK governments concluded

[39] UK Government, 'Moore Welcomes Latest Addition to Scottish Devolution' (25 June 2013) www.gov.uk/government/news/moore-welcomes-latest-addition-to-scottish-devolution.

[40] See C McCorkindale, 'An Accidental Referendum' (*Scottish Constitutional Futures Blog*, 16 August 2013) www.scottishconstitutionalfutures.org/OpinionandAnalysis/ViewBlogPost/tabid/1767/articleType/ArticleView/articleId/2040/Christopher-McCorkindale-An-Accidental-Referendum.aspx.

[41] *cf* A Tomkins, 'The Scottish Parliament and the Independence Referendum' (*UKCLA Blog*, 12 January 2012) https://ukconstitutionallaw.org/2012/01/12/adam-tomkins-the-scottish-parliament-and-the-independence-referendum/; G Anderson et al, 'The Independence Referendum, Legality and the Contested Constitution: Widening the Debate' (*UKCLA Blog*, 31 January 2012) https://ukconstitutionallaw.org/2012/01/31/gavin-anderson-et-al-the-independence-referendum-legality-and-the-contested-constitution-widening-the-debate/.

the 'Edinburgh Agreement'. Based on that agreement, the UK government made a time-limited transfer of power to the Scottish Parliament to hold a single-question independence referendum that would be a fair and decisive expression of the views of the electorate in Scotland, the result of which would be respected on both sides. As support for independence began to increase against (and in at least one poll appeared to overtake) support for Scotland remaining in the Union – it became clear that the single-question referendum could not offer, as its alternative to independence, a mere continuation of the status quo. Once again, the answer from the centre to a rising nationalism was to offer yet more devolution.

Scotland's new deal was given expression shortly before the referendum in a 'vow' by the then leaders of the Conservative Party, the Labour Party and the Liberal Democrats, inter alia, to deliver 'extensive new powers for the [Scottish] Parliament' in the event of a No vote. It was given form, on the morning after Scotland's narrow vote to remain in the UK, with the announcement by the PM that a new commission – chaired by Lord Smith of Kelvin and comprising representatives of all five parties represented in the Scottish Parliament – would be asked to agree to and recommend areas for further devolution. The result was a third Scotland Act (the 2016 Act), which would transform Scottish devolution in a number of ways. First, the 2016 Act raced beyond the fiscal settlement established by the 2012 Act by deepening the Scottish Parliament's income tax powers (notably, devolving the power to set rates and bands of income tax above the personal allowance), devolving new tax powers (air passenger duty and the aggregates levy) and committing the Treasury to allocate 50 per cent of VAT raised in Scotland to the Scottish Government. Second, the dynamics of devolution spending have shifted with – for the first time – the partial devolution of welfare powers and the creation of a new agency, Social Security Scotland, to administer this new public service. Finally, alongside the limited devolution of welfare powers, the devolution of powers over elections to, and the composition of, the Scottish Parliament presents challenges to pan-UK political and social citizenship. Whether through the articulation of a 'human rights based' approach to social security in contrast to the more 'hostile' approach of the UK government, the use of new social security powers to offset unpopular UK government policies such as the (so-called) Bedroom Tax or the extension of the franchise in Scottish Parliament elections to include some prisoners as well as to 16- and 17-year-olds, these new powers of the Scottish Parliament have increasingly marked Scotland's distinctiveness from the UK in areas that once were the Union's lifeblood.

Influenced by constitutional developments in Scotland, as well as by increased support for – and comfort with – devolution in Wales, in 2011 the UK government established a Commission on Devolution in Wales (the Silk Commission) to consider the Welsh Assembly's fiscal and legislative powers as well as aspects of its organisation. In the first of two reports, the Commission made a series of recommendations concerning the devolution of taxation and borrowing powers broadly in line with the 2012 Scottish settlement but with the additional step (contra the Scottish experience) that the devolution of powers over income tax would be conditional on an affirmative vote in a post-legislative referendum.[42] Alongside miscellaneous provisions (including, as in Scotland, a symbolically important change in nomenclature from Welsh Executive to Welsh Government), these recommendations were given effect in the Wales Act 2014. If, for Blair, devolution aimed to bring decision-making closer to the people, for Silk, these reforms – which would 'provide the Welsh Government with an important set of fiscal levers and', for the first time, 'would enable political parties in Wales to offer people real fiscal choices'[43] – were a significant step in that direction. The second Silk Commission report, published in 2014, focused on the Assembly's legislative powers. As with the Calman Commission report, a number of reforms were recommended, some of which were structural (eg increasing the number of AMs), some of which were symbolic (eg that any desire by the Welsh Assembly to change its name to the Welsh Parliament should be – and as of May 2020 has been – respected) and some of which concerned the further devolution of substantive powers (eg policing; responsibility for the water industry; regulatory powers over transport; youth justice; drink-driving and speed limits). More fundamentally, the report recommended a further step change in the Welsh settlement, with the adoption of a reserved powers model and the recommendation that any devolution of youth justice should be followed a decade later with a review of the wholesale devolution of criminal justice.

In contrast to the relatively smooth implementation of the Smith recommendations in Scotland, what followed Silk II was a more tortuous process that juxtaposed stinginess at the centre with the maturation of devolution in Wales itself. As Rawlings has said, these contrasting positions are no surprise. For the UK government, their belated support for a reserved powers model of devolution has been defensive: an opportunity – in response to the Supreme Court's 2014 *Agricultural Sector* ruling that silent subjects (areas not specifically listed as exceptions to competence in devolved fields) fell within devolved competence – to 'reclaim' the content of those subjects through the process of reservation.[44] That stinginess was on display too in the process which led the majority of the Silk II recommendations to be given statutory form in the Wales Act 2017. Described by Rawlings as 'devolution by lowest possible denominator',[45] the St David's Day Agreement, between the Secretary of State for and representatives of the main political parties in Wales, confirmed the devolution of new powers relating to energy, water, Assembly and local

[42] *Report of the Commission on Devolution in Wales: Part 1, Financial Powers to Strengthen Wales* (2012).

[43] Paul Silk, quoted in House of Commons Library Briefing Paper 08318 (n 34) 18.

[44] R Rawlings, 'The Welsh Way/Y Fforrd Gymreig' in J Jowell and C O'Cinneide (eds), *The Changing Constitution*, 9th edn (Oxford University Press, 2019) 304–09.

[45] ibid 305.

government elections, sewerage and transport. However, an absence of consensus and the resistance of the UK government to cede ground on the devolution of justice (from their point of view, to undermine the integrity of the single legal jurisdiction) led to the disappearance of, inter alia, policing, drink-drive limits, youth justice and the establishment of a High Court office in Wales from the reform agenda.[46] From the Welsh Government's perspective, the evolution towards greater legislative and fiscal autonomy – the 2017 Act removed the hurdle of putting new income tax powers to a referendum – followed logically from an increasingly confident assertion of political autonomy. As the then First Minister, Carwyn Jones, said against the backdrop of the second Silk Report, 'Irrespective of thirteenth century history, Wales [today] is part of a voluntary union of four nations, by the consent of the overwhelming majority of Welsh people'.[47] If, then, the UK government sees in the Wales Act 2017 a full and final settlement for Wales, for the Welsh Government the predicament remains one of constitutional *un*settlement: its provisions were not yet fully in force before the First Minister commissioned a review led by the former Lord Chief Justice, Lord Thomas, to investigate the further devolution of powers over justice and the establishment of a separate legal jurisdiction for Wales.[48]

IV. ENTRENCHING DEVOLUTION: AN ENDURING LEGACY?

A second reaction from the centre to persistent nationalist claims in Scotland and Wales has focused less on models and powers of devolution and turned instead to its constitutional status.

When the Scotland Bill and the Government of Wales Bill were introduced into Parliament, much of the constitutional debate concerned the preservation of Westminster's status as the sovereign law-making authority even in devolved areas. When challenged on the absence of any explicit preservation for that status in relation to Wales, the then Secretary of State for Wales, Ron Davies, argued that the nature of sovereignty was such that any specific clause would be 'meaningless': Parliament, he said, 'is supreme, and any statutory assurance to that effect by this or any other Parliament can be set aside by any future Parliament'.[49] In Scotland, however, the question of sovereignty was more

[46] A Evans, 'Out of Sight, Out of Mind? The St David's Day Process and a Welsh Devolution Settlement' (*Centre for Constitutional Change Blog*, 27 February 2015) www.centreonconstitutional-change.ac.uk/opinions/out-sight-out-mind-st-davids-day-process-and-welsh-devolution-settlement.

[47] C Jones, 'Our Future Union – A Perspective from Wales' (speech at the Institute for Government, London, 15 October 2014) www.instituteforgovernment.org.uk/events/keynote-speech-rt-hon-carwyn-jones-am-minister-wales-our-future-union-%E2%80%93-perspective-wales.

[48] Commission on Justice in Wales, *Terms of Reference* https://gov.wales/commission-justice-wales/terms-reference.

[49] HC Deb 8 December 1997, vol 302, col 685 (Ron Davies).

complex: first, because the Scottish Parliament, unlike the Welsh Assembly, would have primary law-making power in devolved areas; and second, because devolution in Scotland could credibly claim to have been underpinned by a rival claim to sovereignty: the sovereignty of the people of Scotland given voice by the Claim of Right and by the Scottish Constitutional Convention. Accordingly, the assurance given by the then Secretary of State for Scotland, Donald Dewar, that 'the United Kingdom Parliament is, and will remain, sovereign in all matters',[50] was given statutory form in section 28(7) of the Scotland Act. The Scottish Parliament's law-making power in devolved areas, it read 'does not affect the power of the Parliament of the United Kingdom to make laws for Scotland'. Devolution, then, according to Dewar, was no limit to the supremacy of the UK Parliament. On the contrary, it was a choice by Parliament to 'exercise that sovereignty by devolving legislative responsibility … without diminishing its own powers'.[51] However, even if initially thought to be legally inconsequential, section 28(7) served an important political purpose: a play to devo-sceptics on the Labour left that reinforced the subservient nature of the new legislature. It also served a constitutional purpose, anticipating and undermining any claim for an enforceable or absolute requirement for the UK Parliament to obtain the consent of the new legislatures before legislating in devolved areas.

The conventional wisdom about section 28(7) – reflected in Davies's answer to the Commons above – has not held. In the *Scottish Continuity Bill reference*,[52] the UK Law Officers invited the Supreme Court, inter alia, to rule that section 17 of the UK Withdrawal from the European Union (Legal Continuity) (Scotland) Bill – which aimed to ensure that Scottish would law continue to function without interruptions or gaps post-Brexit – was ultra vires of the Scotland Act 1998. That provision purported to make the exercise of UK ministers' powers to make subordinate legislation under UK primary legislation, but which affected devolved matters, subject to the consent of the Scottish Government. The Court accepted the invitation. Because section 17 sought to condition the exercise of the UK Parliament's freedom to legislate in devolved areas (Westminster would be incapable of authorising UK ministers to make the relevant subordinate legislation in devolved areas absent the consent of their Scottish counterparts), the Court held that these provisions amounted to an unlawful amendment of a protected provision – section 28(7) – within the category of protected statutes listed in schedule 4.[53] The Court's reasoning here is not obviously clear;[54] however, there are two important consequences that flow from it. First, section 28(7) and (later inserted with the conferral of primary law-making

[50] HC Deb 24 July 1997, vol 298, col 1046 (Donald Dewar).
[51] ibid.
[52] [2018] UKSC 64.
[53] ibid paras 43–54.
[54] See C McCorkindale and A McHarg, 'The Supreme Court and Devolution: The Scottish Continuity Bill Reference' (2019) (2) *Juridical Review* 190.

powers) its Welsh analogue[55] can no longer be assumed to be mere exercises in political and constitutional symbolism. Rather, they create hard legal limits to the legislative competence of the devolved legislatures who may not qualify the UK Parliament's use of its legislative sovereignty. Second, this fits a more general, still emerging, line in the constitutional jurisprudence of the Supreme Court: a conservative radicalism in which judicial activism is justified – and no longer constrained – by concern for the effective exercise of Parliament's legislative and scrutiny functions.[56]

The primary safeguard for devolution lay in the political sphere: a constitutional convention, carried over from the experience of devolution in Northern Ireland, that was articulated in this context by Lord Sewel, the Minister of State in the Scottish Office responsible for steering the Scotland Bill through the House of Lords – that Westminster 'would not normally legislate with regard to devolved matters' without the consent of the devolved legislatures.[57] The scope of the Sewel convention has evolved in Scotland and in Wales so as to apply not only to legislation made by the UK Parliament in devolved areas, but also to legislation made by the UK Parliament that alters the limits of devolved competence. By and large, the procedure has operated without controversy – the UK Parliament regularly legislates in devolved areas, and in the vast majority of cases it does so with the consent (and sometimes at the request) of the devolved institutions.[58]

In 2014, however, driven by that uncertainty about the outcome of the referendum on Scottish independence, focus at the centre turned away from the preservation of Westminster's constitutional status and towards the strengthening of constitutional protections for devolution in Scotland and then in Wales. Building on the agreement expressed in the Vow that 'The Scottish Parliament is permanent', the Smith Commission made two key constitutional recommendations that, in its view, would provide for 'a durable but responsive constitutional settlement'.[59] The first, that 'UK legislation will state that the Scottish Parliament

[55] Government of Wales Act 2006, s 93(5).

[56] See the 'new' understanding of parliamentary sovereignty discussed in M Elliott, 'A New Approach to Constitutional Adjudication: Miller II in the Supreme Court' (*Public Law for Everyone Blog*, 24 September 2019) https://publiclawforeveryone.com/2019/09/24/the-supreme-courts-judgment-in-cherry-miller-no-2-a-new-approach-to-constitutional-adjudication/.

[57] On the evolution of the Sewel Convention, see A McHarg, 'Constitutional Change and Territorial Consent: The Miller Case and the Sewel Convention' in M Elliott, J Williams and AL Young (eds), *The UK Constitution after Miller: Brexit and Beyond* (Hart Publishing, 2016) ch 12.

[58] A Paun et al, *Devolution at 20* (Institute for Government, 2019) 63–68, www.instituteforgovernment.org.uk/sites/default/files/publications/Devolution%20at%2020.pdf. The major exception to the rule lies in the Brexit arena, where the refusal of legislative consent has been one way in which the Scottish and Welsh administrations have sought to register their opposition to – or to shape the terms of – the UK's exit from the EU (see, eg A Paun et al, 'The Sewel Convention' (Institute for Government, 8 December 2020) www.instituteforgovernment.org.uk/explainers/sewel-convention.

[59] *Report of the Smith Commission for Further Devolution of Powers to the Scottish Parliament* (2014) 12 (Smith Report).

and Scottish Government are permanent institutions',[60] finds statutory expression in section 63A of the Scotland Act 1998 (as amended by the Scotland Act 2016). That section restates Smith's recommendation before qualifying it in two important ways. First, having 'declared' in section 63A(2) that the 'purpose' of the permanence clause is 'to signify the commitment of the Parliament and Government of the United Kingdom to the Scottish Parliament and the Scottish Government', Parliament has obscured the question as to whether or not the purpose of the provision also is to create an enforceable legal restriction against the unilateral revocation of devolution by Westminster. Second, section 63A itself explicitly provides for the way in which the devolved institutions (their 'permanence' notwithstanding) may lawfully be abolished: (only) following 'a decision of the people of Scotland voting in a referendum'.[61] The second recommendation, that 'The Sewel Convention will be put on a statutory footing',[62] was reflected in the new section 28(8) of the Scotland Act 1998, which qualifies the continued legislative sovereignty of the UK Parliament by 'recognis[ing] that the Parliament of the United Kingdom will not normally legislate with regard to devolved matters without the consent of the Scottish Parliament'. Identical provisions made for Wales in sections 1 and 2 of the 2017 Act demonstrated the influence of the Scotland Act 2016[63] (and that wider sense that in Wales a significant driver of devolution is comparison between, and catch up with, the evolving Scottish settlement), but here too the democratic justification was grounded in a political nationalism. Whilst nodding at the legal ambiguity – 'the British Constitution,' said Silk, 'does not allow for the entrenchment of any law' and so 'the UK Parliament would still have the power to abolish the National Assembly' – the Commission nevertheless took the view that devolution 'had achieved a constitutional status that means it has become inconceivable that that Parliament would be able to abolish the National Assembly without a clear mandate from the people of Wales'.[64]

Whether or not these provisions strengthen the constitutional status of devolution within the Union remains fully to be tested, but we might make three observations at this stage. First, there is cause for some degree of pessimism following the judgment of the Supreme Court in *Miller I*.[65] There, having held that it would require an Act of Parliament to authorise notification of the UK's intention to leave the EU in accordance with Article 50 of the Treaty on European Union, short shrift was nevertheless given to the argument that, by virtue of it being written into statute, the Court might adjudicate on whether

[60] ibid 13.
[61] Scotland Act 2016, s 1.
[62] Smith Report (n 58) 13.
[63] Rawlings, 'The Welsh Way/Y Fforrd Gymreig' (2019) 305.
[64] *Report of the Commission on Devolution in Wales: Part II, Empowerment and Responsibility – Legislative Powers to Strengthen Wales* (2014) para 13.3.30.
[65] *R (Miller) v Secretary of State for Exiting the European Union* [2017] UKSC 5 (*Miller I*).

any resulting Notification Bill would require legislative consent to be sought from the devolved legislatures. Far from being placed 'on a statutory footing', as the Smith Commission had recommended, the Court took the view that section 28(8) amounted to no more than statutory recognition of the already existing political convention. The purpose of the provision, the Court said, was not to create legal rights and duties on the part of the devolved and UK governments; rather, it was to 'entrench [Sewel] as a convention'.[66] Having established that the rule was political rather than legal in character, the Court then adopted the (somewhat surprising)[67] position that it 'cannot give legal rulings on [the] operation or scope [of the convention, because] those matters are determined within the political world'.[68] It seems unlikely that the permanence provisions will be tested in the same way: the chances of a unilateral revocation of devolution to Scotland and Wales are surely extremely slim. Nevertheless, one might wonder whether these reforms indicate (or might be symptomatic of) a more general evolution towards constitutional entrenchment. We see, in the use of these so-called 'referendum locks', an explicit attempt by the UK Parliament in 2016 and 2017 to bind future Parliaments as to the manner and form of such significant changes to the territorial distribution of power. Whether the Supreme Court will pick up on this signal remains to be seen, but there is a compelling and twofold democratic justification in play. On the one hand, repeal by referendum is a natural analogue to the constitutive referendums held in 1997. On the other hand, to insist on Parliament's continuing sovereignty in this field is to concede that devolution may by right be abolished even where to do so would run counter to the will of the people of Scotland and Wales, the consent of the Scottish and Welsh Parliaments and the views of the MPs elected to represent Scotland and Wales in the UK Parliament.[69]

Second, one might say in light of all of this that the constitutional safeguards in the Scotland Act 2016 and in the Wales Act 2017 amount to no more and no less than the legal constitution catching up with the political constitution: on the one hand, restating in law, but adding little of value to a political rule (Sewel) that for the most part has been respected on all sides; on the other, declaring the permanence in law of institutions that by 2004 had already been said to have been accepted, politically, 'as an integral and 'permanent' feature of Scottish [and later, of Welsh] and UK governance'.[70]

Third, it might nevertheless be argued that, putting aside the legal effects of these provisions, they serve an important symbolic function. As Elliott and Thomas have said:

[66] ibid para 149.

[67] For analysis, see McHarg, 'Constitutional Change and Territorial Consent' (2016).

[68] *Miller I* (n 64) para 146.

[69] For a defence of manner and form entrenchment, see M Gordon, *Parliamentary Sovereignty in the UK Constitution: Process, Politics and Democracy* (Hart Publishing, 2015).

[70] B Winetrobe, 'Scottish Devolution: Developing Practice in Multi-Layer Governance' in J Jowell and D Oliver (eds), *The Changing Constitution*, 5th edn (Oxford University Press, 2004) 193.

> If nothing else, the 'permanence' provisions illuminate just how far the narrative has moved on from the idea that devolution amounts to nothing more than a revocable – and so potentially transitory – sharing by Westminster of part of its law-making power.[71]

Symbols matter, of course. Not only because of what they signal to constitutional actors about how to navigate the political constitution, but – as we have seen with regard to section 28(7) of the Scotland Act 1998 – because from those symbols might crystallise, through processes of legal argument and judicial interpretation, hard legal effects.

V. ANOTHER 20 YEARS: A LEGACY UNDER ATTACK?

What, then, for the future? How might devolution develop – or regress – during the next 20 years? One thing that might be said with some degree of certainty is that with the UK's post-Brexit relationship with the EU still to settle, with its continued membership of the Council of Europe called into question, with Northern Ireland walking a constitutional tightrope, with a new settlement for Wales still taking shape and with Scottish independence firmly on the agenda, the future of the UK's territorial constitution is up for grabs. Indeed, if the first 20 years has been one of a broadening scope and deepening entrenchment of devolution, it is possible that the next two decades will be defined by the vulnerability of devolution in the face of manifold pressures. Some of these pressures are unique to specific settlements; others cut across the devolution settlements and their relationship with the centre.

The clearest threat to devolution in the UK, of course, is the very 'problem' of secession that it was in (no small) part designed to address. When asked by the Institute for Government to reflect, 20 years later, on the success of New Labour's devolution project, Blair himself was equivocal on this point:

> Well, we're still the UK and we're still together so you've got to put a tick there. Are there still pressures for secession? Well, in Scotland, yes, but I still think they won't succeed unless Brexit pushes us into a position where that kind of gets Scottish independence over the line – if you have hard Brexit, which is possible … I don't think there is a strong move for independence in Wales …[72]

In Scotland, secession has barely fallen off the agenda since it was rejected in 2014. Pro-independence majorities have been returned in every Scottish Parliament election and (in terms of Scottish seats) UK Parliament general election that has followed, and polls that were slow to shift in the immediate aftermath of the Brexit referendum appear more recently to have indicated a move towards

[71] M Elliott and R Thomas, *Public Law*, 3rd edn (Oxford University Press, 2017).
[72] Blair, 'Devolution, Brexit and the Future of the Union' (2019) 3.

majority support for independence.[73] Following a strong result for the SNP in the December 2019 general election, when the party won 45 per cent of the (Scottish) vote and 48 of 59 (Scottish) seats (a gain of 13 on the 2017 general election), the Scottish Government published *Scotland's Right to Choose: Putting Scotland's Future in Scotland's Hands*. This document set out the democratic case for a second independence referendum, built on: the characterisation of the UK as being a voluntary union of nations based on the consent of its constituent parts; a 'material change of circumstances' since the 2014 vote, that being Brexit and what the Brexit process has revealed about Scotland's place within the UK; and the mandate conferred by concurrent pro-independence majorities elected at Holyrood and (by the Scottish seats) at Westminster.[74] In addition, the document made clear that the preferred route to independence is via a referendum that is legal, fair and decisive. This is likely to mean putting the legality of the referendum beyond doubt by engaging with the UK government to amend the Scotland Act to make explicit the competence of the Scottish Parliament to enact the necessary authorising legislation. However, if the response by the UK government is to reject the Scottish Government's advances, the latter has made known its intention, as a last resort, to legislate without a section 30 order and to test the legality of a unilateral referendum Bill in the Supreme Court.[75]

As it was in the immediate aftermath of the Brexit referendum (when the then Prime Minister, Theresa May, told Nicola Sturgeon that 'now is not the time' for a second independence referendum),[76] the response by the UK government so far has been dismissive – a short letter by the Prime Minister, Boris Johnson, barely engaged with the substantive arguments made by the Scottish Government before reaching the conclusion that he 'cannot agree to any request for a transfer of power that would lead to further independence referendums'.[77] During the next 20 years, then, the push of nationalism towards independence is likely to continue, but in the face of three related challenges: to persuade the electorate of the advantages of independence in order to build a sufficient political mandate; to use any such political mandate to persuade the UK government to make the desired amendments to legislative competence in order to place any referendum beyond reproach; and to persuade critics within the SNP – impatient with what they see as being an overly cautious approach by its current

[73] See J Curtice, 'Is Brexit Fuelling Support for Independence?' (*What Scotland Thinks*, 3 November 2020) https://whatscotlandthinks.org/2020/11/is-brexit-fuelling-support-for-independence/.

[74] *Scotland's Right to Choose: Putting Scotland's Future in Scotland's Hands* (2019) 13–18.

[75] ibid 20; M Russell, 'This Is the SNP's Routemap to a Scottish Independence Referendum in Full' *The National* (23 January 2021) www.thenational.scot/news/19033561.snps-road-scottish-independence-referendum-plan-full/.

[76] 'Theresa May: "Now Is Not the Time" for Scotland Independence Vote' *BBC News* (16 March 2017).

[77] UK Government, 'Letter from PM Boris Johnson to Scottish First Minister Nicola Sturgeon: 14 January 2020' www.gov.uk/government/publications/letter-from-pm-boris-johnson-to-scottish-first-minister-nicola-sturgeon-14-january-2020.

leadership – that a consensual and unambiguously legal process is the surest way to secure losers' consent, to ensure healthy secession negotiations with the UK and to achieve recognition from the international community and key institutions such as the EU.[78]

Interestingly, too, Blair might have reason to rethink his assessment about support for independence in Wales. There is some considerable distance to travel before the prediction made by Plaid Cymru's leader, Adam Price, that there will be a referendum on Welsh independence by 2030, can be assessed.[79] Nevertheless, opinion polls appear to demonstrate a rise in support for Welsh independence (from approximately 14 per cent in 1997 to a base level of around 21–24 per cent, increasing to around 33 per cent if such a vote would lead to Wales remaining in the EU post-Brexit),[80] whilst the Welsh First Minister, Mark Drakeford, caused a stir when, giving evidence to the Welsh Assembly's External Affairs Committee, he said (albeit with more nuance than headlines might suggest) that Wales's long-term commitment to the Union 'can't possibly be unconditional'.[81] Yet there are two more immediate challenges ahead for devolution in Wales, one indigenous, the other shared with Scotland. The first is structural. Whilst the UK government has demonstrated a reluctance to reopen the settlement once more following the 2017 Act reforms, the Commission on Justice in Wales (the Thomas Commission), has recommended in its final report that justice should be fully devolved.[82] The Commission's findings were presented in stark practical terms, but with constitutional bite. With numerous examples cited throughout, the report opened with the assertion that people in Wales are being 'let down by the system in its current state',[83] exacerbated by the 'pointless complexity, confusion and incoherence in justice and policing' that is created by the current division of responsibilities between Westminster and Cardiff. In order to align justice policy with other (devolved) social and economic priorities, the substantial devolution of justice powers of the kind known to Scotland and Northern Ireland was seen to be the only realistic way

[78] See C McCorkindale and A McHarg, 'Constitutional Pathways to a Second Scottish Independence Referendum' (*UKCLA Blog*, 13 January 2020) https://ukconstitutionallaw.org/2020/01/13/chris-mccorkindale-and-aileen-mcharg-constitutional-pathways-to-a-second-scottish-independence-referendum/.

[79] 'Welsh Independence Referendum "before 2030" Plaid Leader Says' *BBC News* (4 October 2019).

[80] See, eg W Hayward, 'Survey Responses Show How Many People Support Welsh Independence' (*Wales Online*, 7 November 2020) www.walesonline.co.uk/news/politics/welsh-independence-survey-results-yescymru-19233106; M Shipton, 'What the Latest Political Poll Shows as Abolish the Assembly on Course to Win for Four Senedd Seats' (*Wales Online*, 4 November 2020) www.walesonline.co.uk/news/politics/senedd-election-poll-yougov-cardiff-19220474.

[81] 'Independence: Mark Drakeford Rejects Plaid Cymru Claim He's "Indy-curious"' *BBC News* (9 July 2019).

[82] *Justice in Wales for the People of Wales* (2019) 8, 149.

[83] Lord Thomas, quoted in 'Justice Powers for Wales Urged by Commission' *BBC News* (24 October 2019).

to achieve a 'practical long-term solution [that] makes a difference to the people of Wales'.[84] This, the Commission reported, would encompass a number of enabling reforms, including a further devolution Act by the UK Parliament to make the necessary transfer of legislative competence and executive functions, a corresponding transfer of the relevant financial resources, the carving out of a distinct Welsh legal jurisdiction and the creation of a new Justice Department in the Welsh Government led by a cabinet minister.[85] As against the strong findings of the Commission, the response by the UK government has been sceptical, if not outright dismissive: no more than a commitment 'to work closely with the Welsh Government to ensure justice policies are aligned and take into account Welsh needs'.[86] It seems clear, then, that the next 20 years of devolution in Wales will also be a period of substantial unsettlement – this time fought on the terrain of justice.

The second challenge is existential. Devolution in Wales was won on the narrowest of margins and, whilst support for the settlement is now on more solid ground, there exists a persistent, residual, anti-devolution sentiment. This not only finds expression in opinion polls (within the range of 15–20 per cent), but has manifested too in electoral politics, with UKIP winning six seats at the 2016 Welsh Assembly election and, squeezed by the Brexit Party within the Assembly and by the Abolish the Welsh Assembly Party on the outside, has taken an avowedly abolitionist turn.[87] In Scotland too devo-scepticism is a minority sport, but one that ought not to be ignored. Domination by the SNP as the party of government since its breakthrough win in 2007 and the brush with independence in 2014 have reinvigorated that voice: in pockets of public opinion, in opinion columns and now, with UKIP vowing to stand in the 2021 Scottish Parliament election on a commitment to abolish the Scottish Parliament, in electoral politics.[88] Even if these internal challenges to the very existence of devolution in Wales and in Scotland flounder, there is a second-order, external challenge that they serve to fuel: a more aggressive approach to devolution from the centre. When redrawing the boundaries of devolution in Wales in 2017, the UK government was keen not to repeat in Wales what it perceived to be the 'mistake' of conceding too much to Scotland in 1998. The 'clawback' of powers *from* Wales in 2017 and the resistance to calls for the devolution of justice *to* Wales that has followed may portend a more assertive UK attitude in relation to devolution that has already manifested in (dubious) calls for devolution to be suspended in the

[84] *Justice in Wales* (n 81) 464.

[85] ibid ch 12.

[86] M George, 'Getting It Just Right: Delivering Justice in Wales' (*Senedd Research Blog*, 31 January 2020) https://seneddresearch.blog/2020/01/31/getting-it-just-right-delivering-justice-in-wales/.

[87] 'UKIP's Neil Hamilton Wants Election Deal with Abolish the Assembly Party' (*Wales Online*, 10 January 2020) www.walesonline.co.uk/news/wales-news/neil-hamilton-ukip-abolish-assembly-17542281.

[88] 'UKIP Says Next Job Is to Abolish Holyrood' *The Herald* (27 January 2020).

face of a public health emergency,[89] and seems likely over the next stage of devolution to seek to minimise territorial difference across the Union with intrusive regulation from the centre of the UK's internal market.[90]

There was equivocation too when Blair turned to the primary purpose of devolution: to bring decision-making closer to the people of Scotland, Wales and Northern Ireland. On the one hand, he said, 'the people in Wales and Scotland have got the right to elect who they want to elect'.[91] On the other hand, he expressed disappointment (albeit qualified by his view that 'twenty years is not long in a new constitutional settlement')[92] that the devolved governments and assemblies had shown less interest in public service reform than had their counterparts in Westminster and in Whitehall. 'In the end,' he said, 'there will be a market for people who are stepping forward and being in favour of [public service] reform.'[93] Whether this critique of devolution's first 20 years is fair or not, the evolution of devolution during that period has not only seen the scope of devolved powers expand (bringing more areas of responsibility 'closer to the people'), but has also addressed the fundamental problem of political legitimacy that threatened to undermine the pre-devolution Union. There are, however, three caveats that might be added here. First, the political dynamics within each of the devolved legislatures have an actual or potentially distorting effect on the way in which policy debates about the reform of public services are framed and conducted. This is to say that the traditional assumptions that underpin parliamentary democracy – that it is grounded in a battle for ideas (left versus right, collectivism versus individualism, social democracy versus liberalism) and driven by a genuine contest for power that conditions, and is conditioned by, alternativee rule – have been displaced. So, in Scotland and in Wales, we see policy debates give way to constitutional questions about independence (in the case of the former) and about the evolution of the devolution settlement (in the case of the latter). The SNP in Scotland and Labour in Wales both dominate electorally, with little prospect of a meaningful contest for power any time soon.[94] It seems likely, then, that polarisation *about* devolution – a leftward pull towards independence; a rightward pull towards abolition or a more assertive unionism – will characterise the devolution debate in the next period rather than

[89] H Hill, 'Coronavirus Is a Wake Up Call: Devolution Isn't Working' (*CapX*, 7 April 2020) https://capx.co/coronavirus-is-a-wake-up-call-devolution-isnt-working/.

[90] See N McEwen, 'The Internal Market Bill: Impacts for Devolution' (*Centre on Constitutional Change Blog*, 11 September 2020) www.centreonconstitutionalchange.ac.uk/news-and-opinion/internal-market-bill-implications-devolution.

[91] Blair (n 1) 4.

[92] ibid.

[93] ibid.

[94] Indeed, it is striking that in the 2016 Scottish Parliament election the second largest party, the Scottish Conservatives, ran explicitly on a 'programme for opposition' rather than on a programme for government! See Scottish Conservative and Unionist Manifesto 2016, 8 www.scottishconservatives.com/wordpress/wp-content/uploads/2016/04/Scottish-Conservative-Manifesto_2016-DIGITAL-SINGLE-PAGES.pdf.

contestation *within* devolution about which parties should control the levers of power and to what policy ends.

Second, the devolution of power *to* the devolved legislatures has yet to be (and shows little prospect of being) matched by a corresponding devolution *from* those institutions to local government. Local government in Scotland – which had been bitterly divided about devolution in the 1970s – was (largely) won over to the cause in the 1990s by the promise of a more cooperative and consensual relationship with the devolved institutions than had been enjoyed with successive Conservative governments in the 1980s and 1990s.[95] Two decades later, that promise – in Wales as much as in Scotland – remains unfulfilled. Far from local government emerging 'as a powerful institution and [becoming] its own justification',[96] devolution has retained a certain centripetal force – one principle set out in the 1997 devolution White Paper, that 'local authorities should be accountable through local elections', has, as James Mitchell said, been subsumed by another: that it should be for the newly devolved legislatures to 'set the national framework within which local government and other bodies operate'.[97]

Third, there are serious questions about the capacity of the devolved institutions adequately to perform their legislative, scrutiny and executive functions without the further structural reforms needed to accommodate the growing scope of their legislative competences as well as their increased fiscal responsibilities. Indeed, in each of the devolved jurisdictions, we are beginning to see (sometimes tentative, sometimes limited, sometimes frustrated) movements in this area. In Scotland, for example, a number of prominent voices – a former Deputy President of the UK Supreme Court,[98] two former Presiding Officers of the Scottish Parliament[99] and, most recently, a former First Minister[100] – have come to favour the case for a second chamber in the Scottish Parliament, whilst an advisory group to the current Presiding Officer, Ken Macintosh, has made a number of recommendations as to how the Parliament's legislative, scrutiny and engagement functions might be improved.[101] In Wales, despite its recognition that 'Calling for more politicians is unpopular',[102] an Expert Panel on Assembly Electoral Reform has recommended to the Llywdd and the Assembly Commission that the Assembly requires an additional 20–30 members to cope

[95] J Mitchell, 'Local Government and Devolution: Mutual Respect or Parity of Esteem?' (2019) 23 *Edinburgh Law Review* 428.

[96] JAG Griffith, 'Foreword' in M Loughlin et al (eds), *Half a Century of Municipal Decline, 1935–1985* (Allen & Unwin, 1985) xiii.

[97] Mitchell, 'Local Government and Devolution' (2019) 433.

[98] Lord Hope, 'What a Second Chamber Can Do for Legislative Scrutiny' (2004) 25 *Statute Law Review* 3.

[99] 'Presiding Officer Calls for Holyrood Second Chamber' *BBC News* (9 March 2016).

[100] L Paterson, 'Lord McConnell: Ex-first Minister Wants Second Chamber to Keep Holyrood in Check' *The Times* (14 May 2019).

[101] *Report of the Commission on Parliamentary Reform* (2017) www.parliament.scot/parliamentary-business/CurrentCommittees/108084.aspx.

[102] *Report of the Expert Panel on Assembly Electoral Reform* (2017) 6.

with its growing workload without 'risking its ability to deliver effectively for the people of Wales'.[103]

VI. CONCLUSION

If the first 20 years have been marked by the broadening scope and the deepening constitutional status of devolution, we might expect – and certainly we should hope – that, if devolution is to survive its manifold challenges, the next 20 years will see a turn towards the constitutional architecture – structurally, institutionally and procedurally – needed to make it work within and across the UK. Underpinning any such reform, however, must be a shift in structure and a shift in culture at the centre. Devolution too often is thought of from the centre (and too often is taught in our law schools and presented in our textbooks) to be a mere feature of our constitution – a peculiarity at the state's Celtic fringes or of a type with local government and forms of (English) regionalism. It is more than that: it is a (perhaps even the) fundamental principle of the UK constitution that has disturbed the 'bedrock' of parliamentary sovereignty and has reinforced the nature and the implications of this pluri-national state. It is for this reason that Blair's aim to defeat nationalism was always bound to fail – nationalism is (and since the Acts of Union has always been) bound up in the idea of union itself. Whether or not the UK will stand in 20 years' time will depend upon its ability to overcome New Labour's legacy of omission: to reorganise, at the centre, qua union meaningfully to accommodate that reality.

[103] ibid.

7

The 'Evolution' of Devolution: Assessing Labour's Legacy in England

ARIANNA GIOVANNINI

I. INTRODUCTION

DEBATES CONCERNING POLITICAL decentralisation in the UK date back at least to the beginning of the nineteenth century. Yet only over the past two decades have we seen the implementation of devolution across the country, and the Labour Party has undoubtedly played a key role in this process. Whilst, until the late 1970s, Labour's approach to devolution was mainly 'reactive', responding to pressures coming from the 'Celtic nations', proactive discussions within the party and clearer policy lines started to concretise in the 1980s. From 1997 onwards, once back in power, Labour opened a process of constitutional reform and put devolution into practice, adopting an asymmetrical approach tailored around the different nations of the UK – even though divisions were often rife within the party over the subject. After the 2010 general election, however, once in government, the Conservative party has increasingly (and pragmatically) taken ownership of the devolution agenda. Thus, 20 years on, devolution still remains an 'unfinished business' and the process is far from settled.

Against this background, the aim of this contribution is to assess the legacy of the Labour Party in the ongoing process of devolution, focusing on England – which remains, by and large, the 'gaping hole' in the devolution settlement and is therefore one of the most controversial cases within the UK. The chapter will: (i) examine the roots of the English devolution debate within the Labour Party; (ii) offer a critical overview of the way in which devolution was framed, conceived and put into practice by the Labour Party whilst in power (1997–2010) in England, focusing first on policy developments and then assessing the party political dimension of the debate; and (iii) explore how the devolution agenda has evolved from 2010 onwards, concentrating in particular on continuities and changes between Labour and Conservative approaches, and evaluating Labour's legacy in this respect as well as in relation to subsequent developments. The analysis will show that divisions as well as dissonance between different views and approaches within the Labour Party hindered the devolution agenda in England during its time in government. As such, English devolution remained a dilemma within Labour's programme of constitutional reform that the party did not manage to address in full back then, and with which it still struggles to grapple.

II. THE LABOUR PARTY AND DEVOLUTION IN ENGLAND: TRACING THE ROOTS

In many respects, devolution was one of the flagship policies within the process of constitutional reform initiated by the Labour Party after the 1997 election landslide. Debates on devolution started to take prominence around the 1960s, as a means to respond to the 'nationalist wave' and the (re)emergence of the centre–periphery disputes across mainland Britain.[1] However, back then, the Labour Party's position was mostly 'reactive' and pragmatic. Indeed, at the time, Labour's ideological inheritance meant that any clear opening towards devolution could threaten its social and economic philosophy.[2] Caught between the need to respond to the rise of nationalism in the 'Celtic nations' and a desire to stick to the values underpinning the party's ideology, in the late 1960s Harold Wilson's government resorted to a Royal Commission on the Constitution to address issues concerning the territorial distribution of political power in the UK. However, what came to be known as the Kilbrandon Commission produced mixed recommendations that were interpreted in different ways by the various political actors (including MPs and opinion formers) involved in the debate.[3] In the end, the Commission took the view that it was 'not necessary to have a uniform system of government in all parts of Great Britain',[4] and suggested that 'devolution to Scotland and Wales was possible without major constitutional consequences in England'.[5] Indeed, in 1974, when the proposals made by the Commission were examined and translated into a White Paper, it turned out that 'devolution in England would be postponed for further consideration'.[6]

This helps to explain the position of the Labour Party towards devolution up until the 1990s. On the one hand, devolution was mainly seen as a way to address the 'nationalist wave' whilst maintaining political control especially in Scotland and Wales. On the other hand, this also emphasises that from the inception of

[1] V Bogdanor, *Devolution in the United Kingdom* (Oxford University Press, 2001); J Mitchell, *Devolution in the UK* (Manchester University Press, 2010).
[2] Bogdanor, *Devolution in the United Kingdom* (2001).
[3] ibid.
[4] Kilbrandon Commission Report, Cmnd 5460, para 1217.
[5] Bogdanor (n 1) 176.
[6] White Paper, *Democracy and Devolution: Proposals for Scotland and Wales* (Cmnd 5732, 1974).

the debate on devolution within Parliament, the Labour Party did not take any overt stance to address the so-called 'English Question'.[7] Indeed, for a long time the issue of devolution in England was quietly left on the back-burner.

A more proactive approach to English devolution started to emerge within Labour only in the 1980s. This took the form of a growing interest in some form of regionalism among sections of the party, which built on pre-existing, yet fragmented, debates championed by actors in the regions of the North of England that had been going on at a local level since 1919.[8] Whilst, until the late 1970s, the idea of devolution (in particular to Scotland) was perceived almost as a threat by regional Labour leaders in the North, this position started to change in the 1980s. Economic as well as political factors underpinned the shift. In this period, a distinctive form of 'regionalism of discontent'[9] stemmed from concerns about rapid deindustrialisation and its social fallouts. This was coupled with the presence of a Conservative government that was politically and culturally at odds with the North and a willingness on the part of local authorities, business and trade unions to reverse negative economic trends. As a result, in the 1980s, the Labour Party opened an internal discussion over regional devolution strategies as a means to address economic inequalities across England and, above all, to bridge the North–South divide.[10] This, again, was led by regional elites in the North (who sought to redeem regionalist arguments within the party as a way to tackle economic and political weaknesses) and helped to influence a wider debate within Labour in the following decade.[11] At the same time, 'regions' started to emerge as the most suitable scale to develop a devolution policy across England – based on both political and economic arguments.

Labour began to engage more widely, at the national level, with the idea of regional devolution for England in the 1990s, while in opposition.[12] These efforts materialised in the publication, in 1995, of the consultation document 'A Choice for England'.[13] This laid out Labour's plans for English regional government and provided a first blueprint for a regional devolution policy agenda. In essence, the paper outlined a long-term strategy for the creation of directly elected regional assemblies (ERAs) in England. The first phase involved setting up indirectly elected regional chambers (with strategic policy coordination functions); this was to be followed by a second phase in which ERAs would be set up, subject

[7] R Hazel (ed), *The English Question* (Manchester University Press, 2006).

[8] J Tomaney, 'The Idea of English Regionalism' in Hazel, *The English Question* (2006).

[9] ibid 172.

[10] A Giovannini, 'Towards a "New English Regionalism" in the North? The Case of Yorkshire First' (2016) 87 *The Political Quarterly* 590.

[11] Tomaney, 'The Idea of English Regionalism' (2006).

[12] C Jeffery, 'Elected Regional Assemblies in England: An Anatomy of Policy Failure' in M Sandford (ed), *The Northern Veto* (Manchester University Press, 2009); J Tomaney, 'Democratically Elected Regional Government in England: The Work of the North East Constitutional Convention' (2000) 70 *Regional Studies* 383.

[13] Labour Party, 1995.

to public support through referendums, to add democratic accountability to the emerging devolved regional architecture. 'A Choice for England' also proposed the creation of uniform, unitary tiers for local government, to avoid duplication and mismanagement of governance in the English regions.[14]

Thus, the consultation paper can be understood as the key document that laid the foundations for a policy strategy on regional devolution to England. This was subsequently translated into political commitment and became part of the 1997 Labour manifesto.[15] The next section analyses how the Labour Party built on these premises once in government (1997–2010).

III. THE LABOUR PARTY IN GOVERNMENT: DEVOLUTION AND THE 'ENGLISH EXCEPTION'

The 1997 Labour Party manifesto included a section entitled 'Devolution: Strengthening the Union', which recognised the role of territorial distinctiveness across the country.[16] The document presented the UK as 'a partnership enriched by distinct national identities and traditions' and pledged that, once in government, Labour would 'meet the demand for decentralisation of power to Scotland and Wales, once established in referendums'.[17] Other sections outlined plans for Northern Ireland (linking decentralisation to the peace process) and for the establishment of a devolved city government in London, with substantial powers over strategic policy areas.[18]

Devolution to the English regions did feature in the manifesto. This reflected the principles for a regional devolution agenda outlined in 'A Choice for England'. However, in practical terms, the strategy presented was much more vague than the one set for the other nations of the UK and London. No clear commitments were made and, beyond stating that a Labour government would establish regional chambers in England with policy coordination roles for transport, planning, economic development, bids for European funding and land use planning,[19] no details were provided about the powers of these new bodies or their composition. The timing of the proposed reform was also cautious. Clear deadlines were set for the establishment of new devolved institutions in Scotland and Wales and for holding the respective referendums. In the case of the English regions, however, the manifesto went only as far as stating that, since demands

[14] S Leach, J Stewart and G Jones, *Centralisation, Devolution and the Future of Local Government in England* (Routledge, 2018); D Wilson and C Game, *Local Government in the United Kingdom* (Palgrave, 2011).

[15] Tomaney, 'Democratically Elected Regional Government in England (2000); Giovannini, 'Towards a "New English Regionalism"' (2016).

[16] Labour Party Manifesto, 1997.

[17] ibid.

[18] ibid.

[19] ibid.

varied across England, 'in time [Labour] will introduce legislation to allow the people, region by region, to decide in a referendum whether they want directly elected regional government'.[20]

Once elected and in government, Labour pressed ahead with devolution to Scotland, Wales and Northern Ireland, putting this at the core of its ambitious programme of constitutional reform. However, with the exception of London, the plan for regional devolution in England was not rolled out during the first mandate. The only action taken in this direction was the creation of nine Regional Development Agencies (RDAs), ie non-departmental public bodies, tasked with driving economic development, business efficiency, investment and competitiveness, employment, skills and sustainable development in their regions.[21] In addition, RDAs had to contribute to policy on transport, planning and land use, further and higher education, crime prevention, housing, public health, tourism, culture and sport. Crucially, members of RDAs' governing boards were appointed by the government and included mainly business community representatives, as well as voluntary sector, education and local government figures. Thus, they were established from the top-down by central government without public consultation, and they were not directly elected. The Regional Development Agencies Act 1998 did provide for the creation of Regional Chambers to monitor the work of RDAs; however, these bodies were optional and non-binding and, again, were not directly elected (where established, their members were drawn from local authorities).

This suggests that Labour showed some degree of political commitment to devolution in England. Yet, progress in giving legislative form to that pledge was slow and, as Tomaney[22] notes, reflected the deep ambivalence of the Labour government about devolving more powers to the English regions. The capital city was the only area in England where political devolution, in the form of the Greater London Authority with a directly elected mayor, was delivered in 1998. In the rest of the nation, only a fragile, top-down devolution architecture was established, in the form of RDAs and regional chambers. Thus, since its inception, devolution was framed, conceived and put into practice by Labour in very different ways across the country.[23] In short, drawing on the principle of asymmetry, Scotland, Wales and Northern Ireland were granted substantial *political devolution* (although in different forms and with different powers) through mechanisms of representation and policy-making based on communities of identity and principles of autonomy and/or self-government.[24]

[20] ibid.

[21] Regional Development Agencies Act, 1998.

[22] J Tomaney, 'The Evolution of Regionalism in England' (2002) 36 *Regional Studies* 721.

[23] J Willet and A Giovannini, 'The Uneven Path of UK Devolution: Top-Down vs. Bottom-Up Regionalism in England – Cornwall and the North-East Compared' (2014) 62 *Political Studies* 343.

[24] M Keating, 'From Functional to Political Regionalism: England in Comparative Perspective' in Hazel (n 7); Giovannini (n 10).

However, apart from London, England remained the gaping hole in the new devolution settlement, and was only granted a much more limited form of top-down *regionalisation*[25] – ie a (re)organisation of the central state on a regional basis – through the creation of new indirectly accountable bodies for the delivery of (some of) its policies, focusing primarily on regional development ones.[26]

In principle, this 'English exception' within the devolution settlement was to be only temporary. Labour envisioned a 'two-phases' process for England. The first one involved the creation of RDAs and voluntary regional chambers and, as explained, was immediately implemented. The second phase was meant to build on this and was aimed at holding referendums for the establishment of ERAs – although only in the regions that showed an appetite for them.[27] In essence, this second phase would have paved the way towards a shift from *regionalisation* to *regionalism* and political devolution – but it proved very difficult to achieve.

In the 2001 electoral campaign, Labour reaffirmed its commitment to ERAs,[28] and it started to develop this agenda in its second term in government. The publication of the 2002 White Paper *Your Region, Your Choice* (YRYC) was the first attempt to put into practice the second phase of the English regional devolution plan – providing details on ERAs' powers and functions, and on the procedures to set up these bodies. Drawing on the principles laid in 'A Choice for England', YRYC clarified further the terms of the 'two-phases' policy on regional devolution previously mentioned. In the first place, the White Paper suggested a strengthening of existing regional institutions (RDAs and the voluntary regional chambers). Subsequently, regions would have been given the opportunity to create ERAs – but the White Paper affirmed that it could 'take many years before the policy is rolled out across England' and that in the short term 'only one, two or three regions might establish their own ERAs'.[29] YRYC further reinforced that support via referendum was a precondition for any region wishing to set up a regional assembly, although it did not provide specific information regarding the timing of any referendum.

An analysis of *Your Region, Your Choice* reveals the hesitant nature of Labour's approach to regional devolution in England, and an underlying resistance to let go of power in this part of the UK. ERAs were designed to be slimline, strategic authorities, small in size (25–35 members), with the main purpose of setting regional strategies and with no policy delivery duties. The functions of RDAs and regional chambers (including economic development, planning, housing, public health and transport) were to be brought into ERAs. The regional chambers would then be replaced by ERAs; and RDAs were to remain in place

[25] M Keating, 'Devolution and Public Policy in the United Kingdom: Divergence or Convergence?' in J Adams and P Robinson (eds), *Devolution in Practice* (IPPR, 2002) 3; Keating (n 24).
[26] Giovannini (n 10).
[27] ibid.
[28] Labour Party Manifesto, 2001.
[29] *Your Region, Your Choice. Revitalising the English Regions* (Cabinet Office/DLTR, 2002) 63.

under the monitoring of the new assemblies, whilst being operationally independent from them. Although, according to *Your Region, Your Choice*, ERAs would have been able to set RDAs' budgets, appoint their boards, monitor their activities and approve the regional economic strategies, in practice Whitehall maintained key powers, including giving formal approval to most of the decisions taken by ERAs. Moreover, only limited funding was to be under the direct control of ERAs, with central government keeping a tight hold on the regional budget. As such, in practice, the White Paper proposed the creation of very weak regional assemblies, with only few regional functions under their direct control and limited influence. Most of the government policies delivered regionally were to remain under the jurisdiction of Whitehall – leaving ERAs only with indirect levers of power and modest financial capacities, and unable to drive any substantial plan for economic growth or policy outcome.[30]

The following step taken by Labour in 2002 was the publication of a Bill outlining the terms of the Regional Assemblies (Preparation) Act. This set the procedures for the organisation of referendums on ERAs and for the review of local government boundaries that should have accompanied the creation of the assemblies. The Bill also provided for the organisation of a sounding exercise to test the level of support for ERAs across the English regions, using this as a basis to select the first areas to hold referendums. This was carried out by the Office of the Deputy Prime Minister (ODPM), led by John Prescott, and responses were sought from local authorities, regional chambers and stakeholders in all the English regions. Crucially, the data collected omitted any view from the wider public and, for the most part, it conveyed the voice of regional elites, rather than that of the electorate. Moreover, the sampling methods were far from clear: submissions from each region varied widely, with nearly 50 per cent of the total coming from the North West and less than 5 per cent coming from the Midlands.[31] This was perhaps the result of a mixture of poor design and accident – nonetheless, it meant that the consultation process was far from being fully representative of all areas across England.

Despite these flaws, the ODPM published the results of the soundings in the document 'Your Region, Your Say' in June 2003 – stating that the three northern regions of the North East, the North West and Yorkshire and the Humber were to be the first to hold referendums on ERAs. Yet, the process unfolded in a rather convoluted way. Initially, the three referendums were meant to be held in October 2004, but were then rescheduled for November 2004. Finally, in July 2004, the referendums in Yorkshire and in the North West were postponed to a non-specified date, and were eventually cancelled. Officially, this was due to issues with postal voting – but in practice, this decision was taken once the

[30] Jeffery, 'Elected Regional Assemblies in England' (2009).

[31] See ibid; C Jeffery, 'The English Regions Debate: What Do the English Want' (July 2003) ESRC Devolution and Constitutional Change Briefings No 3.

ODPM realised that public support for ERAs in these two regions was low, and the referendums were likely to be lost.[32]

Eventually, the North East was the only region to hold a vote on ERAs. In July 2004, the Draft Regional Assemblies Bill was published, setting the details of referendum process in the North East and the remit of the Assembly. Other than that, the Bill did not involve any major change to the previous Preparation Act 2002 – leaving too many mechanisms for control in the hands of the centre, thus preventing the development of fresh thinking within the region and, crucially, hindering the authority and accountability of ERAs. In short, the Bill set ERAs to be unambitious, incoherent and overregulated bodies,[33] leaving most of the actors supporting ERAs (eg the Campaign for the English Regions, the Constitutional Conventions in the regions, but also the ODPM – which had to lobby the Cabinet on this issue[34]) disappointed with the plan.

The North East went to the polls on the 4 November 2004: nearly 78 per cent of the electorate voted against the creation of a regional assembly, with a 48 per cent turnout.[35] This overwhelming rejection of the North East ERA had a strong impact on the wider English regional devolution agenda. Indeed, the referendum fiasco was interpreted within the Labour Party as a failure of the entire regional devolution project in England.[36] From there onwards, both the idea of directly elected regional assemblies and political devolution, which the ODPM had sought to achieve within its own government with little success, were essentially shelved and never returned to the agenda.

As a result, from the end of 2004, the government focus shifted back to regionalisation, and Labour's 'devolution' strategy for England returned to concentrate primarily on RDAs, as opposed to ERAs. This coincided with a renewed emphasis on the Northern Way, a policy strategy for economic development involving the three northern regions of the North East, the North West and Yorkshire and the Humber aimed at the reduction of the output gap between the North and the South of England.[37] Similarly to the wider regional devolution agenda, the Northern Way was devised and championed by the then Deputy Prime Minister John Prescott. Initial plans for the Northern Way were put in place earlier in 2004, and the policy was conceived as a means to bring together 'the two tracks of the broader regional dimension',[38] ie the constitutional one (in the form of ERAs and devolution to the three northern regions) and the

[32] Willet and Giovannini, 'The Uneven Path of UK Devolution' (2014).

[33] Jeffery (n 30).

[34] Giovannini (n 10).

[35] C Rallings and M Thrasher, 'The North-East Referendum – The Result and Public Reaction' in Sandford (n 12).

[36] Willet and Giovannini (n 23).

[37] S Gonzales, 'The Northern Way. A Celebration or a Victim of the New City-regional Government Policy?' (2006) ESRC & Department for Communities and Local Government Working Paper 28.

[38] J Tomaney and P Hetherington, 'Nations and Regions: The Dynamics of Devolution. Quarterly Monitoring Programme' (2004) ESRC Monitoring the English Regions Report No 16.

economic one (expressed by the work of RDAs and their links with the Treasury and the Deputy PM and his Office). However, the failure of ERAs and the abandonment of regions as the 'preferred scale' for devolution saw the Northern Way emerging as the new overarching narrative that enshrined, in many respects, how 'regional policy was re-imagined within the New Labour logic'.[39]

In practice, the Northern Way became a multi-level governance initiative that was handed over to and implemented by the three northern RDAs. City-regions, understood as engines for economic growth and as a means to redress regional divides, provided another building block of the Northern Way.[40] Eight such bodies were established across the North – reinforcing the idea that economic development was to be at the core of regional devolution policy in England, whilst its political and democratic elements withered away. This was epitomised in the 2007 *Review of Subnational Economic Development and Regeneration*,[41] which set out the gradual 'phasing out' of the voluntary regional chambers. All their remits were passed to RDAs, thus leaving these latter without any scrutiny from local authority representatives, whilst further strengthening the control of central government over regional affairs. Perhaps unsurprisingly, these changes were implemented at the same time as John Prescott left the government in 2007 – exposing both his role as the main champion of regionalism within the government and the presence of diverging views across departments, ministers and MPs on devolution. In this sense, as Jeffery[42] suggests, the review marked the 'final victory of Treasury led competitiveness and national policy delivery agenda over Prescott's concern for greater regional accountability' – confining regionalism to the past as all efforts were now openly concentrated towards a centre-driven and economics-focused process of regionalisation.

This is an important point to note: from that point onwards, the very discourse that presents devolution in England as based primarily on an economic rationale and a need to address the North–South divide (as opposed to the ostensibly more democratic goal attached to devolution to the other UK nations[43]) has never vanished and its legacy is still evident today.[44] Similarly, what has never changed since then is the top-down nature of devolution policy in England, as well as a dismissal of the regional scale in favour of more artificial constructs (at least for some areas) such as city-regions. 'Centralised decentralisation'[45] was the result of this muddled process, and political devolution failed to materialise.

[39] Gonzales, 'The Northern Way' (2006).

[40] S Gonzalez, J Tomaney and N Ward, 'Faith in the City-region?' (2006) 73 *Town and Country Planning* 315; Gonzales (n 37).

[41] HM Treasury, 2007.

[42] Jeffery (n 12).

[43] Mitchell, *Devolution in the UK* (2010).

[44] Giovannini (n 10).

[45] Willet and Giovannini (n 23).

IV. LABOUR'S (DI)VISIONS: REGIONALISATION AND THE DEMISE OF POLITICAL DEVOLUTION IN ENGLAND

The previous section provided an overview of the way in which devolution policy for England was developed by the Labour Party in government, between 1997 and 2010. In doing so, it assessed the process that saw the rise and fall of regional devolution. This culminated in regionalisation strategies prevailing over regionalism, with a clear focus on the economic (rather than the democratic) aspect of devolution.[46] To assess Labour's legacy in this respect in full, though, it is important also to understand the drivers of this uneven process of decentralisation. To this end, this section draws on primary research conducted by the author, including documentary analysis and interviews with key stakeholders.[47]

The analysis suggests that are three main factors that help to explain the process outlined above. First, the regional devolution agenda was met by strong intra-party resistance. Two main 'factions' within the Labour Party emerged, with contrasting views. On the one side stood John Prescott, backed by a small group of (mainly northern) Labour MPs. This current of the party, which can be broadly identified with 'Old Labour', fully subscribed to and supported the cause of political devolution to the English regions. On the other hand, the mainstream of New Labour remained 'sceptical' about regional political devolution.

This view emerged from all the interviews: the Labour government members interviewed strongly emphasised the presence of a cleavage between Old and New Labour, as well as the lack of commitment to regionalism from senior political figures within the government. As summarised by one interviewee:

> Prescott and the ODPM truly supported the case for directly elected regions … there were others, mainly Northern MPs, but no one like Prescott. It was his policy. But you never saw the big hitters, not to mention the PM himself, supporting this. It was very much seen as the last ferment of Old Labour, going back to the old argument about regional inequalities and devolving power, especially for the North.

This is an important point to note as it shows, in line with what was discussed in the previous section, that support for regional devolution was fragmented within Labour and, whilst having a strong champion in the Deputy PM, it came only from a minority of the party. Indeed, many interviewees pointed out how the PM himself, backed by other key Labour ministers, played a crucial role in

[46] Giovannini (n 10).

[47] The discussion developed in this section draws, for the most part, on the results of a programme of research, based on empirical and documentary analysis, undertaken by the author with members of the Labour government and local and regional stakeholders involved in the debate on devolution (1997–2010). The primary research consisted of 28 semi-structured interviews with key stakeholders, including members of the Labour Party at local and national level, members of the Labour government and actors involved in the debate on regional devolution at local, regional and national level. The interviews were conducted between 2009 and 2011. All interviews were fully transcribed and analysed, to inform the arguments contained within this section. The data collected has been anonymised to protect the privacy of the interviewees.

hampering the ERAs' agenda. Some went as far as arguing that 'it was Blair who killed ERAs' (interview data), claiming that the PM was aware of the divisions on this issue within the party,

> so rather than taking a clear position he killed it apart by saying 'yes, as long as it passes the referendum vote' and he knew that you do not win a referendum on more government, with a proposal for regional assemblies with no real powers (interview data).

Others echoed this, suggesting that 'Blair and other ministers hanged the whole process by putting in the referendum clause' (interview data) – whilst also noting that if there was any real support for this policy, it would have been implemented in the first term, when Labour could count on the momentum generated by its landslide victory in 1997. In addition, the lack of direct support from the PM was clearly reflected in the fact that he never openly campaigned for ERAs and, as underlined by an interviewee, Blair 'never went to the North East – in his own constituency – to talk to people, to campaign' (interview data). This helps to explain the presence of 'a dichotomy of beliefs running through the Labour hierarchy'.[48] This materialised as a tension between those, like Prescott, who wanted to achieve political regionalism in full through the establishment of ERAs, and others, including the PM and the majority of government members, who preferred to keep an economic focus for the English regional agenda and were more at ease with institutions like RDAs, which allowed the retention of control over the process by the centre. This lack of collective political will was instrumental in hindering the democratic aspect of devolution, as it was driven by the strongest current of the party.

Second, and related to this, the Treasury and the Cabinet played a key role in undermining Prescott's plan, obstructing any attempt to include substantial powers in the regional assemblies package.[49] As noted by many interviewees involved in the process, Prescott and his Office were left to lead on the ERAs' agenda, shaping the strategy to move towards the establishment of elected regional assemblies in the northern regions. However, this was matched by a lack of engagement from the Cabinet and key ministries, which proved unwilling to give away competences over any substantive policy area and funding. As underlined by a key stakeholder, 'there was a huge amount of work undertaken by Prescott and the ODPM to put together a sensible legislative package … but it got watered down every time by the Cabinet' (interview data). Another interviewee further explained that

> Prescott and his team tried to produce a model of regional government accountable to the regions … They started off with something that looked reasonably coherent … The problem is that then they returned to London … and that's where the plan was

[48] J Harrison, 'The Political-economy of Blair's "New Regional Policy"' (2006) 37 *Geoforum* 932.
[49] Giovannini (n 10).

> continuously chipped away … by rival ministers who didn't buy into the agenda for a variety of reasons, and by Departments in Whitehall [and the Treasury in particular] which kept resisting putting powers into the [ERAs] package (interview data).

This helps explain why the final proposal for ERAs included in the 2004 Regional Assemblies Bill was weak and unsatisfactory, providing only for the creation of regional bodies with few powers, insufficient funding and a high degree of central control. The lack of willingness from the centre to let go of power and create fully accountable, strong regional bodies is also clearly reflected in the content of the Bill, which included 174 clauses, 13 schedules and 229 references to when the Secretary of State would have to be involved[50] – showing that the government would have allowed the creation of ERAs only if it could maintain a strong hold over them. What emerged from this process was a proposal for ERAs that lacked ambition and clout, and was hard to sell to the electorate – both by Prescott and his team and by the regional campaigns. The ODPM's *Housing, Local Government and The Regions Committee* report published in 2005 fully acknowledged this, noting that

> the scope of the powers and responsibilities which the Government was prepared to give to Assemblies was disappointing and would limit their effectiveness. The general power proposed for elected assemblies needed to be more explicit with more specific statements of their functions. This would provide greater clarity, and could also fire the imagination of the general public and potential assembly candidates.[51]

It also highlighted the centripetal views of the Labour government, claiming that 'in many key areas where power [was to be] devolved, central government would have remained the dominant party in the relationship with elected regional assemblies'.[52] These tensions expose the problematic nature of regional devolution policy under Labour. Borrowing Harrison's[53] metaphor, the government sought to devolve powers with one hand, whilst the other (centralised) hand of government was taking powers away from the regions and putting them back into the centre.

Third, the growing chasm between the policy rhetoric in favour of English regionalism and the political reality that saw strong resistance to this within the mainstream of the Labour Party was buttressed by a lack of pressure from the grassroots. This allowed internal party political lines to decide the fate of the regional devolution agenda, without much external consultation or debate. As emphasised by many interviewees, the programme of constitutional reform endorsed by the Labour Party from 1997 was not necessarily driven by a genuine commitment to devolution. Political devolution to Scotland and Wales, and then Northern Ireland, emerged as a strategy aimed at addressing

[50] Harrison, 'The Political-economy of Blair's "New Regional Policy"' (2006).
[51] Housing, Planning, Local Government and the Regions Committee, *Draft Regional Assemblies Bill – First Report*, Vol I (HC 62 I, ODPM, 2005) 3.
[52] ibid 20.
[53] Harrison (n 48).

the territorial cleavage(s) between these areas and central government that widened during the Thatcher years, and also as a means to maintain Labour's political dominance. England, however, was a different case. As previously explained in this chapter, the North–South divide was seen within the Labour Party as the main 'fracture' that had to be addressed through devolution. Yet, this cleavage was not 'read' through the lens of territorial politics, as was the case for the other nations of the UK. Instead, it was primarily interpreted in economic terms. This could be explained by the fact that the North of England – ie the area that was to be the main recipient of regional devolution – was not perceived as bearing any 'political threat' to Labour. Despite being one of the parts of England with stronger regional identities, these were not overly politicised by any regionalist party in the North at this point in time.[54] Instead, 'Northerness' found political expression through support for the Labour Party, and the North as a whole as well as its regions remained a Labour stronghold back then. This suggests that, unlike Scotland, for example, Labour saw the North of England as an 'unproblematic periphery'. In essence, the role of regional identities in the North was underplayed because these did not take any antagonistic political connotation driven by territorially based parties (such as the SNP in Scotland) providing an alternative to Labour and challenging its ascendancy. Thus, political devolution to the northern regions was not seen as a priority by Labour as in the case of Scotland, since it hinged on the recognition of a political cleavage (ie the North–South divide) that the higher echelons of the party were not prepared to politicise – *because they did not have to.*

This is clearly reflected in the fact that Labour did not organise any campaign to support ERAs in the North East ahead of the referendum in 2004. John Prescott was virtually the only member of the government who turned up to pro-ERAs rallies. However, the Yes 4 the North East campaign was not a party political movement, but drew instead on the work of the North East Constitutional Convention (NECC) and its predecessor Campaign for a North East Assembly.[55] The Labour Party played virtually no role in the campaign, and offered very limited support to the pro-ERAs campaigns (in the North East and in the other northern regions). Thus, regionalism in the North of England found expression in civil society campaigns. In principle, this could be read as a positive move to harness a bottom-up momentum for devolution. In practice, however, the NECC did not manage to put any real pressure on central government to relinquish power to the regions or to develop a coherent ERAs agenda that could address concerns for greater regional accountability beyond RDAs. As explained in depth elsewhere,[56] the NECC was very active in the North East,

[54] Giovannini (n 10).
[55] For a full account, see J Tomaney, 'In Search of English Regionalism: The Case of the North East' (1999) 28 *Scottish Affairs* 62; Tomaney (n 12).
[56] See Willet and Giovannini (n 23).

and played a crucial role in shaping a grassroots narrative of regionalism and political devolution. This was epitomised by the publication of the document 'A Time for Change' in 1999, which made the case for a regional assembly, outlining the powers, size and responsibilities this should have.[57] However, as emerged from the interviews, in time, the NECC prioritised lobbying the government over mobilising the nascent North East regional identity and establishing a stronger relationship with the public. As emphasised by many interviewees, the North East Constitutional Convention developed from the beginning a good rapport with John Prescott and the ODPM, even though this did not translate into direct political commitment from Labour. By doing so, though, the NECC ended up lobbying the 'wrong side' of the Cabinet, focusing on a ministry that, as previously explained, was itself in a minority within the Labour government – and thus failing to influence decision-making over regional devolution at the centre. By concentrating their efforts on this, they also missed the opportunity to create the deep, lateral support from the population of the North East that was needed to win the referendum – which, as the Scottish example suggests, could have been key to putting some pressure on the Labour government and making it listen and respond to grassroots demands for powerful regional assemblies.

Taken together, these three factors hindered the progress of regionalism in England. Internal divisions with the Labour Party, coupled with a lack of commitment to relinquish powers from key ministries beyond the ODMP and the absence of any coordinated pressure from the grassroots on the government to let go of powers, help to explain the uneven and tentative process that led to top-down regionalisation prevailing over bottom-up regionalism. It was the combination of these factors, and not just the failure of the North East referendum, as often argued, that sealed the fate of the regional devolution agenda in England – and provide the basis for Labour's devolution legacy.

V. ASSESSING LABOUR'S DEVOLUTION LEGACY WITHIN AND BEYOND THE PARTY

This section seeks to draw together the main points that have emerged so far, and to assess Labour's devolution legacy, both within the party and across the wider political landscape. From an internal perspective, the demise of political devolution to the English regions had at least two effects. First, failure to establish ERAs epitomised by their rejection in the North East referendum of 2004 led to an important scalar and political shift away from regions. From there onwards, the ideology of regionalism[58] never found any support within Labour.

[57] North East Constitutional Convention, *A Time For Change* (NECC, 1999); Tomaney (n 12).

[58] M Keating, *The New Regionalism in Western Europe. Territorial Restructuring and Political Change* (Edward Elgar, 1998); J Lovering, 'Theory Led by Policy: The Inadequacies of the "New Regionalism"' (1999) 23 *International Journal of Urban and Regional Research* 379.

The focus moved away from regions as sites of democratic accountability and economic development, and was recalibrated towards functional geographies (such as city-regions) as drivers of prosperity.

Second, and perhaps more importantly, this shift did not coincide with a consolidation of Labour's position on regional policy. On the contrary, the main result of the long-standing tensions within the party previously analysed was an unfinished and fragmented top-down process of functional regionalism, which started to fade during the last years of government and vanished as soon as the party lost the 2010 general election. In this respect, the main legacy of the 1997–2010 period in government was that Labour lost ownership of the English devolution agenda. Ever since, the party has not managed to come back with a clear policy strategy for devolution in England. Some Labour figures have and still are supporting the idea of devolution – yet the party as a whole has never (re)built a coherent vision on this issue. This is quite remarkable, especially considering: (i) that for a long time Labour was the main party that sought to engage with devolution; and (ii) the importance, if not sheer political necessity, of addressing the North–South divide, as well as regional inequalities across England more broadly, and 'keeping' the North as a Labour stronghold. As some commentators have suggested, this might help to explain why the party has lost ground in the North in recent years, whilst political, social and economic cleavages between the North and parts of the South have widened.[59] The results of the December 2019 general election and the fall of the so-called 'red wall' have brought into even sharper relief how and why Labour cannot take the support of areas like the North for granted any longer. Devolution could be a way to reconnect the party with its traditional heartland in England – yet, even in the recent leadership contest, there has been a deafening silence on this matter.

Another important legacy, in this respect, is that Labour did not manage to solve the issue of over-centralisation in England that lies at the core of the 'English Question'. After 13 years of Labour government, central–local relations as well as the landscape of governance structures in England were still dominated by the centre, whilst the subnational (local and regional) levels were left disempowered and highly fragmented. This stands in sharp contrast to the degree of power passed down by the Labour government through constitutional reform to the other nations of the UK. Remarkably, England continued to be 'the Cinderella of Labour constitutional reform plan'[60] and, perhaps even more importantly, a constitutional conundrum that Labour *could*, but never did, manage to cogently address.

[59] L Raikes, A Giovannini and B Getzel, 'Divided and Connected: Regional Inequalities in the North, the UK and the Developed World' (IPPR, November 2019) https://www.ippr.org/research/publications/state-of-the-north-2019; UK2070 Commission, *Fairer and Stronger. Rebalancing the UK Economy*, First Report, May 2019; A Giovannini and J Rose, 'England: The North–South Divide' in M Garnett and H Pillmoore (eds), *The Routledge Handbook of British Politics and Society* (Routledge, 2020).

[60] J Tomaney, 'New Labour and the English Question' (1999) 70 *The Political Quarterly* 75.

This leads to a consideration of Labour's wider legacy on devolution beyond the party itself. Post-2010 – with the election of a Conservative–Liberal Democrat Coalition government first (2010–15), followed by a Conservative one (2015–present) – there was a sharp 'shift of plans'. To be clear, devolution did not disappear from the political agenda altogether – but was 'reinvented' and ultimately became a Tory project. The lack of drive on English devolution within Labour that emerged especially after John Prescott stepped down meant that, gradually, the Conservative party filled in that policy void, devising its own devolution strategy. Soon after taking office, in the June 2010 Budget, the Coalition government disbanded RDAs and the other structures – in particular, quangos – created by their predecessors, as these were seen as a Labour legacy they did not want to keep.

Post-2010, a new devolution agenda was built on a mixture of continuity with and change from the past. The Conservative party introduced changes in the architecture and focus of devolution. In terms of institutions, RDAs, regional chambers and ERAs were replaced by Local Enterprise Partnerships (LEPs – voluntary partnerships between local authorities and business with a strong focus on economic grown, not too dissimilar from RDAs) and combined authorities (CAs – groups of neighbouring councils collaborating and taking collective decisions over specific policy areas across council boundaries), but city-regions re-emerged as an important scale, too, as they usually provide the basis for CAs.[61] Wider regional devolution strategies have been replaced by two rounds of 'City Deals' (2010–14), aimed at fostering economic development first, and then by 'devolution deals' (2014 onwards), which are partnership agreements between CAs and the government.[62] In addition, directly elected 'metro-mayors' have been introduced to lead some of the existing CAs and deliver devolution deals. However, these new institutions were set up without any real public consultation.

[61] The structures and geography of subnational governance in England is particularly complex. Whilst it is beyond the scope of this chapter to delve into this, it is worth emphasising that the Conservatives' approach to governance restructuring is very top-down and ad hoc. As such, it has led to the creation of a patchwork of new bodies and 'devolution deals' that do not cover the whole of the country and vary in terms of remit, power and scale. For example, at the time of writing, there are 38 LEPs, 10 CAs (nine of which are led by a metro mayor) and ten Devolution Deals in place (including in Cornwall, which is a unitary authority). Some of the LEPs coincide with CAs, but others overlap and span over more than one CA. Similarly, some CAs coincide with city-region, but others do not. In addition, each of these bodies is the recipient of different streams of funding and powers. This clearly shows how under the Conservatives subnational governance in England had become increasingly 'messy', raising questions about its sustainability, effectiveness and accountability (for a full discussion, see A Giovannini, 'The Uneven Governance of Devolution Deals in Yorkshire: opportunities, challenges and local (di)visions' in C Berry and A Giovannini (eds) *Developing England's North. The Political Economy of the Northern Powerhouse* (Palgrave, 2018); see also A Giovannini, 'The 2021 Metro Mayors Elections: Localism Rebooted?' [2021] The Political Quarterly https://doi.org/10.1111/1467-923X.13036.

[62] For a full account, see Berry and Giovannini, *Developing England's North* (2018).

Despite these shifts, there remain many elements of continuity with Labour's devolution agenda. Firstly, in line with the changes that emerged in the final years of the Labour government, devolution in England continues to have a strong economic focus, whilst the democratic element of decentralisation remains in the background. The North–South divide, and regional inequalities more broadly, still play an important role in shaping the Conservatives' devolution agenda. Addressing these divisions was at the core of the narrative used by the former Chancellor George Osborne to build a rationale for devolution deals.[63] The Northern Powerhouse embodies these efforts in many respects. This is a strategy devised by the Conservative government, which in 2016 published its vision and ambitions to address key barriers to productivity in the North through a mix of investment in key sectors such as transport infrastructure and decentralisation.[64] Yet, it is hard not to notice a striking similarity between this new project and John Prescott's Northern Way – which, as previously explained, had virtually the same remit, scale and ambitions.

Devolution also continues to be a top-down, centre-led policy. Central government, and in particular the Treasury, maintains a strong hold over a process that, despite a rhetoric of empowering the subnational levels, still resembles, in practice, 'centralised decentralisation'.[65] In addition, support for devolution remains, once again, fragmented within the government. For example, during the Cameron government years, 'devo deals' and the Northern Powerhouse were conceived and pushed by individual ministers (in particular, George Osborne), with only partial support from the rest of the government and party. This suggests that commitment to devolution is still characterised by a high degree of volatility, and the development/success of the policy hinges on the role and weight of a few champions within the government. As was the case under Labour and Prescott, it is noteworthy that with the departure of Osborne from the Treasury in 2016 devolution has lost its drive and policy development has slowed down considerably. After a long hiatus, it was only with the election of the new Conservative government led by Boris Johnson in December 2019 that we have seen a renewed emphasis placed on devolution – mainly as part of the new 'levelling-up' agenda and, perhaps more cynically, as an attempt at making inroads in traditional Labour strongholds.[66] However, with the outbreak of COVID-19 and Brexit, this initial 'devolution impetus' has now waned.[67]

[63] ibid.

[64] For a full account, see the official government strategy at https://www.gov.uk/government/publications/northern-powerhouse-strategy; for a critique, see Berry and Giovannini (n 61).

[65] Willet and Giovannini (n 23).

[66] J Tomaney and A Pike, 'Levelling Up?' (2020) 91 *The Political Quarterly* 43.

[67] For an account of the most recent developments, see A Giovannini, 'COVID-19 and English Devolution' (2020) 11(3) *Political Insight* 40; A Giovannini, 'Levelling Up' in *Brexit and Beyond*, UK in a Changing Europe Report (2021) https://ukandeu.ac.uk/wp-content/uploads/2021/01/Brexit-and-Beyond-report-compressed.pdf; A Giovannini, 'In the Eye of the Storm: English Local Government and the COVID-19 Crisis' in L Andres, JR Bryson, A Ersoy and L Reardon (eds), *Living with Pandemics: People, Place and Policy* (Edward Elgar, forthcoming).

Finally, and related to this, devolution in England is still a disconnected project and resembles, at best, a patchwork of ad hoc spatial fixes.[68] The new approach still covers only some parts of England (to date, only 10 devolution deals have been signed and nine metro-mayors are in place – mostly in the North). In addition, as recent research shows,[69] in the face of growing inequalities across and within England's regions, there remain doubts about whether devolution has achieved its intended aim of helping rebalance the economy.[70] Relations between central and local government also continue to be problematic. A decade of austerity has seen draconian cuts being imposed on local authorities, leaving many of them – especially in the areas with the highest levels of deprivation and weak economies – close to the tipping point. As a result, the capacity of the local state has shrunk to a nearly unsustainable level, further exacerbating territorial injustice.[71] Against this backdrop, devolution is also still used as a way to deliver local government reform through the backdoor – as, similarly to what happened under Labour, the current government is still trying to impose the creation of unitary authorities across England as part of devolution deals.

VI. CONCLUSION

This chapter has sought to provide an analysis of the way in which plans for a devolution agenda for England emerged within the Labour Party, and how they were translated into policy. The study focused on the roots of the regional devolution strategy, its uneven development during the two Labour governments (1997–2010) and the reasons that led both to the emergence of a functional regionalism approach and the demise of political devolution in England. Finally, it assessed Labour's devolution legacy, both within the party and across the wider political landscape – showing a trend of change and continuity.

All in all, the analysis shows that after 13 years in government, Labour left an unfinished process of devolution in England as its main legacy. This issue was taken onboard by the Conservatives in subsequent years, with a view to providing a new policy strategy for the largest nation of the UK. Yet, little progress has been made: the English Question, understood as the need to address both the role of England within a devolved UK and over-centralisation within England itself, still stands unanswered. Devolution has continued to evolve and is now

[68] A Giovannini, 'The Uneven Path of Devolution Deals in Yorkshire: Opportunities, Challenges and Local (Di)visions' in Berry and Giovannini (n 61).

[69] Raikes et al, 'Divided and Connected' (2019); UK2070 Commission, *Make No Little Plans – Acting At Scale For A Fairer And Stronger Future*, Final Report (2020) http://uk2070.org.uk/wp-content/uploads/2020/02/UK2070-FINAL-REPORT.pdf.

[70] Berry and Giovannini (n 61).

[71] M Gray and A Barford, 'The Depths of the Cuts: The Uneven Geography of Local Government Austerity' (2018) 11 *Cambridge Journal of Regions, Economy and Society* 541,

an established process in the other nations of the UK,[72] but England remains a conundrum in the devolution settlement that still has to be solved. The uncertainties brought in by Brexit and the COVID-19 crisis add a new level of complexity to the English Question, and make it even more imperative to address it.[73] Yet, whilst there have been significant ebbs and flows in the Conservatives' commitment to the English devolution agenda, it is remarkable that Labour as the main opposition party has not come up yet with any concrete alternative proposition. This suggests that the party has not taken stock of its past experience: Labour still remains divided on the issue and, most importantly, has not managed to develop a clear vision and strategy for devolution that could be vital to (re)establish a stronger relationship with its strongholds, especially in the North, and bring it back into power.

[72] The exception here is Northern Ireland, where the devolved assembly was suspended until January 2020, having collapsed in January 2017 due to policy disagreements between its power-sharing leadership.

[73] Giovannini, 'Levelling Up' (2021); Giovannini, 'COVID-19 and English Devolution' (2020); A Giovannini, 'Brexit and Devolution in England: What's at Stake? (*PSA Blog*, 14 March 2019) https://www.psa.ac.uk/psa/news/brexit-and-devolution-england-whats-stake.

8

'Three Harmless Words': New Labour and Freedom of Information

BEN WORTHY

TONY BLAIR'S VIEWS, expressed a decade and a half apart, reflect some of the paradoxes and contradictions that accompany freedom of information (FOI) laws. In 1996, Blair argued:

> A Freedom of Information Act is not just important in itself. It is part of bringing our politics up to date, of letting politics catch up with the aspirations of people and delivering not just more open government but more effective, more efficient, government for the future.[1]

Whereas by 2011 his view had radically shifted:

> *Freedom of Information. Three harmless words. I look at those words as I write them, and feel like shaking my head till it drops off my shoulders* ... The information is neither sought because the journalist is curious to know, nor given to bestow knowledge on 'the people'. It's used as a weapon.[2]

New Labour's experience was typical of how such reforms develop. Openness laws are frequently powerfully championed, often by new governments, and then ruefully regretted. As resistance increases and doubts within government grow, they often emerge from political conflicts as messy compromises.[3]

This chapter maps out the deep roots of FOI reform within the Labour Party, but shows that attempts in the 1960s and 1970s were half-hearted and strongly resisted. For New Labour, in contrast, championing FOI sent out positive signals of its radicalism and new philosophy of governing. In power, Labour's 'radical' initial reforms led to a far-reaching White Paper, but this was then diluted

[1] T Blair, 'Speech by the Rt Hon Tony Blair MP, Leader of the Labour Party' (June 1996, transcript of a tape) www.cfoi.org.uk/blairawards.html.

[2] T Blair, *A Journey* (Hutchinson, 2011) 516–17.

[3] B Worthy, *The Politics of Freedom of Information: How and Why Governments Pass Laws That Threaten Their Power* (Manchester University Press, 2017).

by nervous ministers. There was then a struggle within Parliament between cross-party MPs aiming to strengthen the law and the government seeking a minimal Act. What emerged was a compromise, but the law in operation – the Freedom of Information Act 2000 – has proved unexpectedly resilient.

I. A SHORT HISTORY OF FREEDOM OF INFORMATION

FOI laws, also known as access to information or right to information laws, grant legal access to government information. They are normally subject to a series of exceptions or exemptions, covering, for example, national security and parts of the policy-making process, and are overseen by some form of appeal system, frequently a Commissioner or the courts.

FOI laws have a radical pedigree and somewhat mysterious origin. The idea of 'opening up' government to popular scrutiny became a rallying cry of revolutionaries in England in the seventeenth century and France and America in the eighteenth century.[4] Although the world's first functioning law, a Freedom of the Printing Press Act in 1766, was (briefly) introduced in Sweden, earlier claims have been made for edicts in India and China. Philosophers from Kant to Bentham and from Rousseau to Marx all supported greater openness, though it took until the mid-twentieth century, having been pushed by political outsiders such as Woodrow Wilson and Leon Trotsky, for the idea to become part of mainstream political and legal discourse.[5]

The USA passed an FOI law in 1966, followed by a handful of other countries, including France in 1978 and New Zealand, Australia and Canada in the early 1980s.[6] It was not until the 1990s that FOI laws began making their way into statute books in any significant number, with key countries such as the UK (2000), India (2005) and Nigeria (2011) passing them, and there are now around 100 laws in various forms around the world.[7]

FOI is, in essence, a 'moral idea', stemming from the belief that a government should be 'accountable' and 'open to scrutiny'.[8] It has also become, as Birchall puts it, an 'apparently simple solution to complex problems – such as how to fight corruption, promote trust in government … and foster state accountability'.[9] It is in some senses an 'empty signifier' that can be 'filled' by

[4] ibid.

[5] See C Darch and P Underwood, *Freedom of Information in the Developing World: Demand, Compliance and Democratic Behaviours* (Chandos, 2010); M Fenster, 'The Transparency Fix: Advocating Legal Rights and Their Alternatives in the Pursuit of a Visible State' (2012) 73 *University of Pittsburgh Law Review* 443.

[6] J Ackerman and IE Sandoval-Ballesteros, 'The Global Explosion of Freedom of Information Laws' (2006) 58 *Administrative Law Review* 85.

[7] See Darch and Underwood, *Freedom of Information in the Developing World* (2010); Fenster, 'The Transparency Fix' (2012).

[8] See Darch and Underwood (n 5) 7, 49.

[9] C Birchall, 'Radical Transparency?' (2014) 14 *Cultural Studies ↔ Critical Methodologies* 77, 77.

very different interpretations or emphasis.[10] Though ostensibly a neutral legal reform, it also provokes political conflict because of the threat of exposure and scrutiny: proposed laws often meet closed-door resistance from bureaucracies and politicians. Consequently, as it is developed and once it is in place, transparency remains a 'contested political issue that masquerades as an administrative tool'.[11]

II. THE PARADOXES OF FOI LAWS

Given its radical aura, the passage and operation of FOI has been likened to a 'kind of morality play'.[12] For politicians, such laws are hard to resist in opposition but are hard to escape from once in power.[13] Committing to FOI sends out strong messages of radicalism, change and empowerment that new governments and self-styled radical politicians find difficult to resist. The symbolic power is frequently magnified by the fact that FOI laws are often part of a wider set of legal, constitutional or political reforms, as occurred in the UK.[14]

More practically, FOI laws are, it is argued, often passed out of naivety or inattention by inexperienced and new governments. Some are responding to reformist impulses from within, pressure from the media or as a response to a scandal.[15] Politicians also have more political motives for introducing them, from the simple politics of wrong-footing or neutralising opponents to the longer-term, calculated intent of securing information when they are out of power.[16]

Politicians can, at least in the short term, earn a form of 'moral capital' from supporting openness.[17] FOI laws are symbolically important, especially when they play into the radical self-image of reformists and modernisers. A call for transparency 'tells a transformative narrative' as it 'enables – and, indeed forces [a] virtuous chain of events' towards more accountable and democratic government.[18]

Yet, despite all their power, FOI reforms are voteless policies. Across the world, with the partial exception of India, nowhere has the promise of FOI

[10] R Stubbs and R Snell, 'Pluralism in FOI Law Reform: Comparative Analysis of China, Mexico and India' (2014) 33 *University of Tasmania Law Review* 141.

[11] Fenster (n 5) 449.

[12] PM Wald, 'Freedom of Information Act: A Short Case Study in the Perils and Paybacks of Legislating Democratic Values' (1984) 33 *Emory Law Journal* 649, 649.

[13] Worthy, *The Politics of Freedom of Information* (2017).

[14] M Evans, *Constitution-Making and the Labour Party* (Palgrave Macmillan, 2003).

[15] See D Berliner 'The Political Origins of Transparency' (2014) 76 *Journal of Politics* 479; Darch and Underwood (n 5).

[16] Berliner, 'The Political Origins of Transparency' (2014).

[17] Birchall, 'Radical Transparency?' (2014) 77; G Michener, 'The Surrender of Secrecy? Explaining the Strength of Transparency and Access to Information Laws' (paper presented at the American Political Science Association, Toronto Meeting, 2009) http://ssrn.com/abstract=1449170.

[18] M Fenster, 'Transparency in Search of a Theory' (2015) 18 *European Journal of Social Theory* 150.

attracted significant votes. In the UK, Home Secretary Rees made this explicit in the late 1970s when he pointed out that '*The Guardian* can go on for as long as it likes about open government … but I can tell you that in my own constituency of 75,000 electors I would be hard pressed to find many who would be interested'.[19]

FOI is the story of radical aspirations and symbolism meeting political reality, resistance and disinterest. FOI is often dependent on a small group of key figures, 'lone crusaders' pushing FOI from 'within'.[20] The conventional wisdom is also that politicians rapidly fall out of love with transparency and the potential for exposure, uncertainty and unpleasant surprises it brings.[21]

However, dropping outright a promised policy that speaks of 'freedom', 'information' or a 'right' is problematic. The symbolism, radicalism and 'moral' angle of FOI, even its resonant name, make it difficult to quietly get rid of. The accusation of betrayal from the media, political opponents and factions within the party makes back-pedalling difficult, if not impossible. What happens instead is that FOI proposals are stalled, blocked and channelled away behind closed doors. The classic trajectory of FOI reform is one of survival through dilution.[22] After many lengthy internal battles, FOI laws often emerge, if they emerge at all, as messy compromises.[23]

III. OPEN GOVERNMENT IN BRITAIN

Government secrecy was an obvious target for Labour's reformist impulses since the beginning of the party itself. The commitment to open up government was one of Labour's oldest constitutional reform promises, dating back to its October 1974 manifesto and appearing in every one since. In 1972, it was a Labour politician, Richard Crossman, who famously wrote of the 'English addiction to secrecy'.[24] The UK constitution was, argued reformers, built up of 'secretive components … heaped one on top of the other'.[25] Constitutional conventions and rules, from collective responsibility to the royal prerogative, interlocked with more than 100 laws preventing the release of information, with the infamous all-embracing Official Secrets Act 1911 at its centre. The result was

[19] M Rees, 'The Parameters of Politics' in R Chapman and M Hunt (eds), *Open Government* (Croom Helm, 1987) 31–38.

[20] R Snell, 'Freedom of Information: The Experience of the Australian States – An Epiphany' (2001) 29 *Federal Law Review* 343, 347.

[21] Berliner (n 15).

[22] S Archibald, 'The Freedom of Information Act Revisited' (1979) 39 *Public Administration Review* 311.

[23] Michener, 'The Surrender of Secrecy?' (2009).

[24] R Crossman, *Inside View: Three Lectures on Prime Ministerial Government* (Cape, 1972) 99.

[25] D Leigh, *The Frontiers of Secrecy: Closed Government in Britain* (Junction Books, 1980) 20.

what Rowat described as a 'principle of discretionary secrecy'.[26] The 'English addiction' meant 'it is as natural for the secretary of a village cricket club to stamp the minutes of its committee meetings confidential' as it is for a Cabinet Secretary to keep Cabinet notes secret.[27]

Secrecy was culturally pervasive and almost instinctively 'built in to the calcium of a policy makers bones'.[28] Information control was also lodged deep within the executive dominance, one-party government and strict lines of control of the Westminster system.[29] One 1980s study concluded that 'levels of secrecy [are] a direct consequence of the foundations of British democracy':[30] 'All government information will be seen as having consequences for their ability to exercise the degree of control the structure of responsibility implies and for their political survival since any information may affect their reputation and popularity.'[31]

In the early part of the twentieth century, the Labour Party provided the only sustained push for openness. A very small group of radical Labour MPs, including the future Prime Minister Ramsay MacDonald, had opposed the passage of the Official Secrets Act of 1911.[32] Leading left intellectuals, such as the Webbs, were also 'early champions of the public right to know'.[33] Ramsay MacDonald spoke of how 'bureaucracy … hides itself from the public gaze' and argued 'it is just upon these offices that the wind of public opinion should blow most freely'.[34]

However, Labour's first leaders were themselves torn between the wish to be open and the convenience of secrecy. MacDonald's first government in 1924 issued press releases detailing, for the first time, attendees and subjects at Cabinet meetings, but by 1929 this practice was dropped and MacDonald spoke of the importance of secrecy and complained of leaks.[35] In the 1930s, George Landsbury complained how this 'secrecy business was impossible', but Arthur Henderson opposed reforming the Official Secrets Act 'as we might want to use it when we are back in power'.[36]

The 'long march' to FOI began in the late 1960s, when Harold Wilson began the first serious set of open government reforms. He proposed a minor change to

[26] DC Rowat (ed), *Administrative Secrecy in Developed Countries* (Springer, 1979) 19.
[27] P Hennessy, *Whitehall*, 2nd edn (Pimlico 2003) 347.
[28] ibid 346.
[29] A King, *Who Governs Britain?* (Penguin 2015).
[30] KG Robertson, *Public Secrets: A Study in the Development of Government Secrecy* (Macmillan Press, 1982) 22.
[31] ibid 2.
[32] P Dorey, *The Labour Party and Constitutional Reform: A History of Constitutional Conservatism* (Palgrave Macmillan, 2008) 184.
[33] K Theakston, *The Labour Party and Whitehall* (Routledge, 1992).
[34] ibid.
[35] ibid; Dorey, *The Labour Party and Constitutional Reform* (2008) 184.
[36] Theakston, *The Labour Party and Whitehall* (1992) 164.

the Public Records Act 1958, changing the 50-year rule on document closure to 30 years, and a review of the Official Secrets Act as part of an attempt at 'getting rid of unnecessary secrecy'.[37] Both the Foreign Office and the Ministry of Defence fought back against even these minor proposals. The Cabinet Secretary feared it could result in 'a far too liberally minded report – almost Swedish'.[38] The period for holding information secret under the Public Records Act was reduced to 30 years, but the review never took place.

Pressure then was applied from the left, after a series of controversial Officials Secrets Act trials in the early 1970s. As a result, the Labour administration of 1974 entered power with a manifesto pledge to introduce some form of FOI law. Not for the last time, it was felt that ministers were unaware of what the pledge really meant.[39] Despite the support of Home Secretary Roy Jenkins, the proposals were greeted with disinterest and delayed, and, after Wilson resigned, the new Prime Minister James Callaghan was 'decidedly unenthusiastic' about openness.[40] By 1977, the only clear reform was a voluntarily scheme, the Croham Directive, designed to disclose policy information. Little information was forthcoming and, within two years, *The Times* concluded that 'the government demonstrated blatantly it cannot be relied upon for the voluntary disclosure of official information'.[41]

As Table 1 shows, despite its many promises, in all its time in power in the 1960s and 1970s, Labour consistently failed to fulfil them. The policy was delayed, resisted and compromised with 'a series of non-decisions' at numerous levels.[42] Partly this was about politics. As with New Labour later, Callaghan felt any reform would be electorally valueless, while most other ministers felt open government had 'no votes in it'.[43] But there lay a deeper paradox for reformers. As Diamond explains, 'the structures and processes of central British government ... offer very substantial power to the incumbent administration', and this 'power paradox' is itself 'a formidable obstacle to radical political change'.[44] To pass an FOI law required not only overcoming 'secrecy' laws and layers of culture and practice, but potentially challenging and upending the UK's political system itself, at just the time when a Labour government would be advantaged by it.

[37] P Hennessy, 'The Long March? Whitehall and Open Government since 1945' in S Platten (ed), *Open Government: What Do We Need to Know?* (Canterbury Press, 2003) 20–37; K Theakston, 'Whitehall and Reform' in P Dorey (ed), *The Labour Governments* (Routledge, 2006) 147–68.

[38] Theakston, 'Whitehall and Reform' (2006) 164.

[39] J Michael, *The Politics of Secrecy: Closed Government in Britain* (Penguin, 1982).

[40] Dorey (n 32) 191.

[41] Leigh, *The Frontiers of Secrecy* (1980) 20.

[42] M Burch and I Holliday, *The British Cabinet System* (Prentice Hall, 1996).

[43] Michael, *The Politics of Secrecy* (1982); D Vincent, *The Culture of Secrecy 1832–1997* (Oxford University Press, 1998) 204.

[44] P Diamond, 'Beyond the Westminster Model' (2011) 19 *Renewal* 64, 68.

Table 1 Labour and Transparency Reform, 1924–2000

1924	MacDonald details of Cabinet Meetings
1968	White Paper *Information and the Public Interest* and Public Records Act change
1974 (October)	FOI in manifesto
1977	Croham Directive
1993	Fisher's Right to Know Bill
1996	Blair's CFOI speech
1997	FOI White Paper
1999	FOI draft Bill
2000	FOI law receives assent
2005	FOI law comes into force

Despite social and technological change, secrecy remained firmly in place under Margaret Thatcher's Conservative government, with, it was said, even the brand of tea drunk by ministers technically an official secret. The 1980s were then crucial for the reinvigoration of FOI. A campaign group, the Campaign for Freedom of Information (CFOI), began to build pressure with a series of reforms at local government. Throughout the 1980s and 1990s, CFOI also sought specific public promises from opposition leaders that were then 'recorded and heavily publicised', thus 'pinning them down, committing them to a policy'.[45] As a measure of CFOI's success, in 1984 the new leader Neil Kinnock had promised to make FOI a 'priority' for any future Labour administration.

The push chimed with a current of Labour Party thought on breaking up power that had been given renewed emphasis by Thatcherism. At Westminster, FOI's long support on the Labour backbenches had built into a powerful current of cross-party support, seen through a series of Private Members' Bills in the 1980s and early 1990s, culminating in Mark Fisher's Right to Know Bill, which galvanised wide support from all sides of the House. Kinnock's late 1980s policy review promised 'a FOI Act covering information held by national, regional and local government'.[46] Before the 1992 general election, the Shadow Home Secretary promised that 'a Freedom of Information Act is ready for early enactment. If a Labour government was elected on Thursday I would be able to send the headings of a Bill to parliamentary draughtsman on the following day.'[47]

[45] D Wilson, *Memoirs of a Minor Public Figure* (Quartet Books, 2011) 184–85.

[46] Labour Party, *Final Report of Labour's Policy Review for the 1990s: Meet the Challenge, Make the Change: A New Agenda for the 1990s* (Labour Party, 1989) 59.

[47] K Gundersen, 'Freedom of Information' in P Facey, B Rigby and A Runswick (eds), *Unlocking Democracy: 20 Years of Charter 88* (Politico's, 2008) 226.

IV. NEW LABOUR

While FOI had a long, if uncertain, 'Old Labour' lineage, it was also given a distinctly New Labour spin. Not only did it fit with its tactics and wider reform programme, but it also represented and symbolised key New Labour ideas and aims in the mid-to-late 1990s.

On a narrow, partisan level, in the 1990s, New Labour's push for FOI was opportunistic. In the early 1990s, John Major had explicitly rejected a full FOI law and instead passed a non-statutory Code of Practice on openness that was largely ignored.[48] Blair argued that all the Code really did was to 'underline the need for action on a far greater scale'.[49] Pushing openness reforms shone a harsh light on the secretive and 'sleaze'-ridden Conservative government of John Major. Under the catch-all term 'sleaze', the media revealed a stream of 'corruption, semi-corruption or near corruption', covering sexual 'misconduct', lobbying and financial misdealings.[50] No fewer than nine members of the government stepped down over sex scandals alone.[51] The 'drip' of scandals helped make Major's administration 'the government that could do no right' and meant that it 'plumbed depths of unpopularity never before experienced by a modern government'.[52] Blair himself spoke of how 'it was a media game and as Opposition we played it', and explained that, despite his later regrets, it was 'just too easy to score'.[53] Conveniently for New Labour, the continued exposure was justified as a 'right to know' issue by the media.[54]

Beyond the convenience, FOI exemplified Labour's radicalism and its new approach towards government and the people. It 'symbolised Labour's core values', reflecting its self-image as modernising and anti-establishment.[55] Alongside the Human Rights Act, FOI had become a cause championed by progressive legal and political actors, a 'very fashionable idea' driven by 'radical lawyers' connected to or in the party.[56] The politicians behind it saw themselves as 'outsiders from power' in a party that was, and viewed itself as, distinctly 'non-establishment'.[57]

More concretely, FOI also fitted neatly with several different parts of the constitutional reform programme, from the rights agenda of the Human Rights

[48] Vincent, *The Culture of Secrecy 1832–1997* (1998).

[49] Blair, 'Speech by the Rt Hon Tony Blair MP, Leader of the Labour Party' (1996).

[50] P Dunleavy, S Weir and G Subrahmanyam, 'Public Response and Constitutional Significance' (1995) 48 *Parliamentary Affairs* 602, 603.

[51] D Denver, 'The Government that Could Do No Right' in A King et al (eds), *New Labour Triumphs: Britain and the Polls* (Chatham House Publishers, 1998) 15–48.

[52] ibid 15–16.

[53] Blair, *A Journey* (2011) 127.

[54] AW Turner, *A Classless Society: Britain in the 1990s* (Aurum Press, 2013).

[55] M Scammell, 'The Media and Media Management' in A Seldon (ed), *The Blair Effect* (Little, Brown and Co, 2001) 530.

[56] Interview with David Clark in Worthy (n 3).

[57] ibid.

Act to the democratic innovations promised across local and central government. More broadly, if Labour's constitutional reform programme was about 'breaking up centres of power', then the ruction of information hierarchies offered a simple yet radical way to do it.[58] Professor Peter Hennessy later argued that FOI was a completion of democratic reforms that began with the arrival of the popular vote:

> the Freedom of Information Act … was the completion of the circle that began with the extension of the franchise. It took from 1832 to 1948 to get to one person one vote, but the remaining … test [is whether] an elector could cast an informed vote. The answer was that until the Freedom of Information Act very probably not. It has to be seen as part of completing the virtues of the franchise in an open society.[59]

Blair later described FOI, somewhat ruefully, as a 'revolutionary offer'.[60] In symbolic terms it was, as it represented a radical break with past secretive practices.[61] Foley characterises FOI as

> captivating in its radical simplicity [although] it may appear nothing more than connecting a disjunction between theory and practice … in reality it would represent a profound change in the sources and usage of power within the British government system.[62]

The key question, given past experience, was how committed Labour were in 1997. Blair's own commitment appeared to go a long way back. In 1984, as a newly elected MP, he called on Margaret Thatcher to pass an FOI law in the wake of the prosecution of the civil servant Sarah Tisdall: 'Does the Right Honourable Lady agree that there is an urgent need for legislation so that … the government cannot conceal the scale of what they are doing?'[63]

Between 1992 and 1997, Blair repeated his commitment to FOI in at least eight major interviews, four ministerial statements and one major speech.[64] The key event came with Blair's 1996 speech to the CFOI Awards in 1996. The organisers of the event hoped to obtain a definite commitment to legislate for FOI.[65] Blair's speech, written by Pat McFadden, perhaps exceeded expectations. Blair outlined the centrality of FOI to New Labour's agenda and philosophy in a rich, symbolic, 'justifying narrative', explaining why FOI was needed.[66]

[58] J Straw, 'New Labour, Constitutional Change and Representative Democracy' (2010) 63 *Parliamentary Affairs* 356, 360.

[59] Justice Committee Minutes of Evidence HC 96 – ii: Lord Hennessy of Nympsfield and Lord O'Donnell of Clapham (TSO, 2012) www.publications.parliament.uk/pa/cm201213/cmselect/cmjust/96/120327.htm.

[60] Blair (n 2) 127.

[61] Dorey (n 32) 201.

[62] M Foley, *The Politics of the British Constitution* (Manchester University Press, 1999) 69.

[63] J Rentoul, *Tony Blair: Prime Minister* (Faber & Faber, 2001) 126.

[64] CFOI, 'Research Paper: Labour's Commitments to Freedom of Information', 4–5 www.cfoi.org.uk/labcmits.htm.

[65] Interview with James Cornford Worthy (n 3).

[66] G Michener, 'FOI Laws around the World' (2011) 22 *Journal of Democracy* 145.

In Blair's speech, FOI formed a crucial part of New Labour's vision of how Britain was to be modernised and its government was to function. It sent out a series of signals about Labour's radicalism, its vision of modernisation, a new government morality and its intent to change citizen-government relations.

Blair presented FOI as a practical step in modernising democracy:

> A Freedom of Information Act is not just important in itself. It is part of bringing our politics up to date, of letting politics catch up with the aspirations of people and delivering not just more open government but more effective, more efficient, government for the future.[67]

Blair argued that secrecy created 'disaffection from politics' and 'disillusion', and that FOI was an 'essential' part of the constitutional reform programme, because it was about 'genuinely changing the relationship in politics today' towards a 'partnership'.[68] FOI fitted with a wider, if vague, process of 'democratisation and reconnecting government with the people'. He ended the speech by reaffirming New Labour's commitment to FOI legislation: 'We want to end the obsessive and unnecessary secrecy which surrounds government activity and make government information available to the public unless there are good reasons not to do so.'[69]

Blair joked that people may cynically see his promise as a media ploy, to be quietly changed once Labour were in office: 'people often say to me today: everyone says this before they get into power, then, after they get into power you start to read the words of the government on the screen and they don't seem so silly after all'.[70]

V. NEW LABOUR'S DOUBTS?

Behind the enthusiasm and seeming inevitably, there were doubts about Labour's programme in general and FOI in particular. The wide-ranging constitutional reform programme made Tony Blair, somewhat reluctantly, the 'most far reaching, radical reformer of the formal edifice of the constitution since Oliver Cromwell'.[71] Blair himself, however, 'was always ambivalent about the merits of constitutional reform' and was said to have a curious 'box ticking mentality', pushed by a 'moral and political duty to see it through' as an inheritance of John Smith, rather than any deep belief.[72]

[67] Blair (n 1).
[68] ibid.
[69] ibid.
[70] ibid.
[71] F Matthews, 'Inaction and Reaction – Coalition Government and Constitutional Reform in the United Kingdom' (2015) 10 *British Politics* 308, 312.
[72] M Flinders, *Democratic Drift: Majoritarian Modification and Democratic Anomie in the United Kingdom* (Oxford University Press, 2009).

What reinforced this was the sense that there was no overall grand design holding changes together. The party's ideas 'deliberately eschewed any engagement with first principles, with grand plans and templates'.[73] Instead, it was 'curious and contradictory amalgam of radicalism and conservatism'.[74] Flinders labelled it 'bi-constitutionality', with 'significant change … only in relation to the federal–unitary dimension' but 'no dramatic shift from a majoritarian to a consensual model of democracy at the national level. The Westminster model continues to be the default option in terms of democracy in Britain.'[75] David Marquand described it as a

> revolution without a theory. It is the muddled, messy work of practical men and women … responding piecemeal and ad hoc to conflicting pressures. It was a 'revolution of sleepwalkers who don't know quite where they are going or quite why'.[76]

For FOI in particular, there was a lack of awareness at the top of the party. As with the 1970s, it was an issue that was 'good for a handclap at conference' but nothing more.[77] Blair hinted at this later when he said that FOI was 'agreed by most at the time'.[78] Straw claimed that the 'few words' of the manifesto commitment were 'about all the serious intellectual consideration that the PLP or the Shadow Cabinet had given to this inherently complex issue' and that there was a 'collective naivety' at senior levels about the implications.[79] He claimed that 'FOI was not thought about with any seriousness' before government.[80]

But what of the public? Blair claimed in his 1996 speech that four out of five voters supported the policy. Two 'state of the nation' surveys by Democratic Audit in 1991 and 1995 found strong support for FOI: in 1991, 77 per cent tended to agree or strongly agreed with having a statutory right of access to information, a figure that by 1995 had risen to 81 per cent.[81]

Yet even if support was wide, it was unlikely to be deep. Historically, the British electorate was 'notoriously uninterested' in its constitution. Only the 'Great Reform Act of 1832 and the Parliament Act 1911' stand out as topics of 'intense political and public debate'.[82] Since the 1970s, discussion about constitutional change, Scotland aside, was 'primarily conducted amongst the elite – politicians, academics, lawyers and journalists'.[83] Generally, the public

[73] M Flinders, 'The Problem with Democracy' (2015) 69 *Parliamentary Affairs* 181.
[74] Dorey (n 32).
[75] Flinders, *Democratic Drift* (2009) 63.
[76] D Marquand, 'Populism or Pluralism? New Labour and the Constitution' (1999) ww.ucl.ac.uk/spp/publications/unit-publications/46.pdf.
[77] Private interview in Worthy (n 3).
[78] Justice Committee, letter from Rt Hon Tony Blair to Rt Hon Sir Alan Beith MP, Chair, Justice Committee, re: Post-Legislative Scrutiny of the Freedom of Information Act 2000 (July 2012) www.publications.parliament.uk/pa/cm201213/cmselect/cmjust/96/tb01.htm.
[79] J Straw, *Last Man Standing: Memoirs of a Political Survivor* (Pan Macmillan, 2012) 275–76.
[80] ibid.
[81] Quoted in Worthy (n 3).
[82] Flinders (n 72) 37.
[83] V Bogdanor, *The New British Constitution* (Bloomsbury Publishing, 2009) 6.

was 'little interested' or 'perhaps even unaware' of what Labour wished to do.[84] Gallup found constitutional issues to be the ones that excited the least interest.[85]

VI. FREEDOM OF INFORMATION, 1997–2000: RADICALISM, REACTION AND STRUGGLE

Once in power, FOI entered what was described in the USA as a time of 'back-stage in-fighting and front stage dissembling'.[86] The story of FOI in the UK runs in three distinct stages: a first, 'radical' stage, when a few powerful actors pushed for a far-reaching White Paper; a second period of reaction and reversal, when other ministers and officials watered down the draft Bill; and a third, final struggle within Parliament between cross-party MPs looking to strengthen the law and the government seeking a minimal Act. The story is thus of the mobilisation and counter-mobilisation of small factions supporting first a radical and then a lesser policy.

Table 2 Changes to FOI Policy, 1997–2000

	White Paper	**Draft Bill**	**Bill in Parliament**
Scope	100,000 public bodies (excluding Parliament and police)	100,000 public bodies (including Parliament and police)	–
Harm test	'Substantial' harm	Harm	–
Time scale	?	40 days	20 days
Scope of access	Open ended (include cabinet papers)	Exclude Cabinet papers	–
Veto	None	Veto power for cabinet members and council leaders	Reduced to Cabinet-and must consult
Other exclusions	Privacy?	Health and safety, 'mosaic', ministerial power to create new exclusions	Health and safety, 'mosaic', ministerial power to create new exclusions all removed
Appeal system	Commissioner	Commissioner and Tribunal	–
Justification/ narrative	Anti-establishment popular tool	Local tool	–

[84] ibid.

[85] D Sanders, 'The New Electoral Battleground' in King et al, *New Labour Triumphs: Britain at the Polls* (1998) 241.

[86] G Kennedy. 'Advocates of Openness: The Freedom of Information Movement' (PhD thesis, University of Missouri, Columbia 1978) 115.

VII. THE RADICAL PHASE: YOUR RIGHT TO KNOW, 1997–98

In May 1997, FOI policy was given to the Chancellor of the Duchy of Lancaster, David Clark. However, it was also strongly supported by Blair's formidable Lord Chancellor Derry Irvine, who chaired key constitutional reform cabinet committees, including the CRP-FOI Committee, which oversaw FOI. Together they opted for a radical option, rejecting lesser, smaller changes suggested by officials. Lord Irvine feared FOI would be bogged down and decided to move at speed, drafting his own radical set of proposals described as the 'thoughts of chairman Irvine'.[87] His radicalism and speed had, everyone presumed, the support of the new Prime Minister, and his approach on the committee was compared to Thatcher in the way he directly attacked and criticised those who raised doubts. The other ministers were either uninterested or intimidated. Only the Home Secretary Jack Straw opposed the law, managing to negotiate an opt-out for the police.

By December of 1997, just six months after coming to power, Irvine and Clark had created an eye-catching initial proposal, in the form of a consultation document entitled *Your Right To Know*. It offered, as the radicals hoped, a far-ranging law with very extensive right to information, low-level protections for government and – something to chill the bones of officials and ministers – no veto to stop information being released.[88] The media and activists cheered the new proposals and welcomed its radicalism.[89] Clark described *Your Right to Know* as a 'very, very radical White Paper'.[90] As Table 2 shows, its scope, its approach to judging information release and the power it gave to the commissioner made it a powerful law. Released with an enthusiastic preface from Tony Blair, it was, as David Clark joked, one of the few policies to be welcomed by both *The Guardian* and the *Daily Mail*.[91] It was unclear if the radicals expected the policy to survive intact or hoped that any compromise would retain some of the law's strengths.

Despite its welcome, some commentators expressed concerns. Important issues, such as how FOI interacted with data protection, were left unaddressed, while the innovative tests of whether release causes 'substantial harm' were legally untested.[92] They also found that 'the tone of the White Paper was hopelessly optimistic'. Professor Robert Hazell, an ex-official who had studied FOI, summed up the worries:

> The White Paper offers a very generous Freedom of Information regime, probably the most generous yet seen. It is almost too good to be true. That is the central concern:

[87] Worthy (n 3).

[88] Cabinet Office, *Your Right to Know: The Government's Proposals for a Freedom of Information Act* (Cmnd 3818, 1997).

[89] P Birkinshaw, 'An "All Singin' and All Dancin'" Affair: The New Labour Government's Proposals for Freedom of Information' (1998) 2 *PL* 176.

[90] Worthy (n 3).

[91] ibid.

[92] P Birkinshaw. *Freedom of Information: The Law, the Practice and the Ideal*, 3rd edn (Butterworths, 2001) 292.

> that this is an unreal White Paper brought out without the full understanding or wholehearted commitment on behalf of departments or Ministers.[93]

The concerns came to pass. After the welcome given to the White Paper by the media, FOI policy hit a brick wall. As time passed, the government began to have second thoughts about exposing itself to too much openness. Scandals had begun to hit the new government. Perhaps there should be more protections for government? Perhaps the law was a little too generous? As seen elsewhere, the longer FOI was considered, the less appealing it became.[94] Maurice Frankel, the head of CFOI, warned how the passage of time and changing context would serve to dilute any FOI plans and create more cautious policy:

> The more used to office ministers become the more plausible the case for caution will seem … being caught out is unpleasant … the press is becoming less admiring and more sceptical; even one or two opposition spokesmen are showing the signs of scoring points.[95]

VIII. REACTION AND REVERSAL: THE DRAFT BILL, 1998–99

The Labour government had indeed begun to experience the effect of scandals and scrutiny, from the Ecclestone scandal, which touched on Blair himself, to the Millennium Dome. FOI was not the only area of constitutional reform where doubts crept in. By 1999, Labour had been able to park or freeze progress in other areas of constitutional reform when they proved too difficult, inconvenient or divisive. Voting reform was put on hold, as was later the more complex and politically limiting 'stage two' of House of Lords reform.[96]

In July 1998, responsibility for FOI was then handed to Jack Straw – the minister who had opposed the radical policy in the committee.[97] Crucially, David Clark had been sacked from the Cabinet and Lord Irvine, though still in government, had seen his influence wane amid a series of scandals and missteps. Straw claimed he called a 'temporary halt' to the plans during an 'ill-tempered meeting' of the CRP-FOI Committee.[98] As he began the complex task of legislating, the fears of other ministers, including Tony Blair, began to creep in. One person present at the meetings described them as 'full of worst case scenarios', as officials and ministers from across government became more anxious. Officials nicknamed the CRP-FOI Committee 'Crap FOI'.[99] Blair, rather than realising

[93] R Hazell, 'Commentary on the Freedom of Information White Paper' (Constitution Unit, 1998).
[94] Worthy (n 3).
[95] 'No More Secrets Please!' *The Independent* (26 July 1998).
[96] Flinders (n 72).
[97] Straw, *Last Man Standing* (2012).
[98] ibid 279.
[99] ibid.

'too late' what his generous promises had wrought, specifically instructed Jack Straw to cut them back and even attempted to introduce a blanket protection for 10 Downing Street.[100]

More than a year after the White Paper, in the summer of 1999, a very different set of proposals emerged. Parts of the redrawn Bill were necessarily different as it dealt with the numerous difficult areas, such as privacy, that had been left undone by the consultation paper. It offered a series of new protections from non-disclosure, normal for any FOI law. The new FOI 'Bill' was full of strong protections for those in power, with a government veto and a 40-day turnaround time. In a novel innovation, it gave ministers the power to create new reasons to exclude information. The narrative shifted, as Straw himself showed when he emphasised the 'local' or 'service' aspect of FOI in an article in *The Independent*:

> parents will be better able to find out how schools apply their admissions policies. Patients ... how hospitals allocate resources ... citizens will be able to find out more about their local police force. It's at this local level that constitutional reform matters.[101]

The new draft was heavily criticised. Some questioned whether the new proposals could even be described as 'freedom of information' at all, and felt that the draft was so repressive in order that parts could be 'dropped' to ease its passage through Parliament. The law only survived the revisions because the Committee agreed a five-year implementation gap between passing the law and it coming into force, so that the 2000 Act would come into force in January 2005, a full election cycle away. This decision ostensibly gave records managers more time to prepare, but was also made because Labour believed they would not be in power in 2005 when the law came into force.[102]

IX. FOI IN PARLIAMENT, 1999–2000

In Parliament, a cross-party group of MPs and peers tried to strengthen the law, removing and blunting some of the worse parts. As Table 2 shows, the all-embracing veto power was reduced, as were some of the more repressive parts of the Bill, such as the power to create new exclusions from the law. However, the government used its control of agenda and partisan loyalty to split the alliance and, with a landslide majority of 179, there was limited room for manoeuvre. Straw proved a highly capable strategist in pushing the law, compromising and making concessions at key moments. As happened in other countries, supporters of FOI were nervous of pushing too far when the government seemed so willing to drop the Bill (and said so repeatedly via the whips).

[100] Justice Committee Minutes of Evidence HC 96 – ii: Jack Straw (TSO, 2012) www.publications.parliament.uk/pa/cm201213/cmselect/cmjust/96/120417.htm.
[101] 'Good Government Needs Scrutiny and Challenge' *The Independent* (25 May 1999).
[102] Worthy (n 3).

Whether the government would truly abandon FOI was unclear. Straw claims that the 'slow progress' of the Bill, especially in the later House of Lords stages, 'became the break point', as 'I'd had enough of FOI'.[103] He 'half thought that the best thing might be to bin the whole Bill or kick it into the long grass with a royal commission', but Blair overruled him.[104] A widely predicted 'final battle' in the House of Lords was circumvented when the government did a deal with Liberal Democrat peers, and a similar 'last ditch' battle in the Commons stage was cut short when the Bill was guillotined, with the timing of debate cut short. As happened elsewhere, the radical plans of activists were watered down by the fear of politicians. The FOI Act 2000 was an uneven compromise between reformist hope and politicians' anxieties.

X. WHY DID FOI SURVIVE?

The story of FOI is one of an increasingly reluctant set of politicians, slowly pushing a policy they disliked and feared. So why did FOI not go the way of other New Labour's 'lost' reforms, such as voting reform or stage 2 of the House of Lords, which were quietly put on hold or left to gather dust? Superficially, the political costs of 'losing' FOI were low. It was not a vote winner and, *The Guardian* and *The Independent* aside, large parts of the media were uninterested.

Those involved characterised FOI as a mistake that could not, or was not, stopped in time. Blair claimed it was developed 'with care but without foresight',[105] and wove a picture of a new, inexperienced government blundering naively into passing a radical law whose full consequences became clear 'far too late'. His government legislated 'in the first throes of power' and 'it was only later, far too late in the day, when the full folly of the legislation became apparent'.[106] Straw claimed that CFOI had been 'extremely active' and that ministers had 'become word perfect in the mantra of change' while not foreseeing 'counter-balancing arguments' that would 'hit us in government'.[107]

FOI in part survived because of Labour's unusual commitment to its own pledges. Straw referred to the manifesto as a 'holy text' created with 'immense care'.[108] As McDonald and Hazell point out, Labour

> came to power determined to implement its programme. This … is true of any new administration. But there was a particular edge to New Labour's commitment. This was a party which had been out of power for eighteen years, which had wearied of the charges of betrayal which critics had levelled at the Wilson and

[103] Straw (n 79) 281.
[104] ibid 281.
[105] Blair (n 2) 127.
[106] ibid 517.
[107] Straw (n 79) 275.
[108] ibid 281.

> Callaghan governments and whose leader had spoken often of the need for sustained achievement over two successive terms.[109]

More than this was the symbolic effect. FOI had been trumpeted, not least by Blair himself, as an anti-establishment, transformative tool, a weapon of accountability and a new, central right for citizens. Dropping FOI would make it the party of conservatism and secrecy. FOI was a 'test' of New Labour's own image, as a struggle 'between the … pretensions of New Labour as a party of reform against the instincts of a no-longer new- Labour as a party of government'.[110] If FOI was dropped, each inevitable scandal or secrecy issue would then highlight it. Backbench Labour MPs would continue to push Private Members' Bills. The Liberal Democrats and Conservatives threatened to take over FOI. The symbolism of FOI would boomerang and, crucially, not go away.

For Blair, there was personal credibility attached. As CFOI hoped, he had left several very public hostages to fortune, including his 1996 speech and the preface to the 1997 White Paper. The media repeated quotes and extracts from his speech and promises. Straw recalled, 'I saw Tony [Blair]' was 'exasperated as I was' with FOI. However, Blair had 'made a categorical promise in the John Smith memorial lecture' as well in the manifesto commitment, and had let the White Paper (called the 'David Clark extravaganza') go 'public'.[111] 'How credibly,' Blair asked, 'could we explain dropping a Bill with our names on it which was close to completing its passage through Parliament?', and he concluded that 'we'd better let the Bill go through'.[112]

XI. FOI, 20 YEARS ON

> How many leaders have come into office determined to work for more open government, only to end by fretting over leaks, seeking new ways to classify documents and questioning the loyalty of outspoken subordinates?[113]

Most FOI regimes exist in a constant state of change and flux as legal rulings, political reforms and diverse use continually reshape the boundaries of the laws. Politically, enthusiasm and support also wax and wane in a cycle of 'optimism, pessimism and revisionism'.[114]

FOI remains contested 20 years after the Act received royal assent and 15 years in force. The law has been a success, with high levels of use and deep support for

[109] A McDonald and R Hazell, 'What Happened Next: Constitutional Change under New Labour' in A McDonald (ed), *Reinventing Britain: Constitutional Change under New Labour* (University of California Press, 2007) 6.
[110] 'Poodles or Politicians: Now Is the Time to Decide' *The Guardian* (4 April 2000).
[111] Straw (n 79) 281.
[112] ibid.
[113] S Bok, *Secrets: Concealment and Revelation* (Oxford University Press, 1986) 177.
[114] Snell, 'Freedom of Information' (2001) 350.

it across the media and civil society. While other constitutional reforms simply moved power between elites, FOI is a genuinely popular instrument of accountability.[115] Yet politicians and others have vehemently and publically expressed their dislike. The Act has perhaps come to symbolise something that is 'wrong' or 'right' about contemporary British politics.

The UK's FOI regime is comparatively well functioning, with around 45,000 requests per year and a robust two-stage appeal system.[116] Use is also varied, with requesters made up of members of the public, journalists and non-governmental organisations, with the public representing the largest group.[117] Many of the battles fought before it became law, over the harm test or veto, appear to have had little effect. The veto, which Blair and Straw argued was a 'red line', has only been used nine times since the law was introduced.[118]

While FOI has helped generate high-profile exposures and greater openness, from the MPs' expenses scandal to visitors to Chequers, it is at the local, micro-political level where it has become a valuable tool, with around 80 per cent requests going to local government.[119] In 2012, an FOI request triggered the mass resignation of an entire parish council.[120] As the former Scottish Information Commissioner put it, the success of FOI can be seen in the pages of local newspapers.[121]

There were concerns that the Act would be 'a sheep in wolf's clothing'.[122] However, assessments in 2010 of central government and later local government concluded that FOI had made public bodies more transparent and accountable.[123] Post-legislative scrutiny of the law by a House of Commons Select Committee reached very similar conclusions: 'The Freedom of Information Act has enhanced the UK's democratic system and made our public bodies more

[115] V Bogdanor. 'An Era of Constitutional Reform' (2010) 81(1) *The Political Quarterly* S53: M Fenster, *The Transparency Fix: Secrets, Leaks, and Uncontrollable Government Information* (Stanford University Press, 2017).

[116] See the Cabinet Office, 'Freedom of Information Statistics' https://www.gov.uk/government/collections/government-foi-statistics#2018.

[117] B Worthy and R Hazell, 'Disruptive, Dynamic and Democratic? Ten Years of Freedom of Information in the UK' (2017) 70 *Parliamentary Affairs* 22.

[118] The status of the UK veto is now uncertain following a UK Supreme Court ruling. Despite a commendation to change the veto via primary legislation in 2016, the UK government instead committed only to use it at certain points in the appeal system: see M Elliott, 'A Tangled Constitutional Web: The Black-Spider Memos and the British Constitution's Relational Architecture' (2015) University of Cambridge Faculty of Law Research Paper No 34/2015, http://ssrn.com/abstract=2621451.

[119] Worthy and Hazell, 'Disruptive, Dynamic and Democratic?' (2017).

[120] 'Walberswick Parish Councillors Quit over FOI Requests' *BBC News* (3 October 2012) www.bbc.co.uk/news/uk-england-suffolk-19804046.

[121] See K Dunion, *Freedom of Information in Scotland in Practice* (Dundee University Press, 2011).

[122] R Austin, 'The Freedom of Information Act 2000: A Sheep in Wolf's Clothing?' in J Jowell and D Oliver (eds), *The Changing Constitution*, 6th edn (Oxford University Press, 2007) 387–406.

[123] Hazell et al 2010; B Worthy, 'Some Are More Open Than Others': Comparing the Impact of the Freedom of Information Act 2000 on Local and Central Government in the UK' (2013) 15 *Journal of Comparative Policy Analysis: Research and Practice* 395.

open, accountable and transparent. It has been a success and we do not wish to diminish its intended scope, or its effectiveness.'[124]

In March 2016, a government-appointed Independent Commission on Freedom of Information reinforced this positive assessment: 'The Act is generally working well … It has enhanced openness and transparency … there is no evidence that the Act needs to be radically altered, or that the right of access to information needs to be restricted.'[125]

Experimental work at parish level using FOI requests has shown how the law can work to promote greater openness.[126] Whether it has altered political trust, as Blair hoped, is a more complex question, and it appears to have had little effect either way in an era of declining trust, with surveys showing no change due to FOI.[127] Nor is it clear whether or how voters are influenced by available information.[128] The MPs' expenses scandal of 2009, triggered in part by an FOI request, showed how exposures can reinforce rather than reveal, but also, despite the sound and fury, had little effect on voting patterns in the subsequent general election.[129]

As happened elsewhere, the UK's FOI law has gradually expanded. There was limited change when section 6 of the Act was amended to extend the Act to cover exam bodies and databases in 2012.[130] In 2015, the strategic rail authority was subject to a FOI request, owing to a change in accounting designation and its reclassification as a public body in 2014.[131] In 2017, the government promised

[124] Justice Committee, *Post-Legislative Scrutiny of the Freedom of Information Act 2000, volumes 1 and 2 (HC 96 –i)* (TSO, 2012) 3.

[125] Independent Commission on Freedom of Information. *Independent Commission on Freedom of Information Report* (TSO, 2016) 3.

[126] See P John, B Worthy and M Vannoni, 'Transparency at the Parish Pump: A Field Experiment to Measure the Effectiveness of Freedom of Information Requests in England' (2017) 27 *Journal of Public Administration Research and Theory* 485. This experiment used a series of FOI requests and non-legal 'asks' to English parish councils to measure the effectiveness of FOI as opposed to simply seeking information. It found requests to be twice as effective as asks. A replication of the experiment in the Netherlands found even stronger differences.

[127] See P Whiteley, HD Clarke, D Sanders and M Stewart, 'Why Do Voters Lose Trust in Governments? Public Perceptions of Government Honesty and Trustworthiness in Britain 2000–2013' (2016) 18 *British Journal of Politics and International Relations* 234; Justice Committee, *Post-Legislative Scrutiny of the Freedom of Information Act 2000* (2012).

[128] M Bauhr and M Grimes, 'Indignation or Resignation: The Implications of Transparency for Societal Accountability' (2014) 27 *Governance* 291.

[129] C Pattie and R Johnston, 'The Electoral Impact of the UK 2009 MPs' Expenses Scandal' (2012) 60 *Political Studies* 730; N Allen and S Birch, 'Tempests and Teacups: Politicians' Reputations in the Wake of the Expenses Scandal' in J van Heerde-Hudson (ed), *The Political Costs of the 2009 British MPs' Expenses Scandal* (Palgrave Macmillan, 2014) 132–52.

[130] Protection of Freedoms Act 2012, ss 102–03.

[131] 'The Office for National Statistics announced its intention to reclassify Network Rail as a Central Government Body in the UK National Accounts and Public Sector Finances with effect from 1 September 2014. This was a statistical change driven by new guidance in the European System of National Accounts 2010 (ESA10)': Network Rail 'What Reclassification Means for Investors' https://www.networkrail.co.uk/industry-commercial-partners/third-party-investors/investor-relations/information-for-investors/reclassification/.

greater proactive transparency over pay and FOI statistics through a revision to the Code of Practice in 2018, issued under section 45 of the law.[132] Scotland's separate Freedom of Information (Scotland) Act 2002, covering devolved matters, was extended to cover independent schools and certain leisure trusts. Since 2016, the Information Commissioner has championed the inclusion of private sector bodies directly under FOI (rather than simply using contractual clauses on FOI in procurement agreements) – something the independent review suggested and MPs have continually pushed through a series of Private Members' Bills.

Yet a reaction also exists. Looking across the 10 years, there is evidence of a clear slowdown in responses at central government level: 'Since 2010, departments have become less open in response to FOI requests': while 39 per cent of requests were 'fully or partially withheld' in 2010, a full 52 per cent were 'fully or partially withheld' in 2017.[133] There have been a series of attempts at 'dismantling' or chipping away at the law since 2005, with roughly one attempt floated every 18–24 months. Tony Blair proposed introducing a fee for requests (2006), a Private Members' Bill attempted to remove Parliament from the law (2007) and, under Gordon Brown, the Monarch and Heir were removed from the ambit of the law (2010). The Conservative–Liberal Democrat Coalition then mooted a clampdown on 'industrial users' (2012–13) and the subsequent Conservative government suggested amending the veto (2015–16). In 2015, the Cameron government announced an independent inquiry into the FOI Act and gave it a remit to examine the potential effect on decision-making and costs of the law. Despite fears that it would seek to water down the law, the FOI Commission's clear endorsement of the Act in 2016 and the sheer scale of the resistance to change by the media and civil society halted any attempt to limit it.[134] Of all these attempts, only the removal of the Monarch and Heir to the Throne, pushed through at the end of the 2010 Labour government with little publicity, was successful, though Brown also opened up government through records reforms.[135]

One key to the strength or weakness of a law is the level of political support. While Blair was ambivalent, Gordon Brown and then David Cameron both made strong speeches in favour of openness. Nevertheless, it was openness on their terms: Cameron pledged 'true freedom of information' through a 'transparency revolution', with th eaim of 'making our government one of the most open and transparent in the world'.[136] However, while he pushed a series of apparently radical open data reforms as a badge of his own radicalism from 2010 onwards,

[132] See Cabinet Office, *Freedom of Information Code of Practice* (2018) https://www.gov.uk/government/publications/freedom-of-information-code-of-practice.

[133] Institute for Government, *Whitehall Monitor 2018. The General Election, Brexit and Beyond* (2018).

[134] Worthy and Hazell (n 117).

[135] Constitutional Reform and Governance Act 2010, s 46.

[136] Prime Minister's Office, 'PM's Podcast on Transparency' (29 May 2010).

many of which were aimed at the private sector, in 2015 he also set up the FOI Commission to restrict the Act and described the law as something that was 'furring up the arteries of government'.[137]

For some senior politicians and officials, FOI is part of a narrative of failure and abuse. Blair argued his FOI law was a twofold failure.

First, it had stopped government decision-making:

> If you are trying to take a difficult decision and you're weighing up the pros and cons, you have frank conversations ... And if those conversations then are put out in a published form that afterwards are liable to be highlighted in particular ways, you are going to be very cautious. That's why it's not a sensible thing.[138]

The former Cabinet Secretary Gus O'Donnell claimed that it had 'hamstrung' the government, though when pressed he could only offer isolated examples.[139] O'Donnell's successor as Cabinet Secretary, Jeremy Heywood, while praising the Act, agreed that FOI was 'sand in the machine' and that 'there are some extra costs that come with the Freedom of Information Act, there are some chilling effects'.[140]

Research points towards a minimal effect across government as a whole. The Justice Committee 'was not able to conclude, with any certainty that a chilling effect has resulted from FOI'.[141] In central government, there was concern, with isolated instances of resistance but no general trend, and at local government level similarly there appear to be a few exceptional cases but no systematic effect.[142] In both Scotland and England, there was some concern about informal recording, but also some evidence of a positive professionalising effect.[143]

However, there appears to be growing resistance and avoidance at the top. In 2018, following complaints by Scottish journalists, a report by the Scottish Information Commissioner concluded that the government had sought to create a 'two-tier' system delaying journalists' or politically sensitive requests.[144] At the same time, Northern Ireland's most senior civil servant, David Sterling, informed the Renewable Heat Incentive 'cash for ash' inquiry, over the failed renewable heating policy, that records had not been kept of certain sensitive

[137] Worthy and Hazell (n 117).

[138] 'World Exclusive: Tony Blair Interview' *The Guardian* (1 September 2010).

[139] Worthy (n 3). O'Donnell cited a hypothetical situation and the 2010 coalition negotiations, but also admitted that FOI had not changed how minutes were taken.

[140] Institute for Government, 'The Role of A Modern Cabinet Secretary' (2015) http://www.instituteforgovernment.org.uk/events/role-modern-cabinet-secretary-conversation-sir-jeremy-heywood.

[141] Justice Committee (n 124) 32.

[142] Worthy, 'Some Are More Open Than Others' (2013); E Shepherd, A Stevenson and A Flinn, 'Records Management in English Local Government: The Effect of Freedom of Information' (2011) 21 *Records Management Journal* 122.

[143] P Richter and R Wilson, '"It's the Tip of the Iceberg": The Hidden Tensions between Theory, Policy and Practice in the Management of Freedom of Information in English Local Government Bodies – Evidence from a Regional Study' (2013) 33 *Public Money & Management* 177.

[144] Scottish Information Commissioner, *Intervention Report Scottish Government* (2018).

political meetings – 'safe space where they could think the unthinkable and not necessarily have it all recorded' – with the DUP and Sinn Féin having 'got into the habit' of not recording all meetings.[145]

The second problem, according to Blair, was that FOI was being misused. As he put it:

> The truth is that the FOI Act isn't used, for the most part, by 'the people'. It's used by journalists. For political leaders, it's like saying to someone who is hitting you over the head with a stick, 'Hey, try this instead', and handing them a mallet.[146]

Though the evidence does not support this claim, it tells us much about how politicians see it. Blair regretted it, while Cameron described FOI as a 'buggeration factor'.[147] FOI is seen as a symptom of creating too much openness and too little knowledge. In a 'low trust high blame' environment like the UK, FOI is viewed a 'gotcha tool' for shock exposure.[148] Others argue that such 'hyper-democratic problems' are less a failure of 'openness' as an ideal, and instead represent the failure of elites to respond properly to the politics of a new age.[149] Moreover, any successful FOI should make politicians nervous and upset – public laments should be seen as markers of success.

XII. CONCLUSION

At a distance of 20 years, FOI has a complex and unpredictable legacy as a constitutional reform, and demonstrates the extent to which this is as much about perceptions of success (or failure) as it is about concrete realities. That a popularly supported change is so deeply disliked in government is especially revealing of its impact. Indeed, few leaders have addressed themselves so forcefully as Blair after passing reforms their party have pushed for 30 years:

> You idiot. You naive, foolish, irresponsible nincompoop. There is really no description of stupidity, no matter how vivid, that is adequate. I quake at the imbecility of it.[150]

[145] 'RHI Inquiry: Minutes Not Taken to Frustrate FOIs' *BBC News* (4 March 2018); 'RHI Inquiry: Foster Says Note-taking Claim "Nonsense"' *BBC News* (18 April 2018).

[146] Blair (n 2) 516–17.

[147] Worthy and Hazell (n 117).

[148] A Fung and D Weil, 'Open Government, Open Society' in T Lathrop and L Ruma (eds), *Collaboration, Transparency, and Participation in Practice* (O'Reilly Media, 2010) 105–14.

[149] D Richards and MJ Smith, 'In Defence of British Politics against the British Political Tradition' (2015) 86 *The Political Quarterly* 41, 48–49.

[150] Blair (n 2) 516.

9

What Was New Labour's Vision for Parliament? And Did It Succeed?

LOUISE THOMPSON

I. INTRODUCTION

DAVID MARQUAND DESCRIBES the constitutional reforms implemented during the early New Labour years as 'a revolution of sleepwalkers who don't know quite where they are going or quite why'.[1] Some of the biggest reforms implemented during this period involved aspects of the constitution which may have been badged as parliamentary reform, but which were largely external to the institution of the UK Parliament, such as devolution to Scotland and Wales. Within Parliament, most emphasis was (and still is) placed on reform of the House of Lords and, as such, discussion usually begins and ends with the 1997 Parliament. This chapter draws on the Labour Party's manifestos, speeches and parliamentary material to consider the internal reforms to Parliament implemented during the New Labour years. In doing so, it asks what the New Labour vision for Parliament actually was, and whether or not it succeeded. The reforms made to Parliament were generally thought of as piecemeal and ineffective at the time of the Labour governments, but a longer-term view, particularly taking into account the context of minority government, tells a different story.

II. A STRONG PARLIAMENTARY ATTITUDE?

In his final remarks as Prime Minister in the House of Commons on 27 June 2007, Tony Blair noted that he had 'never pretended to be a great House of Commons man',[2] but placed on the record his unswerving 'respect' for the

[1] D Marquand, 'Populism or Pluralism? New Labour and the Constitution' (Mischon Lecture, UCL, May 1999) www.ucl.ac.uk/political-science/publications/unit-publications/46.pdf.
[2] HC Deb 27 June 2007, col 333.

debating chamber.[3] These comments are strengthened by the relative (un) importance he seemed to attach to appearing in Parliament during his time as Prime Minister. His consolidation of Prime Minister's Question Time into one 30-minute session sat hand in hand with a tendency to brief the media before Parliament[4] and a very low (8 per cent) record of prime ministerial attendance in divisions.[5] In sum, they constituted a dwindling of prime ministerial presence in the House of Commons chamber, though it should be noted that Blair has placed on the record his disagreement with this characterisation.[6] This apparent lack of respect for parliamentary convention and the lack of parliamentary participation was not confined solely to Tony Blair. Indeed, Riddell notes that this was simply a feature of political life for all senior politicians, but was 'accentuated' further under Blair's premiership.[7] The Prime Minister and his Cabinet colleagues were often absent from the Commons division lobbies, something later governments with far smaller parliamentary majorities would seldom dare to do. Alongside the individual relationship between the Prime Minister and Parliament was the attitude of the New Labour government itself towards its own parliamentarians. Rawnsley describes the party's conception of parliamentary democracy as one in which 'government MPs exist almost solely to sustain the government',[8] while Foley talks of the obligation of backbench MPs 'to the leadership and to its judgements and decisions',[9] which, in a parliamentary sense, meant that any opposition was squeezed out of the party.[10] Foley cites early decisions by the government, such as the imposition of guillotine motions on the Referendums (Scotland and Wales) Bill, as examples of these attempts to curtail any opposition from backbenchers.[11]

Yet there were times at which Blair pursued a more overt parliamentarian style in his dialogue. In particular, he actively spoke of the UK Parliament in a historical sense, recognising its position as a key institution of British democracy and the role it had played in the country's modernisation and development. In his first conference speech as Prime Minister, he told delegates that 'we are one of the great innovative peoples – from the Magna Carta to the first Parliament to the industrial revolution to an empire that covered the world'.[12] At a broad

[3] HC Deb 27 June 2007, col 334.

[4] A Finlayson, *Making Sense of New Labour* (Lawrence and Wishhart, 2003) 174.

[5] P Riddell, 'Members and Millbank: The Media and Parliament' (1998) 69B *The Political Quarterly* 8.

[6] Liaison Committee, Oral Evidence from the Prime Minister, HC 2002–03, Q15.

[7] Riddell, 'Members and Millbank' (1998).

[8] A Rawnsley, *Servants of the People: The Inside Story of New Labour* (Hamish Hamilton, 2000) 3.

[9] M Foley, *The British Presidency* (Manchester University Press, 2000) 307.

[10] ibid.

[11] ibid 308.

[12] T Blair, speech to Labour Party Conference (Brighton 1997) www.britishpoliticalspeech.org/speech-archive.htm?speech=203.

level then, there is clear respect for Parliament as an institution of democracy and an understanding of its centrality to British political life. At a personal level, though, the institution of Parliament would play a rather secondary role during the New Labour years.

III. (DIS)INTEREST IN PARLIAMENTARY REFORM?

Tony Blair's activity in Parliament may provide somewhat mixed messages about his attitude towards the institution. His biographer Anthony Seldon, however, is clear about Blair's disdain for constitutional or parliamentary reform policies, noting that he was both 'bored absolutely rigid by it' and 'supremely uninterested in the details'.[13] Blair himself would later write that he was 'not passionate about it', but that despite this he felt that the reform of Parliament was 'inevitable'.[14]

Evidence of this can be found in the way in which Blair maintained a degree of separation between himself and parliamentary or constitutional reform legislation. Where previous Prime Ministers had introduced this legislation in the Commons themselves, Blair 'left other ministers to open and close the second reading debates'.[15] The creation of a new Department for Constitutional Affairs in 2003 perhaps reinforced this detachment further.[16] Similar attitudes can be found among other members of government. Jack Straw, for instance, writes that it was simply not high on the agenda; 'there were other more important issues for us to deal with'.[17] This was particularly true after the 2001 general election, when, it seemed, New Labour's priorities had changed and 'constitutional fatigue had set in'.[18] Once the initial constitutional and parliamentary reforms had been dealt with in the 1997 Parliament, 'constitutional apathy' set in during Blair's second term, with no significant reform plans on the agenda.[19] Although further House of Lords reform following the removal of the hereditary peers remained in the Labour Party's 2001 manifesto, it was given a very low priority.[20]

Neither the party leader nor his senior colleagues therefore seemed to have invested a great deal of time or interest in aspects of parliamentary reform.

[13] A Seldon et al, *Blair Unbound* (Simon & Schuster, 2007) 202.

[14] T Blair, *A Journey* (Hutchinson, 2010) 251.

[15] K Theakston, 'Prime Ministers and the Constitution: Attlee to Blair' (2005) 58 *Parliamentary Affairs* 17, 33.

[16] For the contrasting argument that the creation of a Department for Constitutional Affairs was 'most welcome', see R Brazier, *Constitutional Reform: Reshaping the British Political System* (Oxford University Press, 2008) ch 2.

[17] J Straw, *Last Man Standing: Memoirs of a Political Survivor* (Macmillan, 2012).

[18] M Flinders, 'Majoritarian Democracy in Britain: New Labour and the Constitution' (2005) 29 *West European Politics* 61, 64.

[19] Seldon et al, *Blair Unbound* (2007) 202.

[20] ibid.

An analysis of some of the key policy forums (speeches to party conference and the general election manifestos) across the New Labour years presents an ever more disheartening picture. Writing in 2003, Alan Finlayson spoke of what he describes as the 'consistency of vision' emanating from Blair's conference speeches.[21] Ardent parliamentary reformers would probably agree with him, but in a slightly different way. An analysis of all of the Labour leaders' conference speeches between 1995 and 2009 and the party's general election manifestos across this period share one very consistent absence: the lack of any real interest or vision in the area of parliamentary reform. That is, although there is an abundance of discussion of broader constitutional reform, particularly in the early New Labour years and the commitment to devolution, discussions of specific parliamentary reforms became increasingly sparse. It should be noted that in the run up to 1997 the lack of 'detailed definition' was widespread across New Labour policy,[22] but for parliamentary reform policy this continued far beyond the 1997 general election. Three features of parliamentary reform policy can be drawn from these speeches and manifestos.

First, where parliamentary reform is mentioned, it is often not actually about the institution of Parliament at all. Rather, it is about the reform of central government. The 1997 Labour Party manifesto, for instance, talks of 'over-centralisation of *government* and lack of accountability' (emphasis added) as one of the party's key objectives. There is no mention of Parliament here. Later on in the document, House of Lords reform is discussed within a broader section on 'reforming *government*'[23] (emphasis added) and cleaning up politics. The manifesto links it clearly to government, stating that the Conservatives support 'hereditary peers, unaccountable quangos and secretive government'. An apparent confusion or muddling of government and Parliament is perhaps reflective of the broader New Labour attitude towards Parliament. Scholars would go on to document the seemingly engrained view of executive dominance or governing through Parliament.[24]

Second, parliamentary reform became something of an umbrella term used most frequently to describe reforms which were *external* to the institution itself. The 1997 manifesto's discussion of an effective House of Commons talked more about the selection of candidates, the funding of political parties and the choice of electoral system than about internal reform. In the Gordon Brown years, this was replaced by the phrase 'political reform', which is perhaps a better fit. Only one piece of constitutional legislation in the 1997 Parliament actually focused on Parliament as an *institution* (the 1999 House of Lords Act). Other reforms may have affected Parliament in some way, but the institution was not

[21] Finlayson, *Making Sense of New Labour* (2003) 82.
[22] Rawnsley, *Servants of the People* (2000) 6.
[23] Labour Party, *New Labour: Because Britain Deserves Better* (1997).
[24] See A Seldon *The Blair Effect* (Little, Brown & Co, 2001).

the focus of it. Section 19 of the Human Rights Act 1998, for instance, would require ministers to make a statement to the House regarding the compatibility of government legislation with the Act prior to its second reading. Similarly, while the Scotland Act 1998 and the Wales Act 1998 created institutions external to the UK Parliament, the introduction of the Sewel Convention would mean that Parliament would not ordinarily legislate on devolved matters without the passage of legislative consent motions in the devolved Parliaments.

Third, where issues of parliamentary reform are highlighted, the overwhelming focus is on the House of Lords rather than the House of Commons, implying that most of the New Labour vision is about reform of the upper chamber, rather than full parliamentary reform encompassing both chambers of the institution itself. Lords reform is allocated much more space in the 1997, 2001 and 2005 manifestos compared to Commons reforms. Of the latter, the majority are devoted to discussions of diversity in the Commons and the need to increase the number of women MPs. Those that would become key House of Commons reforms, such as the changes made to Prime Minister's Question Time, are given very little explanation. Indeed, Burch and Holliday describe how this change was 'mentioned rather ambiguously in the [party's] manifesto'.[25] It was in fact discussed in just a few words: 'Prime Minister's Questions will be made more effective'.[26] No indication is given as to how or why it should be 'more effective'. Kelso argues that Commons reforms were often turned inward by Blair, focusing on specific procedures and rules which minimised change rather than promoting comprehensive reform of the institution as a whole.[27] We can see this in the way that the 1997 manifesto discusses the creation of a new select committee to 'review' House of Commons procedures.[28] Kevin Theakston sums up the mix of Blair's attitude towards reform and the actual plans put in place by the Labour government. He describes Blair as 'shying away from theory … [with] … no roadmap or blueprint for constitutional reform' and a rather piecemeal approach to addressing constitutional or parliamentary problems as they appear rather than the implementation of any overarching strategy.[29]

IV. NEW LABOUR'S COMMITMENTS

With this in mind, we must consider what New Labour's commitments to parliamentary reform entailed. Doing so is complicated by the fact that the language used by New Labour in this area was, on the whole, vague at best. Flinders

[25] M Burch and I Holliday, 'New Labour and the machinery of government' in D Coates, P Lawler, PA Lawler *New Labour in Power* (Manchester University Press, 2000) 89.

[26] Labour Party (n 23).

[27] A Kelso, *Parliamentary Reform at Westminster* (Manchester University Press, 2009).

[28] Labour Party (n 23).

[29] Theakston, 'Prime Ministers and the Constitution' (2005) 35.

speaks of the 'lack of clear goals or principles in relation to constitutional policy as a whole',[30] but this was especially so in relation to Parliament. Even more so when we consider the House of Commons. As Leader of the Opposition, Blair says that we should reform Prime Minister's Questions so that it 'does Parliament credit',[31] but there is no discussion of its current failings. The word 'effective' is used quite liberally across all the party's manifestos. We see in the 1997 manifesto that PMQs will be 'made more effective'.[32] Indeed, this falls under a section entitled 'an effective House of Commons'.[33] The 2001 version picks up this theme, stating that the Commons needs to 'effectively fulfil its functions'.[34] Another term used frequently in relation to parliamentary reform is 'modernisation'. Although synonymous with the New Labour programme as a whole, use of modernisation here is equally vague. The 1997 manifesto affirms that 'we believe the House of Commons is in need of modernisation',[35] while in 2001 the party talks of continuing 'to modernise the procedures of the House of Commons'.[36] No detail is provided here as to what this modernisation involves. Blair himself admitted in his 2002 speech to the party conference that 'reform is just a word. It has no meaning in itself.'[37] This lends weight to the views expressed by academic and political observers that parliamentary reform occurred without a theory,[38] founding principles or a final destination.[39] It was, in essence, 'riddled with ambiguity'.[40]

The most significant attempt to explain New Labour's plans for Parliament comes from Alexandra Kelso.[41] Although her work takes a more longitudinal account of parliamentary reform, she makes the crucial distinction between efficiency and effectiveness reforms. Whereas the former involve changes to assert executive power over Parliament, particularly when dealing with legislation, the latter enhance opportunities for Parliament to influence the government. The difficulty in the New Labour period is that most of the reforms can be seen to be efficiency reforms even where they have been branded by the party as reforms of effectiveness. It implies that New Labour hoped to minimise Parliament's legislative and debating roles and prioritised the notion that a government with

[30] M Flinders, New Labour and the Constitution' in S Ludlam and MJ Smith (eds), *Governing as New Labour: Policy and Politics Under Blair* (Palgrave, 2003) 126.

[31] Tony Blair, speech to Labour Party Conference (Blackpool 1996).

[32] Labour Party (n 23).

[33] Labour Party (n 23).

[34] Labour Party, *Ambitions for Britain* (2001).

[35] Labour Party (n 23).

[36] Labour Party (n 34).

[37] T Blair, speech to Labour Party Conference (Blackpool 2002) www.britishpoliticalspeech.org/speech-archive.htm?speech=185.

[38] Marquand 'Populism or Pluralism?' (1999).

[39] P Toynbee and D Walker, *Better or Worse? Has Labour Delivered?* (Bloomsbury, 2005) 273.

[40] V Bogdanor, 'Labour and the Constitution: Part 1: The Record' in B Brivati and T Bale (eds), *New Labour in Power: Precedents and Prospects* (Routledge, 1997) 117.

[41] Kelso, *Parliamentary Reform at Westminster* (2009).

a solid mandate and a parliamentary majority has a right to get its business through Parliament in a timely and largely unobstructed manner. The remainder of this chapter discusses what impact Blair's reforms to Parliament had on the institution as a whole. They are divided into reforms which prioritised efficiency over effectiveness; reforms that stalled; and reforms which saw something of a delayed drop in terms of their significance for the institution of Parliament.

V. EFFICIENCY REFORMS: PRIME MINISTER'S QUESTION TIME AND LEGISLATIVE TIMETABLING

The primary efficiency reforms introduced by Blair were changes to PMQs and the introduction of timetabling for government legislation. Both were designed to maximise the government (and Prime Minister's) use of parliamentary time. Prime Minister's Question Time is a prime example of a change to parliamentary procedure which was originally marketed as an effectiveness reform by Blair. As a mechanism which underpins the entire system of accountability in Parliament, PMQs is a highlight of the parliamentary calendar. The Prime Minister had previously had to come to the House of Commons chamber twice a week – on Tuesdays and Thursdays – to endure 15 minutes of questions from MPs. Commons Speaker John Bercow has spoken of how 'it cannot be said that the whole House received these changes with rapture'.[42] Neither did outside observers have a very favourable attitude to the change, describing it as 'symptomatic of New Labour's impatience' with traditional parliamentary accountability.[43] As the key forum for prime ministerial accountability in the Commons, PMQs required a lot of preparation for a Prime Minister. Alistair Campbell writes about the extensive preparation Blair undertook for his first PMQs as Prime Minister on 21 May 1997, shutting himself away to 'write out answers on the tough questions'.[44] Although Blair had discussed his plans with the Procedure Committee before the 1997 general election, there was no formal parliamentary debate on the change, leading to a sense around the institution that 'the House has been bounced into new arrangements which suited the Prime Minister rather more than they did Parliament'.[45] Blair himself would later agree with this view, admitting that he had 'hatched a plot before the election' to reform PMQs and that his pitching of it in the party's general election manifesto was somewhat disingenuous.[46]

[42] J Bercow, speech at the Centre for Parliamentary Studies (9 June 2010) www.johnbercow.co.uk/content/speech-centre-parliamentary-studies.

[43] Foley, *The British Presidency* (2000) 308.

[44] A Campbell and R Stott, *The Blair Years: Extracts from the Alistair Campbell Diaries* (Hutchinson, 2007) 204–05.

[45] Bercow, speech at the Centre for Parliamentary Studies (2010).

[46] Blair, *A Journey* (2010) 108.

Academic analysis of Prime Minister's Questions suggests that this change contributed to PMQs becoming rowdier and that the session is now dominated by the Prime Minister and the Leader of the Opposition.[47] Although this trend continued after the Blair and Brown premierships, the condensing of the two PMQs slots no doubt facilitated this way of working in the chamber. Fewer questions were posed to the Prime Minister during Blair's PMQs than during the Major or Thatcher years,[48] suggesting that Blair and his opponents became more adept at giving extended answers in response to questions from the opposition. The Leader of the Opposition would have a total of six question slots to use, while the leader of the third largest party (the Liberal Democrats throughout the New Labour years) were guaranteed a further two. Eight questions from the party leaders and eight extended responses from Blair would regularly take up most of the session. The resulting fall in the time available for backbench questions suggests that this reform was not aimed at enhancing parliamentary accountability; it had become more difficult for the average Member of Parliament to put a question to the Prime Minister. It would take until the 2010 Parliament and the speakership of John Bercow for this to be rectified, with Bercow himself regularly extending PMQs beyond the by now usual 30-minute slot to 'ensure that more MPs have the opportunity to speak' in the chamber.[49]

The changes to PMQs may have freed up parliamentary time for other purposes, but it was, in the eyes of the Prime Minister himself, much more of an efficiency reform designed to alleviate some of his parliamentary schedule. Although Kelso's definition of efficiency reforms encompasses those designed to expedite the handling of government legislation, here we see a reform designed to increase the efficiency of the Prime Minister. By reducing the number of appearances in the Commons, preparation for PMQs could be consolidated and Thursdays could become a PMQs-free day. Although beneficial to the Prime Minister, it did little to increase either the accountability of the Prime Minister or the ability of MPs to quiz him. As Bates et al note, the increasing use of PMQs as a partisan joust between the two main party leaders rather than as a serious accountability tool for backbench MPs serves only to reinforce the notion 'that Parliament is a weak institution, dominated by the executive'.[50]

Also falling into this category are the changes made to the passage of legislation. A new system of legislative timetabling during government Bills was implemented in 1997, following recommendations by the Modernisation Committee that it be trialled as part of a wider package of reforms of the legislative process. The issue of timetabling had been considered by those within[51]

[47] S Bates, S Kerr and R Serban, 'Questioning the Government' in C Leston-Bandeira and L Thompson (eds), *Exploring Parliament* (Oxford University Press, 2017) 174–86.

[48] SR Bates, P Kerr, C Byrne and L Stanley, 'Questions to the Prime Minister: A Comparative Study of PMQs from Thatcher to Cameron' (2012) 67 *Parliamentary Affairs* 253, 263.

[49] J Bercow, speech at the University of Cape Town (16 August 2012).

[50] Bates et al, 'Questioning the Government' (2017) 176.

[51] See, eg the Jopling Report, Session 1991–92, HC 20.

the House and externally[52] on many previous occasions. Jack Straw describes it as a tool for making the legislative process more 'rational' and preventing opposition games and tactics whereby hundreds of amendments to the early clauses of a Bill are tabled.[53] The Modernisation Committee agreed with this interpretation, also highlighting the greater certainty it provided, giving MPs 'a clear idea of which parts of a bill will be debated when'.[54]

Backbench MPs, however, were less than impressed with the changes. For them, the changes were an indication of the government's desire to restrict the opportunities for debate of Bills.[55] The significant number of Bills passing through the Commons in which large numbers of clauses went unscrutinised would be a feature of the New Labour era. Peter Luff told Blair during his evidence to the Liaison Committee in 2007 that 'the Commons Library could not even estimate for me the number of clauses that have not been considered in the Commons' as a result of timetabling.[56] This is even more significant given the growing volume and complexity of legislation in the twenty-first century. Korris describes how the number of pages of legislation passed in a parliamentary session almost doubled from 8940 pages in 1990 to 16,031 by the 2006 parliamentary session.[57] Although the Modernisation Committee cautioned against using statistics showing the number of clauses going undebated as a measure of poor scrutiny, it did agree that 'concern about the volume of legislation which passes undebated is entirely legitimate' and cited nine Bills in which the addition of internal 'knifes' as a result of timetabling had left a large number of clauses undebated.[58] In particular, it cited the Planning and Compulsory Purchase Bill (2002–03) as an example of the disadvantages of the new timetabling procedures. A total of 73 clauses and schedules, along with 50 groups of amendments, were lost to internal knifes.[59]

Alongside the greater control of the legislative timetable came the introduction of 'carry-over' of Bills, meaning that a Bill which had not completed its scrutiny by the end of the parliamentary session could be 'carried over' into the next. In some respects this provided opportunities for greater scrutiny of legislation, but in others it simply provided government with more time and less opportunity for humiliating losses of their own Bills. Combined, these changes

[52] Hansard Society, *Making the Law: The Report of the Hansard Society Commission on the Legislative Process* (1992).

[53] Straw, *Last Man Standing* (2012) 551.

[54] Modernisation of the House of Commons Select Committee, First Report, Session 2003–04, 29 October 2003.

[55] M Goodwin and M Atkins, 'Parliament and Modernization' in Leston-Bandeira and Thompson, *Exploring Parliament* (2017) 297.

[56] Liaison Committee, Oral Evidence from the Prime Minister, HC 2007–08, Q141.

[57] M Korris, 'Standing Up for Scrutiny: How and Why Parliament Should Make Better Law' (2011) 64 *Parliamentary Affairs* 564.

[58] Modernisation of the House of Commons Select Committee, First Report, Session 2003–04, 29 October 2003.

[59] ibid.

to PMQs and the scrutiny of legislation may have been marketed as reforms designed to empower backbenchers in their scrutiny of government, but in practice they caused frustration on the green benches.

VI. REFORMS THAT STALLED: THE HOUSE OF LORDS

As with other aspects of parliamentary and constitutional reform, New Labour (and Blair in particular) were not overly passionate about House of Lords reform. Blair had inherited the commitment to reforming the upper chamber from Neil Kinnock.[60] The Labour Party's 1997 election manifesto committed it to a staggered reform process, with the first step being the removal of hereditary peers, before delegating the future of the House to a Joint Committee. This is perhaps the result of Blair's own attitude to the future of the Lords, which was somewhat ambiguous.[61] Lords reform was never an issue that New Labour wanted to dominate the news agenda.[62] Other policy areas were considered much more pressing and to resonate with the public in a much more positive way. Peers would prove a nuisance to the passage of New Labour's flagship policies at times and the number of government defeats in the upper house would escalate throughout the 2001 Parliament as peers became more assertive,[63] but even cabinet ministers agreed that the upper chamber brought about significant improvements to New Labour's legislation[64] and there was a lack of enthusiasm among them about the various reform options.[65]

Nevertheless, the removal of the hereditary peers was a relatively smooth process, albeit with a compromise that 92 would remain. The swift decision-making in this regard helped to make Blair's constitutional change reforms in the first term both successful and straightforward.[66] Although Blair invested some personal capital in the initial stage of Lords reform, negotiating the removal of all but 100 hereditary peers with the Conservative Party, we see him begin to distance himself from any further reform plans during the 2001 Parliament. The delegation of the problem to a new Joint Committee on Lords Reform in 2002 is an example of this, as is the commitment to give MPs a free vote on the possible reform options in 2003. He was no doubt relieved that MPs could not agree on a final option for the Upper House. It was, in Seldon et al's words, 'a political battle he wanted to avoid'.[67]

[60] P Dorey, 'Stumbling Through "Stage Two": New Labour and House of Lords Reform' (2008) 3 *British Politics* 22, 25.
[61] ibid 26.
[62] Campbell and Stott, *The Blair Years* (2007) 336.
[63] M Russell, 'A Stronger Second Chamber? Assessing the Impact of House of Lords Reform in 1999 and the Lessons for Bicameralism' (2010) 58 *Political Studies* 866, 872.
[64] Straw (n 17) 476.
[65] Dorey, 'Stumbling Through "Stage Two"' (2008) 33.
[66] Seldon et al (n 13) 20.
[67] ibid 203.

Progress was delayed throughout the rest of the Parliament – a clear sign of things to come. Stage Two of the Lords reform would cause a bigger headache for the Labour government. Kelso describes the 'muddled' nature of New Labour's policy on the Lords, with a contrast between the reform options outlined in the White Paper and the apparent commitment to an elected or 'democratic' Lords in the party's 2001 election manifesto.[68] Even when a Bill was finally drafted, Blair gave it little priority.[69] He would later write that although he was happy to be carried along by his ministers' hopes for a part-elected House, he still felt that the appointments system was unique and worth preserving,[70] something which explains the 'cautious' approach taken by the Prime Minister to talk of an elected upper chamber.[71] When the Commons was finally given a free vote on four possible options for Lords reform in 2003, it 'made a fool of itself',[72] voting against every single option in what Dorey describes as a 'fiasco'.[73] By March 2007, MPs had finally agreed on both an 80 per cent and a 100 per cent elected Lords, and the Brown government was supposedly ready to publish a draft Bill on Lords reform in 2010.[74] With defeat in the general election, however, such a Bill never saw daylight.

The one other aspect of Lords reform which could ostensibly be judged as an effective parliamentary reform under New Labour was the separation of the executive, legislative and judicial powers of the Lord Chancellor in 2003 and the removal of the Law Lords as part of the Constitutional Reform Act 2005. This had an immediate impact on Parliament in terms of the removal of some of its members and the creation of a new elected post of Lord Speaker, which was initially filled by Baroness Hayman. This was significant, establishing a clearer separation of powers. The removal of the Law Lords took a source of legal expertise from the upper house which some saw as crucial. Richard Cornes, for instance, argued that their contributions to debates on New Labour's devolution and human rights legislation had 'self evident merit'.[75] However, it is clear that Blair did not actually consider this to be a parliamentary reform. Rather, although it involved Parliament, it was first and foremost a reform of the judiciary.[76] He writes in his autobiography that it was the court, not Parliament, which 'matters first to me'.[77] Likewise, moving constitutional issues out of the remit of the Home Office as part of this reform meant it would not be distracted

[68] A Kelso, 'Reforming the House of Lords: Navigating Representation, Democracy and Legitimacy at Westminster' (2006) 44 *Parliamentary Affairs* 563, 570.

[69] Seldon et al (n 13) 202.

[70] Blair (n 14) 649.

[71] Liaison Committee, Oral Evidence from the Prime Minister, HC 2007–08, Q148.

[72] Straw (n 17) 477.

[73] Dorey (n 60) 33.

[74] Straw (n 17) 524.

[75] R Cornes, 'Reforming the Lords: The Role of the Law Lords' (UCL, 1999) 6.

[76] This perspective is reflected in G Gee, ch 5 in this volume.

[77] Blair (n 14) 631.

by constitutional issues and could focus on the important work of crime and immigration.[78]

We must judge New Labour's initial efforts at House of Lords reform as contributing to a more effective, legitimate[79] or perhaps less anachronistic legislature. But their later Lords reform legacy was one of 'almost constant deferral and indecision' about the future role and composition of the upper chamber;[80] hardly a sign of an effective parliamentary reform.

VII. DELAYED DROP REFORMS: SELECT COMMITTEES AND PARLIAMENTARY VOTES ON MILITARY ACTION

There were two areas of parliamentary reform under New Labour which had merit at the time, but whose significance only became clearer much later on, after the end of the New Labour era. These were the decision to allow the Commons to give its approval for military action in Iraq in 2003 and the changes made to the select committee system. In both cases, it would not be until the 2010 Parliament and the Cameron–Clegg Coalition government that the true impact of the changes would become apparent.

A. A Parliamentary Prerogative over Military Action

The decision on whether or not to commit British troops to military intervention overseas had traditionally rested with the Prime Minister, as one of the prerogative powers exercised on behalf of the monarch. Prime Ministers are not 'statutorily bound' to consult Parliament before committing troops overseas and have traditionally chosen not to do so.[81] While debates on military action had been a feature of many previous Parliaments, with the Commons discussing intervention during the Thatcher and Major premierships to name just two, no substantive vote had been held in which the Commons was asked to approve military action since the Churchill government of 1950.[82]

This would change in New Labour's second term in office as foreign policy decisions made Blair's time in office more difficult than in the honeymoon period of the 1997 Parliament. With public, parliamentary and intra-party tension over the possibility of war in Iraq (something which would later lead to the resignation of Robin Cook), Blair agreed to allow the House of Commons to have a debate and a vote on Britain's participation in the conflict. Strong notes the frustration

[78] ibid.

[79] Russell, 'A Stronger Second Chamber?' (2010).

[80] Dorey (n 60) 24.

[81] House of Lords Constitution Committee, 'Waging War: Parliament's Role and Responsibility' (2006) HL Paper 236, 8.

[82] ibid 10.

of MPs with Blair's refusal to allow a debate on Iraq for many months, despite the course of action to come seeming to be very clear.[83] Although those closest to the Prime Minister saw no need for a vote,[84] there was clear support for giving the Commons a stronger voice from other central Labour figures. Jack Straw, for instance, writes that he had long found it 'preposterous' that Parliament had not been asked for approval and describes his lobbying of Blair on the issue, alongside Robin Cook.[85] Seldon et al confirm the importance of these two figures in pressing the rest of the Cabinet for the vote.[86] Thus, although the granting of the debate marked a significant milestone in the influence of the twenty-first century Parliament over military intervention, it was somewhat overdue.

Although Blair notes his confidence in winning the vote,[87] he still describes his appearance in the Commons on 18 March 2003 as 'the most important speech I had ever made'.[88] Seldon et al also describe the meticulous preparation that went into his parliamentary performance.[89] The strong sense that should the vote not have gone to plan Blair and his team would have had to go[90] makes the decision to continue with the vote a brave one. The eventual debate in the Commons and the final vote of 412–149 in favour of intervention was a significant event for observers of parliamentary politics. It demonstrated both the legitimation function of Parliament as an institution and something of a move away from the centralised, presidential style of decision-making associated with New Labour.[91] The true significance of Blair's decision to allow the vote would not, however, become clear until a decade later.

Under the Brown premiership, focus on the issue of Parliament and decisions on war remained on the agenda. Brown's *Governance of Britain* White Paper reaffirmed that crown prerogative powers should be moved to Parliament,[92] proposing that where there were to be any 'significant, non-routine deployments' of troops, the Commons should be consulted and asked to give its consent.[93] This was restated in his speech to Labour Party Conference, where he announced that 'parliament will make the final decisions about peace and war'.[94] Badged as a change which would 'make the executive more accountable',[95]

[83] J Strong, 'Why Parliament Now Decides on War: Tracing the Growth of the Parliamentary Prerogative through Syria, Libya and Iraq' (2015) 17 *British Journal of Politics and International Relations* 604, 608.

[84] Seldon et al (n 13) 158.

[85] Straw (n 17) 375; RF Cook, *The Point of Departure* (Simon & Schuster, 2003) 190.

[86] Seldon et al (n 13) 159.

[87] Blair (n 14) 436; Seldon et al (n 13) 170.

[88] Blair (n 14) 436.

[89] Seldon et al (n 13) 171.

[90] ibid 170.

[91] Foley (n 9) 321.

[92] HM Government, *The Governance of Britain* (CM 7170, 2007) 16.

[93] ibid 18.

[94] G Brown, speech to Labour Party Conference (Bournemouth 24 September 2007) http://news.bbc.co.uk/1/hi/uk_politics/7010664.stm.

[95] ibid.

no further substance could be given to the issue; no debates on military action were necessitated throughout the remaining years of Labour government and thus there was no opportunity to put his intention into practice.

The Commons would not be asked to give its consent to intervention again until 2011, when intervention in Libya was approved. Strong writes that it was only at this point that we can see the precedent set by Blair actually being applied once more.[96] The debate in the Commons only took place after the first air strikes had occurred in Libya and this watered down the significance of the precedent somewhat. It seemed that Parliament was simply being asked to approve intervention which had already begun. Eight years after Blair's Iraq vote, we could only really say that Parliament was being given greater opportunity to debate war powers which still resided with the Prime Minister.[97] In August 2013, however, this would change and Cameron would ask the Commons to once again consider intervention, this time against the Assad regime in Syria. When the House voted 285–272 against air strikes, Cameron became the first Prime Minister to lose a vote on intervention since 1782.[98]

Although Blair's decision to allow the Commons a vote in 2003 was not without importance, it was this vote that was seen to be the 'game changer',[99] challenging 'the conventional wisdom that Westminster has little influence in security policy'[100] and suggesting the existence of a political, if not constitutional, convention that it is 'Parliament [that] now decides when Britain goes to war'.[101] Although the 2013 vote had no legal underpinnings,[102] it was David Cameron's immediate acceptance of the decision and his express commitment to follow Parliament's wishes[103] which appeared to establish the 'political convention that parliament ultimately decides when Britain goes to war'.[104] Blair's 'innovation'[105] may have taken place over a decade ago, but it had finally proved its real worth; the Commons had exerted its voice and veto power as a constraint on military intervention, and the executive had listened and stood by the decision.[106] It may not have been quite what Blair originally anticipated, but the substance was very similar.

[96] Strong, 'Why Parliament Now Decides on War' (2015) 612.

[97] Only at this point, in 2011, shortly before MPs ratified military intervention in Libya, did the government formally acknowledge that a convention had developed that Parliament would be consulted before troops were committed: HC Deb 10 March 2011, col 1066.

[98] J Strong, 'Interpreting the Syria Vote: Parliament and British Foreign Policy' (2015) 91 *International Affairs* 1123.

[99] R Rogers and R Walters, *How Parliament Works*, 7th edn (Routledge, 2015) 368.

[100] J Kaarbo and D Kenealy, 'No, Prime Minister: Explaining the House of Commons' Vote on Intervention in Syria' (2015) 25 *European Security* 28.

[101] Strong (n 83).

[102] Strong, 'Interpreting the Syria Vote' (2015).

[103] HC Debs 29 August 2013, col 1555.

[104] Strong (n 83) 617.

[105] ibid 616.

[106] A subsequent challenge to this convention came in April 2018, when Prime Minister Theresa May committed the UK to participate in air strikes in Syria without a prior vote in the House

B. A More Powerful Select Committee System

The Prime Minister is something of an outsider when it comes to the formal accountability mechanisms of the UK Parliament.[107] The changes made by Blair to PMQs seemed to emphasise this even further, minimising the quantity of prime ministerial visits to the House of Commons chamber. Although statements and important debates may require prime ministerial presence, the accountability relationship between the Commons and the Prime Minister has always been relatively 'fluid' and dependent on prime ministerial goodwill.[108]

Blair was asked on several occasions to give evidence to select committees, but it was only in 2002 that he agreed to appear before the House of Commons Liaison Committee twice a year to answer MPs' questions, in something Kelso et al describe as a 'significant realignment of parliamentary scrutiny infrastructure'.[109] Though Blair seemed to portray the impression that he was attending under his own initiative, Robin Cook was once again reported to be a driving force behind the decision.[110] Blair implied that his appearance was a response to a changing parliamentary environment, one in which there was now much less focus on what 'actually happen[s] in Parliament and parliamentary debates'.[111]

His first appearance before the Committee on 16 July 2002 marked the first time a Prime Minister had appeared before a select committee for 65 years.[112] There was nothing sensational about this first session. A large committee of MPs and a series of questions on aspects of the machinery of government, decision-making and Parliament meant that the Prime Minister's answers were fairly mundane. The Chair, Labour MP Alan Williams, had told observers that 'the wider we cast our net the shallower our questioning inevitably becomes',[113] yet despite this realisation the questioning style throughout the first sessions remained very broad and disparate, moving between topics at a fairly rapid pace. It was a 'fundamental design flaw'[114] which did not bring a positive glow to the extra scrutiny being provided by Parliament. By the time of Blair's final Liaison Committee session in 2007, the committee had undergone a period of 'institutional learning'.[115] A smaller group of MPs and greater cooperation and

of Commons; on the uncertain implications for the convention, see, eg V Fikfak and H Hooper, 'Whither the War Powers Convention? What Next for Parliamentary Control of Armed Conflict After Syria?' *UK Constitutional Law Association Blog* (20 April 2018).

[107] M Bennister and P Larkin, 'Accountability in Parliament' in Leston-Bandeira and Thompson (n 47) 148; A Kelso, M Bennister and P Larkin, 'The Shifting Landscape of Prime Ministerial Accountability' (2016) 18 *British Journal of Politics and International Relations* 740.

[108] Bennister and Larkin, 'Accountability in Parliament' (2017) 148.

[109] Kelso et al, 'The Shifting Landscape of Prime Ministerial Accountability' (2016) 741.

[110] ibid 744.

[111] Liaison Committee, Oral Evidence from the Prime Minister, HC 2002–03, Q2.

[112] ibid Q1.

[113] ibid Q1.

[114] Kelso et al (n 107) 746.

[115] M Bennister, A Kelso and P Larkin, 'Questioning the Prime Minister: How Effective is the Liaison Committee?' (2016) 36 http://create.canterbury.ac.uk/16761/1/16761_Final%20PMAP%20Report_MBPL%20July2017.pdf.

discussion about questioning and strategy brought about more focus to the session. Kelso et al write that Liaison Committee members at this time were disappointed that they had been unable to land any major blows on the Prime Minister through five years of evidence sessions.[116] The perceived lack of impact from those present at these early sessions, however, did not really matter. The real significance was that a new parliamentary practice had been established; future Prime Ministers would routinely appear before the committee.

Comparison between Blair's evidence to the Liaison Committee and more contemporary sessions with Theresa May demonstrate how far the Committee has evolved since 2002. The number of questions asked may still seem unwieldly, with May facing even more questions[117] than the 123 which directed at Blair in his first session,[118] but the questions asked have become more confident. MPs routinely pressed May on her own decisions and the questioning was more intensive. These 'sharper exchanges'[119] could be seen during discussions of Brexit, with MPs quizzing the Prime Minister in great detail on the possible outcomes of the parliamentary vote on the original Brexit deal in 2018[120] and on the next steps for negotiations in May 2019.[121] Just as select committee chairs have grown in confidence and stature since the New Labour years, Liaison Committee Chairs have seen a similar growth in self-assurance, becoming much more 'interventionist' in style,[122] with Andrew Tyrie and Sarah Wollaston being prominent examples of this. It has become a key forum for prime ministerial accountability to Parliament, putting it on a 'more systematic footing'.[123] Once again, we see that New Labour had played a fundamental role in setting 'a new precedent',[124] but that the significance of the Prime Minister's appearances before the Liaison Committee would take another decade or so to be fully realised.

VIII. CONCLUSION: WAS THE NEW LABOUR VISION A SUCCESS?

Speaking at the Labour Party's annual conference in 2004, Tony Blair claimed that his government had produced 'a happy ending because rarely has a political party been able to deliver so much of what it promised'.[125] Blair's optimism seems misplaced; political scientists have tended to conclude that Labour's

[116] Kelso et al (n 107) 749.
[117] Liaison Committee, Oral Evidence from the Prime Minister, HC 2017–19.
[118] Bennister and Larkin (n 107) 149.
[119] ibid 149.
[120] Liaison Committee, 2018, Q1–8.
[121] Liason Committee, Oral Evidence from the Prime Minister, HC 2017–19.
[122] Bennister and Larkin (n 107) 150.
[123] Bennister et al, 'Questioning the Prime Minister' (2016).
[124] Liaison Committee, Oral Evidence from the Prime Minister, HC 2006–07, Q199.
[125] T Blair, speech to Labour Party Conference (Brighton, 28 September 2004) http://news.bbc.co.uk/1/hi/uk_politics/3697434.stm.

commitment to constitutional reform on paper was not matched by its implementation of reforms in practice.[126] Perhaps this explains the fact that the party's 2010 manifesto still called for a further 'strengthening the power of Parliament to hold the executive to account'[127] and Gordon Brown's almost immediate support for Labour MP Tony Wright's request for the creation of a new committee on parliamentary reform.[128] The Wright Committee would go on to suggest a comprehensive package of reforms, including the election of select committee members and chairs, and the creation of a backbench business committee which had a 'tangible effect on the relationship between Parliament and the executive'.[129] Clearly the new Labour leadership recognised that there was still further work to be done to enhance the power and voice of backbench MPs.

Writing in the middle of Labour's period in office, Flinders argued that we should view constitutional reform as 'a chain reaction or process' which could deliver intended or unintended consequences.[130] Given that parliamentary reforms take time to evolve, analysis of the government's parliamentary reforms during the 2001 or 2005 Parliaments was in many respects premature. New Labour may not have had a clear and streamlined vision for parliamentary reform – and there was certainly no firm understanding of what a reformed Parliament should look like beyond that perennial word 'effective' – but we must not underestimate the significance of their reforms in this area.

Crucially, if we look back on the reforms discussed in this chapter in the context of the recent minority governments led by Theresa May and then Boris Johnson between 2017 and 2019, and in light of Parliament's scrutiny of Brexit in this period, then we can see the significance of some of these internal reforms. In particular, the ability of MPs to hold the Prime Minister to account through the Liaison Committee has been of huge importance. For example, Theresa May's appearance before the committee in November 2018 saw her pressed heavily on the consequences of the vote on the final Brexit deal (which she would eventually lose) and the planning taking place in government for what would happen in the event of a defeat.[131] The heavy questioning and persistent probing on this issue demonstrates perfectly the evolution of the Liaison Committee since Blair's original agreement to appear before it. Although the Prime Minister will have anticipated a heavy grilling on this issue, the precedent set by Blair in agreeing to be scrutinised on an annual basis meant that Theresa May (and Boris Johnson since then) had little choice but to attend.

[126] Flinders, 'Majoritarian Democracy in Britain: New Labour and the Constitution' (2005).

[127] Labour Party, *A Future Fair For All* (2010) 9:3.

[128] M Russell, 'Never Allow a Crisis to Go to Waste: The Wright Committee Reforms to Strengthen the House of Commons' (2011) 64 *Parliamentary Affairs* 618.

[129] N Le Roux, 'The Wright Reforms Changed Parliament, but There Remains Scope for Further Reform' (Democratic Audit, 2014) www.democraticaudit.com/2014/02/25/committees-scotland-and-the-right-of-recall-the-potential-for-parliamentary-reform/.

[130] Flinders, 'New Labour and the Constitution' (2003) 143.

[131] Liaison Committee, Oral Evidence from the Prime Minister, HC 2017–19.

David Marquand may have been correct when he described New Labour's reforms as a 'revolution of sleepwalkers',[132] but there is no doubt that they succeeded – whether intentionally or not – in waking up a rather dormant House of Commons. The context of minority government under Theresa May amplified several of the reforms initiated by New Labour which had been masked by Blair's convincing parliamentary majorities. Her rocky relationship with the Commons and the growing confidence of MPs in challenging the executive during this period were an antidote to any earlier claims that the Commons had been 'marginalised as a political institution'[133] under New Labour.

[132] Marquand (n 1).
[133] Foley (n 9) 309.

10

New Labour's Judicial Power Project

ROGER MASTERMAN

I. INTRODUCTION

THE IMPLEMENTATION OF New Labour's constitutional reforms between 1997 and 2005 began at a point in time when – as a result of, inter alia, significant changes to governmental infrastructure,[1] perceived failures of political frameworks of accountability[2] and the inability of existing legal mechanisms to defend individual rights[3] – pressure for constitutional change was widespread.[4] The impact of the Blair governments' reforms on the powers and institutional positioning of the judiciary was considerable. The Human Rights Act 1998 enabled the courts to determine – informed by the jurisprudence of the European Court of Human Rights – the European Convention on Human Rights (ECHR)-compliance of both legislation and public body decision-making. Its primary function was to give 'further effect' in domestic law to rights previously only enforceable against the state by the European Court of Human Rights but, as a proto-Bill of Rights for the UK,[5] it also served to implicitly endorse the constitutionalist credentials of the judiciary through facilitating the legislative review of primary legislation on human rights grounds. Structural reforms brought into effect pursuant to the Constitutional Reform Act 2005 meanwhile served to underpin a more explicit

[1] RAW Rhodes, 'The Hollowing out of the State: The Changing Nature of the Public Service in Britain' (1994) 65 *Political Quarterly* 138.

[2] See A Tomkins, *The Constitution After Scott: Government Unwrapped* (Clarendon Press, 1998).

[3] eg TH Bingham, 'The European Convention on Human Rights: Time to Incorporate' (1993) 109 *LQR* 390.

[4] On which see Charter 88, https://unlockdemocracy.org/resources-index/2016/07/04/charter-88); Institute for Public Policy Research, *The Constitution of the United Kingdom* (1991); R Dworkin, *A Bill of Rights for Britain* (Chatto & Windus, 1990); Scottish Constitutional Convention, *Scotland's Parliament, Scotland's Right* (1995); Labour Party/Liberal Democrats, *Report of the Joint Consultative Committee on Constitutional Reform* (1997).

[5] F Klug, 'A Bill of Rights for the United Kingdom: Do We Need One or Do We Already Have One?' [2007] *PL* 701.

institutional separation of judicial power from the other personnel and institutions of government. Severing the links between Parliament and the apex court and stripping the judicial role from the office of Lord Chancellor gave succour to consideration of the judiciary as a separate 'branch' of government, institutionally and physically independent of the executive and legislature.[6]

Given the extent of Labour's programme of constitutional reforms, and the rate at which they were implemented, assessments which have emphasised the transformative consequences of the Blair reforms for the constitutional order are not difficult to find.[7] As early as 2000, Anthony King's Hamlyn Lectures asked whether the pre-1997 constitution remained intact.[8] King's follow up – *The British Constitution* – further developed the premise that the 'traditional' constitution had been so radically amended that it could not be 'reconstituted'.[9] In 2009, Vernon Bogdanor similarly argued that core tenets of the old order had been jettisoned and a 'new' constitution – based on separation of powers and a federal principle – brought into being.[10] Both accounts provided deeper and richer narratives of constitutional development in the UK, but the influence of the Blair reforms was a central – indeed necessary – pillar of both theses.

In vital respects, the Blair reforms marked a turning point, and a modification of the principles of accountability core to the 'political constitution'.[11] The enhancement of judicial oversight of public decision-making with potential implications for individual rights can be understood as a partial response to perceived deficiencies in the traditional doctrine of ministerial accountability to Parliament.[12] More than this, and in contradistinction to efforts by the judges themselves to develop the rights-protecting dimensions of the common law, the adoption of the Human Rights Act 1998 represented an amendment to the framework of legal accountability that was proposed and endorsed by those to whose actions it was to apply. The enactment of the Human Rights Act ensured that the specific means by which the protected rights were to be realised in claims against public bodies and via the construction of legislation enjoyed legislative endorsement. And although the adoption of a weak form of statutory review fell short of empowering courts to 'disapply'[13] statutes that unjustifiably interfered with human rights, it was nonetheless a notable innovation in a system that had traditionally resisted testing primary legislation on (legal) constitutionalist

[6] On which see R Masterman, *The Separation of Powers in the Contemporary Constitution: Judicial Competence and Independence in the United Kingdom* (Cambridge University Press, 2011).

[7] The most preposterously titled is K Sutherland (ed), *The Rape of the Constitution?* (Imprint Academic, 2000).

[8] A King, *Does the United Kingdom Still Have a Constitution?* (Sweet and Maxwell, 2001).

[9] A King, *The British Constitution* (Oxford University Press, 2007) ch 3, 362.

[10] V Bogdanor, *The New British Constitution* (Hart Publishing, 2009) 289.

[11] JAG Griffith, 'The Political Constitution' (1979) 42 *MLR* 1.

[12] J Jowell and D Oliver (eds), *The Changing Constitution*, 4th edn (Oxford University Press, 2000) viii.

[13] *R v Secretary of State for Transport, ex parte Factortame (No 2)* [1991] 1 AC 603.

grounds.[14] The cumulative effect of these functional and institutional changes was to expand the spheres in which the influence of judicial power might be felt[15] and – by providing the judicial branch with a prominent, visible, focal point[16] – enhance the standing of the courts within the constitution.

Yet, extensive though the New Labour reforms undoubtedly were, they cannot be understood as standing apart from the more incremental, less explicit constitutional developments of the latter years of the twentieth century. Nor should they be understood as marking a complete abandonment of core constitutional principles and characteristics; in important respects, the Blair reforms displayed conservative tendencies, and were projected as being consistent with – rather than a departure from – established features of the constitutional architecture. The modernising desires of the Labour government were therefore tempered by something of a tendency towards continuity. The impact of the New Labour constitution on the judiciary can be seen in this light. It is therefore possible to simultaneously view the New Labour project as both a radical reformation of the judicial function and a more incremental continuation of the constitutionalisation of the formal role of judicial review traceable at least back to the 1960s.[17] The adoption of a statutory rights instrument can be viewed as a rejection of the common law's rationalisation of freedom as 'an immunity from interference by others'[18] and a complement to the (then) nascent efforts of the judges to recognise constitutional rights as existent within the common law,[19] as well as to the (then) relatively stable position of EU norms in the domestic constitution. Similarly, the establishment of a Supreme Court can be understood as both an endorsement of the arguably alien concept of separation of powers and as consistent with a long-standing domestic commitment to judicial independence.

This chapter examines the ostensibly competing (yet coexisting) narratives of constitutional continuity and constitutional realignment that, taken together, illuminate the judicial role within, and following, the Blair governments' constitutional reforms. It suggests that although the Blair reforms to the powers and position of the courts were considerable, they should not be solely understood as precipitating fundamental constitutional renewal. Through the lenses of decisions concerning (i) the interpretation of rights under the Human Rights Act, (ii) the exercise of the interpretative function under section 3(1) of the Act

[14] *Cheney v Conn* [1968] 1 WLR 242, 247: 'What the statute itself enacts cannot be unlawful, because what the statute says and provides is itself the law, and the highest form of law that is known to this country.'

[15] G Gee, R Hazell, K Malleson and P O'Brien, *The Politics of Judicial Independence in the UK's Changing Constitution* (Cambridge University Press, 2015) 2.

[16] K Malleson, 'The Evolving Role of the Supreme Court' [2011] *PL* 754, 764–66.

[17] See *Ridge v Baldwin* [1964] AC 40; *Padfield v Minister for Agriculture, Fisheries and Food* [1968] AC 997; *Anisminic v Foreign Compensation Commission* [1969] 2 AC 147.

[18] *Wheeler v Leicester City Council* [1985] AC 1054, 1065 (Lord Browne-Wilkinson).

[19] eg *R v Secretary of State for the Home Department, ex parte Leech (No 2)* [1994] QB 198; *R v Lord Chancellor, ex parte Witham* [1998] QB 575.

and (iii) the apex court's 'federal' jurisdiction (each a core feature of the Blair constitution's judicial architecture), this chapter examines the attempted reconciliation of the 'continuous' and 'transformative' in the post-1997 era. While accepting that the scope and prominence of judicial power has increased, this chapter argues that the experience of the post-Blair years should be viewed as an exercise in reconciling this enhanced judicial role with the constitution's more long-standing features, rather than marking an abandonment of the *ancien régime*.

II. THE NARRATIVE OF CONSTITUTIONAL CONTINUITY

Though the New Labour programme of constitutional reform was undoubtedly ambitious, it did not amount to a comprehensive scheme of constitutional renewal.[20] The Blair governments' project – significant though its individual components undoubtedly were – was more limited in scope, and was not informed by any overarching constitutional vision. Instead, the Blair reforms were targeted at pragmatically addressing a series of distinct politico-constitutional issues: the absence of a catalogue of individual rights enforceable against public bodies;[21] strengthening the Union through the devolution of power;[22] the modernisation of the House of Lords;[23] excessive secrecy in government;[24] and so on. If a broad vision could be said to have existed, it served rather more obviously political than constitutional objectives, with the early Blair reforms presented as an attempt to 'clean up government' after the scandal-mired twilight years of the preceding Conservative administration. In the light of this, the very notion of a 'New Labour' or 'Blair' constitution is perhaps something of a portmanteau concept.

A tendency towards constitutional continuity can also be evidenced in what was *not* delivered by New Labour's reforms. While the removal of the hereditary peers from the House of Lords was largely achieved as a result of the House of Lords Act 1999, momentum towards 'stage two' of the process quickly dissipated in the post-Wakeham period, and Lords reform did not feature in Labour's 2001 general election manifesto. Other proposals were similarly found to be lacking the requisite political and/or popular support. Reform of the voting system for Westminster elections stalled following the publication of the report of the

[20] The prospect of wholesale constitutional reconfiguration taking the form of a written constitution was later mooted – with little practical effect – by Gordon Brown's administration: *The Governance of Britain* (Cm 7170, 2007) [211]–[215].

[21] Human Rights Act 1998.

[22] Scotland Act 1998; Government of Wales Act 1998; Northern Ireland Act 1998.

[23] House of Lords Act 1999.

[24] Freedom of Information Act 2000.

Jenkins Commission,[25] and a promised referendum on first-past-the-post did not take place.[26] The implementation of a regional layer of devolved government in England was exposed as severely lacking in grassroots support.[27] And even though the Blair governments were bolstered by the size of their House of Commons majorities in the 1997–2005 period, a number of significant proposals either lacked the necessary Westminster traction (the 1997 manifesto's suggestion of a referendum on adoption of the euro, for instance) or otherwise were scaled back in the light of the pressures of occupying office (for example, the proposals which became the Freedom of Information Act 2000[28]).

Far, then, from amounting to an explicit and sweeping reshaping of constitutional fundamentals, the flagship reforms of the early New Labour years consciously sought to demonstrate continuity with constitutional orthodoxy. Ministers were at pains to situate the government's programme of reform as being in accordance with – rather than a departure from – the UK's constitutional *grundnorm*.[29] As a result, the devolution of (limited) legislative powers from Westminster was not to formally diminish the legal ability of Parliament to legislate in fields of devolved competence.[30] Similarly, the scheme of rights protection afforded by the Human Rights Act 1998 – although centred on the enhancement of judicially policed protections for rights[31] – did not permit invalidation or disapplication of rights infringing primary legislation[32] and was designed to uphold the ability of the legislature to enact measures which might contravene the protected rights.[33] The Human Rights Act model was therefore championed as an efficient accommodation of fundamental rights[34] and a departure from the experience of those Bills of Rights overseas that explicitly curtailed the law-making competence of the legislature by permitting judicial invalidation

[25] *The Report of the Independent Commission on the Voting System* (Cm 4090-I/Cm 4090-II, 1998) (Jenkins Commission).

[26] A referendum on the adoption of the Alternative Vote system for use in UK general elections was later promised as a part of the agreement securing the Conservative–Liberal Democrat Coalition government of 2010–15. The referendum – held in 2011 – saw almost 68% of voters reject the change.

[27] See *Your Region, Your Choice: Revitalising the English Regions* (Cm 5511, 2002).

[28] On which see R Austin, 'The Freedom of Information Act 2000 – A Sheep in Wolf's Clothing?' in J Jowell and D Oliver (eds), *The Changing Constitution*, 5th edn (Oxford University Press, 2004); B Worthy, ch 8 in this volume.

[29] eg HL Deb 3 November 1997, vol 582, col 1228; HC Deb 16 February 1998, vol 306, col 772.

[30] See, eg Scotland Act 1998, s 28(7).

[31] Human Rights Act 1998, ss 2, 3, 6.

[32] Human Rights Act 1998, ss 3(2)(b), 3(2)(c), 4(6)(a).

[33] Human Rights Act 1998, s 19(1)(b).

[34] Lord Irvine of Lairg QC, 'The Impact of the Human Rights Act: Parliament, the Courts and the Executive' [2003] *PL* 308. In 2006, the (short-lived) Department for Constitutional Affairs continued to maintain the narrative of constitutional continuity, responding to criticisms of the Human Rights Act by suggesting that 'arguments that the … Act has significantly altered the constitutional balance between Parliament, the executive and the judiciary have … been considerably exaggerated': Department for Constitutional Affairs, *Review of the Implementation of the Human Rights Act* (July 2006) 4.

of rights-infringing measures.[35] Even the Act's innovation of legislative review had been partially anticipated by Parliament's acceptance of EU norms into the domestic legal order and the testing of primary legislation against a catalogue of 'external' standards that accompanied EU membership.[36]

If the mechanisms by which rights were to be given effect against public bodies and in the interpretation of legislation were demonstrative of a certain consistency with the past, so too was the catalogue of rights to which the Human Rights Act gave effect. Adoption of the core rights protected by the ECHR provided the Human Rights Act with both a normative backbone and a substantive content (in the case law of the Strasbourg Court) that the UK had been committed to uphold since 1951. The absence of social and economic rights from the protections afforded by the Act also provided further continuity with those rights indirectly upheld by the common law.[37] While giving domestic effect to the core provisions of the ECHR was – initially at least – seen as an interim step towards the adoption of a modern Bill of Rights,[38] Labour's momentum towards this more fundamental piece of constitutional engineering did not carry into the period following the implementation and enforcement of the Human Rights Act.[39]

The narrative of constitutional continuity was also in evidence in relation to the proposals that formed the backbone of the Constitutional Reform Act 2005. The establishment of the UK Supreme Court and removal of the Lord Chancellor's core judicial functions was premised on a desire to 'reflect and enhance the independence of the judiciary from both the legislature and the executive'.[40] Again, however, the government sought to place emphasis on the pragmatism of the proposed change and downplayed the constitutional consequences of this formalisation of the institutional separation of powers. Potentially inventive options for the new Supreme Court – innovations which would have undermined the narrative of continuity, including recognition of the court as an explicitly constitutional organ or permitting abstract judicial review – were ruled out during the consultation process as 'a departure from the UK's constitutional traditions'.[41] In parallel with the reforms of the first Blair administration, the preservation of parliamentary sovereignty was of central

[35] CA Gearty, *Can Human Rights Survive?* (Cambridge University Press, 2006) 94–98.

[36] *R v Secretary of State for Transport, ex parte Factortame (No 2)* [1991] 1 AC 603.

[37] *Rights Brought Home: The Human Rights Bill* (Cm 3781, 1997) [1.3]–[1.5].

[38] R Brazier, *Constitutional Reform: Reshaping the British Political System*, 3rd edn (Oxford University Press, 2008) 28.

[39] Croft recorded that, as early as September 2000 (before the Act had come into full effect), 'political enthusiasm for the Human Rights Act ha[d] diminished' and that 'the … Act [bore] the hallmark of a proposal conceived in opposition that comes to be viewed differently in the cold harsh light of government': J Croft, *Whitehall and the Human Rights Act* (Constitution Unit, 2000) 27.

[40] Department for Constitutional Affairs, *A Supreme Court for the United Kingdom* (CP 11/03, 2003) 4.

[41] ibid [23], [24]. But see Scotland Act 1998, s 33; Northern Ireland Act 1998, s 11; Government of Wales Act 2006, s 112.

concern.[42] The proposals were – as Robert Stevens noted at the time of their publication – 'intensely conservative'.[43]

In the absence of constitutionally allocated functions and of formal institutional divisions at the apex of the executive, legislative and judicial branches, the under-theorised and uneven nature of separation of powers in the UK constitution gave credence to the then government's continuity narrative. Those elements of separation of powers that could be said to enjoy normative purchase – the role of the judge as interpreter of law and the independence of the individual judge – provided the backbone to the court's expanded powers under the Human Rights Act and the establishment of a Supreme Court. The separation of powers as reflected on the face of the Human Rights Act was hierarchical, derivative of the supremacy of the legislature and consistent with a binary division of functions between legislature and interpreter.[44] In casting judicial powers as primarily interpretative, a connection could be drawn between the innovation of positive, enforceable rights and the traditional, interpretative means by which those rights were to be realised. Similarly, in portraying the reforms to the office of Lord Chancellor and the removal of the Law Lords from Parliament as reflections of pre-existing commitments to judicial independence, the implications of a structurally independent judicial branch of government were underemphasised.

III. THE NARRATIVE OF CONSTITUTIONAL TRANSFORMATION

The continuity narrative can only provide a partial reflection of reforms which undoubtedly saw significant transfers of political power away from the traditional loci of governmental authority in Whitehall and Westminster towards alternative seats of constitutional authority in the devolved nations and – as a result of the Human Rights Act 1998 – to the courts.[45] To an extent at least, Labour's decentralisation of powers from core institutions of government (including from Parliament to courts) provided a formal counterpart to the administrative and managerial redistribution of powers to quangos, executive agencies and contracted-out services that had taken place (since at least the 1980s) under preceding Conservative governments. The market-driven antipathy towards established governmental institutions that had driven the 'hollowing out of the state'[46] was not, however, explicitly recognised or promoted as a case of constitutional engineering. By contrast, the programme of reforms proposed

[42] Department for Constitutional Affairs, *A Supreme Court for the United Kingdom* (2003) [23].
[43] R Stevens, 'Reform in Haste and Repent at Leisure: Iolanthe, The Lord High Executioner and *Brave New World*' (2004) 24 *Legal Studies* 1, 33.
[44] *Duport Steel v Sirs* [1980] 1 WLR 142, 157.
[45] KD Ewing, 'The Human Rights Act and Parliamentary Democracy' (1999) 62 *MLR* 79.
[46] Rhodes, 'The Hollowing Out of the State' (1994).

by the new administration was clearly directed towards addressing perceived deficiencies in the UK's political and constitutional arrangements.

At the level of principle, the Human Rights Act – in the words of Lord Irvine – 'represent[ed] Britain's recognition that freedom in the Diceyan sense is not coterminous with the protection of fundamental human rights'.[47] The consequence of the constitution's failure to secure personal freedoms had seen the residue of liberty – the sphere within which individuals were free to act without being subject to the coercive powers of the state – slowly eroded through the statutory allocation of powers to the government. The common law, in spite of its historical claim to uphold rights[48] and more recent recognition of constitutional rights, lacked the structural and remedial armoury to offer robust protections for a catalogue of rights equivalent to that found in the ECHR.[49] At a stroke, statute domesticated what was previously only accessible to litigants at Strasbourg, and embraced – in the positive recognition of individual rights, enforceable against the state at large – elements of the continental constitutional paradigm.

In order to address the enforcement deficits of the pre-Human Rights Act years, the Act allocated new powers to the courts – powers that, in the absence of enabling/incorporating legislation, had previously lain beyond the constitutional Rubicon.[50] While the constitution's divisions between legislation and interpretation and between law and policy had always been dynamic, the Human Rights Act offered the prospect of increased fluidity and therefore of greater opportunity for the engagement of the courts in matters previously considered non-justiciable. Permitting courts to enforce the ECHR rights against public bodies[51] and interpret legislation (so far as is possible)[52] to achieve compliance with those rights amounted – for Ewing – to 'an unprecedented transfer of power to the judiciary and a fundamental realignment of our "political constitution"'.[53] Even in the light of the sovereignty-safeguarding provisions of section 4, it was acknowledged at the highest judicial levels that the Human Rights Act held the potential to 'subject the entire legal system to a fundamental process of review and, where necessary, reform by the judiciary'.[54] The sheer range of governmental decisions to be potentially subjected to judicial scrutiny on the basis of the Human Rights Act, and the appointment of the judges as arbiters of the legality of alleged public body interferences with rights, provided

[47] Lord Irvine of Lairg, 'Keynote Address' in Cambridge Centre for Public Law, *Constitutional Reform in the United Kingdom: Practice and Principles* (Hart Publishing, 1998) 1.

[48] eg *Beatty v Gilbanks* (1882) 9 QBD 308 (*cf Thomas v Sawkins* [1936] 1 KB 249; *Duncan v Jones* [1936] 1 KB 218).

[49] *Malone v Metropolitan Police Commissioner (No 2)* [1979] Ch 344; *Kaye v Robertson* [1991] FSR 62.

[50] *R v Secretary of State for the Home Department, ex parte Brind* [1991] 1 AC 696, 761–62.

[51] Human Rights Act 1998, s 6.

[52] ibid s 3.

[53] Ewing, 'The Human Rights Act and Parliamentary Democracy' (1999) 79.

[54] *R v Director of Public Prosecutions, ex parte Kebiline* [2000] 2 AC 326, 374–75 (Lord Hope).

the potential to collapse the separation between policy makers and judges; for Bevir, the Act effectively 'welcome[d] the court[s] into the policy-making process'.[55]

The creation of a UK Supreme Court was a divergence from both the model of final appeal court that had endured since the Appellate Jurisdiction Act 1876 and the government's own previously stated position: in November 2001, the Blair administration had been 'committed to maintaining judicial membership of the House of Lords';[56] by June 2003, it had come to endorse the establishment of a Supreme Court. This *volte-face* was (from a legal perspective, at least[57]) prompted by an earlier piece of the government's own constitutional engineering: the then recently domesticated Article 6(1) ECHR had prompted concerns that the position of the Law Lords within the House of Lords was structurally compromised.[58] The web of convention and understanding that hitherto had served to protect the independence of the Appellate Committee[59] looked increasingly unlikely to be reconciled with the more formal approach to the segregation of judicial and legislative powers required by the Strasbourg Court.[60] The removal of the Law Lords from the legislature provided the logical solution to further suggestions of 'structural impartiality'[61] and also amounted to a partial rejection of the approach to judicial independence which had traditionally tolerated a degree of 'fusion' at its apex with the legislative and executive branches.

By contrast with earlier reforms impacting on the judiciary, the Constitutional Reform Act explicitly sought to amend the institutional divisions between the core branches of state. 'The very purpose of the Constitutional Reform Act 2005 (CRA) was to increase the formal separation of powers between the political and judicial branches of government and to reduce the role of the executive in judicial matters.'[62] The constitution has enjoyed something of an ambivalent relationship with theories of separation of powers, but the Constitutional Reform Act ended the 'anomaly'[63] of an apex court housed within the legislature. This step brought with it the promise of a 'purer separation of powers'[64] and that

[55] M Bevir, 'The Westminster Model, Governance and Judicial Reform' (2008) 61 *Parliamentary Affairs* 559, 571.

[56] *The House of Lords – Completing the Reform* (Cm 5291, 2001) [81].

[57] For analysis of the political circumstances surrounding the decision to establish a UK Supreme Court, see A Le Sueur, 'From Appellate Committee to Supreme Court: A Narrative' in L Blom-Cooper, B Dickson and G Drewry, *The Judicial House of Lords 1876–2009* (Oxford University Press, 2009) esp 67–73.

[58] See in particular *Procola v Luxembourg* (1996) 22 EHRR 193; *McGonnell v United Kingdom* (2000) 30 EHRR 289. For discussionm see R Cornes, '*McGonnell v United Kingdom*, The Lord Chancellor and the Law Lords' [2000] *PL* 166.

[59] HL Deb 22 June 2000, vol 614, cols 419–20.

[60] *Starrs v Ruxton* 2000 JC 208, 250 (Lord Reed): 'It would be inconsistent with the whole approach of the Convention if the independence of the courts itself rested upon convention rather than law.'

[61] *Procola v Luxembourg* (1996) 22 EHRR 193, [45].

[62] Gee et al, *The Politics of Judicial Independence in the UK's Changing Constitution* (2015) 254.

[63] Department for Constitutional Affairs (n 40) [3].

[64] A Patterson, *Final Judgment: The Last Law Lords and the Supreme Court* (Hart Publishing, 2013) 258.

decisions of the new court would enjoy the 'added authority' attached to decisions of an apex court structurally separated from the legislature.[65] This newly found autonomy facilitated the only formal change to the jurisdiction of the court. Though the Law Lords (sitting as the Judicial Committee of the Privy Council) had previously discharged the jurisdiction stemming from the 1998 legislation that gave effect to devolution, it was nonetheless a notable modification of the new court's responsibilities. Because of its position within the legislature, the Appellate Committee of the House of Lords was felt to be an inapt mediator of disputes concerning the relationships between the devolved bodies and Westminster.[66] Allocation of this 'federal' jurisdiction to the Supreme Court provided implicit acknowledgement that the achievement of the structural independence of the Supreme Court actually enhanced the position of the court as an independent, and as a constitutional, arbiter.

Further, by adopting the nomenclature associated with explicitly constitutional organs elsewhere, the creation of a Supreme Court for the UK invited comparisons with authoritative/determinative apex courts in other jurisdictions. Though it would lack powers of strong-form judicial review, the creation of a *Supreme* Court alluded to a model of constitutionalism quite unlike the political constitution, in which the courts were explicitly identified as standing structurally apart from the other core institutions of the state and enjoying the constitutional function of policing an abstracted catalogue of legal rights. The Supreme Court has succinctly captured this tension – in the context of its devolution jurisdiction – in the following terms: 'The powers of the Scottish Parliament, like those of Parliaments in many *other* constitutional democracies, are delimited by law.'[67] The combination of statutory devolution and human rights jurisdictions – alongside powers exercisable resulting from EU membership, and by virtue of the common law's principle of legality – added weight to the claim that the UK Supreme Court was to exercise a constitutional jurisdiction, and function as a proto-constitutional court.[68]

IV. TWENTY YEARS AFTER

The cumulative effect of New Labour's reforms was to reposition and empower the judicial branch of government within the constitutional architecture. The

[65] Lord Hope, Barnard's Inn Reading, 'The Creation of the Supreme Court – Was It Worth It?' (24 June 2010).

[66] A Le Sueur, *What Is the Future for the Judicial Committee of the Privy Council?* (Constitution Unit, 2001) 11.

[67] *UK Withdrawal from the European Union (Legal Continuity) (Scotland) Bill* [2018] UKSC 64, [12] (emphasis added).

[68] R Masterman and JEK Murkens, 'Skirting Supremacy and Subordination: The Constitutional Authority of the UK Supreme Court' [2013] *PL* 800.

Blair reforms acknowledged that the courts play an active and distinctive role in the articulation, and potentially enforcement of, constitutional standards (a point emphasised in the post-1997 period as the diet of the apex court took on a distinctly public/constitutional law flavour[69]). The Human Rights Act became emblematic of a constitutional rejection of arbitrary power and – for some judges – represented the establishment of a 'new legal order'.[70] The devolution legislation further pointed to a 'division'[71] of sovereignty and – in establishing democratic assemblies that were to legislate within parameters established by law – towards a broader sense that public powers, including legislative powers, were amenable to judicial scrutiny.[72]

In the light of this, it is unsurprising that the New Labour reforms have played a part in provoking a body of literature critiquing the extent to which the constitutional balance has been irrevocably altered, and the political (democratic) constitution compromised, by positioning law as 'the cordon within which politics is allowed to take place'.[73] Parliamentary sovereignty, it is argued, is threatened – if not displaced[74] – by this 'new', inexorably expanding, judicial role, while an expansive vision of the rule of law fuels 'ever more searching judicial review', judicial 'misuse of ordinary techniques of statutory interpretation' and review of legislative and policy choices on their merits.[75]

In short, the Blair reforms impacting on the powers and status of the judiciary have come to be understood as radical, and the importance of the narrative of continuity has somewhat faded. Yet it is clear – and has been noted explicitly by many senior judges during this period – that the sovereignty doctrine retains its position at the core of the constitution.[76] Indeed, one of the most politically significant Supreme Court decisions in recent years – *R (Miller) v Secretary of State for Exiting the European Union* – amounted in key respects to a reaffirmation of the centrality of parliamentary legislative power in the domestic constitution.[77] The judicial record since 1997 displays a more complex embrace of the functions attached to the Blair governments' reforms, and often can be seen to veer between extremes of judicial adventurism and judicial restraint.

[69] T Poole and S Shah, 'The Impact of the Human Rights Act on the House of Lords' [2009] *PL* 347.

[70] *R (Jackson) v Attorney General* [2006] 1 AC 262, [102].

[71] ibid.

[72] On this point, see *R (on the application of Miller) v The Prime Minister; Cherry and others v Advocate General* [2019] UKSC 41, [2020] AC 373.

[73] D Nicol, 'Law and Politics after the Human Rights Act' [2006] *PL* 722, 722.

[74] Bogdanor, *The New British Constitution* (2009).

[75] R Ekins, *The Dynamics of Judicial Power in the New British Constitution* (Policy Exchange, 2017) 19. As with the 'transformative' accounts of Bogdanor and King noted above, Ekins's position considers a broader range of influences on this 'new' judicial role, but the influence of the Human Rights Act 1998 (and the courts' 'misuse' of the Act (11)) is central.

[76] *R (Jackson) v Attorney General* [2006] 1 AC 262, [9] (Lord Bingham); Lord Neuberger, 'Who Are the Masters Now?' Lord Alexander of Weedon Lecture (6 April 2011).

[77] *R (Miller) v Secretary of State for Exiting the European Union* [2017] UKSC 5, [2018] AC 61. On which see T Poole, 'Devotion to Legalism: On the Brexit Case' (2018) 80 *MLR* 696.

Emphasising the radical elements of the New Labour reforms makes it easy to lose sight of the narrative of continuity, and the importance of that narrative to articulating the judicial function in the aftermath of the Blair reforms and sustaining this 'new' judicial role into the longer term.

A. Bringing Rights Home

The New Labour project to bring rights 'home' positioned the implementation of the Human Rights Act – and the enforcement of its catalogue of rights – as being consistent with the UK's existing (international) obligations,[78] and was a pragmatic step towards repatriating rights that were 'originally developed with major help from the United Kingdom Government'.[79] Some judges – Laws LJ chief among them – saw the enactment of the Human Rights Act as a confirmation of the common law's burgeoning jurisprudence of constitutional rights,[80] and in so doing adopted their own variant of the continuity narrative by seeking to explain the advent of the Human Rights Act as an endorsement of a trend already evident in common law reasoning. On this view, the relationship between the common law and the ECHR was to be complementary, with the emergence of a 'municipal law of human rights' a product of the incremental blending of the two sources of rights jurisprudence.[81] An alternative position, articulated by Lord Hoffmann, sought to minimise the transformative effect of the Strasbourg case law by postulating that the effect of the Human Rights Act was:

> to create domestic rights expressed in the same terms as those contained in the Convention. But they are domestic rights, not international rights. Their source is the statute, not the Convention. They are available against specific public authorities, not the United Kingdom as a state. And their meaning and application is a matter for domestic courts, not the court in Strasbourg.[82]

Hoffmann's view – expanded upon extrajudicially as a theory of human rights that are 'universal in abstraction but national in application'[83] – sought to preserve those dualist elements of the constitution that the Human Rights Act threatened to dissolve, and in doing so emphasised that the role of the domestic courts was to enforce the Act itself, rather than to position themselves as domestic proxies for the Strasbourg Court.[84]

[78] *Rights Brought Home: The Human Rights Bill* (1997) [1.18].

[79] ibid [1.14].

[80] *International Transport Roth GmbH v Secretary of State for the Home Department* [2003] QB 728, [71].

[81] *Runa Begum v Tower Hamlets London Borough Council* [2002] 2 All ER 668, [17]. See also *R (ProLife Alliance) v British Broadcasting Corporation* [2002] 2 All ER 756, [33]–[34].

[82] *In Re McKerr* [2004] UKHL 12, [63].

[83] Lord Hoffmann, 'The Universality of Human Rights' (2009) 125 *LQR* 416, 422.

[84] *R v Secretary of State for Foreign and Commonwealth Affairs, ex parte Quark Fishing* [2005] UKHL 57, [2006] 1 AC 529, [34] (Lord Nicholls): 'The [Human Rights] Act was intended to provide

In relation to the meaning and application of the Convention rights, however, it was an approach that accentuated the transformative influence of the new (external) source of the Convention rights that came to be seen as dominant. The principle that domestic courts should effectively 'mirror'[85] the requirements of the Strasbourg case law – articulated in *Ullah* by Lord Bingham as the 'duty of national courts to keep pace with the Strasbourg jurisprudence as it evolves over time: no more, but certainly no less'[86] – dominated the courts' approach to the application of the Act's protected rights for almost a decade. This 'internationalist'[87] reading of the courts' obligations under the Act tended towards emphasising the superior status of the Strasbourg case law in Human Rights Act disputes and led to a 'baleful and unnecessary' tendency to overlook the rights-protecting capacity of the common law.[88] Rather than seeing the Convention rights 'woven into' domestic law as the Labour government had hoped,[89] this approach gave rise to suggestions that the Convention rights were alien impositions[90] and – unfortunately – chimed with politically motivated caricatures of expansionist, imperialising decision-making by the European Court of Human Rights.[91]

The *Ullah* approach 'suggest[ed] a position of deference [to the Strasbourg Court]',[92] which in turn intimated the imposition of the Strasbourg rights jurisprudence to the detriment of distinct characteristics of national law. The increased propensity – since at least the Supreme Court decision in *Horncastle*[93] – of the courts to reconceive of their human rights jurisdiction as an enterprise shared between the domestic institutions and the European Court of Human Rights has somewhat diminished this trend. It has both facilitated the re-emergence of the common law as a means by which rights might be upheld and promoted the willingness of domestic courts to seek to engage in 'dialogue' with the European Court of Human Rights. The sense of unquestioning acceptance of the Strasbourg case law has reduced, as the Supreme Court has steadily carved out a series of exceptions to the mirror principle which either seek to maintain the distinctive approaches of the existing domestic law[94] or otherwise

a remedy where a remedy would have been available in Strasbourg. Conversely, the Act was not intended to provide a domestic remedy where a remedy would not have been available in Strasbourg.'

[85] J Lewis, 'The European Ceiling on Rights' [2007] *PL* 720.

[86] *R (Ullah) v Special Adjudicator* [2004] UKHL 26, [2004] 2 AC 323, [20].

[87] B Dickson, *Human Rights and the United Kingdom Supreme Court* (Oxford University Press, 2013) 56.

[88] *Kennedy v Information Commissioner* [2014] UKSC 20, [133].

[89] *Rights Brought Home: The Human Rights Bill* (n 37) [1.14].

[90] Commission on a UK Bill of Rights, *A UK Bill of Rights? The Choice Before Us* (December 2012) [24]–[40].

[91] See, eg M Pinto-Duschinsky, *Bringing Rights Back Home: Making Human Rights Compatible with Parliamentary Democracy in the UK* (Policy Exchange, 2011).

[92] N Bratza, 'The Relationship between the UK Courts and Strasbourg' [2011] *European Human Rights Law Review* 505, 512.

[93] *R v Horncastle* [2009] UKSC 14, [2010] 2 AC 373.

[94] ibid; *Poshteh v Kensington and Chelsea LBC* [2017] UKSC 36, [2017] AC 624.

seek to preserve the decision-making competence of the relevant domestic authority.[95] As a result, Lord Reed has argued against the apparently transformative demands of the *Ullah* approach:

> The importance of the [Human Rights] Act is unquestionable. It does not however supersede the protection of human rights under the common law or statute, or create a discrete body of law based on the judgments of the European Court.[96]

Instead – and in line with the approach taken by Laws LJ in the years following implementation – Lord Reed emphasised that the 'fundamentally subsidiary' nature of the Strasbourg Court demands that 'the Convention rights should be protected primarily by a detailed body of domestic law'.[97] The recent jurisprudence of the Supreme Court therefore emphasises that the Human Rights Act should be understood as allowing for the principled integration of the ECHR case law with existing domestic laws, tending towards continuity through emphasising that the Strasbourg jurisprudence should not *necessarily* usurp established domestic rules or decision-making.

B. Interpreting Rights

The judicial approach to the Human Rights Act's interpretative clause has seen similar trends, by turns emphasising the radical and rather more restrained potential of section 3(1). The permeable division between the (legitimate, or at least statutorily endorsed) task of 'interpretation' pursuant to section 3(1) of the Human Rights Act and the (questionable, potentially constitutionally illegitimate) exercise of judicial 'legislation' has provided a focal point of argument over the nature of the judicial role following the enactment of the Human Rights Act. If the traditional separation of powers drew a rudimentary distinction between legislator and interpreter,[98] the functional division between interpretation and judicial law-making was brought into sharper focus by the enforcement of the Human Rights Act. While the Human Rights Act suggests that interpretative functions fall within the remit of the courts and legislative functions fall to be exercised by Parliament (or – as a result of the section 10 procedure – to the executive), a precise delineation between the two functions remains elusive.[99]

Adjudication under the Act has revealed the section 3(1) species of 'interpretation' to be a multifaceted process that requires focus on issues beyond the intention of the legislature as evidenced in statutory language. Though

[95] *R (Animal Defenders International) v Secretary of State for Culture, Media and Sport* [2008] UKHL 15, [2008] 1 AC 1312; *In Re P* [2008] UKHL 38, [2009] 1 AC 173.

[96] *R (Osborne) v Parole Board* [2013] UKSC 61, [2014] AC 1115, [57].

[97] ibid [56].

[98] *Duport Steel v Sirs* [1980] 1 WLR 142, 157.

[99] The most comprehensive assessment can be found in A Kavanagh, *Constitutional Review under the UK Human Rights Act* (Cambridge University Press, 2009).

pre-Human Rights Act adjudication had already demonstrated the waning of formalist/literalist approaches to statutory construction, the reconciliation of (interpreted) statute and Convention rights (and attendant case law) within the remedial framework provided by the Act is a process arguably demanding of a purposive approach, as it subjects *all* legislation to the meta-requirement of Convention compliance in so far as that is 'possible'. In the sense that section 3(1) added – at a minimum – judicial assessment of external influences (Strasbourg decisions) as well as new questions of institutional competence (which remedial provision to employ) to linguistic, legislative intent-focused processes of statutory construction, then it should be considered a departure.

Early decisions deploying the provision in practice emphasised this impression, drawing parallels with the experiences of the Judicial Committee of the Privy Council in interpreting *constitutional* Bills of Rights and suggesting that the Human Rights Act ought to be afforded a 'generous and purposive'[100] interpretation in order that individuals fully benefit from its protections.[101] The so-called 'radical' approach to interpretation[102] drew on this expansive (judicially focused) understanding of the Act, conceiving of the courts' powers under section 3(1) as potentially remedial of all inconsistencies other than those explicitly 'stated in terms' by statute. This approach in turn viewed the declaration of incompatibility as a 'measure of last resort' to be avoided 'unless … plainly impossible to do so'.[103] While the radical approach was inspired by the Privy Council experiences of the Law Lords[104] and was contextualised by reference to the 'weaker'[105] model of the New Zealand Bill of Rights Act, it nonetheless sat uneasily with the constitutional 'balance'[106] that the government had sought to preserve. The remedial architecture of the Human Rights Act does not clearly support a judicio-centric construction of its protections; although the courts are a central means through which the Convention rights might be upheld, it is clear that the Act was not designed to displace the ability of Parliament to legislate in connection (and potentially inconsistently[107]) with the protected rights, and it is implicit in the Act's schema that the protection of the Convention rights is an enterprise shared.[108]

The expansive view, however, quickly ceded ground to a more contextual approach under which the dividing line between interpretation and law-making will be contingent on a range of issues, including – but not limited to – linguistic

[100] *Minister of Home Affairs v Fisher* [1980] AC 319, 329 (Lord Wilberforce). See also *R v Director of Public Prosecutions, ex parte Kebilene* [2000] 2 AC 326, 375; *Brown v Stott* [2003] 1 AC 681, 703.

[101] Lord Steyn, 'The New Legal Landscape' [2000] *European Human Rights Law Review* 549, 550.

[102] A Kavanagh, 'Unlocking the Human Rights Act: The "Radical" Approach to s 3(1) Revisited' [2005] *European Human Rights Law Review* 259.

[103] *R v A (No 2)* [2002] 1 AC 45, [44] (Lord Steyn).

[104] ibid [38] (Lord Steyn).

[105] ibid [44] (Lord Steyn).

[106] Lord Irvine of Lairg QC, 'The Impact of the Human Rights Act' (2003).

[107] Human Rights Act, s 19(1)(b).

[108] ibid s 4.

matters,[109] perceived constitutional competence,[110] the impact of the proposed interpretation on the impugned legislation,[111] the weight to be attached to the relevant/applicable Strasbourg jurisprudence[112] and so on. In the abstract, the formal possibilities of interpretation pursuant to this contextual approach to section 3(1) are tolerably clear: although section 3(1) falls short of permitting interpretations which would 'vandalise'[113] statutory provisions or allow for interpretations which run 'against the grain'[114] of primary legislation, it does permit the implication of words and phrases with potentially significant implications for the legislation under consideration.[115]

Rejection of the 'radical' approach to interpretation permits greater space for use of section 4. While the declaration of incompatibility mechanism lacks – from the perspective of the Strasbourg Court – the definitive characteristics of an 'effective remedy'[116] it preserves the right of the sovereign Parliament to sustain legislation which may fail to meet the requirements of the Convention. But perhaps just as importantly, the contextual approach to section 3(1) suggests that the determination of legislative intent remains at the core of the interpretative exercise; consistency with the intention behind the impugned legislation will condition whether or not an interpretative remedy is 'possible' or not. The broader point here is that recognition of the decision-making autonomy of the primary decision-maker remains as important to the processes of Human Rights Act judicial review as it is to judicial review more broadly considered. Indeed, the availability of a primary decision-maker's 'discretionary area of judgment'[117] became seen as 'the classic separation of powers device in the post-Human Rights Act era'.[118] Yet, even in this sphere, the 'new' language of deference was often presented as a continuation of the '*ordinary judicial task* of weighing up the competing considerations on each side …'[119]

C. 'Federal' Adjudication

Predictions that the courts would play a significant role in policing the boundaries of the devolutionary settlement[120] initially appeared to be unfounded. While

[109] *Bellinger v Bellinger* [2003] UKHL 21, [2003] 2 AC 467.
[110] *Bellinger v Bellinger* [2003] UKHL 21, [2003] 2 AC 467.
[111] *R (Anderson) v Secretary of State for the Home Department* [2002] UKHL 46, [2003] 1 AC 837.
[112] *Secretary of State for the Home Department v AF (No.3)* [2009] UKHL 28, [2010] 2 AC 269.
[113] *R (Anderson) v Secretary of State for the Home Department* [2002] UKHL 46, [2003] 1 AC 837, [30].
[114] *Ghaidan v Godin-Mendoza* [2004] 2 AC 557, [121].
[115] ibid [32].
[116] *Burden v United Kingdom* (2008) 47 EHRR 38.
[117] *R v Director of Public Prosecutions, ex parte Kebilene* [2000] 2 AC 326, 380–81 (Lord Hope).
[118] S Tierney, 'Determining the State of Exception? What Role for Parliament and the Courts?' (2005) 68 *MLR* 668, 670.
[119] *Huang v Secretary of State for the Home Department* [2007] UKHL 11, [16] (emphasis added).
[120] See, eg R Cornes, 'Intergovernmental Relations' in R Hazell (ed), *Constitutional Futures: A History of the Next Ten Years* (Oxford University Press, 1999).

adjudication over devolution matters was by no means uncommon following the establishment of the devolved bodies, its focus was in larger part on the ECHR-compatibility of elements of the Scottish criminal justice system, rather than competence disputes arising on 'federal grounds'.[121] Hazell concludes that a partial reason for this can be found in both the hierarchical structuring of the devolutionary arrangements and in the 'flexibility' provided by the sovereignty concept (the latter evidenced in early amendments to the devolved frameworks and accommodation of devolved interests into Westminster legislation).[122] From one perspective at least, the enduring influence of centralised government offered a partial explanation for the lack of 'federal' adjudication in the early years of the devolution project.

Evidence from the early case law on the nature of this 'federal' jurisdiction was somewhat polarised. On the one hand, Lord Rodger in *Whaley v Lord Watson of Invergowrie* appeared to suggest that the legal limits on the powers of the Scottish Parliament were to be understood similarly to those attaching to 'any other statutory body'. Lord Rodger – in characterising the Scottish Parliament as a body 'created by statute and deriv[ing] its powers from statute' – implicitly rejected suggestions that the 'constitutional' status of the Scotland Act and devolutionary settlement were to have any bearing on the method of interpretation adopted in resolving questions of competence. By contrast, the House of Lords in *Robinson v Secretary of State for Northern Ireland* advocated a devolutionary counterpart to the radical approach to interpretation under section 3(1) of the Human Rights Act. Lord Bingham, in the majority, found that the Northern Ireland Act 1998 was 'in effect a constitution' and that it followed that its provisions should be 'interpreted generously and purposively'.[123] Similarly, Lord Hoffmann found that the Act should not be interpreted 'rigidly' and that giving effect to the broader political agreement it rested upon 'required … flexibility'.[124] In so finding, the Law Lords were able to dismiss a challenge to the validity of elections to the positions of First Minister and Deputy First Minister on the basis that they had fallen outside the statutory time limit.

Subsequent decisions have indicated an intermediate – sub-federal – approach, which seeks to reconcile the distinctive, democratic characteristics of the devolved bodies with their statutory heritage. As such, the Scottish Parliament is no ordinary statutory body, but a 'democratically elected legislature'[125] enjoying 'plenary powers'[126] subject to the limitations stated in the Scotland Act[127] and 'constitutional review' on the basis of the common law principle of legality.[128]

[121] R Hazell, 'Out of Court: Why Have the Courts Played No Role in the Resolving of Devolution Disputes in the United Kingdom?' (2007) 37 *Publius* 578, 581.

[122] ibid.

[123] *Robinson v Secretary of State for Northern Ireland* [2002] ULHL 32, [11].

[124] ibid [32].

[125] *AXA General Insurance Ltd v HM Advocate* [2011] UKSC 46, [2012] 1 AC 868, [145].

[126] ibid [147].

[127] Scotland Act 1998, s 29(2).

[128] *AXA General Insurance Ltd v HM Advocate* [2011] UKSC 46, [2012] 1 AC 868, [149]–[153].

Further – as recognised by Lord Hope in the *Imperial Tobacco* decision – while the Scotland Act might be regarded as a constitutional statute, that 'cannot be taken, in itself, as a guide to its interpretation. The statute must be interpreted like any other statute.'[129] *Robinson* – as Lord Reed has argued – now appears 'best understood as a decision concerned with its own specific circumstances'.[130] The balance to be struck was outlined by the unanimous Supreme Court in the reference on the *UK Withdrawal from the European Union (Legal Continuity) (Scotland) Bill* in the following terms:

> The Scotland Act must be interpreted in the same way as any other statute. The courts have regard to its aim to achieve a constitutional settlement and therefore recognise the importance of giving a consistent and predictable interpretation of the Scotland Act so that the Scottish Parliament has a coherent, stable and workable system within which to exercise its legislative power. This is achieved by interpreting the rules as to competence in the Scotland Act according to the ordinary meaning of the words used.[131]

As such, the courts have sought to recognise – within the frameworks provided by the devolution legislation – the distinctive constitutional status of the devolutionary arrangements without sanctioning general departures from the legislative intent-driven techniques of interpretation to be applied.

Consideration of the effects of the Sewel Convention – recognised in statute since the Scotland Act 2016[132] – in *Miller* also emphasised that the devolutionary functions of the Supreme Court would not necessarily authorise departures from established precedents. In *Miller*, the Supreme Court was asked to determine whether the government's proposal to trigger Article 50 TEU and commence the UK's departure from the EU could be achieved through use of the foreign relations prerogative. The applicants contended that this power could only be conferred upon the government by primary legislation. As a subsidiary question, the Supreme Court was asked whether, if primary legislation was required to bestow upon ministers the power to initiate Article 50, the Sewel Convention in turn required that the consent of the devolved legislatures was a necessary precursor to Westminster enacting the authorising legislation.

Consistently with the tenor of the Supreme Court's decision more broadly construed[133] the majority's treatment of Sewel tended towards the support of

[129] *Imperial Tobacco v Lord Advocate* [2012] UKSC 61, 2013 SC (UKSC) 153, [15].

[130] Lord Reed, 'Scotland's Devolved Settlement and the Role of the Courts', Dover House Lecture (27 February 2019).

[131] *UK Withdrawal from the European Union (Legal Continuity) (Scotland) Bill* [2018] UKSC 64, [2019] AC 1022, [12].

[132] Section 28(8) of the Scotland Act 1998, as amended by the Scotland Act 2016, reads: 'But it is recognised that the Parliament of the United Kingdom will not normally legislate with regards to devolved matters without the consent of the Scottish Parliament.'

[133] Poole, 'Devotion to Legalism' (2017).

orthodox constitutional principles. The majority recognised the established position that constitutional conventions are not judicially enforceable, finding that the coercive effect of the Sewel convention was 'a political restriction on the activity of the UK Parliament'.[134] Judges, the majority added,

> are neither the parents nor the guardians of political conventions; they are merely observers … they can recognise the operation of a political convention in the context of deciding a legal question … but they cannot give legal rulings on its operation or scope, because those matters are determined within the political world.[135]

Though 'legislative recognition' of Sewel had had the effect of entrenching its status as a 'convention',[136] it did not – given the qualified language of section 28(8) – 'convert [the convention] into a rule which can be interpreted, let alone enforced, by the courts'.[137] In sum, Sewel was regarded as a political 'means of establishing cooperative relationships between the UK Parliament and the devolved administrations'[138] rather than a stronger regulatory tool capable of protecting devolved interests from central incursion. Accordingly, the majority found that the UK Parliament was subject to no justiciable/enforceable obligation resulting from the Sewel convention.

The delineation of the (distinct) legal and political spheres of the *Miller* dispute provides something of a leitmotif of the majority judgment in the Supreme Court (as indeed it had done in the Divisional Court). This is, in a sense, unsurprising: the majority decision was both largely supportive of constitutional orthodoxy and alert to the prospect of inflaming an already incendiary public debate surrounding Brexit. The compartmentalising by the majority of the legal and the political elements of the decision – only the former of which fell to the court for determination – therefore provided insulation in substantive and procedural terms. The institutional position of the Supreme Court may also provide some explanation for its failure to fully account for the complexities of the interplay between the forces of devolution and those of Brexit. While it is true to say that the Supreme Court exercises constitutional functions in relation to human rights adjudication and consideration of devolution issues, for instance, it is not explicitly a 'constitutional court'. Instead, the court – in cases with constitutional implications – adjudicates in relation to disputes which intersect law and politics,[139] and its findings may tend towards to emphasising the requirements of the law when confronted with circumstances with a particularly clear (and perhaps singularly controversial) political flavour. Resolution of

[134] *R (on the application of Miller) v Secretary of State for Exiting the European Union* [2017] UKSC 5, [2018] AC 61, [145].
[135] ibid [146].
[136] ibid [149].
[137] ibid [148].
[138] ibid [136].
[139] Masterman and Murkens, 'Skirting Supremacy and Subordination' (2013).

the primary substantive issue – as the majority recognised – rendered it unnecessary to fully unpack those arguments pertaining to the UK's devolutionary arrangements. The relatively myopic view of the constitution provided shows that – despite acknowledgements from within the Supreme Court that devolution has transformed it into something 'more and more like a constitutional court'[140] – the Supreme Court carries the baggage of a system constitutionally dominated by the sovereignty of a centralised legislature.

V. CONCLUSION

The confluence of (i) legislatively mandated review, (ii) the creation of an independent, politically influential Supreme Court and (iii) a growing propensity towards utilising courts as a means by which high-level politico-legal disputes might be addressed has produced circumstances in which the Supreme Court might be regarded as a constitutional actor (in a way in which the Appellate Committee of the House of Lords perhaps never was). A trajectory towards an increasingly 'constitutional' judicial function was, however, evident prior to the Blair reforms – the seeds of a common law rights jurisdiction and of a constitutional hierarchy of statutes had already been sown – but it was given increased impetus by the explicit direction and structural realignments of the New Labour reforms. As a result, the role of the courts in articulating constitutional standards is more firmly established than it was pre-1997,[141] and the Supreme Court in particular exercises functions that can be likened to those explicitly held by constitutional courts elsewhere.[142] But it cannot be said that the old order has been dispensed with.[143] In both articulating and interpreting rights, and in expounding the constitutional implications of the devolutionary arrangements, characteristics of the pre-1997 constitution remain essential to the post-1997 judicial architecture and function. It is perhaps better to understand the consequence of these developments, not as a radical redrawing of judicial power, but as an explicit demarcation of the judicial function as central to the mapping of constitutional power as it is exercised within and across the UK.

[140] Lady Hale, 'Should the Law Lords have left the House of Lords?' Michael Ryle Lecture 2018 (14 November 2018).

[141] Masterman and Murkens (n 68) 819.

[142] Lord Phillips, 'The Challenges of the Supreme Court', Gresham Lecture (2 June 2010).

[143] The tension between continuity and more radical change is also arguably evident in other fields of the Supreme Court's 'constitutional' jurisdiction: see, eg *R (Evans) v Attorney General)* [2015] UKSC 21; *R (Buckinghamshire CC) v Secretary of State for Transport* [2014] UKSC 3, [2014] 1 WLR 324.

11

New Labour's Secret National Security Constitution

PAUL F SCOTT

I. INTRODUCTION

THIS CHAPTER ADDRESSES the law of investigatory powers during the New Labour era, arguing that under New Labour there existed a 'secret' national security constitution which augmented and even at times departed from the openly avowed and clearly communicated law in this area. Having first considered the question of what legal – as opposed to, say, factual – secrecy might mean and provided some of the relevant background, the chapter makes its key claim in two stages. The first considers the reform of the law of investigatory powers by the enactment of the Regulation of Investigatory Powers Act 2000 (RIPA), which significantly expanded the prior law, then contained (mostly) in the Interception of Communications Act 1985. Though the relevant powers appeared clear on the face of the legislation, in a few areas RIPA operated so as to confuse and even conceal the nature of the contribution which it made to the national security constitution. This chapter therefore considers the ways in which – and the techniques by which – this gap between appearance and reality was created and sustained. A second element of the law of investigatory powers under New Labour – to which attention turns in the second half of the chapter – makes RIPA seem, however, a model of transparency. That is, only in the post-New Labour period have key features of the national security constitution as it existed between 1997 and 2010 attracted legal and political attention commensurate with their significance: not because they were uncontroversial, but because they were unknown and in many cases unknowable. The most important such features include equipment interference ('hacking') by the state[1] and the bulk acquisition of communications data under the authority not

[1] Discussed at length in PF Scott, 'General Warrants, Thematic Warrants, Bulk Warrants: Property Interference for National Security Purposes' [2017] *Northern Ireland Legal Quarterly* 99.

of RIPA, but of the Telecommunications Act 1984.[2] All of these – and others[3] – have been subjects of attention by the courts in recent years and the relevant law is now largely superseded by the clear authority of the Investigatory Powers Act 2016.[4] In each case, however, the powers were used – often widely, and in some cases, perhaps, for the first time – under New Labour.

This chapter therefore takes as its focus not only what was done by New Labour in the field of national security, but also what was not done; or, rather, what was done in the shadows, without public explanation and so without the fact, or even the possibility, of scrutiny. It considers how the powers in question were tweaked over time and how the associated oversight varied, as well as the strategies employed in order to ensure that basic (domestic) legality was achieved without disclosing to the public at large the reality of the powers in question. Its argument is that it is here, in the shadows – the gaps left in RIPA; the powers which were employed and amended without their centrality to the national security project being acknowledged – that the true nature of New Labour's national security constitution emerges, and that the picture is considerably gloomier than would be a consideration which restricted itself to the constitutional surface. The chapter's final section considers some of the broader issues raised by these facts: how this story was unable to unfold the way it did, and what might be done to prevent its reoccurrence.

II. 'SECRET LAW'

Elsewhere, a significant aspect of modern national security constitutionalism has been what has been dubbed 'secret law', this being, on one important account, 'legal authorities that require compliance that are classified or otherwise withheld from the public'.[5] Approaching the matter from the point of view of the US Constitution and its requirements, that contribution argues for a distinction between matters of 'secret law' and those involving 'secret fact'.[6] In the UK, the continued obscurity of 'secret fact' is secured in a number of ways within the executive, the courts and, to a lesser extent, the legislature and its offshoots.[7] Though the necessity and efficacy of the mechanisms in question are contested,

[2] See PF Scott, *The National Security Constitution* (Hart Publishing, 2018) 85–97.

[3] One such example is the retention and use of what are known as 'bulk personal datasets', for which explicit authority was provided only by the Investigatory Powers Act 2016: see ibid 97–103.

[4] ibid ch 2. The fullest treatment of the 2016 Act is found in S McKay, *Blackstone's Guide to the Investigatory Powers Act 2016* (Oxford University Press, 2018).

[5] DS Rudesill, 'Coming to Terms with Secret Law' [2015] *Harvard National Security Journal* 241, 249.

[6] ibid 310–25.

[7] For the position in the courts, see A Tomkins, 'Justice and Security in the United Kingdom' (2014) 47 *Israel Law Review* 305. For that in the executive, see the discussions in Scott, *The National Security Constitution* (2018) 222–34. For that in the legislature, see V Fikfak and HJ Hooper, *Parliament's Secret War*, Hart Publishing (2018) ch 5.

they themselves are generally well understood, not least because those mechanisms are implemented by laws which are not themselves secret. Secret facts are therefore – at the general level – 'known unknowns'.[8]

In discussing secret law in the UK, we might distinguish between secret law which is, like these secret facts, a 'known unknown' and that which is an 'unknown unknown', with the public not even knowing that there is something it does not know. A related way of making a similar point is to distinguish between 'shallow' and 'deep' secrecy.[9] 'Deeply' secret law – that which is an 'unknown unknown' – is, of course, more objectionable, although its very nature is such that we cannot know if it exists in the UK. What we have encountered in the UK is law which is instead 'shallowly' secret: what is unknown is not the existence or content of the primary (usually statutory) norm, but rather relevant information regarding, for example, its interpretation or the use to which it is put. Here, on the basis of the consideration of some of the techniques which have been used to secure 'shallow' secrecy in the national security context, I argue that such secrecy is only marginally less obnoxious than is deep secrecy, and may in many cases be in fact more so, for two reasons. One is that the result of the techniques outlined here may be that what is known is in fact not known. As will be discussed below, several of the secret elements of New Labour's national security constitution were hidden, as it were, in plain sight: they were found in the statute books, but were not present in the consciousness of observers of the matters to which they related. The second reason is that, as a result of some of the techniques of shallow secrecy discussed below, what is known may actively mislead as to the nature and scope of the unknown: an interpretation may be given to a known norm which cannot be predicted from its terms, or which appears to be incompatible with those terms. Unless and until that interpretation is endorsed (or rejected) by somebody with the jurisdiction to rule authoritatively on the question, there is no mechanism for ensuring that the relevant actors – at a minimum, the legal community – really know what they think they know.

III. BACKGROUND

Before the 1980s, two legal regimes were relevant to the interception of communications: one was that permitting the interception of what would now be called

[8] Rudesill, 'Coming to Terms with Secret Law' (2015) 281ff. The phrase is, of course, now somewhat deprecated by reason of its association with Donald Rumsfeld, then US Secretary of State for Defense, who answered a question regarding the (absence of) evidence linking Iraq with the supply of weapons of mass destruction to terrorists by saying that: 'Reports that say that something hasn't happened are always interesting to me, because as we know, there are known knowns; there are things we know we know. We also know there are known unknowns; that is to say we know there are some things we do not know. But there are also unknown unknowns – the ones we don't know we don't know.' D Rumsfeld, Department of Defense News Briefing (12 February 2002).

[9] Rudesill (n 5), using language previously used in DE Pozen, 'Deep Secrecy' (2010) *Stanford Law Review* 275.

'external' communications (that is, those which are either sent to or from a place outside of the UK;[10] those which are both sent from and received within the UK are 'internal' communications) was found in the Official Secrets Act 1920.[11] The second, permitting the interception of internal communications, did not have a statutory basis.[12] Both the internal and external regimes were overtaken by the Interception of Communications Act 1985, enacted in response to the decision of the Court of Human Rights in *Malone v United Kingdom*,[13] in which it was held that the interception of communications was an interference with Article 8 rights that was not 'in accordance with law'.[14] In opposition before 1997, the Labour attitude towards national security questions was relatively restrained. The 1983 Labour Party manifesto referred to 'widespread concern' about the security services and the intention that 'they should become properly accountable institutions':

> We outline in Labour's Programme, 1982 our proposals for a new Security Act, to define the powers and responsibilities of the services, including those concerned with the interception of communications. We will also extend parliamentary accountability ... which will be assisted by a new select committee; prohibit, under the Security Act, unauthorised surveillance; and abolish 'D' notices.[15]

In the years following that commitment, the Conservative government enacted the Interception of Communications Act 1985 and the Security Service Act 1989,[16] which between them did much of what the 1983 manifesto had

[10] Technically, we are dealing here not with the UK, but rather the 'British Islands', defined in sch 1 of the Interpretation Act 1978 to mean 'the United Kingdom, the Channel Islands and the Isle of Man'.

[11] Official Secrets Act 1920, s 4.

[12] Indeed, its legal basis was astonishingly weak. The Birkett report of 1957 could provide no better an account than this: 'The power to intercept letters has been exercised from the earliest times, and has been recognised in successive Acts of Parliament. This power extends to telegrams. It is difficult to resist the view that if there is a lawful power to intercept communications in the form of letters and telegrams, then it is wide enough to cover telephone communications as well.' Report of the Committee of Privy Councillors Appointed to Inquire into the Interception of Communications (1957) [51].

[13] *Malone v United Kingdom* (1985) 7 EHRR 14.

[14] In those pre-HRA days, the domestic court had held that legal authority was necessary only where the individual's legal rights were interfered with; at common law there was no right to privacy, and so no such authority was required here: *Malone v Metropolitan Police Commissioner* [1979] Ch 344.

[15] Labour Party, *The New Hope for Britain* (1983). The reference is to a pamphlet published the previous year: Labour Party, *Labour's Programme, 1982* (1982).

[16] For contemporary discussion, see IJ Lloyd, 'The Interception of Communications Act 1985' (1986) 49 *MLR* 86; I Leigh and L Lustgarten, 'The Security Service Act 1989' (1989) 52 *MLR* 801. Notably, the 1989 Act was prompted in part by *Hewitt and Harman v United Kingdom* [1989] ECHR 29, where it was decided that the 'Maxwell-Fyfe Directive' on which MI5 relied was not sufficient legal basis to ground a lawful interference with the applicants' Art 8 rights. The interferences – carried out when Hewitt and Harman worked the National Council of Civil Liberties, later Liberty – were revealed in 1984 by whistleblower Cathy Massiter, by which point Harriet Harman was a Labour MP, becoming Secretary of State for Social Security in the Labour government formed in 1997. Patricia Hewitt joined her in the House of Commons in that same year.

committed a Labour government to doing. The 1992 manifesto promised only that 'The security services will be brought under the scrutiny of a Parliamentary Select Committee',[17] reflecting arguments made during the passage of both the 1985 and 1989 Acts (with considerable support, on the latter occasion, from the government benches).[18] Though Labour of course failed to win the 1992 election, that change was made by the Intelligence Services Act 1994, which gave a statutory basis to MI6 and GCHQ.[19] Rather than – as had been argued for – instituting a select committee or a committee of Privy Councillors, however, the government constituted the Intelligence and Security Committee – a 'unique and special' committee doing a 'unique and special job' – with members appointed by the Prime Minister following consultation with the Leader of the Opposition.[20] Labour nevertheless chose not to force a vote on the second reading of the Bill, which it said represented 'another step towards ending the deeply conservative, secretive culture of government in our country' and gave Parliament 'more, although not sufficient, powers to scrutinise what is done at taxpayers' expense and in the national interest'.[21] It was, Labour claimed, a 'victory for the arguments that we have advanced over the years'.[22] Though a number of amendments aimed at rendering the ISC more like a true select committee were moved, none made it into the final Act,[23] and its eventual reform took place only after the New Labour era.[24] Labour's 1997 manifesto made no direct reference to matters of domestic security policy.[25]

The first legislative intervention by New Labour in the field of investigatory powers was RIPA, which received Royal Assent just a week after the Terrorism Act 2000 gave effect to a radical overhaul of the law on terrorism. RIPA's enactment took place against a background of a series of changes: the growth in technology (including the facts that 'Mobile telephones have developed from being virtually unheard of to the mass ownership which is seen today' and

[17] Labour Party, *It's Time to Get Britain Working Again* (1992). Interesting background on the 1989 Act is found in the autobiography of Stella Rimington: *Open Secret* (Arrow Books, 2002) 194–97.

[18] See H Bochel, A Defty and J Kirkpatrick, *Watching the Watchers: Parliament and the Intelligence Services* (Palgrave Macmillan, 2014), 56–65.

[19] Intelligence Services Act 1994, ss 1–4.

[20] HC Deb 22 February 1994, vol 238 col 164, quoted in Bochel et al, *Watching the Watchers* (2014) 61.

[21] HC Deb 22 Feb 1994, vol 238 col 174.

[22] ibid.

[23] Bochel et al (n 18) 64–5.

[24] See Justice and Security Act 2013, ss 1–3 and sch 1. For a discussion of the reforms to the ISC, see H Bochel, A Defty and J Kirkpatrick, '"New Mechanisms of Independent Accountability": Select Committees and Parliamentary Scrutiny of the Intelligence Services' (2015) 68 *Parliamentary Affairs* 314.

[25] Labour Party, *New Labour – Because Britain Deserves Better* (1997). One of the first things the New Labour government of 1997 did upon taking power was, however, to reverse the ban on trade union membership at GCHQ, which had been the subject of ongoing dispute since it was first implemented in the 1980s and was the subject of the seminal decision in *Council of Civil Service Unions & Others v Minister for the Civil Service* [1985] AC 374.

'Communications via the Internet have grown dramatically in the last few years, and this part of the market continues to grow') and, in particular, the use of networks not operated by 'public telecommunications operators' as defined by the 1985 Act.[26] Also cited by the government were the need to encompass private networks[27] and to create a legal framework for the acquisition of 'communications data' – data about communications other than its content.[28]

The Investigatory Powers Act 2016 supersedes RIPA in respect of (almost) all of the powers discussed in this chapter. It contains fresh regimes for the interception of communications and the acquisition of communications data.[29] It also contains, however, a number of 'new' powers: powers of bulk acquisition of communications data, powers of 'equipment interference' or hacking (both targeted and bulk), and powers permitting the retention and use of 'bulk personal datasets'.[30] It is tempting, therefore, to construct a narrative whereby the 2016 Act is simply the next step in the expansion of the state's investigatory powers: in a new national security (and technological) era, the state required new capabilities to counter the emerging threats, and the 2016 Act provided them. Such a narrative is, however, untenable. The 'new' powers, that is, are in reality anything but. Rather, they had existed elsewhere in the statute book, obscure and almost entirely unnoticed, being avowed only at the point at which they were to be supplanted by the 2016 Act. Though, in all three cases, the powers in question – found in the Telecommunications Act 1984 (bulk acquisition of communications data),[31] the Security Service Act 1989 and the Intelligence Services Act 1994 (the bulk personal dataset powers)[32] and the Intelligence Services Act 1994 (equipment interference)[33] – had been put in place before Labour's return to power in 1997, they were in each case modified by and used under the Labour government, and so form part of New Labour's 'secret' national security constitution. Before considering these powers – hidden, as they were, in plain sight – it is necessary to say something about elements of the

[26] Secretary of State for the Home Department, *Interception of Communications in the United Kingdom: A Consultation Paper* (Cm 4368, 1999) 2–3.

[27] Private telecommunications were not included in the 1985 Act – a gap demonstrated by the decision of the Court of Human Rights in *Halford v United Kingdom* [1997] ECHR 32.

[28] Secretary of State for the Home Department, *Interception of Communications in the United Kingdom* (1999) 3. The powers in question are found in RIPA, Pt I, Ch II. RIPA also implemented powers relating to relating to surveillance and 'covert human intelligence sources', which are not discussed herein: RIPA, Pt II.

[29] The power to acquired communications data is now bolstered by powers – much broader even than those contained in the lapsed Data Retention and Investigatory Powers Act 2014 – requiring communications data to be retained, in order that it might be acquired under these new powers See Investigatory Powers Act 2016, Pt 2 (interception), Pt 3 (communications data) and Pt 4 (data retention).

[30] See IPA 2016, Pt 5 (equipment interference), Pt 6, Chs 2 (bulk acquisition) and 3 (bulk equipment interference) and Pt 7 (bulk personal datasets).

[31] Telecommunications Act 1984, s 94.

[32] Security Service Act 1989, s 2(2)(a); Intelligence Services Act 1994, ss 2(2)(a) and 4(2)(a).

[33] Intelligence Services Act 1994, ss 5 and 7.

RIPA regime itself which demonstrate some of the subtler forms of legal secrecy employed in New Labour's national security constitution.

IV. RIPA IN RETROSPECT

RIPA contained a number of powers related to surveillance, interception and so on. These provisions by definition met the requirement that there be a suitable legal basis for interferences with private and family life.[34] They were also held to meet the further requirements applied to secret surveillance law to ensure that such powers cannot be utilised arbitrarily (the '*Weber* requirements').[35] RIPA therefore seems another chapter in the story of the rationalisation of the national security constitution in response to pressures deriving from the European Convention on Human Rights and its transposition into domestic law by the Human Rights Act 1998. It was a whiggish development, to which the later Investigatory Powers Act 2016 is the bigger and better sequel: more rational, more comprehensive. Even on its own terms, however – ignoring matters not dealt with until the IPA was enacted – there are elements of RIPA which challenge that narrative.

The first relates to the definition of 'person' employed in RIPA. RIPA interception warrants were, on their face, 'targeted', internal warrants being required to 'name or describe either':

(a) one person as the interception subject; or
(b) a single set of premises as the premises in relation to which the interception to which the warrant relates is to take place.[36]

The provision on its face therefore requires warrants thereunder to be specific: they must sit at one pole of a spectrum at whose other pole sit the general warrants condemned by the common law in a series of eighteenth-century cases, including *Entick v Carrington*.[37] The difficulty comes with the (general) interpretation section of RIPA (rather than the section making provision specifically for the interpretation of terms used in part I),[38] which provides that 'person' 'includes any organisation and any association or combination of persons'.[39]

[34] Found, most relevantly for the purposes of surveillance measures, in Art 8 of the ECHR.

[35] *Kennedy v United Kingdom* (2011) 52 EHRR 4. For the requirements, see *Weber and Saravia v Germany* (2008) 46 EHRR SE5, [95].

[36] RIPA, s 8(1).

[37] *Entick v Carrington* (1765) 19 St Tr 1029. A general warrant is one which does not name the person to whom it relates, leaving those executing the warrant to decide for themselves whether there is sufficient evidence that, in the case of the relevant warrants, a particular person is amongst the 'authors, printers and publishers' of the seditious material. In truth, *Entick* itself did not relate to a general warrant – the warrant at issue named John Entick as its subject – though other cases of the same era did: for discussion of the case, see A Tomkins and P Scott, *Entick v Carrington: 250 Years of the Rule of Law* (Hart Publishing, 2015).

[38] That is RIPA, s 81 rather than s 20.

[39] RIPA, s 81(1). See, before RIPA, the Interception of Communications Act 1985, s 10(1).

The effect was that, although it was not possible to grant a warrant which was general, nor one which was, in the modern terminology, 'bulk' (including within its effect persons of no interest to the security services, as well as those who were), it was possible under RIPA to grant a 'thematic' interception warrant, one which identified persons not individually but by virtue of a category to which they belonged. Though the IPA similarly makes such thematic interception warrants available (as well as a variety of other thematic warrants), it – by contrast – does so with explicit words, found in each of the relevant places.

A case can be made for the interception power under RIPA being excluded from the category of 'secret law': the disparity between the terms of the power and its effect when read together with the interpretation section is unfortunate, but all the necessary interpretative material is available within the statute itself. And yet the feeling persists that there is something materially misleading about its structuring, which complicates unnecessarily (and so, one might speculate, deliberately) the process of reasoning out from dense statutory language to an understanding of what that language permits in practice. This sort of 'secrecy' – if that designation is accepted – is, paradoxically, perhaps more pernicious than any other: the meaning of 'person' is clearly central to the operation of the interception regime, yet was not addressed in any of the early case law on the act, and seems to have attracted little attention while still in force.[40] Nor is there any obvious legal means of combatting this drafting technique. Neither common law canons of interpretation nor any requirement under the ECHR will see it condemned. The wording is neither 'general' nor 'ambiguous'.[41] The ECHR does not condemn outright 'bulk' interception, never mind that which is merely 'thematic' – in fact, the Strasbourg Court would seem to be becoming more tolerant of it in an era in which more and more states are legislating to permit it[42] – and so the interpretative obligation of the Human Rights Act does not bite here. Similarly, the requirement of 'foreseeability' read into the 'prescribed by law' aspect of the qualified Convention rights would seem to be insufficiently demanding for this approach to drafting to fall foul of it.

A second criticism which might be made of the clarity of RIPA relates to an issue of perhaps even greater importance: the distinction between 'internal' and 'external' communications. The reason that this distinction mattered is that the requirements of specification applied only to warrants for interception of internal communications;[43] as they did not apply to external warrants, such communications could be intercepted in bulk and, by virtue of an omnipresent indemnity provision, any other conduct necessary to give effect to an external

[40] For example, in the leading work on investigatory powers, the point does not appear to be discussed: see S McKay, *Covert Policing*, 2nd edn (Oxford University Press, 2015) [3.146].

[41] *R v Secretary of State for the Home Department, Ex p Simms* [2000] 2 AC 115.

[42] See *Centrum för Rättvisa v Sweden* [2018] ECHR 520, holding the regime of bulk interception in Sweden to be compatible with the ECHR.

[43] RIPA, s 8(4).

intercept warrant was permitted by it, including – crucially – the interception of communications which were in fact internal.[44] To ensure that external warrants were not used in a way which effectively bypassed the limits on internal warrants, a number of (additional) limits existed upon the selection for examination of the material acquired thereunder.[45] Though the relevant rules were complex on their own terms, understanding of their operation was hampered by an absence of clear definitions.[46] Only with the post-Snowden litigation was some certainty offered, in the unhelpful guise of a witness statement to the Investigatory Powers Tribunal (IPT) by Charles Farr, then Director of the Office for Security and Counter-Terrorism and later Chairman of the Joint Intelligence Committee and Head of the Joint Intelligence Organisation. Farr noted that a communication sent from a person in the British Islands to another such person was internal even if routed through servers outside the British Islands,[47] and clarified the executive's understanding of the application of the distinction to internet platforms: 'Making a post on Facebook … entails placing a message upon a web-based platform' and in such a case 'the recipient … is the platform itself, because the platform is both the repository for the message, and the means by which it is broadcast to those with access to the relevant … Facebook page'.[48] If a person posted a message to a Facebook server located in a data server outside the British Islands, then that communication was 'external'.[49] The effect is that something that may not have been understood to be a 'communication' at all was in fact such a thing,[50] and – given the dominance of modern technology by American firms – was likely to be an external communication, which could therefore be acquired as part of a 'bulk' warrant which did not identify the 'sender' of the 'communication'.

The third point on which RIPA was potentially misleading was one of those addressed in post-Snowden litigation, after the fact (and scale) of the National Security Agency's interception of internet traffic had become known. A group of human rights and privacy non-governmental organisations brought a case before the Investigatory Powers Tribunal alleging that material was being passed by the US authorities to their British counterparts. This potentially circumvented the

[44] ibid s 5(6)(a).

[45] ibid s 16.

[46] RIPA said only that an 'external communication' was one 'sent or received outside the British Islands', with the category of 'internal communications' created solely by implication: RIPA, s 20.

[47] C Farr, witness statement in Case IPT/13/92/CH (16 May 2014), [126]–[141].

[48] ibid [136].

[49] ibid [137].

[50] As it was put by David Anderson QC in his review of investigatory powers, certain of the implications of the law as interpreted by the government were 'not clear prior to the publication of Mr Farr's statement' and, indeed, some of them might be the opposite of what a reader of the legislation might have anticipated: 'Some have considered those distinctions counter-intuitive: for example, many people might not consider a Google search to be a communication at all, let alone an external communication.' D Anderson, *A Question of Trust*: *Report of the Investigatory Powers Review* (2015) [6.52].

limitations found in RIPA upon the targeting of interception and the use made of material acquired via such interception.[51] Within the litigation, however, it was disclosed that – notwithstanding the absence of such limitations on the face of RIPA – a request for intercept material from foreign partners might be made only where a warrant under RIPA was in place (and so its requirements were not being circumvented) or where making the request without such a warrant did 'not amount to a deliberate circumvention of RIPA' or 'otherwise contravene' the *Padfield* principle.[52] In the latter scenario, not only would requirements of necessity and proportionality be implemented, but the decision to make such a request would be taken personally by the Secretary of State, and – it was later added – no such request had ever occurred 'as at the date of this statement'.[53] Moreover, any material obtained under these processes was subject – on an informal basis – to the same 'internal rules and safeguards' as applied to material obtained in accordance with RIPA. Though the effect was that RIPA could not be bypassed in the most egregious of fashions – any attempt to do so being stymied, if that is not too strong a term, by a mix of voluntary safeguards and pleasingly mundane principles of English administrative law – it was nevertheless later held that the regime for acquiring intercept material from foreign partners was not compliant with the ECHR prior to the point at which the relevant disclosures were made.[54] There seems no reason why the rules in question could not – and indeed should not – have been placed upon a statutory footing, rather than implemented in this manner.

These specific issues, however, are potentially dwarfed in their significance by the saving provision of RIPA, which reads as follows:

> Nothing in any of the provisions of this Act by virtue of which conduct of any description is or may be authorised by any warrant, authorisation or notice, or by virtue of which information may be obtained in any manner, shall be construed –
>
> (a) as making it unlawful to engage in any conduct of that description which is not otherwise unlawful under this Act and would not be unlawful apart from this Act;
>
> (b) as otherwise requiring –
>
> (i) the issue, grant or giving of such a warrant, authorisation or notice, or
>
> (ii) the taking of any step for or towards obtaining the authority of such a warrant, authorisation or notice,
>
> before any such conduct of that description is engaged in; or
>
> (c) as prejudicing any power to obtain information by any means not involving conduct that may be authorised under this Act.

[51] *Liberty v GCHQ* [2015] 3 All ER 142.

[52] [2015] 3 All ER 142, [47]. The reference is to *Padfield v Minister of Agriculture, Fisheries and Food* [1968] AC 997.

[53] [2015] 3 All ER 142, [48].

[54] *Liberty v Secretary of State for Foreign and Commonwealth Affairs* [2015] 3 All ER 212, [23].

Considerations of space preclude a full treatment of this provision,[55] which nevertheless encapsulates perhaps better than anything else the constitutional approach – both of New Labour and its many predecessors – to investigatory powers. The provision does two things of relevance. First, it means that information which might be acquired under RIPA could continue to be acquired under any other power permitting its acquisition. This would prove crucial later. Second, and more strikingly, it makes clear – in keeping with the logic of the British constitution, whereby legal authority is required only for those acts which are incompatible with the rights, in public or private law, of some person (legal or natural)[56] – that the fact that the conduct can be authorised under the Act does not in itself make it unlawful to engage in such conduct. Not only is such action not unlawful, but it can be carried out without even such authorisation as is available under RIPA. This creates some problems in practice. That is, certain of the conduct which might be authorised under RIPA was clearly unlawful when engaged in without authorisation under the Act: the key example is the interception of communication.[57] But much was not, and that conduct might, notwithstanding the possibility of having it authorised under RIPA, lawfully be engaged in without such authorisation. One example is covert surveillance under RIPA, of which it has been noted that 'Surveillance by public authorities (or, indeed, by anyone else) is not in itself unlawful at common law, nor does it necessarily engage Article 8 of the Convention'.[58] The effect of section 80 is therefore that even though RIPA provides for the authorisation of surveillance, it 'does not require prior authorisation to be obtained by a public authority in order to carry out' that surveillance.[59] The problem, however, is knowing exactly which conduct falls into which category; which must be authorised and which need not be. To know for sure requires a consideration of both the public and private law rights applicable to a given situation, including what has been (or might in some hypothetical case be) said by the Court of Human Rights at Strasbourg, and the approach (still unsettled) of the courts to the so-called 'third source' or 'common law' powers of the Crown.[60] And so the savings provision may have saved much conduct, or may have saved little: it is difficult to know for sure, and impossible to determine the point by consulting RIPA itself.

We thus have two points at which central provisions of RIPA were potentially misleading: one because a definition found in the act's interpretation section

[55] See McKay, *Covert Policing* (2015) [5.21]–[5.25]. For judicial consideration, see *AKJ v Commissioner of Police of the Metropolis* [2013] EWHC 32 (QB), [155]–[181].

[56] See the chapters by Scott and Endicott in Tomkins and Scott, *Entick v Carrington* (2015).

[57] See RIPA, s 1.

[58] *C v The Police* IPT/03/32/H, [42].

[59] IPT/03/32/H, [62].

[60] See, eg A Tomkins, 'The Authority of *Entick v Carrington*' in Tomkins and Scott (n 37); A Perry, 'The Crown's Administrative Powers' (2015) 131 *LQR* 652. The issue was considered by the Supreme Court in *R (New London College) v Secretary of State for the Home Department* [2013] UKSC 51.

resulted in a meaning that was – at the very least – in tension with the ordinary meaning of the provision; and the other because, in the absence of a clear statutory directive or judicial consideration of the point, the executive read it as meaning something which, though certainly defensible as reading of the law, was nevertheless difficult to foresee from its terms. Alongside that, we have the possibility – not precluded by the legislation itself – of the restrictions therein being circumvented by the sharing of data with international partners. But we also have a much more fundamental difficulty, applying beyond the context of interception: the terms of the savings provision made it difficult to be sure what investigatory powers existed outside of RIPA; what might be done on the basis of other authority – and, if so, what authority? – and what might be done without any authority at all. Nothing in RIPA answers these questions. Not only was the RIPA regime of investigatory powers not exhaustive even in those areas in which it was the primary or seemingly original authority (to say nothing of the area of investigatory powers generally), but it left a glaring uncertainty as to what other measures – if any – might share those domains. The combined effect was that RIPA's practical effect could be very different indeed from what even a reasonably informed observer of its provisions might have assumed. This difficulty was compounded many times over by limits imposed by RIPA on the possibility of challenging the use made of the powers it contained.[61] Though these sins are – compared to those discussed in the next section – perhaps minor, they are nevertheless a crucial aspect of the inadequacies of New Labour's national security constitution, and so must inform both our understanding of New Labour constitutionalism and that period's more general lessons for national security constitutionalism.

V. THE SECRET NATIONAL SECURITY CONSTITUTION BEYOND RIPA

In this part, I first consider two non-RIPA powers which were utilised under New Labour and so form part of what must count as its national security constitution. Neither, however, originated – or was rationalised – in RIPA. Rather, they were found elsewhere, in obscure statutory provisions, and entered the public consciousness only as a result of the Snowden revelations of 2013, and exist now – in modified form – in the Investigatory Powers Act 2016. They were therefore secret in different ways, and for different reasons, than the RIPA powers discussed above.

[61] The extent and use of many of the powers under RIPA could, in effect, be challenged only in the Investigatory Powers Tribunal, which operates in a regime of considerable secrecy: for an overview, see Tomkins, 'Justice and Security in the United Kingdom' (2014).

A. Equipment Interference under the 1989 and 1994 Acts

The first of these 'secret' powers is that of property interference, contained in section 5 of the Intelligence Services Act 1994 and its companion in section 7 of that statute.[62] The two powers vary along a number of axes: that in section 5 permits interferences with property and wireless telegraphy, while an authorisation under section 7 can encompass the doing of any act. The section 5 power can see a warrant granted to do an act anywhere; a section 7 authorisation can permit the doing of an act only outside of the British Islands. Most importantly, section 7 is, unlike section 5, explicit in permitting the granting of authorisations of broad scope: an authorisation granted thereunder may, it says, 'relate to a particular act or acts, to acts of a description specified in the authorisation or to acts undertaken in the course of an operation so specified'. Between the enactment of the 1994 Act and New Labour's entry into power, a major change was made to the regime governing the security and intelligence agencies (SIAs): the Security Service Act 1996 added to the functions of MI5 that of acting 'in support of the activities of police forces and other law enforcement agencies in the prevention and detection of serious crime'.[63] The effect of this was to extend its powers of property interference and interference of wireless telegraphy to the domain of 'ordinary' criminality, rather than just that which touched national security.[64] Though the 1996 Act purported to limit the implications of that extension,[65] the limitation was very weak.[66] The further modifications made under New Labour were, by comparison, minor.[67] The post-9/11 Anti-terrorism, Crime and Security Act 2001 extended section 7 authorisations to the carrying out of the functions of GCHQ, where they had previously been restricted to those of MI6.[68] Alongside this, section 7 was amended so as to provide that the

[62] See the account in Scott, 'General Warrants, Thematic Warrants, Bulk Warrants' (2017).

[63] Security Service Act 1989, s 1(4).

[64] For discussion of the 1996 Act, see M Hunt and P Duffy, 'Goodbye Entick v Carrington: The Security Service Act 1996' (1997) *European Human Rights Law Review* 11.

[65] Providing that a warrant could relate only to conduct which 'constitutes … one or more offences, and either … involves the use of violence, results in substantial financial gain or is conduct by a large number of persons in pursuit of a common purpose; or the offence or one of the offences is an offence for which a person who has attained the age of twenty-one and has no previous convictions could reasonably be expected to be sentenced to imprisonment for a term of three years or more': ISA 1994, s 5(3B) (as amended).

[66] As pointed out at the time, 'The Secretary of State is empowered to issue warrants in any case involving violence or substantial financial gain, regardless of the penalty likely to be imposed … The executive warrant power is [also] widely available in relation to industrial disputes and to political demonstrations': Hunt and Duffy, 'Goodbye Entick v Carrington' (1997) 13.

[67] RIPA amended the conditions under which a s 5 warrant could be granted, introduced a requirement of proportionality and removed the requirement that the senior official under whose hand a s 7 authorisation was granted in urgent circumstances be one from the relevant Secretary of State's own department: ISA 1994, ss 5 and 7, as amended by RIPA 2000.

[68] ATCSA 2001, s 116.

reference to an act done outside the British Islands included a reference to acts done therein which 'is or is intended to be done in relation to apparatus that is believed to be outside the British Islands'.[69] In the original enactment, there had been no reference to 'apparatus'.

In terms of the 'secrecy' of these powers (which appear, on their face, transparent), two particular issues stand out, both demonstrating the sort of 'shallow' secrecy discussed above. The first is the very fact of using the power of property interference to carry out 'computer network exploitation' (CNE – now, under the Investigatory Powers Act 2016 (IPA 2016), called 'equipment interference'). As part of the challenge to the use of CNE in the IPT,[70] it was argued that the use of the Intelligence Services Act 1994 (ISA 1994) powers for such acts did not meet the *Weber* criteria because – quite apart from the sufficiency of safeguards – it was not foreseeable that the powers would be used in that way, it never having been avowed by the government nor identified within the relevant Code of Practice as an activity they encompassed. This was rejected by the IPT, which said that it was 'quite clear that at least since 1994 the powers of GCHQ have extended to computer interference' and it was:

> thus apparent in the public domain that there was likely to be interference with computers, 'hacking' being an ever more familiar activity, namely interference with property by GCHQ (and see in particular the 1990 Hansard references ... above) ... Use of it was thus foreseeable, even if the precise form of it and the existence of its use was not admitted.[71]

The Hansard reference is to the following passage in the IPT's judgment, discussing an amendment which had been moved to the Bill which became the Computer Misuse Act 1990.[72] Two points should be made here: the first is that we are in the realm of mild desperation if we are relying not upon the debate on the 1994 Act or its 1989 predecessor, but rather on what was said in debate on the Computer Misuse Act (enacted between the two, and the relationship of which with the 1994 Act was part of the discussion in the IPT).[73] The second is

[69] ISA 1994, s 7(9) (as amended). The newly inserted provision continued 'and in this subsection "apparatus" has the same meaning as in the Regulation of Investigatory Powers Act 2000'. Finally, the Terrorism Act 2006 extended the lifetime of a s 7 authorisation: ISA 1994, s 7(6) (as amended). It also introduced a series of provisions governing property believed to be outside the British Islands: an act which might be done under a s 5 warrant can be done under a s 7 warrant to property in the British Islands if the property is believed to be outside those Islands at the time, or within a five-day grace period following the point at which it was realised that the property was in fact within the UK: ISA 1994, s 7(10)–(14) (as amended).

[70] *Privacy International v The Secretary of State for Foreign and Commonwealth Affairs* [2016] UKIP Trib 14/85-CH (*Privacy/GreenNet*).

[71] [2016] UKIP Trib 14/85-CH, [81].

[72] 'This amendment ("to prevent hacking or similar activities by the Security Service") was not pressed. It would seem therefore that it was accepted that the 1989 Act, already on the statute book, was not affected by the CMA. A fortiori the subsequent 1994 Act is not either': [2016] UKIP Trib 14/85-CH, [18].

[73] The CMA contains a saving provision of its own which was amended by the Serious Crime Act 2015 – after knowledge of the government's use of equipment interference had entered the public

that a visit to the source shows that the matter was hardly made explicit in that context either. To quote from the remarks of the MP who moved the amendment in question:

> Amendment No. 7 … refers to the security services and their powers. We need some answers as to what powers they have in relation to hacking because that matter has never been discussed in the House … I was appalled to learn from the Minister, in asides in Committee … that the Security Services Act 1989, by default, legitimises hacking by the security services … Until the Minister spoke in Committee there was no sign that the warrant could authorise MI5 staff to hack into any computer whenever they wanted … That power to give a warrant to legalise computer hacking was not discussed in debates on the Security Services Act.[74]

So, while there does seem to have been an awareness of the ability to use the powers under the 1994 Act in this way, it was a knowledge which emerged from the shadows, not being discussed during the passage of the 1989 Act itself, and having – it seems – faded back into those shadows by the time the 1994 Act was passed to renew and expand those powers. If the carrying out of CNE was as reasonably foreseeable as the IPT – on this thinnest of evidence – asserted, it is not at all clear why it could not have been openly acknowledged, either before 1997 or by New Labour.

The second element of 'shallow' secrecy associated with the 1994 Act's powers of property interference is the availability, under section 5, of 'thematic' warrants. It was noted above that section 7 explicitly provides that authorisations made thereunder may have a broad scope, while section 5 does not: the crucial formulation of the provision permits the grant of a warrant which authorises 'the taking … of such action as is specified in the warrant in respect of any property so specified or in respect of wireless telegraphy so specified'.[75] This seems to create a fairly stark divide, with an obvious rationale: section 7 (which relates to acts outside the British Islands) does not require the particular person to whom an act is done, or the specific act itself, be identified in the authorisation; section 5 (which relates to a narrower category of acts, which might take place within the British Islands) requires specification of the act and the property in relation to which it is to be done. It is, on its face, a power to grant what we would now call a 'targeted' warrant. As revealed by the Intelligence Services Commissioner in his 2014 report, however, the security bodies (SIAs) interpreted section 5 as permitting warrants which, rather than specifying the property in question, were 'thematic'.[76] Could section 5 permit such warrants? The ISC

arena and proceedings had been brought in the IPT. In *Privacy/GreenNet* (n 70), it was argued that the amendments demonstrated that the use of the powers in the 1995 Act to carry out equipment interference was unlawful under the 1990 Act. The Tribunal, however, accepted the government's position that the amendment was 'simply clarificatory': [2016] UKIP Trib 14/85-CH, [20].

[74] HC Deb 4 May 1990, vol 171, cols 1299–1300.

[75] ISA 1994, s 5.

[76] M Waller, *Report of the Intelligence Services Commissioner for 2014* (HC 225, 2015) 18. He noted the distinction between ss 5 and 7 of the Act: 'ISA section 7 makes specific reference to

thought it arguable that it could not, for the provision 'does not expressly allow for a class of authorisation' and

> the words 'property so specified' might be narrowly construed requiring the Secretary of State to consider a particular operation against a particular piece of property as opposed to property more generally described by reference for example to a described set of individuals.[77]

The SIAs contested this, arguing that 'the property does not necessarily need to be specifically identified in advance as long as what is stated in the warrant can properly be said to include the property that is the subject of the subsequent interference'.[78]

In siding with the SIAs to endorse a reading of section 5 which permitted the granting of 'thematic' warrants, the IPT rejected the claim that such an interpretation was precluded by the common law opposition to general warrants demonstrated by cases such as *Entick v Carrington*:

> Eighteenth Century abhorrence of general warrants issued without express statutory sanction is not in our judgment a useful or permissible aid to construction of an express statutory power given to a Service, one of whose principal functions is to further the interests of UK national security, with particular reference to defence and foreign policy. The words should be given their natural meaning in the context in which they are set.[79]

The problems with this are numerous. First, the notion that the general warrant cases are not a useful aid to interpretation is one thing; to deem them impermissible represents a major leap from that. Second, there is, notwithstanding what is implied here, no exception to the principle of legality in the context of national security.[80] Third, it is hardly the case that the natural meaning of the statutory language in question is such as to permit thematic warrants, and so even if the interpretative approach taken by the IPT is a plausible one, it does not follow that – as it held – what is required is that the property to be interfered with be

> so defined, whether by reference to persons or a group or category of persons, that the extent of the reasonably foreseeable interference caused by the authorisation of CNE in relation to the actions and property specified in the warrant can be addressed.[81]

The IPT's decision for these reasons fails to convince, and the better view must be that there was a double lack of foreseeability: as to the use of the provisions

thematic authorisations (what are called class authorisation) because it refers "to a particular act" or to "acts" undertaken in the course of an operation' but 'section 5 is narrower referring to "property so specified".'

[77] ibid 18.

[78] An interpretation which the ISC held to be 'very arguable': ibid 18.

[79] [2016] UKIP Trib 14/85-CH, [37].

[80] See, eg *Ahmed*, in which the principle of legality was employed by the Supreme Court in holding that certain interferences with fundamental rights (primarily the right to property) could not take place on the broad and general authority of the United Nations Act 1948. *HM Treasury v Ahmed* [2010] UKSC 2.

[81] [2016] UKIP Trib 14/85-CH, [38].

of the 1994 Act to permit equipment interference and as to the use of section 5 in particular to permit 'thematic warrants'.

The lack of foreseeability was accompanied by a lack of oversight: the provisions were the subject of a Property Interference Code of Practice, but it had nothing specific to say of equipment interference; warrants under section 5 and authorisations under section 7 were subject to the oversight of the Intelligence Services Commissioner, but until the 2014 report noted above, no relevant information was disclosed. From the point of view of both oversight and foreseeability, therefore, the continuing existence of the 1994 Act powers after the enactment of RIPA significantly undermined the system which had been put in place by it, particularly as equipment interference could be used to acquire 'stored communications' which would – if intercepted in transmission or following it – have had to be the subject of a RIPA warrant.[82] Where RIPA thematic warrants were justified by plain statutory language here the secrecy was greater, being caused by the confluence of two factors. The first was statutory language which encompassed something not immediately apparent from its face (ie a power to physically interfere with property permitted electronic interference). The second was the interpretation of a statutory provision to stretch it beyond what the language of the provision clearly permitted. Though CNE (rebranded as equipment interference) is now explicitly provided for by the 2016 Act – in both targeted (including thematic) form and bulk form – it was a central plank of the UK's national security powers for decades before that avowal, including for the entirety of the New Labour period, but without being known, or knowable, to the public at large.

B. Bulk Communications Data under the Telecommunications Act 1984

A second example of non-RIPA secrecy is that prefigured above, where it was noted that in RIPA there was no general prohibition upon the acquisition and disclosure of communications data. Such acquisition was provided for by RIPA. It eventually became clear, however – long after the New Labour era – that this was not the sole, perhaps not even the primary, means by which communications data might be acquired. That is, communications data could be and was collected (in bulk) in pursuance of 'directions' given to telecommunication providers under section 94 of the Telecommunications Act 1984. This use of the power was avowed only in November 2015, more than 30 years after the statutory authority was first put in place, when the draft Investigatory Powers Bill was presented to Parliament.[83] It was originally introduced – it seems – to prevent the privatisation of the telecommunications system from obstructing the use of

[82] See, eg *Coulson v R* [2013] EWCA Crim 1026, which confirms that a voicemail message is still 'in the course of transmission' even after it has been listened to by the intended recipient.

[83] In the review of investigatory powers which preceded the publication of the Bill, the Independent Reviewer of Terrorism Legislation identified s 94 as one of the 'non-RIPA powers' relevant to the

that system to pursue national security ends,[84] though there is little information available as to the use to which it was put prior to 11 September 2001. Avowal of the power was followed by a number of belated attempts at oversight: a report by the Interception of Communications Commissioner on the use to which the power had been put,[85] a legal challenge to the use of the power (encompassing both domestic law grounds and the power's compatibility with EU law and the ECHR),[86] and the power's replacement and repeal by the Investigatory Powers Act 2016.[87] Useful information about the section 94 power and its use therefore became available only at the point at which it was being confined to history.

Originally, section 94 applied to 'any person who is a public telecommunications operator', permitting the Secretary of State (after consultation) to 'give to that person such directions of a general character as appear to the Secretary of State to be requisite or expedient in the interests of national security or relations with the government of a country or territory outside the United Kingdom'.[88] It further provided that:

> If it appears to the Secretary of State to be requisite or expedient to do so in the interests of national security or relations with the government of a country or territory outside the United Kingdom, he may … give to that person a direction requiring him … to do, or not to do, a particular thing specified in the direction.[89]

These, it goes almost without saying, were powers of staggering breadth. And though directions were to be laid before Parliament, this was subject to an exception where the Secretary of State was of the opinion that disclosure was 'against the interests of national security or relations with the government of a country or territory outside the United Kingdom, or the commercial interests of any person'.[90] In practice, none of the directions were – it seems – ever laid before Parliament. Certain features of the power stand out in comparison to the analogous RIPA power: where RIPA authorisations required monthly renewal,[91] directions under section 94 could last indefinitely; directions were not subject to a Code of Practice; and they were subject only to belated and partial oversight

topic, but he noted that, of such powers, there was 'little or nothing in the public domain that explains how frequently (if at all) they are used': Anderson, *A Question of Trust* (2015) [6.16]–[6.20].

[84] The tale of interception in the years leading up to privatisation of British Telecom is well told in P Fitzgerald and M Leopold, *Stranger on the Line: Secret History of Phone Tapping* (The Bodley Head, 1987).

[85] S Burnton, *Report of the Interception of Communications Commissioner: Review of Directions Given under section 94 of the Telecommunications Act (1984)* (2015–16, HC 33).

[86] *Privacy International v Secretary of State for Foreign and Commonwealth Affairs* [2016] UKIP Trib 15/110-CH.

[87] IPA 2016, Pt 6, Ch 2.

[88] TA 1984, s 94(1).

[89] ibid s 94(2).

[90] ibid s 94(4).

[91] RIPA, s 23(4). Though where directions were given by the Secretary of State, communications data authorisations under RIPA were given by a 'designated person': RIPA, s 22(3).

by the Commissioners.[92] As with the RIPA power to acquire communications data, there was no requirement of a 'foreign focus', so the communications data of persons within the British Islands could be acquired in bulk. The powers therefore coexisted in the arsenal of the security services, but with significant incentives for them to make use of the Telecommunications Act power rather than that put in place by the New Labour government. When it was first avowed, the government said of the 1984 Act power that it was 'first used at scale in the UK in 2001 after the 9/11 attacks in New York, and later extended following the attacks on the London transport system on 7 July 2005 to respond to the domestic terrorist threat'.[93] The report of the Interception of Communications Commissioner on section 94 reported the existence of 23 directions at that time, all of which 'specified that they were necessary under section 94(1) of the Telecommunications Act 1984 "in the interests of national security"'.[94] Of the 23 directions, 15 related to the acquisition of bulk communications data.[95] Data acquired under the directions was examined on an industrial scale, such that, for example, 'In 2015 the Security Service made 20,042 applications to access communications data obtained pursuant to section 94 directions'. These related to a total of '122,579 items of communications data'.[96] By contrast, the final report of the Interceptions of Communications Commissioner (IOCCO) relating to the acquisition of communications data under RIPA shows that in 2016, MI5 accessed only 39,364 items of communications data in pursuance of those powers.[97] The known power was more carefully limited and overseen than its 'unknown' counterpart, yet the latter was relied upon far more heavily by the SIAs.

Meanwhile, the power had been challenged in the IPT. The primary claim was that the RIPA regime was the exclusive means by which communications data might be acquired by the security services. In rejecting this contention, and holding that RIPA and section 94 of the 1984 Act in fact represented 'two lawful routes' by which communications data might be acquired, the IPT noted section 45 of the 1984 Act, which had originally made it an offence for a person operating a public telecommunications system to intercept communications

[92] See the details given in Burnton, *Report of the Interception of Communications Commissioner* (2015–16) 3–7.

[93] HM Government, *Operational Case for Bulk Powers* (November 2015) [9.7].

[94] Note, though, that certain challenges were faced by IOCCO in establishing the extent of the use of s 94 directions for a number of reasons: 'the directions are secret as allowed for by statute; they can be given by any Secretary of State; they do not automatically expire after a defined period; and there was not, at the time of the July 2015 report, any comprehensive central record of the section 94 directions that had been given by the various Secretaries of State.' Burnton (n 85) [5.9].

[95] ibid [7.1]–[7.5]. 'The remaining eight extant section 94 directions were given on behalf of the Security Service, the three agencies collectively, or the [Metropolitan Police Counter Terrorism Command]' and related to 'the provision of services in emergencies, for civil contingency purposes or to help the agencies in safeguarding the security of their personnel and operations'.

[96] Burnton (n 85) [8.7].

[97] S Burnton, *Report of the Interception of Communications Commissioner Annual Report for 2016* (2017–19, HC 297) Annex A.

(except 'in obedience to warrant under the hand of the Secretary of State') and for such a person to disclose 'otherwise than in the course of his duty' the 'contents of a statement of account' specifying the telecoms services provided to a person other than that to whom the services were provided. The reference to the course of duty could, the Tribunal stated, have only been a reference to the section 94 duty to comply with a direction given by the Secretary of State.[98] Though the new section 45 inserted into the 1984 Act a year later was perhaps even more oblique than the original in its acknowledgement of the power and related duty under section 94 (referring to 'any disclosure … which is made in the interests of national security'),[99] the IPT held that a natural reading of that provision showed it preserved them.[100] This was amended again by RIPA, with the relevant wording now making an exception for disclosure carried out 'in compliance with any requirement imposed … in consequence of the exercise by any person of any statutory power exercisable by him for the purpose of obtaining any document or other information'.[101] The IPT held this to similarly preserve the section 94 power, that conclusion being 'put beyond doubt' by the RIPA saving provision discussed above.[102] The relevance of that provision might, however, be doubted, and it is not clear from its judgment which of subsections (a) (which provides that nothing in RIPA that allows conduct to be authorised should be understood 'as making it unlawful to engage in any conduct of that description which is not otherwise unlawful under this Act and would not be unlawful apart from this Act') and (c) (which states that the same fact does not prejudice 'any power to obtain information by any means not involving conduct that may be authorised under this Act') the Tribunal took to have acted to 'save' section 94: that it cited both suggests that it harboured a degree of uncertainty on the point.[103]

As discussed above, statutory oversight of the acquisition of bulk communications data (BCD) by the relevant commissioner took place only in respect of that portion of its acquisition carried out under either RIPA or the ISA 1994. Though (non-statutory) oversight of the accessing of BCD acquired via (some) section 94 directions did take place, no oversight took place of the giving of those directions, nor of the retention, storage or destruction of data acquired thereunder.[104] As a result, the IPT concluded, the oversight of the BCD regime prior to November 2015 was inadequate.[105] In the 'absence of the necessary oversight and supervision by the [Interception of Communications Commissioner],

[98] [2016] UKIP Trib 15/110-CH, [32]–[33].
[99] ibid [36]–[37].
[100] ibid [37].
[101] TA 1984, s 45(2) (as amended by RIPA 2000).
[102] [2016] UKIP Trib 15/110-CH, [41].
[103] ibid [41].
[104] ibid [75]–[78].
[105] ibid [80].

the secondary roles of the [IPT] and the ISC were no replacement'.[106] The IPT later held, further, that the making of a large number of directions amounted to an unlawful delegation of power to GCHQ because the Secretary of State had made directions of a general character the specific effect of which was determined not by him or her (as the statute requires) but by GCHQ itself:

> Officials decided, in discussion with the [communication service provider], what types of data the CSP could provide to meet a current intelligence requirement. The CSP would then be informed that the Foreign Secretary had made a general direction, but the effect of that direction would depend entirely on the datasets which GCHQ selected for provision ... The power exercised by GCHQ was thus a substantive power to determine the content and duration of the requirement to be imposed under the direction.[107]

The secrecy inherent in the process thus permitted it to operate in a fashion which was ultimately illegal – both as a matter of domestic law and also (as a consequence) in terms of the ECHR: as an interference with the Convention rights which takes place in accordance with a direction that is unlawful cannot be 'in accordance with the law', violations of Article 8 had taken place on a significant scale.[108] The Tribunal was nevertheless keen to offer some context in mitigation:

> It was entirely understandable that in the aftermath of the 9/11 attack on New York the directions made in November 2001 should have been drafted broadly so as to allow GCHQ to vary the data it sought as intelligence requirements rapidly developed. But the scope of those directions should have been reviewed after s.94 was amended in 2003.[109]

It declined to make any declaration, or to grant any further relief of any sort, in respect of data obtained under the unlawfully made directions.

Though it had not enacted the power, (heavy) use was nevertheless made of it under New Labour. As the above extract demonstrates, it also amended it, but without drawing attention to it. The relevant changes were made by the Communications Act 2003. They are as follows: the requirement that directions be 'requisite or expedient' in the interests of national security etc was replaced with a requirement that they be 'necessary'; and a requirement was introduced that the Secretary of State believe the conduct required by a direction be 'proportionate to what is sought to be achieved by that conduct' before making it.[110]

[106] ibid [80].

[107] *Privacy International v Secretary of State for Foreign and Commonwealth Affairs* [2018] UKIP Trib 15/110-CH, [46].

[108] ibid [52]–[53].

[109] ibid [55].

[110] TA 1984, s 94, as amended by the Communications Act 2003. Additionally, references to directions applying notwithstanding anything in the 1984 Act were replaced with references to the 2003 Act itself; for a reference to 'public telecommunications operators' there was substituted one to 'providers of public electronic communications networks'; a reference to the Director General of Telecommunications was replaced with one to OFCOM.

The Joint Committee on the Draft Telecommunications Bill report gives some sense of the approach taken to this element of the legislation:

> the Government's original memorandum on issues on which new or amended Clauses will appear when the Bill is presented referred to further consideration being undertaken on national security issues. We asked the Government to elucidate this opaque reference. It told us that this was a reference to continued consideration on how to 'update' section 94 of the Telecommunications Act 1984 …

The Committee continued by saying that the government 'sees the need to update these powers to reflect the removal of the concept of public telecommunications operators',[111] but that was, of course, not the only change made to section 94 by the 2003 Act. The Committee's recommendation on the provision was as follows:

> Before undertaking a technical revision of section 94 of the Telecommunications Act 1984, the Government should ask itself the prior question of whether such broad powers are either required or compatible with Convention rights. If the provision is retained in an amended form, we recommend that the Government, in its response to this Report, give an account of the use to which the provision has been put and an explanation of how it is envisaged it might be used in future.[112]

The government responded that it believed that 'a provision broadly equivalent in effect to Section 94 of the 1984 Act is still necessary to address a number of issues that are not addressed' by any of the related legislation. It addressed, briefly, the use of the power:

> Directions which have been issued in the past have dealt with matters including aspects of emergency planning, adherence to appropriate standards in the security vetting of staff … and sensitive operational matters considered necessary for protecting national security, some of which were issued in the aftermath of the events of 11th September 2001.[113]

The Joint Committee on Human Rights' report on the Bill did not engage with the reforms to section 94 at all.[114] The effect was that the powers were tweaked so as to bring them in line with the modern human rights framework, but with the use that was already being made of them only hinted at. While the law of counterterrorism was being challenged incessantly through the courts, other elements of the national security constitution remained shrouded in secrecy, emerging into public view only occasionally and fleetingly, and with the political institutions accordingly limited in their ability to challenge the necessity or the wisdom of the powers.

[111] Joint Committee on the Draft Communications Bill, Draft Communications Bill (2001–02, HL 169-I, HC 876-I) [141] (references omitted).

[112] ibid [141].

[113] Department of Trade and Industry and Department of Culture, Media and Sport, *Government's Response to the Report of the Joint Committee on the Draft Communications Bill* (Cm 5646, 2002) [55].

[114] Joint Committee on Human Rights, *Draft Communications Bill* (2001–02, HL 149, HC 1102).

VI. LESSONS OF NEW LABOUR'S SECRET NATIONAL SECURITY CONSTITUTION

To identify the secrecy of law as a key feature of the UK's national security constitution under New Labour is not to make a partisan point. The key statutory provisions predate Labour's return to power, and though the gaps in the public record make it impossible to be sure, it seems very likely that the powers described in the second part of this chapter were utilised (perhaps heavily) even before New Labour came into power in 1997. And although the system of 'secret law' underpinning certain of these powers was beginning to fray at the edges even beforehand, there is no strong reason to believe that the rationalisation which has recently taken place – in the form of the 2016 Act – would have taken place as quickly or as extensively in the absence of the Snowden revelations of 2013: what was done after the New Labour era was done not because those who followed possessed some greater commitment to legal or constitutional principle, but because an external factor laid bare the flaws of a system which had long been hidden from public view. Nevertheless, we can identify from the material discussed above a number of lessons, regarding both the New Labour approach to government (and the governance of national security) and legal secrecy generally.

A first constitutional point which these matters raise relates to the point made at the start of this chapter about the phenomenon of 'secret law' and its general absence (so far as we can tell) from the UK's legal orders. All of the rules discussed herein were publicly available, even if – as is often the case in the context of surveillance – the full picture could not be ascertained without knowledge of the internal interpretation of certain key provisions (discussed below) and of the internal arrangements which govern the use made of material acquired thereunder. But even discounting the situation whereby the law is 'hidden in plain sight', the claim that there is no 'secret law' in the UK relies upon an implicit distinction between law and executive action: after all, warrants issued under RIPA are not publicly available, and even though it might be argued that they should be, it seems a stretch to claim that the norms which apply to legislation should apply also to such warrants, or – say – their equivalents under the 1994 Act. The legislative/executive distinction, however, cannot be a purely formal one, but must allow a degree of functional assessment. Something which masquerades as an executive act might nevertheless be understood to be a legislative one when considered from the point of view of the generality of its application. That is exactly the case for at least some of the section 94 directions discussed above: not only might such directions be 'of a general character', but the directions could be and were given to communications providers generally. What resulted from the use of the power, therefore, were rules which might easily have (perhaps should have) appeared in a piece of primary legislation, and to diminish directions by labelling them executive acts is to do them the favour of applying a weaker set of constitutional standards than might apply to legislative acts.

The point about generality is not, of course, unique to the national security context, but the ability to keep secret the directions distinguishes this example from the modern reliance on law-making by statutory instrument. On one view, therefore, section 94 directions were secret law in the fullest sense. And even if that claim is not accepted, the example seems to suggest that it may be necessary to rethink the boundary between legislative and executive action in the UK.[115]

In light of what has gone before, a second point can be made briefly. It was noted above in relation to the RIPA savings provision that there remains considerable uncertainty about the basic rule-of-law position in the UK: for what does the executive require legal authority and when? And this uncertainty, despite having a special significance where the executive seeks to interfere surreptitiously with individual interests (whether protected by public or private law), is more general, and has in fact only been exacerbated by the Supreme Court's consideration of the matter.[116] There is no room here to answer the following relevant questions, but only to flag them up. What is the scope of the tort of misuse of private information such that certain acts will – where they did not previously – require some positive legal authority? What are the nature and extent of the common law powers of the Crown, such that it can act incompatibly with legally protected interests of legal or natural persons, or alter their legal position? Are there – as has sometimes been suggested – any limitations on the use of such powers over and above those which apply to the exercise of statutory powers? And is the distinction between those public authorities which are and those which are not emanations of the Crown, which takes on a new significance in the context of these powers, fit for the modern constitutional environment? What about those things which can be done without legal authority of any sort, because they do not have legal effect – sometimes called the Crown's 'ordinary powers'?[117] Can those 'powers' be subject to judicial review or is the idea of a legal challenge to an act with no legal effect nonsensical? While these issues remain so grossly uncertain, a saving provision like that found in RIPA has a black hole at its heart, and cannot be interpreted or applied with any certainty.

Another point, of particular importance in the national security context but not logically limited to it, has similarly been prefigured above. Several of the forms of secrecy discussed – of greater or lesser democratic obnoxiousness – related to an internal interpretation of key statutory terms which was not, and often could not have been, shared by those external to government called upon to understand and perhaps apply the relevant provisions. To take only the most

[115] See, eg the Human Rights Act 1998, which recognises as 'primary legislation' not only public and general, local and personal, and private acts of Parliament, but also eg prerogative orders in council: HRA 1998, s 21(1). Though this final designation is a plausible one, it has the effect of lending to prerogative act the status of an act of Parliament, notwithstanding the almost complete absence of scrutiny and accountability associated with prerogative orders in council. It must, in fact, be doubted that it is ever constitutionally appropriate to make prerogative legislation.

[116] In *R (New College London Ltd) v Secretary of State for the Home Department* [2013] UKSC 51.

[117] Perry (n 60).

obvious examples: it is plausible, if contestable, to claim that the use of power of property interference in section 5 of the Intelligence Services Act 1994 to ground equipment interference ('hacking' of various sorts) was foreseeable. Evidence to that effect was available and, as importantly, clear evidence to the contrary was not. The same cannot be said for the use of the provision to ground thematic warrants, which flies in the face of the interpretative canons of the common law going back hundreds of years – canons neatly and cursorily discarded by the IPT. Even if the Tribunal's eventual conclusion was correct, therefore, an internal interpretation was at work for some time – perhaps decades – before it was described in the report of the Intelligence Services Commissioner and so could be challenged before the courts. To make the point clear: we are dealing here with specialised statutory authority which will be 'used' only by the state, and only by a small and necessarily shadowy facet thereof. Any interpretation adopted by those actors is likely to be of considerable importance to the practical powers which exist, but is similarly unlikely to be challenged in the courts. Strained interpretations are therefore more problematic here than they would be elsewhere. The examples we have might well be accompanied by any number of others – the problem, of course, is that we do not and cannot know. A number of key provisions of surveillance legislation remain without authoritative interpretation by the courts, and some terms (including 'national security' itself) have been interpreted only in a loose fashion which leaves room for more or less expansive interpretations. How to deal with this problem? One way would be to permit advisory references to be made to the IPT, so that it could determine the point. To do so would, however, represent a significant departure from key elements of the common law tradition, and unless any opinions were published the problem of secrecy would remain, and there would be no possibility of challenging them before the higher courts. Another method which has been suggested would be to require the government to publish its own internal interpretations of relevant statutory provisions. There are at least two problems with that idea, however. The first is that to publish interpretations of all the relevant statutory provisions would seem excessive, but the line between what is crucial and what is not would be difficult, if not impossible, to draw in a highly technical context. The second is that any provision of which an interpretation was not published would attract more rather than less suspicion: the government is damned if it does, but also damned if it doesn't. So, while a clear and workable solution does not immediately suggest itself, it is certain that what has been done in recent decades in terms of pushing the limits of statutory language will continue to bedevil the national security constitution for a long time to come. Those attempting to reason from the 2016 Act to the actual capabilities of the state will do so against a background of justified suspicion.

Finally, there is an obvious (verging on trite) point that must be made, and again has been prefigured above, about the possibility of accountability in this context. All observers of the UK's constitution understand that there exist venues for both legal and political accountability, and are familiar with debates about what is or should be the balance between the two types. This chapter suggests some of the limitations of that debate, which we see now reflects certain assumptions which do not always hold: most importantly, that those in a position to pursue accountability are aware (or are capable of becoming aware) of the relevant facts. This has not always been the case. The institutional or discursive merits or demerits of courts and legislature are therefore irrelevant: no one can ask a question in Parliament, carry out a select committee inquiry or launch proceedings in the IPT or the Court of Human Rights if he or she does not know that there is something there to challenge. So factual secrecy not only weakens the process of constitutional accountability, but also underpins the associated legal secrecy, allowing the provisions discussed in this chapter to have sat, mostly unnoticed, on the statute books for many years without their significance – actual or even potential – being recognised. But this difficulty is accounted for within the system: that is, it is widely accepted that the national security context involves issues which are simply so sensitive that it is not just justifiable, but in fact obligatory, to keep them secret. We do not, for the most part, simply throw up our hands when we encounter such an issue; rather, we seek to rely upon institutional forms which reflect the sensitivities of national security law and policy. Often, we rely upon what I have called elsewhere 'hybrid' institutions, which marry certain features of legal and political institutions – with, for example, legally qualified individuals carrying out oversight that is general in scope, rather than focused upon specific disputes – in order to do what neither legal nor political institutions are themselves well-suited to doing.[118] Here, such institutions were involved only in part, and in many cases not at all: though property interference warrants were overseen by the Intelligence Services Commissioner, there was no separate treatment of those authorising equipment interference or of those which were thematic. Though the involvement of these hybrid institutions would not necessarily have sufficed to bring the matter to the attention of the public – their reports can and sometimes do remain secret – they would have ensured that when the veil was lifted, the picture which it revealed was not nearly so unedifying as it has in fact been revealed to be in recent years.

VII. CONCLUSION

The New Labour constitutional project presented itself outwardly as one of modernisation and rationalisation. This was no less true in the field of national security than elsewhere. The material discussed in this chapter shows the limits of that process. Though RIPA represented a major advance over its predecessor, capable of meeting many of the demands of new technology and of the ECHR regime, it both left gaps and left in place certain obscure and poorly

[118] PF Scott, 'Hybrid Institutions in the National Security Constitution' (2019) 39 *Legal Studies* 432.

understood powers. Some of these were capable of being used so as to subvert the RIPA regime, with the remainder augmenting it. In both cases, their exclusion had the effect of giving a deeply misleading impression of the powers of the SIAs. As with the Terrorism Act 2000, it would not have been possible to foresee the extent to which the needs of national security would see these various non-RIPA powers operationalised during the New Labour period of government. Nor would it have been possible to predict the extent to which the actions of one rogue contractor would lead to the relevant powers being avowed and – soon after – repealed. Nevertheless, the events discussed in this paper put the New Labour modernisation of the national security constitution in a very different light. While RIPA was systematic and heavily circumscribed the powers of interception and the acquisition of communications data, the heaviest of national security lifting was being done by a series of powers which were hidden in plain sight, lacking both the relative foreseeability of the RIPA powers and – mostly – the oversight associated with them.

12

Individual Terrorist Suspects as the New Folk Devil: New Labour, Rights Tokenism and Security Compulsions

RUMYANA VAN ARK (NÉE GROZDANOVA)[1]

On a certain May morning of 1997, a new dawn had broken over Britain.[2] A triumphant Tony Blair was celebrating Labour's long-awaited victory at the polls. By October of the same year, his government was already working on fulfilling their pledge to modernise British politics and deliver on its commitment for a comprehensive programme of constitutional reform.[3] A key component of this agenda was increasing individual rights by introducing legislation to incorporate the European Convention on Human Rights (ECHR) into domestic law. The rationale behind the proposed Human Rights Bill was twofold: to enhance national awareness of human rights and to place the promotion of human rights at the forefront of foreign policy.[4] The Human Rights Act 1998 (HRA) came into force with much fanfare on 2 October 2000.[5]

Yet, by early 2002, the UK was the only Council of Europe Member State to have derogated from the ECHR under the provisions of Article 15 as a response to the events of 9/11.[6] The derogation allowed for the adoption of certain extended powers of arrest and detention under the Anti-Terrorism, Crime

[1] With special thanks to Bart van Ark and the editors of this edited collection.

[2] *The Guardian* (11 April 2017).

[3] *Rights Brought Home: The Human Rights Bill*, https://assets.publishing.service.gov.uk/government/uploads/system/uploads/attachment_data/file/263526/rights.pdf.

[4] ibid, preface.

[5] *The Independent* (4 February 2003).

[6] Declaration contained in a Note Verbale from the Permanent Representation of the United Kingdom, dated 18 December 2001, registered by the Secretariat General on 18 December 2001.

and Security Act 2001 (ATCSA), which would have otherwise been in breach of Article 5 of the ECHR. Only a year before, Parliament had introduced the Terrorism Act 2000 (TA),[7] a wide-ranging piece of legislation that created a permanent UK-wide counterterrorism legislative framework.[8] Nevertheless, the ATCSA was described as essential in order to 'strengthen legislation in a number of areas to ensure that the Government, in the light of the new situation arising from the September 11 terrorist attacks … have the necessary powers to counter the increased threat to the UK'.[9] Some such measures included the now abolished provisions under Part 4 of the ATCSA allowing for indefinite detention of non-nationals who had been certified by the Home Secretary as terrorists.[10] With reference to these and other powers, the Act was once described as 'the most draconian legislation Parliament has passed in peacetime in over a century'.[11]

The comprehensive and highly restrictive nature of the provisions and counterterrorism measures contained within the ATCSA set the stage for New Labour's post-2001 approach towards human rights and national security: a perfunctory or token respect for individual rights in comparison to the exhaustive commitment to counterterrorism measures and policies. By early 2003, Tony Blair expressly stated that he was prepared to 'reconsider our obligations under the Convention on Human Rights' as the 'rising tide of asylum-seekers, combined with the renewed terrorist threat was unacceptable'.[12] At the same time, the government was privately developing a long-term counterterrorism strategy, known as CONTEST, which aimed to reduce the risk from international terrorism.[13] The strategy was made publicly available in late 2006; the focus of the strategy was a deepening of the counterterrorism effort and strengthening of the powers needed to tackle those who facilitate and promote terrorism. In March 2008, the government adopted the first National Security Strategy, which outlined proposals to address and manage the security challenges facing

[7] The 2000 Act was introduced in order to supersede and replace the Prevention of Terrorism (Temporary Provisions) Act 1989 and the Northern Ireland (Emergency Provisions) Act 2006 (as amended by the Northern Ireland (Emergency Provisions) Act 1998. For a more detailed explanation of the rationale behind the 2000 Act, see, eg the 1998 Consultation Paper on a Legislation Against Terrorism.

[8] This permanent footing of many of the provisions and powers contained in the 'temporary' emergency legislation aimed at 'The Troubles' is ironic in the context of statements made in 1974 by the then Home Secretary Roy Jenkins. He stated as follows: 'I do not think that anyone would wish these exceptional powers to remain in force a moment longer than is necessary.' Official Report, 25 November 1974, vol 882, col 642.

[9] Anti-Terrorism, Crime and Security Bill Explanatory Notes, https://publications.parliament.uk/pa/cm200102/cmbills/049/en/02049x–.htm.

[10] See ss 21–30 of ATCSA 2001 in particular.

[11] A Tomkins, 'Legislating against Terror: The Anti-Terrorism, Crime and Security Act 2001' (2002) 2 *PL* 205.

[12] *The Independent* (4 February 2003).

[13] For more details on the substance and rationale of the strategy, see https://assets.publishing.service.gov.uk/government/uploads/system/uploads/attachment_data/file/272320/6888.pdf.

Britain and their underlying drivers.[14] The consideration afforded to human rights as part of the set of core values, which grounded both strategies, was limited.

If New Labour's legislative and policy record on security matters post-9/11 is to be summarised, it would be thus: when faced with a choice between a prompt legislative response to close perceived legal and policy gaps[15] or first exhausting the wide range of legal powers already available within the statute books, the government chose the former. Furthermore, rather than demonstrating a deep commitment to human rights, the legislation and policies adopted from the year 2000 onwards were more reflective of the following two interrelated considerations: how much interference with various human rights could be proportionate and acceptable to allow for pre-emption of acts of terrorism as early as feasible? Concomitantly, how restrictive can the measures immobilising a terrorist suspect be before they are seen as unpalatable and/or found to be disproportionate?

The arguments on the onerous and problematic nature of certain legislative definitions, provisions and powers adopted between 2000 and 2010 and related judicial decisions are well rehearsed.[16] Thus, rather than dwelling on them in detail, this chapter proposes to instead focus on the catalyst(s) behind New Labour's penchant to update counterterrorism legislation annually or biennially and the longer-term impact(s) of this legislative fever. In doing so, the following discussion will first address how the individual terror suspect became one of New Labour's folk devils.[17] The contemporaneous entrenchment of the 'their rights versus our security' dichotomy, facilitated by the folk devil narrative, resulted in a tokenistic approach towards existing rights obligations. This tokenism has arguably led to the hollowing out of a number of individual rights, such as the right to fair trial, which will be the focus of the latter sections. What is perhaps one of New Labour's more disconcerting legacies is that this hollowing out has been mostly achieved from within the rule of law through persistent modification of counterterrorism legislation, including broader utilisation of bespoke judicial processes initially intended for limited use in immigration cases only.

[14] *The National Security Strategy of the United Kingdom: Security in an Interdependent World*, https://assets.publishing.service.gov.uk/government/uploads/system/uploads/attachment_data/file/228539/7291.pdf.

[15] New Labour tended to legislate as an instant response either to specific events (9/11 – ATCSA 2001) or judicial decisions (*A and Others v the United Kingdom* [2004] UKHL 56 – Prevention of Terrorism Act 2005).

[16] K Ewing, 'The Political Constitution of Emergency Powers: A Comment' (2007) 3 *International Journal of Law in Context* 31; KD Ewing, *The Bonfire of Liberties* (Oxford University Press, 2010); H Fenwick, 'The Anti-Terrorism, Crime and Security Act 2001: A Proportionate Response to 11 September?' (2002) 65 *MLR* 724; VV Ramraj et al (eds), *Global Anti-Terrorism Law and Policy* (Cambridge University Press, 2005).

[17] The concept of a 'folk devil' is magisterially discussed in S Cohen, *Folk Devils and Moral Panics*, 3rd edn (Routledge, 2002).

I. NEW LABOUR ON COUNTERTERRORISM PRE- AND POST-2001: MORAL PANIC AND THE FOLK DEVILS

In recent years, there have been many speculations over the executive's legal interpretation and decision-making, particularly in relation to matters of national security and counterterrorism.[18] The debates on how and why the executive arrives at a certain understanding of its legal constraints and the extent to which expansive national security and counterterrorism measures proposed by the executive can be adequately restrained by existing legal obligations have persevered.[19] The current legal scholarship has predominantly focused on rational, political and structural arguments[20] to explain executive action. However, the diverse manner in which legal questions arise for the executive following a moral panic such as 9/11 should also be considered.[21] Understanding these distinct triggers or 'interpretation catalysts' for legal decision-making is important as they can have a significant effect on the executive process and resulting decisions.[22] In particular, these catalysts can have a role in driving and shaping the executive decision-making when balancing national security and counterterrorism considerations against existing international law and human rights obligations.[23] New Labour's pre- and post-9/11 approach towards national security, counterterrorism and human rights is quite illustrative of the impact of an intense moral panic as such a catalyst and the questions it can trigger for the executive.

A. From the Human Rights Act 1998 to the Anti-Terrorism, Crime and Security Act 2001

The aplomb of New Labour's White Paper on the Human Rights Bill, stressing that the 'time has come to bring rights home',[24] suggests that at that particular time this Bill was considered to be the government's flagship legislation.

[18] R Ingber, 'Human Rights, National Security, and Executive Branch Legal Decision-making' [2013] *Administrative and Regulatory Law News* 19, 19. This issue is explored in PF Scott, ch 11 of this volume.

[19] ibid. See also EA Posner and E Vermeule, *Terror in the Balance: Security, Liberty, and the Courts* (Oxford University Press, 2007); A Kavanagh, 'Constitutionalism, Counter-Terrorism and the Courts: Changes in the British Constitutional Landscape' (2011) 9 *International Journal of Constitutional Law (ICON)* 172.

[20] R Ingber, 'Interpretation Catalysts and Executive Branch Legal Decision-making, (2013) 38 *Yale Journal of International Law* 359; see also N Rao, 'Public Choice and International Law Compliance: The Executive Branch Is a They Not an It' (2011) 96 *Minnesota Law Review* 194; E Magill and A Vermeule, 'Allocating Power within Agencies' (2011) 120 *Yale Law Journal* 1032.

[21] Ingber, 'Human Rights, National Security, and Executive Branch Legal Decision-making' (2013) 19.

[22] ibid 19–20.

[23] ibid.

[24] *Rights Brought Home: The Human Rights Bill* (n 3).

Yet, New Labour's penchant to emphasise and promote the importance of security is not a strictly post-9/11 occurrence. 'The fight against terrorism has taken on new urgency ... terrorism should have no hiding place, no opportunity to raise funds ... there should be no let-up in our determination to bring its perpetrators to justice.'[25] This statement, made by Tony Blair on 21 September 1998 at the 53rd session of the UN General Assembly, could easily be mistaken for having been delivered in the post-2001 environment. Similarly, the following comments by Jack Straw,

> the wide ranging and evolving threat from terrorism will not go away. The Bill therefore sets in place an appropriate and effective range of provisions, which is proportionate to the reality of the threat that we face and of practical operational benefit[26]

delivered in December 1999 during the second reading of the Terrorism Bill 2000 have been echoed since, when new counterterrorism legislation is put forward. While perhaps less prominent than subsequent statements made after 9/11, both are nevertheless revealing of New Labour's approach towards national security – the available national security toolkit will be updated if or when it is deemed necessary and appropriate to do so to counter a perceived threat. As indicated in Tony Blair's full statement to the UN General Assembly, revising and improving domestic legislation in addition to effective new measures to counter terrorism agreed at international level could 'make a real difference' in the fight against terrorism.[27]

In the context of the above statements, it is unsurprising that New Labour's first government sought to create permanent and UK-wide counterterrorism legislation shortly after the introduction of the HRA. The TA was presented as necessary in order to address the 'special difficulties' terrorism poses; these challenges were described as quite distinct from those caused by regular crime.[28] The overarching aim behind the reform and extension of the existing, area-specific, counterterrorism legislation was to ensure that all forms of domestic and international terrorism could be effectively addressed by the proposed provisions. To put it differently, the Terrorism Bill 2000 was intended to close what were perceived as gaps in the existing laws and remove 'certain anomalies'.[29] However, as the New Labour government had taken 'great exception to particularly arbitrary aspects of the [preceding] prevention of terrorism Acts', there were safeguards put in place to prevent the disproportionate use of powers contained within the Bill – namely, the HRA and the rights protections it affords.[30] The Terrorism Act came into force in July 2000.

[25] UN General Assembly 53rd Session, A/53/PV.7.
[26] HC Deb 14 December 1999, vol 341, cols 152–231.
[27] UN General Assembly 53rd Session, A/53/PV.7.
[28] HC Deb 14 December 1999, vol 341, col 152.
[29] ibid cols 159–62.
[30] ibid col 160.

The provisions of the Act vastly expanded previous definitions of terrorism solely as politically motivated violence to include politically and religiously motivated serious property damage and interference with electronic systems.[31] The Act also outlined a proscription regime based on intelligence evidence and introduced offences relating to being a member of or identifying with a proscribed organisation.[32] Other newly introduced offences, potentially applicable to individuals suspected of terrorist activities, appeared to push the boundaries of inchoate or pre-crime liability by criminalising the possession of articles.[33] The Act further provided for broad police powers, including preventative arrests on suspicion and without charge and random stop and search powers for articles that can be used in connection with terrorism.[34] Counterterrorism measures such as proscription, limitations on speech, administrative detention based on secret evidence, emergency-based legislation, the use of immigration as an aid to counterterrorism and derogation from rights were given a firmer basis.[35]

Yet, by November 2001, the 2000 Act was deemed insufficient to allow the UK government to effectually engage in the 'war with terrorism'.[36] The Anti-Terrorism, Crime and Security Act 2001 was fast-tracked through Parliament and was in force within a month of being introduced in the House of Commons.[37] The Act's perceived necessity was heavily criticised on the basis that the TA was an already comprehensive piece of counterterrorism legislation providing for a broad range of powers and preventive measures, as well as giving an exhaustive definition of terrorism.[38] Further, as the 2000 Act had come into force only a few months earlier, it was arguably still in the process of embedding. As such, any evaluation on the effectiveness of its provisions would be unlikely to adequately assess what the full impact of the adopted measures and powers had been or currently was. More tellingly – there is no indication that such an appraisal was in actuality carried out. Rather, the UK government chose to engage in a 'classic

[31] Part I – Introductory, Section 1 Terrorism Interpretation of the Terrorism Act 2000.

[32] Part II – Proscribed Organisations of the Terrorism Act 2000.

[33] K Roach, *The 9/11 Effect: Comparative Counter Terrorism* (Cambridge University Press, 2011) 241.

[34] Part V – Counter-terrorist Powers and Part VIII General of the Terrorism Act 2000.

[35] See, eg Northern Ireland (Emergency Provisions) Act 1973; the Prevention of Terrorism (Temporary Provisions) Act 1974 and the Terrorism Act 2000, which maintained similar provisions; see also the Immigration Act 1971. See further J Jackson, 'Many Years on in Northern Ireland: The Diplock Legacy' (2009) 60 *Northern Ireland Legal Quarterly* 213; L Donohue, 'Terrorism and Trial by Jury: The Vices and Virtues of British and American Criminal Law' (2007) 59 *Stanford Law Review* 1321.

[36] For the full text of Tony Blair's speech to Parliament indicating incoming new legislation, see *The Guardian* (4 October 2001).

[37] The Act was introduced in the House of Commons on 12 November 2001 and came into force on 14 December 2001.

[38] See, eg H Fenwick and G Phillipson, 'UK Counter-Terror Laws Post-9/11: Initial Acceptance of Extraordinary Measures and the Partial Return to Human Rights Norms' in Ramraj et al, *Global Anti-Terrorism Law and Policy* (2012) 481–513.

example of rushed legislation which was in fact unnecessary'.[39] While lamentable, this approach is not surprising.

B. From the 9/11 Moral Panic to Indefinite Detention of Terrorism Suspects

In the immediate aftermath of a national security exigency and at the onset of a moral panic, the executive's positioning tends to be the initial and at times pivotal declaration of how the state will respond legally, politically and/or militarily. As such, there is, by now, a fairly common pattern in the aftermath of a terrorism act – a pattern applicable in respect of events which have occurred both within and outside the relevant state's territory. First, questions of whether the state has the necessary means, information and powers to prevent the current level of terrorism threat tend to arise. Then, in order to be seen to respond appropriately to the immediate events as well as be able to pre-empt future attacks, governments usually seek to expand their counterterrorism and security toolkit with more far-reaching and, at times, controversial powers.[40] Legislative bodies – driven by the agendas of the political parties within them – loathe to be seen by the voting public as being soft on terror or, worse, as indifferent to terror.[41] With the stakes this high, legislators tend to consent to contentious provisions which may have a significant impact on individual rights[42] – the indefinite detention of those certified as international terrorists under the ATCSA being an apt example. What does, however, differentiate New Labour's immediate legislative approach after 9/11 to other, similarly rushed legislation is the draconian nature of the provisions, the longevity of its folk devil and the enduring impact on individual human rights.

In 2003, David Dyzenhaus observed that in the aftermath of 9/11 a number of states were gripped by a profound 'moral panic'.[43] While periods of moral panic are not new to societies – particularly in the context of national security emergencies – what tends to change is the episode, person or group of persons

[39] House of Lords Constitutional Committee, *Fast-track Legislation: Constitutional Implications and Safeguards*, 15th Report, Session 2008–09.

[40] The range of measures introduced as part of the Anti-Terrorism, Crime and Security Act (ATCSA) 2001 (now repealed) would fall within this category. The post-2015 French approach to counterterrorism legislation and regular renewal of the state of emergency is similarly illustrative. Following a series of coordinated terrorist attacks in Paris on 13 November 2015, France first declared a state of emergency (renewed on several occasions) and then proceeded to implement and impose a number of new criminal and administrative measures. See further B Boutin, 'Administrative Measures in Counter-Terrorism and the Protection of Human Rights' (2017) 27 *Security and Human Rights* 128.

[41] See, eg Ewing, 'The Political Constitution of Emergency Powers' (2007); L Donohue, *The Cost of Counter-Terrorism: Power, Politics and Liberty* (Cambridge University Press, 2008).

[42] ibid.

[43] D Dyzenhaus, 'Humpty Dumpty Rules or the Rule of Law: Legal Theory and the Adjudication of National Security' (2003) 28 *Australian Journal of Legal Philosophy* 1, 2.

that becomes defined as a threat to society.[44] The object of the panic can be quite novel; however, it can also be something which has been in existence for a long time and has suddenly reappeared in the limelight.[45] The threat of terrorism and public acts of terrorism are certainly not new, yet the events of 9/11 were perceived as unique; the threat by international terrorist organisations was (and still is) persistently depicted as unprecedented.[46] One explanation behind this strong reaction could be the correlation between the volatility or intensity of the moral panic and the decisions taken by the relevant government or governments as a response to the event(s) triggering the panic.[47]

For an event to be a moral panic, three key elements are required: a suitable enemy or folk devil;[48] a suitable victim;[49] and a consensus that the actions being denounced are not insulated entities but can become integral parts of society or regular occurrences unless decisive action is taken.[50] Once blame is allocated, ie an individual or a group has been identified as being responsible for causing the damage, the relevant government will then assess the level of risk and, by proxy, the measures required to both apprehend those responsible and pre-empt further occurrences of the violence.[51] Aside from the potential longevity of the measures adopted as a response, the volatility or intensity of the particular moral panic could also result in an expansive and assertive immediate reaction targeting everyone deemed responsible for the events triggering the panic.[52]

The events of 9/11 – the scale of destruction, the callousness of the attack and the number of casualties – arguably touched a chord within numerous states in a manner previous terrorist attacks had not.[53] The immediate multifaceted and multifronted response led by the USA and strongly supported (and operationalised) by the UK, amongst many other European and non-European countries, is illustrative of how much the events of that day impacted on the international community.[54] The intensity of the post-9/11 moral panic and the lingering fear of whether or when another attack might occur challenged the

[44] Cohen, *Folk Devils and Moral Panics* (2002) 1. See also M Tushnet, 'Defending *Korematsu*?: Reflections on Civil Liberties in Wartime' [2003] *Wisconsin Law Review* 273; J Young, *The Vertigo of Late Modernity* (Sage Publications, 2007).

[45] Cohen (n 17) 1.

[46] See the public comments of Tony Blair, George W Bush, Theresa May and Francois Holland, amongst others, who at various times since 9/11 have described the threat of terrorism countries as 'unprecedented' and requiring more commensurate and contemporary means to combat terrorism. The immediate public statements by NATO and the UN Security Council took a similar approach.

[47] Cohen (n 17) xxxii.

[48] Described as a soft and easily denounced target with little power.

[49] Someone with whom individuals could easily identify with.

[50] Cohen (n 17) xii.

[51] ibid xxxii.

[52] ibid xix.

[53] D Jenkins et al (eds), *The Long Decade: How 9/11 Changed the Law* (Oxford University Press, 2014) 5.

[54] Otherwise known as the infamous 'War on Terror' and including counterterrorism measures such as the 'High Value Detainee' programme and extraordinary renditions.

ability of states to provide and guarantee security.[55] Thus, governments had to be seen to respond forcefully, nationally and transnationally, through legislation and all other means deemed necessary.[56]

The ensuing domestic legislative fever, particularly in the UK, has resulted in severe and lengthy restrictions of the rights and liberties of individual terrorist suspects – restrictions which have perhaps permanently recalibrated[57] the relationship between such suspects and the state. The disproportionate and discriminatory nature of measures such as the indefinite detention of those certified as international terrorists,[58] the control orders regime which replaced the indefinite detentions[59] and the stop and search powers[60] under section 44 of the TA have been widely dissected within academia as well as in domestic and regional court rooms.[61] In 2004, the House of Lords (before its replacement by the Supreme Court) found that the indefinite detention powers under Part 4 of the ATCSA were incompatible with Articles 5 and 14 of the ECHR.[62] The powers were found to be disproportionate and to allow for the detention of suspected international terrorists in a manner that discriminates on the ground of nationality or immigration status. Of particular interest are the comments made by Lord Hoffmann on both the existence of a state of emergency and the impact of the legislation in question.[63] He first noted that 'terrorist violence, serious as it is, does not threaten our institutions of government or our existence as a civil community'.[64] Thus, he felt that the Special Immigration Appeals Commission had made an error of law on the question of whether there was an emergency threatening the life of the nation. On this point, he discernibly differed from many of his colleagues. He then strongly criticised the use of indefinite detention in any form as incompatible with the UK's constitution (again, diverging noticeably from other Law Lords). He famously concluded his judgment as follows: 'the real threat to the life of the nation, in the sense of a people living in accordance with its traditional laws and political values, comes not from terrorism but from laws such as these'.

The problematic nature of these provisions thus does not require detailed elaboration other than to note that while New Labour may initially have been an advocate for human rights, induced by the post-9/11 moral panic, it ultimately

[55] Jenkins et al, *The Long Decade* (2014) 9.
[56] ibid.
[57] The concept of 'downward recalibration' of rights has been discussed in detail in F De Londras, *Detention in the 'War on Terror': Can Human Rights Fight Back?* (Cambridge University Press, 2011); H Fenwick, 'Recalibrating ECHR Rights and the Role of the HRA Post-9/11: Reasserting International Human Rights Norms in the "War on Terror"?' (2010) 63 *Current Legal Problems* 153.
[58] See the findings in *A and Others* (n 15).
[59] See the Prevention of Terrorism Act 2005 and the Explanatory Notes attached to it.
[60] *Gillan and Quinton v the United Kingdom* [2010] ECHR 28.
[61] A particularly thorough account is provided by Ewing, *The Bonfire of Liberties* (2010).
[62] *A and Others* (n 15) [73].
[63] ibid [96].
[64] ibid [96].

became a champion for counterterrorism and over-securitisation. The prevention of terrorism crept into the pre-criminal/pre-terrorism spaces where an individual who may be influenced to support terrorism-related activities also became a folk devil. Thus, within this environment, the downward recalibration of rights captured not only individuals (suspected of) engaging in acts of terrorism, but gradually also those who were yet to engage in any terrorism-related activities but may potentially be influenced to do so in the future, as the subsequent discussion will illustrate.[65]

II. IMMOBILISING THE FOLK DEVIL

Lurking behind the utilisation of the powers under Part 4 of the ATCSA, the subsequent imposition of control orders and the exclusion of individuals from the UK on national security grounds[66] was the reliance on a procedure first employed strictly within the Special Immigration Appeals Commission (SIAC). Section 5(3) of the SIAC Act of 1997 introduced to the UK's legislative and judicial framework the use of both secret evidence and closed proceedings – within immigration cases only.[67] Under a closed material procedure (CMP), secret intelligence evidence can be considered by a judicial body without the defendant or his legal team being given the access to hear the evidence. A Special Advocate (SA) is tasked with representing the interests of the excluded party in closed hearings and subjecting the sensitive material to scrutiny, thereby enhancing the fairness of the proceedings.[68] Upon introduction, the CMPs were perceived as a legal abnormality and, thus, were heavily criticised on human rights grounds.[69] Nevertheless, they have gradually become a more permanent fixture within the UK judicial framework.

The founding of a specialised tribunal accommodating the use of secret evidence could be viewed as a rather serendipitous pre-9/11 occurrence, the utility of which was more fully appreciated and exploited in the post-9/11 environment. It should be noted, however, that SIAC and its procedures were

[65] See, eg H Duffy, *The 'War on Terror' ad the Framework of International Law*, 2nd edn (Cambridge University Press, 2015); Donohue, *The Cost of Counter-Terrorism* (2008); Ramraj et al (n 16); A Masferrer and C Walker (eds), *Counter-Terrorism, Human Rights and the Rule of Law* (Edward Elgar, 2013). See also the UK Counter Extremism and Safeguarding Bill 2016 and the UK Investigatory Powers Act 2016.

[66] See Case C-300/11 *ZZ v the Secretary of State for the Home Department*, judgment of 4 June 2013; *IR and GT v the United Kingdom* App nos 14876/12 and 63339/12, judgment of 28 January 2014.

[67] The Act also established SIAC to have purview over appeals of deportation, detention or exclusion decisions due to national security considerations; SIAC has the same powers as a High Court. See further the SIAC Act 1997 and SIAC (Procedure) Rules 2003 No 1034 in force since April 2015.

[68] The role of Special Advocate was also introduced by s 6 of the SIAC Act 1997.

[69] E Nanopoulos, 'European Human Rights Law and the Normalisation of the 'Closed Material Procedure': Limit or Source?' (2015) 78 *MLR* 913, 913.

established as a direct response to the findings in *Chahal v the United Kingdom* in respect of Article 5 of the ECHR.[70] The 1997 Act sought to directly address the European Court of Human Right's (ECtHR) decision and ensure that there continues to be a specialised tribunal with a bespoke procedure that accommodates the use of closed evidence in immigration matters where national security considerations are engaged.

SIAC heard only three cases in a CMP prior to 2001.[71] In all three cases, the UK was seeking to deport the individuals in question as they were considered to pose a threat to national security due to (suspected) terrorism-related activity.[72] The limited number of cases and SIAC's strict purview strongly suggest that pre-9/11 the reliance on CMPs was exceptional. Nevertheless, although there were only three cases, they opened up the possibility that the government could rely on secret evidence when seeking to deport a certain category of individuals. As this specialised procedure was deemed to be of benefit in a post-9/11 environment, New Labour's legislative fever gradually expanded its operation to a number of other preventative counterterrorism measures, eventually resulting in the CMPs' entrenchment within the UK judicial structures.

Part 4 of the ATCSA, now repealed, was devoted to targeting those suspected of international terrorism, their certification, removal and/or detention. What should be highlighted, aside from their controversial and highly restrictive nature, is that the operation of these measures was grounded in immigration and asylum law. Under section 21(9) of the ATCSA, an action of the Home Secretary taken wholly or partly in reliance on a certificate could only be questioned in legal proceedings involving SIAC, ie proceedings within which, if necessary, a CMP could be relied on. As SIAC has purview over deportations, any immigration removal proceedings and/or related appeals under section 22 of the ATCSA would thus involve SIAC and, again, potentially a CMP. While awaiting departure or removal from the UK, an individual certified as a suspected international terrorist could be detained either temporarily or indefinitely under section 23. Further, under section 30 of the Act, SIAC had exclusive jurisdiction over derogation matters as pertaining to the ATCSA.

What Part 4 of the ATCSA thus appeared to do is transform SIAC from a bespoke immigration tribunal to one specialising in counterterrorism cases within the ongoing state of emergency. As a result, once certified under

[70] App no 22414/93, judgment of 15 November 1996. The Advisory Panel procedure, the predecessor of SIAC, fully reviewed the evidence relating to the national security threat Mr Chahal was deemed to pose and agreed with the determination that Mr Chahal ought to be deported. While there was no violation of Art 5(1), neither the proceedings for *habeas corpus* and the judicial review of the detention decision nor the Advisory Panel procedure complied with the requirements of Art 5(4).

[71] All three were heard between 1999 and 2000, ie during New Labour's first government.

[72] *Secretary of State for the Home Department v Shafiq Ur Rehman* [2000] EWCA Civ 168; *Mukhtiar Singh and Paramjit Singh v Secretary of State for the Home Department* (Special Immigration Appeals Commission, 31 July 2000).

section 21, and therefore transformed into a folk devil, an individual faced the prospect either of indefinite detention or of challenging closed evidence which neither he nor his core legal team had any access to. If an individual was to contest the (dis)proportionality of the measures imposed by disputing the existence of the state of emergency, which accommodated certain derogations, under section 30 they again faced the possibility of a CMP. The history of counterterrorism cases suggests that, once depicted as a folk devil within an emergency, an individual tends to encounter significant legal difficulties in challenging the imposition of restrictive or preventative security measures.[73] Yet, the measures contained within Part 4 of the ATCSA were particularly onerous and disproportionate. They were therefore unsurprisingly found to be in breach of existing rights obligations by the House of Lords in 2004.[74] While the Law Lords made references to the use of closed materials within the proceedings in SIAC, they felt that the impact of these materials did not go further than to substantiate and strengthen the openly available evidence.[75] Thus, they found that SIAC had made no error in law in reaching the conclusion that a public emergency threatening the life of the nation existed.[76] Following the House of Lords' decision, the government replaced Part 4 of the ATCSA with the provisions of new counterterrorism legislation. The reliance on CMPs, closed evidence and SAs in the context of preventative counterterrorism measures continued unabated.

Before the decision in the *A and Others* case, SIAC could consider three possible outcomes when deliberating on immigration appeals: exclusion or removal from the UK; detention under Part 4 of the ATCSA; and removal of citizenship.[77] Following the decision, New Labour acted swiftly to ensure that SIAC's now defunct detention function was replaced by another regime capable of similarly immobilising terror suspects. The Prevention of Terrorism Bill 2005, introduced to the House of Commons on 25 February 2005, proposed a new system of control orders under which an individual may be subjected to various obligations deemed necessary to prevent or restrict further involvement in terrorism-related activity.[78] The Bill was specifically designed to address the imminent release of 10 of the foreign nationals detained under Part 4 of the ATCSA following the ruling in the *A and Others* case.

[73] See, eg Tushnet, 'Defending *Korematsu*?' (2003); Jackson, 'Many Years on in Northern Ireland' (2009); R English, *Terrorism: How to Respond* (Oxford University Press, 2009).

[74] *A and Others* (n 15). In its decision, the House of Lords approached the issue of whether there was a state of emergency as a primarily political question, ie one that needs to be addressed and resolved by the government (para 29). ATCSA 2001, s 23 was, however, found to be incompatible with Arts 5 and 14 of the ECHR. A Declaration of Incompatibility under s 4 HRA was thus issued.

[75] ibid [27].

[76] ibid [166].

[77] House of Commons Constitutional Affairs Committee, *The Operation of the Special Immigration Appeals Commission (SIAC) and the Use of Special Advocates*, 7th Report of Session 2004–05, HC 323-I.

[78] Prevention of Terrorism Bill 2005 Explanatory Notes, Session 2004–05.

The obligations imposed could include restrictions on movement to or within certain areas, restrictions on communications and associations, and requirements as to place of residence, amongst others. Each control order was envisioned as being tailored to the particular risk posed by the individual in question. A control order could be imposed against any individual engaged in terrorism-related activity, irrespective of nationality or terrorist cause, thus arguably addressing the problem with Part 4 of the ATCSA. Judicial scrutiny over the imposition, renewal or modification of a control order was entrusted with the High Court; control order proceedings could involve the hearing of evidence in both open and closed sessions.[79] Within 17 days, the Prevention of Terrorism Act 2005 (PTA) was in force and all 10 individuals had been placed under a control order.[80]

The PTA was strongly criticised as a legislation 'pushed through in Parliament … to meet an artificial deadline imposed [by the government's] own earlier emergency legislation of 2001'.[81] The adoption process surrounding the PTA and the introduction of a control order regime based on the indefinite detention one are illustrative of the longer-term impact of emergency counterterrorism laws. What the indefinite detention and control order regimes aimed to achieve is restrict or prevent an individual from any further involvement in terrorist-related activity by in essence immobilising them through unorthodox court proceedings. The immediate replacement of one extraordinary regime with another, similar one indicates that a vested interest in such measures had already been created. As the history of emergency counterterrorism legislation suggests, once enacted, the relevant agencies tend to be reluctant to relinquish powers which could be used to address other threats to national security or diminish crime.[82] Similarly, an executive which has compelled the introduction of such measures tends to do so on the basis that it perceives these measures to be necessary; as such, a government has an ongoing vested interest in reaffirming and defending its overall security and counterterrorism strategy. Replacing one measure with another of a similar spirit is a means to achieve the latter.

III. THE ENTRENCHMENT OF FOLK DEVILS AND OVER-SECURITISATION

The manner in which the PTA was pushed through Parliament[83] and the practical operation of the control order regime demonstrate a particular danger

[79] Ibid; Prevention of Terrorism Act 2005 (now repealed).

[80] House of Commons Constitutional Affairs Committee, 7th Report of Session 2004–05 (n 77).

[81] House of Lords Constitutional Committee, *Fast-track Legislation: Constitutional Implications and Safeguards*, 15th Report of Session 2008–09.

[82] Donohue (n 41) 15.

[83] See, eg the House of Lords Constitutional Committee, 15th Report of Session 2008–09 (n 81) and the evidence featured therein.

of adopting extraordinary counterterrorism measures within an emergency. Once such procedures are implemented, their continued use has a normalising effect – either on the restrictiveness of the specific processes or by paving the way for similar, if marginally less onerous, measures in the future. Arguably, in a pre-9/11 environment, the control order regime might have been deemed unacceptable and never legislated for. However, in the post-9/11 moral panic and particularly after the operation of Part 4 of the ATCSA, while criticised prior to introduction, control orders nevertheless became a feature in the UK counterterrorism toolkit until 2011.[84] Their use, similar to the provisions of the 2001 Act, underwent several high-profile judicial challenges, some of which will be briefly outlined in the subsequent section. While the control order regime was repealed in 2011, its operation between 2005 and 2011 normalised the broader utilisation of CMPs and SAs across a range of pre-emptive counterterrorism measures.

A. (Future) Folk Devils and the Courts

In 2007, the House of Lords gave its judgment in one of the first cases challenging a non-derogating control order made by the Home Secretary under sections 2 and 3(1)(a) PTA – the joined cases of *AF and MB*.[85] The court had to decide, inter alia, whether the CMP and SA procedures provided for under the Act were compatible with Article 6 of the ECHR. It should be noted that neither MB nor AF were charged with having committed any breach of the law, but rather that they *might* engage in unlawful behaviour in the future. This was a particularly pertinent issue in respect of one of the appellants (AF) – the use of a CMP had resulted in the case against him being in essence entirely undisclosed, with no specific allegations of terrorism-related activity being contained in open material.[86] The court was tasked with addressing four particular issues, including whether the procedures provided for by section 3 of the PTA and the Rules of Court were compatible with Article 6 in circumstances where they have resulted in a case based in essence on entirely closed evidence.

In addressing this specific issue, Lord Bingham felt that neither AF nor MB had 'enjoyed a substantial measure of procedural justice';[87] he further noted that the very essence of the right to a fair hearing had been impaired.[88] The majority

[84] The PTA and the control order regime were repealed by the Terrorism Prevention and Investigation Measures Act 2011. The 2011 Act introduced the Terrorism Prevention and Investigation Measures (TPIMs); the Counter-Terrorism and Security Act 2015 made some modifications to the TPIM regime.

[85] *Secretary of State for the Home Department v MB (FC), Secretary of State for the Home Department v AF (FC)* [2007] UKHL 46. The PTA drew a clear distinction between a 'derogating control order' defined in s 15(1) and a 'non-derogating control order' defined in s 1(10).

[86] ibid [3].

[87] See further the findings in the *Chahal v United Kingdom* (1996) 23 EHRR 413, para 131.

[88] *AF and MB* (n 85) [42]. He also relied on *R (Roberts) v Parole Board* [2005] UKHL 45 to emphasise that 'the concept of fairness imports a core, irreducible minimum of procedural protection'. This 2005 case addressed the question whether the Parole Board had the power to adopt a special advocate regime, ie employ a CMP or similar process.

did, however, take the view that the cases should be remitted for reconsideration to the trial judge on the basis that issues relating to a fair trial, when a CMP is employed, can be fact specific. This conclusion was based on the view that in many cases a CMP and the reliance on SAs would provide a sufficient counter-balance where the Home Secretary wished to utilise closed evidence; each case had to be considered individually and would depend on whether the controlled person had been given 'a meaningful opportunity to contest the factual basis' for the order.[89]

By the time the Supreme Court was delivering its judgment in the *AF (No 3)* case,[90] the ECtHR had established that the subject of a control order must be given sufficient information about the allegations against him to enable him to give effective instructions to challenge the allegations.[91] The Court of Appeal confirmed that non-disclosure of evidence cannot go as far as denying a party knowledge of the essence of the case against him, at least where an individual is at risk of consequences as severe as those normally imposed under a control order.[92] Some of these consequences have included, in essence, 'a form of internal exile' or severe impact on family life.[93] The onerous nature of control orders was subject to criticism both within the courts and in Parliament until the PTA was eventually repealed. However, the reliance on closed evidence through the CMP and SA procedures has endured despite comments made by current Special Advocates that in their experience 'CMPs are inherently unfair' and do not deliver real procedural fairness.[94]

Nevertheless, aside from the aforementioned scenarios under the now repealed ATCSA and PTA, CMPs have also been used in a variety of cases involving proscription as a terrorist organisation,[95] domestic asset freezing orders,[96] terrorism prevention and investigation measures[97] and employment disputes,[98] which raise questions of national security. The recent cases relating to employment disputes – *Tariq* and *Kiani* – are quite illustrative of how much the counterterrorism legislative and judicial landscape has shifted post-9/11.

[89] *AF and MB* (n 85) [65]–[66], [74]. Lady Hale, in the majority, did expressly note that it was unlikely that the ECtHR would hold that '*every* control order hearing in which the special advocate procedure had been used … would be sufficient to comply with Article 6.'

[90] *Secretary of State for the Home Department v AF and Another (No 3)* [2010] 2 AC 269.

[91] *A and Others v the UK* [2009] ECHR 301.

[92] [65].

[93] Human Rights Joint Select Committee, *Counter-Terrorism Policy and Human Rights (Sixteenth Report): Annual Renewal of Control Orders Legislation 2010*, HL 64/HC 395.

[94] See response by Special Advocates within the 2011 Justice and Security Green Paper.

[95] TA.

[96] Counter-Terrorism Act 2008.

[97] Terrorism Prevention and Investigation Measures Act 2011.

[98] See, in particular *Home Office v Tariq* [2011] UKSC 35; *Kiani v Secretary of State for the Home Department* [2015] EWCA Civ 776. In April 2018, the ECtHR found that even though some of the proceedings were held in a closed session, Mr Tariq had been provided with proper safeguards for his right to fair trial, including a Special Advocate. The application was declared inadmissible: *Gulamhussein and Tariq v the United Kingdom* App nos 46538/11 and 3960/12, judgment of 26 April 2018.

There was no suggestion in either case that the individuals in question had engaged in terrorism-related activities. Rather, the concerns were that they *might be vulnerable* to future outside attempts or duress to have them abuse their positions as immigration officers. By 2010, the CMP and SAs procedure had been used in at least 21 different contexts, including parole hearings.[99] Following the adoption of the Justice and Security Act 2013 (JSA), the applicability of CMPs has been extended to all civil proceedings.[100]

The JSA was a response to somewhat embarrassing legal proceedings stemming from a transnational strand of New Labour's counterterrorism policies – support for the US 'War on Terror' and facilitation of the rendition programme mentioned above. Binyam Mohamed[101] was one of several individuals subjected to an extraordinary rendition after 9/11 who subsequently challenged various aspects of the UK's alleged (in)direct involvement in the rendition process.[102] The contentious issue of the case was the potential public disclosure of seven paragraphs which provided a summary of reports by the CIA on the circumstances of Mr Mohamed's detention and interrogation in Guantánamo Bay. During the parliamentary discussions around the Justice and Security Bill, yet another case threatening to cause some embarrassment for the UK government arose out of a claim for damages.[103] The civil claim related to the detention of the six claimants by foreign authorities at various locations. The most recent high-profile case raising the issue of a CMP was also a highly charged rendition case – *Belhaj and Another v Director of Public Prosecutions and Others*[104] – which temporarily raised the prospect that a CMP could be utilised in proceedings *concerning* a criminal cause or matter.[105] This case was also settled and followed by an unreserved apology.[106]

[99] For the full list, see Human Rights Joint Select Committee, *Counter-Terrorism Policy and Human Rights (Sixteenth Report): Annual Renewal of Control Orders Legislation 2010*, HL 64/HC 395, 51–53; Human Rights Joint Select Committee, *Counter-Terrorism Policy and Human Rights (Seventeenth Report): Bringing Human Rights Back In*, HL 86/HC 111, 21–22.

[100] Part 2 JSA.

[101] *R (Binyam Mohamed) v Secretary of State for Foreign and Commonwealth Affairs (No 1)* [2008] EWHC 2048 (admin); *R (Binyam Mohamed) v Secretary of State for Foreign & Commonwealth Affairs (No 2)* [2010] EWCA Civ 158. Mr Mohamed was detained in Guantánamo Bay as a suspected enemy combatant for several years.

[102] In February 2008, the then Foreign Secretary David Miliband admitted that two US aircrafts carrying rendered suspects had landed on Diego Garcia Island in 2002. See also the Open Society Justice Initiative, *Globalizing Torture: CIA Secret Detention and Extraordinary Rendition* (GHP Media, 2013) and the December 2013 interim report, 'The Report of the Detainee Inquiry', by Sir Peter Gibson.

[103] *Al Rawi and Others v The Security Service and Others* [2011] UKSC 34.

[104] [2018] UKSC 33.

[105] See further the 2017 Divisional Court decision in *Belhaj and Another v Director of Public Prosecutions and Others* [2017] UKSC 3. This limb of the Belhaj legal proceedings concerned a challenge to a decision by the Crown Prosecution Service. The Court decided that whilst the judicial review application could be seen as proceedings concerning a criminal cause or matter, it was certainly not proceedings in a criminal cause or matter (a CMP cannot be utilised in the latter scenario).

[106] 'Britain Apologises for "Appalling Treatment" of Abdel Hakim Belhaj' *The Guardian* (10 May 2018).

Thus, since New Labour utilised this bespoke procedure within the ATCSA and subsequently expanded its use beyond SIAC's proceedings, (i) CMPs have become the standard governmental response when facing highly sensitive and potentially embarrassing cases relating to counterterrorism operations (both transnational and domestic) and (ii) CMPs should no longer be described as exceptional or extraordinary. More significantly, post-9/11, the use of CMPs has altered the courts' approach towards the core principles of open and natural justice.[107] It should be noted that a CMP does have most of the trappings of an adversarial procedure: the possibility to challenge closed evidence, the presence of a security cleared and highly trained counsel, and a hearing in front of experienced justices. However, in the words of Dinah Rose QC, who has acted as a Special Advocate: 'The case that an appellant thinks they are meeting may not be simply different in extent but wholly different in kind from the case they are actually meeting.'[108] In other words, an individual is effectively placed in the quintessential Kafkaesque scenario when closed evidence is employed – one can only prevail in a trial if they can rebut all the undisclosed evidence against them. To do so successfully, however, an individual would have to prove that they are not a terrorist or engaged in terrorism-related activity regardless of what might be implied by the government's closed evidence. An individual must do so without always knowing who provided the evidence or how it was obtained. Alternatively, as the aforementioned cases illustrate, the use of a CMP can either result in the imposition of onerous counterterrorism measures or be used by the executive to avoid some embarrassment.

B. New Labour's Counterterrorism Legacy: Entrenchment of the Exceptional

Having gradually become normalised during New Labour's counterterrorism legislative fever, CMPs could be viewed as yet another means of recalibrating compliance with state obligations in respect of individual terror suspects. As suggested in a number of relevant cases,[109] these specialised proceedings are used in order to balance the need of the state to protect sensitive intelligence information and gathering techniques with the rights of the individual terror suspect.

[107] See the extensive judicial scrutiny and references to the importance of 'open and natural justice' in *Al Rawi* (n 103). Lord Dyson described the principle of open justice as a 'fundamental common law principle' (para 11). Natural justice and its various strands were discussed as core foundations of court trials (paras 12–15).

[108] See oral evidence before the Joint Committee on Human Rights, 'The Justice and Security Green Paper' (24 January 2012) 13 https://www.parliament.uk/documents/joint-committees/human-rights/JCHR%2024%20January%20transcript.pdf.

[109] See cases such as *AF (No 3) v Secretary of State for the Home Department* [2010] 2 AC 269; *Bank Mellat v Her Majesty's Treasury* [2013] UKSC 38; *XH and AI v the Secretary of State for the Home Department* [2017] EWCA Civ 41; *K, A, B v Secretary of State for Defence and Secretary of State for Foreign and Commonwealth Affairs* [2017] EWHC 830 (Admin).

Engaging the concept of 'balancing' in this context is, however, misguided as it suggests that perhaps there is an equal starting point or equilibrium between individual rights on one scale and national security on the other. It further implies that human rights are somehow an impediment on defence, security and counterterrorism policies. The preambles and texts of the relevant regional and international human rights documents demonstrate that while individual rights should be respected at all times, the human rights framework has been designed to afford states some flexibility when they need to respond to exigent circumstances through provisions such as Article 15 ECHR. In order words, ensuring continuing respect for human rights does not impede states from seeking to restore and reassert the security of the nation during a state of emergency; rather, the required respect for human rights is intended as a guarantee that any exceptional measures are legitimate, proportionate and ultimately short-lived, in line with the (ideally) temporary nature of an emergency.

However, as aptly demonstrated by the aforementioned replacement of one extraordinary preventative regime with another, once enacted, counterterrorism measures create an institutional interest.[110] This is particularly so when these powers can be used in other areas to, for example, manage immigration, reduce crime or pre-empt additional threats to national security. From this perspective, counterterrorism law is perhaps better seen as a spiral rather than a pendulum,[111] which swings from side to side – one side being individual rights and the other security. The discourse on individual rights versus security assumes that they align on a fulcrum; when there is a terrorist threat, the pendulum swings in the direction of security over human rights and dignity. However, viewing counterterrorism laws as a spiral arguably offers a more apt understanding.[112] During times of normalcy, rights and security could be seen as being affixed to their places. When a state experiences an emergency, rights begin to slide down the spiral while security keeps moving to the top, creeping into numerous aspects of governmental policies in the process.[113] As emergency measures become entrenched and normalised within the legislative framework, for those immediately impacted there is no return to normalcy.

The jurisprudence, both within and beyond the UK, suggests that there is perhaps an inherent disparity in the relationship between the individual folk devil and the state within national security cases.[114] Within this context, the pre-emptive counterterrorism toolkit championed by New Labour since the year 2000 onwards can be seen as formalising this inequality further by hollowing

[110] Donohue (n 41) 1–17.
[111] ibid.
[112] ibid.
[113] ibid.
[114] See, eg B Dickson, *The European Convention on Human Rights and the Conflict in Northern Ireland* (Oxford University Press, 2010); C Gearty, *Liberty and Security* (Polity Press, 2013), RA Wilson (ed), *Human Rights in the 'War on Terror'* (Cambridge University Press, 2005); Jenkins (n 53).

out the protections and scope of rights such as the right to liberty and the right to fair trial. The impact of indefinite detentions and control orders on individual dignity and liberty has been widely discussed and criticised, as mentioned previously. In the particular example of the fair trial rights of individuals facing a CMP, without access to the closed judgment, it is naturally difficult to analyse how individual rights obligations are addressed. However, as the aforementioned cases and comments by the SAs suggest, while the CMP process can afford individuals a procedural measure of justice,[115] it may not necessarily result in a substantive measure of justice.

In other words, as a result of New Labour's counterterrorism policy of oversecuritisation, human rights, individually and in general, were approached in an increasingly more formalistic or empty manner, resulting in the mere appearance or pretence of respect for human rights and dignity. The divergence from the standard legal processes to accommodate the imposition of onerous counterterrorism measures is an example of where the executive's approach to the rule of law in times of security emergencies is at its most dangerous – through various legislative processes, a legal grey hole or an exploitable space within the law can be created.[116] In a legal grey space, while there are legal constraints on state actions, these constraints are weak enough to permit governments to operate in any manner it desires. Such an approach to the rule of law is highly problematic not just in itself, but also in combination with what has been described by Joseph Raz as the 'danger created by law itself'.[117] Law can be uncertain, unstable or obscure, and thus potentially infringe on individual rights and freedoms; however, the rule of law is designed to prevent such dangers.

The argument can thus be made that the rule of law failed under New Labour. The operation, updating and impact of various counterterrorism measures and provisions suggests that New Labour persistently sought to create and exploit legal grey spaces through legislation. While gradually the counterterrorism legislation provided for perhaps more palatable preventative measures,[118] the executive's desire to identify, capture, detain and/or immobilise individual terror suspects as early as feasible did not wane. The adoption of counterterrorism measures such as indefinite detention and control orders and the executive's arguments to defend and justify them have embedded a perception that anyone defined as a terrorist suspect is undeserving of the full protections afforded by law. As such, within this context, the rule of law was defeated during New Labour's time in government. However, the causes behind this defeat lie firmly within New Labour's policies. Driven by a desire to persistently address all

[115] *IR and GT* (n 66) para 58.

[116] D Dyzenhaus, *The Constitution of Law: Legality in a Time of Emergency* (Cambridge University Press, 2006).

[117] J Raz, *The Authority of Law: Essays on Law and Morality* (Oxford University Press, 1979).

[118] The longevity of the control order regime in comparison to indefinite detention suggests that arguably the former were deemed less onerous and less objectionable.

existing and perceived security risks and to be seen to respond effectively to the threat of terrorism, New Labour substantially prioritised the adoption of stringent counterterrorism legislation over the preservation of the rule of law and the promotion of human rights. In persistently upgrading counterterrorism policies, measures and strategies, New Labour exploited and weaponised the law to target all those considered to be a folk devil. As such, the opposite is perhaps more apt – New Labour failed the rule of law.

IV. CONCLUSION

In another, by now ritualised pattern, legal scholarship tends to reflect extensively on the insinuated tensions between individual liberty and national security demands in the aftermath of a terrorist event. However, as New Labour's various domestic and transnational counterterrorism legislative and policy measures often demonstrated, it is equally appropriate to describe these tensions as due process protections versus security considerations.[119] The indefinite detention of those certified as international terrorists, the subsequent imposition of onerous control orders, the normalised reliance on closed evidence and the indirect involvement in extraordinary renditions are particularly illustrative examples of where the post-9/11 security demands substantially eclipsed the importance of protecting human dignity. While rights might have been 'brought home' by the HRA, New Labour's subsequent tokenistic approach to individual human rights, particularly in the context of counterterrorism, left the promotion of human rights in the background rather than placing them at the forefront as promised. From an intrinsic part of the New Labour project, individual rights thus became a peripheral consideration. This is perhaps one of New Labour's most lamentable policy failures. If a similar legislative and political effort and support had been afforded to the HRA after its adoption as was given to all counterterrorism acts enacted from 2000 onwards, then perhaps the HRA would have had the constitutional impact that had initially been pledged.

Instead, the new dawn that broke over Britain on a May morning in 1997 ushered in a legislative decade (2000–2010) dominated by security and counterterrorism priorities and considerations. Yet, despite receiving disparate attention and prominence post-2000, the counterterrorism and human rights legislative and policy strands are equally reflective of one of New Labour's most enduring legacies: New Labour's legislative innovations have become embedded and have expanded despite significant changes in the circumstances which precipitated their development.[120] From this perspective, certain parallels could perhaps

[119] For similar comments, see A Tomkins, 'National Security and the Due Process of Law' (2011) 64 *Current Legal Problems* 215.

[120] The HRA has weathered heavy criticisms and suggestions that it should be replaced; since 2001, SIAC's bespoke and rarely used CMP process has been embedded across a variety of proceedings, including civil ones.

be drawn between these distinct legislative strands – their longevity within the constitutional framework of the UK despite many criticisms and calls for reform being one such parallel. This longevity has come at a cost, however. The distinct precedence afforded to counterterrorism considerations has resulted in the entrenchment of the fallacy that a 'balance' must be struck between human rights and security to achieve effective counterterrorism policies. This particular entrenchment – both politically and legislatively – could prove to be New Labour's longest lasting legacy.

13

Revisiting the Administrative Justice Legacy of New Labour

JOE TOMLINSON AND RICHARD KIRKHAM[1]

I. INTRODUCTION

THE PERIOD THAT New Labour was in power – 13 years when taken to include both Blair and Brown's time in No 10 – saw significant social, political and economic evolution. Given the rich material the New Labour years produced for those with an interest in constitutional law and constitutional reform, it is perhaps unsurprising – especially given administrative law's long-standing position as the 'hard-working, unglamorous cousin laboring in the shadow of constitutional law'[2] – that much more has been written by public law scholars about New Labour's impact on the constitution than its impact on the system of administrative justice. Yet, a wide range of important reforms, as well as innovations, were put in place concerning the way administrative decisions by government departments are made and the avenues for challenging those decisions. For this reason alone, in order to comprehend fully the long-term impact of New Labour on governance and the constitution in the UK, it is important to consider the contemporaneous evolution of administrative justice across the same period. There are, however, other important reasons to pay specific attention to the experience of administrative justice under New Labour. Reflecting on this period can help us learn lessons and inform analysis of current and future reform proposals, including about how to approach reform. It can also assist in developing our understanding of the significant relationship between administrative justice and constitutional legitimacy, which

[1] We are very grateful to Nick O'Brien, Adam Tucker and Mike Gordon for comments on various drafts.

[2] T Ginsburg, 'Written Constitutions and the Administrative State: On the Constitutional Character of Administrative Law' in S Rose-Ackerman and PL Lindseth (eds), *Comparative Administrative Law* (Edward Elgar, 2010) 117.

remains a surprisingly underdeveloped link in the densely populated field of public law scholars interested in the performance of constitutions.[3]

In this chapter, we address the issue of how the legacy of New Labour's administrative justice reform is best characterised. In what has been written thus far on New Labour's development of the administrative justice system, the central narrative is one of a 'rise' before a post-2010 'fall'.[4] This account – which we will call the 'standard account' – runs broadly along the following lines. New Labour, in what many considered to be a revolutionary step, recognised the need for a coherent overall approach to the administrative justice system and that the system ought to be friendly for the 'users' (ie citizens) which depend on it. Due to this approach, the New Labour administrations were said to represent the first time that a government had set out a 'vision for administrative justice that aimed to give it parity with civil and family justice'[5] and, as a consequence, administrative justice had 'emerge[d] from the shadows'.[6] Eventually, New Labour established, as part of a wider reform package, the Administrative Justice and Tribunals Council (AJTC), to provide coherent oversight of the system and advance a principled, research-based approach to the area. The AJTC was an institutional solution, designed to provide coherent oversight of the system and advance a principled, research-based approach to the area. This body, along with its new functions, became an institutional symbol of progress. This apparent success story then transforms to a tragedy when the Coalition government arrives in Westminster in 2010, reduces public spending under a programme of austerity and makes multiple changes to decision-making and redress procedures.[7] This fall was, in turn, also given institutional expression when the Coalition government decided to abolish the AJTC under the Public Bodies Act 2011. In its place was put the lighter-weight Administrative Justice Forum (AJF), with a budget that rendered it incapable of being anything more than an occasional talking shop. The step from the AJTC to the AJF thus symbolised the end of 'a brief period during which administrative justice had seemingly come of age … [the] revolution has been quelled, its vision of a transformed, and transformational, future consigned to the Whitehall archives'.[8] Some suggested that

[3] See, eg AZ Huq, 'Constitutionalism, Legitimacy, and Public Order: A South African Case Study' in R Dixon and T Roux (eds), *Constitutional Triumphs, Constitutional Disappointments* (Cambridge University Press, 2017).

[4] M Adler, 'The Rise and Fall of Administrative Justice – A Cautionary Tale' (2012) 8(2) *Socio-Legal Review* 28.

[5] N O'Brien, 'Administrative Justice: A Libertarian Cinderella in Search of an Egalitarian Prince' (2012) 83 *The Political Quarterly* 494.

[6] M Adler (ed), *Administrative Justice in Context: Mapping the Terrain for Further Study* (Hart Publishing, 2010) xv–xvi.

[7] N O'Brien, 'Administrative Justice in the Wake of I, Daniel Blake' (2018) 89 *The Political Quarterly* 82. For analysis of the post-2010 landscape, see R Thomas and J Tomlinson, 'Mapping Current Issues in Administrative Justice: Austerity and the "More Bureaucratic Rationality" Approach' (2017) 39 *Journal of Social Welfare and Family Law* 380.

[8] O'Brien, 'Administrative Justice: A Libertarian Cinderella in Search of an Egalitarian Prince' (2012) 494.

the move provided 'a strong case' that a 'Leggatt-style inquiry' should consider 'the wider administrative justice environment post-AJTC'.[9] When the Ministry of Justice abolished the AJF in 2017, the narrative of the rise and fall of administrative justice, as articulated in institutional form, was seemingly complete.

While not disagreeing with the general thrust of the standard account, in this chapter we use the standard account as a springboard for further developing the existing understanding of New Labour's influence on the administrative justice system. After explaining briefly what administrative justice is and introducing the standard account, we suggest four 'subplots' to the standard account which we think require and deserve attention by public law scholars studying the New Labour period. Each of them also sheds new light on the constitutional reforms discussed elsewhere in this collection. We do not suggest our account is comprehensive and are conscious that we are speaking at a high level of generality about a complex and fragmented system. Instead, our hope is to develop the existing narrative and enhance understandings of what the New Labour years represent in the ongoing development of administrative justice.

This chapter has three main parts. First, we provide an introduction to administrative justice, particularly for those who may be less familiar with this subfield of public law. Second, we trace the standard account of the New Labour years. Finally, we set out four underexplored and important administrative justice developments from the New Labour years, with the aim of stimulating further discussion about the developments themselves and also how they relate to New Labour's constitutional legacy.

II. ADMINISTRATIVE JUSTICE

In simple terms, administrative justice, which can be understood as a subfield of public law but also engaged with a wider range of other disciplines, concerns the making of administrative decisions by public bodies.[10] It also concerns the redress systems for challenging such decisions. The Tribunals, Courts and Enforcement Act 2007 defined the administrative justice system as:

> The overall system by which decisions of an administrative or executive nature are made in relation to particular persons, including: (a) the procedures for making such decisions; (b) the law under which such decisions are made, and (c) the systems for resolving disputes and airing grievances in relation to such decisions.[11]

[9] C Skelcher, 'Reforming the Oversight of Administrative Justice 2010–2014: Does the UK Need a New Leggatt Report?' [2015] *PL* 215.

[10] J Mashaw, *Bureaucratic Justice: Managing Social Security Disability Claims* (Yale University Press, 1983).

[11] Tribunals, Courts and Enforcement Act 2007, Sch 7, para 13(4). The Schedule within which this provision was set was repealed by the Public Bodies (Abolition of Administrative Justice and Tribunals Council) Order 2013 (SI 2013/2042), Art 1(2), Sch para 36, but the statement remains the clearest legislative expression of administrative justice in the UK.

Given the fact that much of the work of governing is, in practice, exercised primarily in the administrative domain, administrative justice remains an understudied aspect of public law. The routine decisions that public officials take day-to-day and the redress options available when things go wrong shape many everyday experiences of justice in the modern state. In shaping these experiences, public law is interpreted, and indeed often made, not just by the ordinary courts, but by a wide range of interpretative communities, from tribunal judges through to frontline officials. This combined body of decision-making has a huge social and economic effect, and can be linked directly with seemingly distant themes of constitutional law, such as legitimacy and authority.

This administrative justice system is constituted of myriad processes and vast amounts of law, including different types of soft law. This makes it a complex terrain to cover at a macro level. It could be seen to be constituted of (and therefore studied as) various different processes (eg judicial review, tribunals, ombuds) or different subareas of policy-tied activities (eg social security, immigration, housing). The scale of the administrative justice system is difficult to comprehend, and what is known about how it works is, from one perspective, only a drop in the ocean. Collectively, millions of initial decisions are made by public officials each year, forging 'street-level' experience of policy.[12] If public law is made meaningful for ordinary citizens, it is largely through adherence to it when these initial decisions are taken. Yet, we have very little understanding of the role of law in these processes. There is also a growing volume of internal reviews which take place within departments such as the Department of Work and Pensions, as well as many hundreds of thousands of tribunal appeals where the decisions of departments such as the Home Office are challenged.[13]

The design of the administrative justice system is in practice under the control of multiple actors.[14] Designers include multiple government bodies – at central, local, devolved and international levels – as well as courts and other redress institutions, and their separate initiatives are often uncoordinated. Notwithstanding this complexity, parliamentary sovereignty has continued pre-eminence in the UK's constitutional order. As a result, a government with a majority in Parliament and with what one may see to be positive plans to change the administrative justice process can usually act relatively quickly and easily. Indeed, the sense of 'routine bureaucracy' around many administrative justice issues may lead to less political scrutiny being provided, with the risk of any political frustration often being low. At the same time, a government often

[12] M Lipsky, *Street Level Bureaucracy: Dilemmas of the Individual in Public Services* (Russell Sage, 1980).

[13] For a recent summary of the interaction between these systems, see R Thomas and J Tomlinson, 'A Different Tale of Judicial Power: Administrative Review as a Problematic Response to the Judicialisation of Tribunals' [2019] *PL* 537.

[14] V Bondy and A Le Sueur, *Designing Administrative Justice* (Nuffield Foundation, 2012).

wears the two hats of being 'designer' and 'player' in the administrative justice system, creating obvious tensions around the maintenance of effective and fair process.[15]

III. THE STANDARD ACCOUNT OF THE NEW LABOUR YEARS

Given the diversity of designers in control of the system and its scale, administrative justice is in constant flux. This makes it difficult, though not entirely impossible, to track or identify coherent overarching changes in the system. For those who have sought to identify the arc of the New Labour years vis-à-vis administrative justice, a 'standard account' has emerged, albeit one containing some differences of both substance and presentation, which we trace in this part of the chapter.

Michael Adler's analysis of the New Labour years, written in 2012, is the most extensive. In providing his account, Adler's particular focus is both the 'unique institution' of the AJTC and the 'successive emergence of different dominant conceptions' of administrative justice.[16] Adler starts his account of the New Labour's administrative justice 'cautionary tale'[17] by noting the constitutional backdrop: that 'a "progressive" government with a majority in the House of Commons can pass "progressive" legislation, but there is nothing to stop a "reactionary" government, as long as it has a majority in the House of Commons, from reversing it'.[18] A consequence of this constitutional framework is that dominant conceptions of administrative justice can be 'transient'.[19] It was through this constitutional framework that the AJTC was established by statute in 2007,

> with a wider and more ambitious remit than its predecessor, the Council on Tribunals (COT), to keep the administrative justice system of the United Kingdom under review and to ensure that the relationships between the courts, tribunals, ombudsmen and alternative dispute resolution mechanisms promote justice and reflect the needs of citizens.[20]

The AJTC was subsequently abolished under legislation enacted by the Coalition government to reduce the amount of non-departmental public bodies.[21]

Adler observes that, at the start of the New Labour years, administrative justice was a concept that few were familiar with in policy circles, and also in the scholarly community.[22] He contrasts this situation to the field of

[15] See, eg Thomas and Tomlinson, 'A Different Tale of Judicial Power' (2019).
[16] Adler, 'The Rise and Fall of Administrative Justice' (2012) 29.
[17] ibid 28.
[18] ibid 30.
[19] ibid 30.
[20] ibid 31.
[21] Public Bodies Act 2011.
[22] Adler (n 4) 32–33.

administrative law, which had – in the decades since its very existence was questioned by constitutional lawyers – become 'a recognised component of English (and Scots) law'.[23] This was true in both scholarship and practice. Yet the lens of administrative law, as Adler understands that term, is narrow: for him, the concept ignores 'the plethora of administrative tribunals, complaints systems and ombudsmen which very large numbers of people in the United Kingdom have occasion to use'.[24] New Labour being in government saw a change to this, with Adler specifically pointing to the publication of the UK government's White Paper *Transforming Public Services: Complaints, Redress and Tribunals* in July 2004 as a defining moment.[25] This White Paper had a whole chapter considering 'The Administrative Justice Landscape' and its recommendations were eventually enacted in the form of the Tribunals, Courts and Enforcement Act 2007. More scholarly interest emerged around the same time.[26]

Adler saw these changes – the White Paper, the creation of the AJTC and the Tribunals, Courts and Enforcement Act 2007 – as reflecting a fundamental shift in the dominant conception of administrative justice. One approach, as he conceptualises it,

> sees administrative justice in terms of the principles formulated by the superior courts and, to a lesser extent, by the top tiers of other redress mechanisms that come into play when people who are unhappy with the outcome of an administrative decision, or with the process by which that decision was reached, challenge the decision and seek to achieve a determination in their favour.[27]

A second conception of administrative justice is one

> that sees administrative justice in terms of the justice inherent in routine administrative decisions. This approach does not accept that the formulation of principles by the courts and other redress mechanisms is sufficient and emphasises the importance of efforts that aim to improve first-instance decision-making directly, such as recruitment procedures, training and appraisal, standard setting and quality assurance systems'.[28]

The former approach he characterises as 'top-down', with the latter being 'bottom-up'.[29] A third approach

> sees the merits in both of the above approaches and seeks to combine them … It sees administrative justice as something that applies to an end-to-end process that begins

[23] ibid 33.

[24] ibid 33.

[25] Department for Constitutional Affairs, *Transforming Public Services: Complaints, Redress and Tribunals* (July 2004).

[26] See, eg Adler (n 4); M Partington and M Harris (eds), *Administrative Justice in the 21st Century* (Hart Publishing, 1999).

[27] Adler calls this the 'traditional administrative law conception of administrative justice': Adler (n 4) 34.

[28] The 'justice in administration conception of administrative justice': ibid 34.

[29] ibid 34–35.

> with an administrative decision and ends, in a small minority of cases, with the decision of an ombudsman, a tribunal or a court.[30]

This approach 'places considerable importance on "feedback", i.e. on first-instance decision-makers drawing lessons from judgments made in cases that are subject to challenge'.[31]

For Adler, the New Labour years can be understood as taking the UK away from operating on the basis of an 'administrative law conception' and towards an 'integrated conception' of administrative justice. At the start, the 'administrative law' conception was dominant. Textbooks largely focused on judgments of the superior courts, and policy officials were 'relatively inactive'.[32] A small but committed group of socio-legal scholars undertook empirical studies on different aspects of the administrative justice system, but there was limited focus on frontline decision-making. With New Labour's stimulation, a new conception of administrative justice became dominant – demonstrated by how broadly the administrative justice system was defined in the Tribunals, Courts and Enforcement Act 2007.[33] This integrated definition was underpinned by an integrated vision, with the White Paper approaching administrative justice through 'the perspective of the normative expectations held by members of the public':[34]

> We are all entitled to receive correct decisions on our personal circumstances; where a mistake occurs we are entitled to complain and to have the mistake put right with the minimum of difficulty; where there is uncertainty we are entitled to a quick resolution of the issue; and we are entitled to expect that, where things have gone wrong, the system will learn from the problem and will do better in the future.[35]

There was a new policy mantra in town too: 'proportionate dispute resolution'.[36] This shift to an integrated conception of administrative justice was, for Adler, a 'most welcome change and pointed the way to a real enhancement of administrative justice for millions of people who are on the receiving end of administrative decisions'.[37]

The implementation of this 'integrated conception' of administrative justice would require a proactive state, priorities being set and administrative justice concerns being given precedence over (or at least a fighting chance next to) other operational pressure (eg cost and efficiency). Adler suggests that, to an extent, this vision was starting to be realised by New Labour administrations.

[30] Adler calls this the 'integrated conception of administrative justice': ibid 35.
[31] ibid 35.
[32] ibid 35.
[33] Tribunals, Courts and Enforcement Act 2007, Sch 7, para 13(4).
[34] Adler (n 4) 36.
[35] Department for Constitutional Affairs, *Transforming Public Services: Complaints, Redress and Tribunals* (July 2004) [1.5].
[36] ibid. See also M Adler, 'Tribunal Reform: Proportionate Dispute Resolution and the Pursuit of Administrative Justice' (2006) 69 *MLR* 958.
[37] Adler (n 4) 37.

There was an extensive review of the tribunals systems by Sir Andrew Legatt,[38] followed by transformative legislation.[39] There was the creation of the new office of the Senior President of Tribunals,[40] with oversight of a more coherent tribunals system and under a duty to 'innovate'.[41] The AJTC set about researching the administrative justice system and devising principles for public bodies to improve processes, accompanied by a set of recommendations for 'getting it right first time' in decision-making.[42] While, for Adler, this was all cause for 'optimism', the mood changed when, as part of its overall Spending Review, the new Coalition government reviewed the position of so-called 'arm's-length bodies' and ultimately abolished the AJTC. The new conception of administrative justice was effectively trampled on in the pursuit of cost-cutting and less bureaucracy. For Adler, this action weakened both 'government and civil society'.[43] The new conception of administrative justice fell too:

> [A]s far as administrative justice in the UK is concerned, it looks very much as if the rise of the pendulum set in motion by the Leggatt Report … [was followed] … by its fall. The shaft of light which fell on administrative justice is likely to be followed by its renewed eclipse by civil justice.[44]

Adler's account of the New Labour years has gone largely unchallenged and was reflected in many of the submissions to Public Administration Select Committee when the AJTC was abolished.[45] Similarly, O'Brien conceives administrative justice as a 'Cinderella' area of policy and research.[46] He, too, saw the decision to abolish the AJTC as bringing 'to an end a brief period during which administrative justice had seemingly come of age'.[47] The White Paper, for O'Brien, was, 'for the first time in more than a generation', a worthy attempt at setting out:

> [A] vision for administrative justice that aimed to give it parity with civil and family justice: it spoke ambitiously of an administrative justice 'system' that would comprise not just courts and tribunals, but ombudsmen and departmental first-instance decision makers, too; it proposed as the guiding principle for the construction of this 'system' the principle of 'proportionate dispute resolution'; and it elevated the 'user' of the system to a position of pre-eminence at the expense of judges and administrators, for whose benefit other parts of the judicial system seem so often to have been organised.[48]

[38] A Leggatt, *Tribunals for Users – One System, One Service* (2001).
[39] Tribunals, Courts and Enforcement Act 2007.
[40] Tribunals, Courts and Enforcement Act 2007, s 2.
[41] Tribunals, Courts and Enforcement Act 2007, s 2(3)(d).
[42] Administrative Justice and Tribunals Council, *Right First Time* (2011).
[43] Adler (n 4) 47.
[44] ibid 54.
[45] Public Administration Select Committee, *Future Oversight of Administrative Justice: The Proposed Abolition of the Administrative Justice and Tribunals Council* (2012).
[46] O'Brien (n 5).
[47] ibid 494.
[48] ibid 494.

This all represented 'a quiet revolution in administrative justice … With the abolition of the AJTC, that revolution has been quelled, its vision of a transformed, and transformational, future consigned to the Whitehall archives'.[49] Now, O'Brien concludes, 'Like every other Cinderella, administrative justice awaits its invitation to the ball'.[50] This narrative of rise under New Labour and fall when they left office appears to be the widely accepted story.

IV. DEVELOPING THE STANDARD ACCOUNT

There is much in the standard account with which we concur. However, with the benefit of a few extra years of observation, there is space to develop further the story of New Labour's impact on administrative justice – in other words, to add subplots to the story that the standard account offers. Some of these subplots add depth to the standard account, while some challenge aspects of the standard account. Others propose new dimensions to it. In this part of the chapter, we suggest four such possible subplots to the standard account – the introduction of the Senior President of Tribunals (SPT), the increased focus on the user, the attempts to add a layer of oversight to the administrative justice system and the devolution of the delivery of administrative justice – all of which demand further exposition and reflection by public law scholars.

A. A Senior President of Tribunals

One significant part of tribunal reform undertaken in the New Labour years which has had a lasting impact was the introduction of the SPT.[51] The SPT is a lawyer appointed by the Queen on the advice of the Lord Chancellor, who himself operates on the recommendation of the Judicial Appointments Committee. The SPT's key job is to maintain the functioning of the large tribunals judiciary and to oversee the system itself. In carrying out his mandate, the SPT is statutorily mandated to 'have regard' for the need for 'tribunals to be accessible',[52] for 'proceedings before tribunals to be fair and handled quickly and efficiently',[53] for 'members of tribunals to be experts in the subject-matter of, or the law to be applied in, cases in which they decide matters'[54] and for 'the need to develop innovative methods of resolving disputes that are of a type that may be brought before tribunals'.[55] The SPT also has the role of reflecting the views of tribunal

[49] ibid 494.
[50] ibid 500.
[51] Tribunals, Courts and Enforcement Act 2007, s2.
[52] ibid s 2(3)(a).
[53] ibid s 2(3)(b).
[54] ibid s 2(3)(c).
[55] ibid s 2(3)(d).

members to Parliament, the Lord Chancellor and government ministers. Thus far, there have only been four holders of this office: Lord Carnwath, Sir Jeremy Sullivan, Sir Ernest Ryder and Sir Keith Lindblom.

The Office of the SPT was ostensibly part of the widely discussed tribunal reforms carried out by New Labour, and the post was recommended by Sir Andrew Leggatt in his review of tribunals. The explanatory notes accompanying the legislation which brought the Office into existence explain that the 'post is intended to provide unified leadership to the tribunals judiciary'. However, the Office also fits into other attempts by New Labour to reconfigure the structures surrounding the separation of powers, judicial independence and judicial leadership.[56] From this wider constitutional perspective, the creation of the SPT's Office is not just an artefact of the tribunal system, but a critical part of a new, or at least finessed, constitutional settlement between the senior judiciary, Parliament and the executive – a settlement which also involved reformed roles for the Lord Chancellor and Lord Chief Justice. These are all reforms that have not only survived the fall of the New Labour government, but have become important tools through which subsequent administrative justice policy-making has been channelled.

The current (at the time of writing) judge's predecessor, Sir Ernest Ryder, who held the Office for a number of years, was the most publicly prominent SPT to date. This is in part because Ryder himself was a dynamic figure, open to new, evidence-based approaches to administrative justice and in search of solutions to improve access to justice. He also seemed to fit the 'administrative' and 'leadership' demands of the role particularly well, with journalist Joshua Rozenberg describing him as a 'technocrat who has several different computer systems running in his room, he is well used to managing staff and resources'. Ryder speaks to diverse audiences across the country. Through his many speeches, though designed principally to inform audiences about ongoing reforms, he sought to outline a new approach. In 2018, he set out 10 principles underpinning judicial leadership from the SPT's Office: open justice; accountability; accessible justice; democratic participation and civic engagement; diversity and inclusivity; specialism and expertise; localism; proportionality, including speed and efficiency; innovation that is evidence-based and tested; and coherent governance.[57]

Not only was Ryder a reform-minded judge, but he was in office at a time when some of the largest reforms to the tribunal system, as well as the justice system more broadly, were occurring. He, with the Lord Chancellor and the Lord Chief Justice, was one of three names signing-off on the Transforming Our Justice System policy, which paved the way for an ongoing £1 billion+ reform of the entire justice system.[58] These reforms – including court closures,

[56] See G Gee, ch 5 in this volume.

[57] Sir E Ryder, 'The Duty of Leadership in Judicial Office' (Centre for Contemporary Coronial Law, 22 October 2018).

[58] HMCTS, *Transforming Our Justice System* (2016).

high court staff reductions and a globally pioneering project to introduce technology to dispute resolution – are an attempt to modernise the entire justice system while reducing how much the government spends.[59] Within this context, Ryder oversaw many important changes to tribunals, including the introduction of 'continuous dispute resolution' and new online processes, in key jurisdictions such as social security and immigration.[60] He also had to ensure that smaller tribunal jurisdictions were not left behind. Moreover, with the reform programme coinciding with a changeover in Lord Chief Justice and with a whole string of Lord Chancellors (due to tumultuous post-Brexit referendum politics) coming and going, Ryder was the most constant figure in reform leadership. If anyone was the 'public face' of these reforms in the legal community, it was him. As part of his leadership, he proactively set up the Administrative Justice Council to promote research and discussion of the system. Designed to mirror the influential Civil Justice Council, the SPT became the first Chair, attempting to bring together practice, policy, pro bono and academic communities. It is so far proving to be more active than the Administrative Justice Forum.

As with any public office, much hinges on the approach of the office holder. It could well be the case that more sanguine, less innovative replacements follow in his wake. Yet, Ryder has demonstrated the dynamic potential of the Office of the SPT to exercise real and influential leadership over administrative justice, as well as the wider justice system. The SPT's Office is proving to be one of the most important legacies of New Labour's institutional reforms around administrative justice and is now a key constitutional player. Despite this, the role of the SPT remains far more marginal in public law thought than the reforms carried out under the Constitutional Reform Act 2005.

B. The Rise and Rise of the 'User-Focused' Administrative Justice System

One trend which was made prominent during the New Labour years, and is a key part of the standard account, was further focus on 'users' in administrative justice (ie the citizen, as well as others who use decision-making and redress processes). From one perspective, this was New Labour carrying on the focus on 'customer service' which was inculcated by New Public Management and market-inspired approaches to governance that came to prominence in

[59] J Tomlinson, *Justice in the Digital State* (Bristol University Press, 2019) ch 3; J Rozenberg, *The Online Court: Will IT Work?* (Legal Education Foundation, 2017); H Genn, 'Online Courts and the Future of Justice' (The Birkenhead Lecture, Gray's Inn, 2017).

[60] J Tomlinson and B Karemba, 'Tribunal Justice, Brexit, and Digitalisation: Immigration Appeals in the First-tier Tribunal' (2019) 33 *Journal of Immigration, Asylum & Nationality Law* 47; J Tomlinson and R Thomas, 'Remodelling Social Security Appeals (Again): The Advent of Online Tribunals' (2018) 25 *Journal of Social Security Law* 84.

the 1980s.[61] Arguably, the standout early moment for the recognition of the user-perspective was John Major's Citizens' Charter initiative in 1991,[62] when it was briefly heralded as 'becoming part of both a philosophy of government and a means of government'.[63] By the time New Labour came to power, the Citizens' Charter had largely faded from all official language, to be replaced by the brand 'Service First', but the underlying philosophy of being user-focused remained a big part of New Labour's approach to public administration and its modernisation agenda.[64] The policy language deployed by New Labour may have been less market-orientated, but it effectively took the idea of user-focus from the Charter and ran with it.

Multiple policy initiatives evidence New Labour's continuation of the same underlying consumer-driven premises of the Major government that preceded it. For instance, it was visible in the 'choice agenda' that Blair's government pushed in schools and the health sector,[65] the basing of public provider targets on user-based metrics[66] and the introduction of the NHS Constitution.[67] This ethos was advanced in particular administrative justice reforms too. For instance, in his landmark report on tribunals, Leggatt suggested the need for a tribunal system that was centred on empowering the user:

> It should never be forgotten that tribunals exist for users, and not the other way round. No matter how good tribunals may be, they do not fulfil their function unless they are accessible by the people who want to use them, and unless the users receive the help they need to prepare and present their cases.[68]

Similarly, the 2004 White Paper *Transforming Public Services* sought to set out a vision of a user-focused administrative justice system.

Rather than falling away after New Labour left office, the emphasis on designing justice systems for users has, if anything, increased. The important Transforming Our Justice System proposals, discussed above, directly explained that new online tribunals should be 'specifically designed to meet user needs' and be 'focused around the needs of individuals so that claimants can be more confident that their needs will be understood'. On top of this, the user-focused approach to administrative justice has now found a new method of design to accompany it – so-called 'agile' design – which uses techniques premised

[61] See generally C Pollitt, *Managerialism and the Public Services*, 2nd edn (Blackwell, 1993); P Dunleavy and C Hood, 'From Old Public Administration to New Public Management' (1994) 14(3) *Public Money & Management* 9.

[62] Cabinet Office, *The Citizen's Charter: Raising the Standard* (Cm 1599, 1991).

[63] N Lewis, 'The Citizens' Charter and New Steps: A New Way of Governing' [1993] *The Political Quarterly* 316.

[64] Cabinet Office, *Modernising Government* (Cm 4310, 1999).

[65] J Clarke, J Newman and M McDermont, 'Delivering Choice and Administrative Justice: Contested Logics of Public Services' in Adler, *Administrative Justice in Context* (2010).

[66] I Lapsey and J Lonsdale, 'The Audit Society: Helping to Develop or Undermine' in Adler (n 6).

[67] NHS England, *The NHS Constitution: The NHS Belongs to Us All* (2009).

[68] Leggatt (n 38).

on the user being central.[69] There is no precise definition of the agile method. However, the core of the approach appears to rest on emphasising the perspective of 'users' of systems, developing prototype systems and consistently testing systems with users.[70] These core tenets are commonly expressed in the five-part, non-linear design method of: empathising with users; defining the problem; ideating; prototyping; and testing.[71] Within this framework, multiple tools to support each of these exercises have also been developed.[72] For instance, the use of 'journey mapping' tools are increasingly common in the design of administrative justice system. These tools help system designers trying to understand how users come to use a service and what they experience at each step of the process. The agile approach has been influential in many sectors, including architecture, business and management.[73] It has been particularly prominent in technology circles, and in UK government the approach has been most prominently pushed by technologists in government, including the influential Government Digital Service. Academic research trends in administrative justice have now also turned towards emphasising the importance of engaging with users and their viewpoints.[74]

It would be wrong to think, however, that the connecting thread between the New Labour years and the subsequent and previous administrations is straightforward. There appears to be different conceptions of this movement towards 'user focus' operating beneath the surface.[75] This was particularly evident in the recent UK Supreme Court decision in *UNISON*, which appeared to offer

[69] Tomlinson, *Justice in the Digital State* (2019) ch 4. On this approach generally, see L Kimbell, 'Rethinking Design Thinking: Part 1' (2012) 3 *Design and Culture* 285; L Kimbell, 'Rethinking Design Thinking: Part II' (2012) 4 *Design and Culture* 129. See also K Dorst, 'The Core of "Design Thinking" and Its Application' (2011) 32 *Design Studies* 521; R Buchanan, 'Wicked Problems in Design Thinking' (1992) 8(2) *Design Issues* 5.

[70] H Plattner, C Meinel and L Leifer (eds), *Design Thinking* (Springer, 2011) 14–15.

[71] These stages have been expressed in various ways, see eg M Hagan, *Law by Design* (2017) (ebook).

[72] R Alves and NJ Nunes, 'Towards a Taxonomy of Service Design Methods and Tools' in JF e Cunha, M Snene and H Sampaio da Nóvoa (eds), *Exploring Services Science*, LNBIP 143 (Springer, 2013).

[73] See, eg FP Brooks Jr, *The Design of Design: Essays from a Computer Scientist* (Addison-Wesley, 2010); RL Martin, *Design of Business: Why Design Thinking is the Next Competitive Advantage* (Harvard Business School Press, 2009).

[74] See, eg UK Administrative Justice Institute, *Research Roadmap: Where Have We Been and Where Do We Need To Go with Research on Administrative Justice?* (2017). For a recent example, see C Gill and N Creutzfeldt, 'The "Ombuds Watchers": Collective Dissent and Legal Protest among Users of Public Services Ombuds' (2018) 27 *Social and Legal Studies* 367. For further examples, see H Genn, 'Tribunals for Diverse Users' (Department for Constitutional Affairs, 2006); G McKeever and B Thompson, *Redressing Users' Disadvantage* (Nuffield Foundation, 2010). This research has also gone beyond administrative justice to other areas of the justice system: see, eg H Genn, *Paths to Justice: What People Do and Think About Going to Law* (Hart Publishing, 1999); A Barlow, R Hunter, J Smithson and J Ewing, *Mapping Paths to Family Justice: Resolving Family Disputes in Neoliberal Times* (Palgrave Macmillan, 2018).

[75] J Tomlinson, 'The Grammar of Administrative Justice Values' (2017) 39 *Journal of Social Welfare and Family Law* 524.

a critique of focusing on users.[76] Lord Reed, in striking down a tribunal fee on access to justice grounds, stated that:

> The importance of the rule of law is not always understood. Indications of a lack of understanding include the assumption that the administration of justice is merely a public service like any other, that courts and tribunals are providers of services to the 'users' who appear before them, and that the provision of those services is of value only to the users themselves and to those who are remunerated for their participation in the proceedings. The extent to which that viewpoint has gained currency in recent times is apparent from the consultation papers and reports discussed earlier. It is epitomised in the assumption that the consumption of [tribunal] services without full cost recovery results in a loss to society, since '[tribunal] use does not lead to gains to society that exceed the sum of the gains to consumers and producers of these services'.[77]

In contemporary administrative justice policy discussions and commentary, finding similar criticism of the phrase 'user' is not difficult, despite the fact that having user-friendly justice processes is widely seen as a universal good. Therefore, although government of different political orientations now seems ready to maintain a commitment to user-focused public services, the nature of that commitment – as manifest in the patterns of thought, texts and actions of designers of the administrative justice system – appears to be subtly shifting. What the New Labour years represent in the overarching story of 'user-focus' is therefore more ambiguous than it may seem.

C. The Oversight Cycle

As noted above, the standard account has it that New Labour brought to the field of administrative justice a fresh strategic approach which included an independent statutory advisory body that could oversee and offer critical advice on how to enhance coordination, not just of tribunals, but of the sector as a whole.[78] In aspiration, this was potentially a major step forward as, for the first time, independent of Parliament and the executive, there was a standing body with sufficient resources, expertise and reputation that was capable of offering continuous reflection on the government's delivery of its administrative justice obligations. To perform this role, the AJTC was made up of a specialised body of relevant professionals, with practitioner or academic experience. The body was staffed by permanent civil service posts and had sufficient budget to commission research and produce reports.[79] In something of a

[76] *R (UNISON) v Lord Chancellor* [2017] UKSC 51.

[77] ibid [66]. For context, see A Adams and J Prassl, 'Vexatious Claims: Challenging the Case for Employment Tribunal Fees' (2017) 80 *MLR* 412.

[78] The AJTC replaced the Council on Tribunals, which was first introduced by the Tribunals and Inquiries Act 1958, s 1.

[79] On budget, see the annual reports of the AJTC, eg Administrative Justice and Tribunals Council, *Annual Report 2007/08* (HC 2008/09, SG/2008/132) 36.

bipartisan coup for New Labour, the first Chair of the AJTC was Lord Newton, a senior Conservative politician with a long-standing interest in administrative justice issues from his time as Health and Social Security Minister. He was replaced in 2009 by Richard Thomas, a public lawyer and former Information Commissioner. The introduction of this body was, according to the standard account, a serious public policy signal in the direction of bringing the profile of the administrative justice system into line with the civil and criminal justice systems. However, two important qualifications need to be made to the 'rise and fall' narrative of the standard account: the lack of evidence that the AJTC ever fulfilled its worthy aspirations; and the subsequent cyclical process of oversight which suggests that the 'fall' has not been so straightforward.

On the first qualification, through no fault of its own, the AJTC was never allowed the opportunity to grow into the institution that it was designed to be. In its brief life, we suggest that the AJTC operated through three short phases. First was an 'establishment phase', during which the AJTC landscaped the terrain. Amongst other things, this phase produced a report that provided insight into hitherto undermapped areas of the administrative justice system.[80] Second, there was an 'action phase', which involved the AJTC identifying issues for special attention, providing guidance and disseminating information and proposals through reports, quarterly newsletters, an annual conference and general lobbying activities. Notable reports included *Administrative Justice Principles* (2009); *Right First Time* (2011); *Patients' Experiences of the First-Tier Tribunal* (Mental Health) (2011); *Securing Fairness and Redress: Administrative Justice at Risk?* (2011); *Putting It Right (Proportionate Dispute Resolution)* (2012); and *Guidance on Schools Admissions and Exclusions Appeals* (2012). This phase represented the beginnings of a role that might have made a difference in the long term, if such studies could have been used as vehicles to influence public policy based on a detailed evidence base. Indeed, the AJTC was beginning to organise itself as a body capable of demonstrating a clear voice[81] and helped to raise the profile of important issues.[82] However, this period of activity was too short to evidence lasting impact.

By 2008, the New Labour government had been forced to refocus its energies due to the global economic crisis. By 2010, a new Coalition government had been formed, with a goal of reducing the number of public bodies in operation. Tellingly, during the parliamentary debates on the AJTC's abolition, little concrete evidence could be presented of its impact, though there were strong defences.[83] This is not a critique of the members of the body, but a simple

[80] eg Administrative Justice and Tribunals Council, *The Developing Administrative Justice Landscape* (2009).

[81] See, eg Administrative Justice and Tribunals Council, *Annual Report 2011–12* (HC 2012/13, SG/2013/18).

[82] See, eg R Smith, 'Beyond Satirical Debate?' *New Law Journal* (13 February 2009).

[83] Justice Committee, *Scrutiny of the Draft Public Bodies (Abolition of Administrative Justice and Tribunals Council) Order 2013* (2012/13, HC 965).

consequence of the brevity of its existence and its lack of opportunity to make a difference. A final 'closure phase' of the AJTC, therefore, was largely spent fighting its abolition and securing a legacy arrangement for its services,[84] but the battle was finally lost on 19 August 2013.[85] A sister advisory council lasted slightly longer in Wales (the Committee for Administrative Justice and Tribunals, Wales (March 2016)),[86] as did an interim Scottish Tribunals and Administrative Justice Advisory Council, before it too was disbanded in November 2015. The AJTC was a low-cost outfit and the financial benefit gained from abolition was small, but the value of the policy being pursued was seen as sufficient to justify the decision.[87] In any event, there was little evidence that the Coalition government was going to be heavily influenced by its work. The AJTC, therefore, might have appeared to its advocates as a bold step forward, but it never got up to full speed, still less did it get close to becoming settled as a quasi-permanent fixture of the constitutional architecture. In such circumstances, it would seem unwise to rest too much of any evaluation of New Labour's impact on administrative justice on the AJTC's contribution.

Likewise, care should be taken not to claim too much about New Labour's approach to administrative justice as being more systematic than any predecessor government. Save for the review of the tribunal service in the 2004 White Paper and the aspiration of the AJTC,[88] the links between the different components of the administrative justice system were often as uncoordinated during the New Labour era as any other, with the complaints sector, for instance, overseen through a range of different government departments and multiple ombudsman schemes.[89] Where there were attempts at widespread systematic reform, such as of the ombudsman sector[90] or the introduction of public law monetary remedies,[91] they did not always go very far.

A more positive narrative, however, could perhaps be drawn from the lasting, albeit subtler, impact that the idea of the AJTC has had on the sector. Certainly, the goal laid out in Sir Andrew Leggatt's original proposal, within which an advisory council would become the 'hub of the wheel of administrative justice',

[84] See, eg Administrative Justice and Tribunals Council, *Research Agenda* (2013).

[85] The Scottish and Welsh Committees for Administrative Justice and Tribunals were abolished at the same time, see The Public Bodies (Abolition of Administrative Justice and Tribunals Council) Order 2013.

[86] C Jones, 'Written Statement – Publication of the Legacy Report of the Committee for Administrative Justice and Tribunals, Wales and the Welsh Government's Response' (1 August 2016).

[87] Ministry of Justice, *Response to Consultation on Reforms Proposed in the Public Bodies Bill* (Cm 825, 2011).

[88] Department for Constitutional Affairs, *Transforming Public Services: Complaints, Redress and Tribunals* (Cm 6243, 2004).

[89] For a critique of the complaints system overseen by New Labour, see P Dunleavey, S Bastow, J Tinkler, S Goldchluk and E Towers, 'Joining Up Citizen Redress in UK Central Government' in Adler (n 6).

[90] Cabinet Office, *Review of the Public Sector Ombudsmen in England* (April 2000).

[91] Law Commission, *Administrative Redress: Public Bodies and the Citizen* (Law Com 322, 2010).

was a long way from being realised.[92] However, notwithstanding the clear loss for those advocating independent administrative justice scrutiny, the idea that administrative justice should be seen as a coherent field of policy which would be better coordinated has not evaporated from public policy. The Ministry of Justice, for instance, still organises its work around administrative justice being a distinct policy area. As for the demand for independent oversight of the administrative justice system, this remains strong and has resurfaced on multiple occasions.

Since 2012, there has been an almost cyclical pattern in which successive efforts have been made to acknowledge the oversight needs of the administrative justice system. Initially, the Ministry of Justice committed to retain a government-sponsored advisory service, by establishing an Administrative Justice Forum (AJF), an advisory group composed of stakeholders with an interest in the tribunal system which met twice a year. The AJF was chaired and managed by the Ministry of Justice and lacked any realistic ability to develop a collegiate identity. Nor did it possess its own website or ability to generate research, and as a result left little footprint before being abolished in March 2017. Its budget was pocket change in government spending terms. As had been widely anticipated, the AJF's existence was little more than a cosmetic exercise.

The charitable and academic sectors have subsequently intervened. In 2014, the Nuffield Foundation awarded the University of Essex a grant to fund the establishment of the UK Administrative Justice Institute (UKAJI), a research-focused enterprise which had a remit to 'kickstart the expansion of empirical research on administrative justice in the UK'.[93] UKAJI has built up an extensive database of up-to-date knowledge and commentary on the administrative justice system, and remains a platform for debate. This initiative has been followed by the establishment of the Administrative Justice Council (AJC), supported by the charity JUSTICE, an organisation with a long-standing interest in administrative justice affairs. Currently, it also has support from the Ministry of Justice. The aspiration of the AJC is different to UKAJI, describing itself as the successor body to the AJF. Chaired from the beginning by Sir Ernest Ryder, now the former Senior President of Tribunals, and made up of a wide cross-section of relevant stakeholders, it is akin to the Civil Justice Council. It has been very active in its short lifespan so far. The potential capacity and longevity of the AJC should not, however, be overestimated. Its long-term funding is uncertain and its work is reliant on a large amount of pro bono and voluntary contributions. Without formal power, its capacity to effect change may be limited. Even so, the initiative illustrates the lasting power of the AJTC idea.

Within our constitutional order, an oversight body is permanently vulnerable to the politics of the day and any short-term objectives. Added to this, there is a

[92] A Leggatt, *Tribunals for Users, One System One Service: Report on the Review of Tribunals* (2001) [7.45]–[7.51].

[93] See UKAJI's website, https://ukaji.org/about/.

clear and powerful incentive for government to prefer to regulate its own decision-making internally. This incentive will always be likely to rankle with accepting the need for independent oversight.[94] Nor can it be safely presumed that a future government of the left would be any more interested in replacing the AJTC than governments of a right-leaning disposition. Not only did the Coalition government, partially formed of Liberal Democrats, reject the idea that independent oversight of the sector was a priority, but once austerity provided a cost-based rationale for abolition, the Scottish and Welsh governments also rejected the model despite being made up of parties of very different political persuasions. The 2015 discontinuation of an equivalent governmental body in Australia, the Administrative Review Council, a body with a 40-year history, provides another example of the challenges of sustaining political support in this context.[95] There are thus complex lessons to be learnt about general-level administrative justice oversight from the New Labour years. Yes, there was a 'fall', as Adler characterises it. However, the reasons for this are perhaps not as straightforward as just changing governments with new politics.

D. Devolution of Administrative Justice

Of all the themes that could be explored around New Labour's contribution to administrative justice, perhaps the most influential area of activity in the long term is devolution. The shift during the New Labour period of office towards separate, territorially distinct spheres of policy and implementation represented a concrete and lasting institutional change. Many of the areas of policy devolved involve key parts of the administrative justice system, and the result has been an incremental movement towards a different approach to administrative justice in the devolved nations. If anything, this institutional difference has become more pronounced since the New Labour years came to an end than during them. Three areas of difference illustrate this growing divergence.

First, there is now an organisational difference towards administrative justice under devolution. An early distinctiveness that occurred on devolution was the settling of the perennial debate about how best to organise ombudsman offices.[96] Rather than splitting different functions between multiple specialised offices, in the devolved nations the trend was towards integrating functions into a single office with the aim of reducing the complexity of the system. A key part of the acceptance of the single-ombudsman model had to do with the difference in scale involved, a devolution factor that also lay behind the Crerar

[94] Skelcher, 'Reforming the Oversight of Administrative Justice 2010–2014' (2015) 223.

[95] Minister for Finance, 'Smaller Government – Transforming the Public Sector', media release, May 2015.

[96] Scottish Public Services Ombudsman Act 2002; Public Services Ombudsman (Wales) Act 2005.

Review in Scotland.[97] The Crerar Review examined the structure and distribution of public bodies across a broad spectrum of public sector regulation and governance, and recommended a wholesale restructuring and merging of institutions. For administrative justice, an important organisational difference that was emphasised by the Crerar Review process was a perceived need to interlink administrative justice scrutiny agents more firmly with legislators. In Scotland, a series of bodies were set up as Commissioners and made directly accountable to Parliament, not the executive. A similar set-up is developing in Wales, with the embedding of the Commissioner network within the Senedd's sphere of influence also being proposed, albeit as yet not followed through.[98]

The Welsh example illustrates a second potential distinct outcome of devolution: a cultural difference in approach towards administrative justice.[99] In Wales, a sympathetic approach towards broader administrative justice values has evolved through a willingness to recognise those values institutionally.[100] Thus, the investigative and guidance roles of the Language Commissioner, Future Generations Commissioner and Older People's Commissioner are distinct to Wales, and sit alongside institutions such as the Children's Commissioner, the Equalities and Human Rights Commission and ombudsman that exist elsewhere in the UK.[101] The impact and efficiency of such institutional solutions will always require ongoing evaluation, but their introduction is indicative of a distinct statement of intent to integrate into the Welsh administrative justice system a firm commitment towards such issues as language rights, environmental protection and the safeguarding of vulnerable sections of society. Further evidence of Welsh distinctiveness can be seen in the moves in recent years towards constructing a separate legal and tribunal jurisdiction for Wales.[102] Local researchers have also observed that, contrary to the individualistic and user-focused cultural bias that dominates in Whitehall, in Wales a more egalitarian cultural bias is evident, one which is 'driven [more] by accountability and dialogue'[103] than by marketisation.

Another example of cultural difference that has been encouraged by devolution comes from Northern Ireland. In Northern Ireland, human rights legislation

[97] L Crerar, *Report of the Independent Review of Regulation, Audit, Inspection and Complaints Handling of Public Services in Scotland* (Scottish Government, 2007).

[98] The Shooter Report, *An Independent Review of the Role and Functions of the Children's Commissioner for Wales* (Government of Wales, 2016) 45.

[99] On cultural bias and administrative justice, see S Halliday and C Scott, 'A Cultural Analysis of Administrative Justice' in Adler (n 6).

[100] S Nason, 'Administrative Justice in Wales: A New Egalitarianism?' (2017) 39 *Journal of Social Welfare and Family Law* 115.

[101] A Sherlock, J Williams and E Royles, 'A Welsh Model of Commissioners' (2015) 45 *Cambrian Law Review* 74.

[102] See S Nason, 'Understanding Administrative Justice in Wales' (Bangor University, 2015); D Gardner, *Administrative Law and the Administrative Court in Wales* (University of Wales Press, 2016); Law Commission, *Form and Accessibility of the Law Applicable in Wales* (Law Com 366, 2016).

[103] P Williams, *Commission on Public Service Governance and Delivery* (2014).

is not seen purely as a reserve mechanism for the purpose of protecting individual rights, but has become engrained in the methods of accountability agents seeking to promote good administration. For instance, through a partnership between the Northern Ireland Human Rights Commission and the Northern Ireland Ombudsman, guidance has been produced on good administration which positively promotes the human rights connection.[104] By way of contrast, none of the other UK-based ombudsman schemes use human rights concepts in their work to any great degree.

A third difference in administrative justice that has flowed from devolution has been a degree of *legislative* willingness to engage in reform in all three devolved nations to a degree only intermittently apparent in Whitehall and Westminster. Thus, whereas in the UK and English jurisdictions the public services ombudsman sector has struggled to obtain scraps of legislative amendment through both the New Labour and later Conservative periods of government,[105] in the devolved nations bold reforming legislation has been passed.[106] Partly this has come about through the powers of select committees in the devolved chambers to promote legislation,[107] and may well be a facet of the lighter burden carried by lawmakers in devolved bodies. But the outcome also potentially demonstrates a greater executive willingness in the devolved nations to experiment in forms of autonomous administrative justice oversight than in Whitehall. The Welfare Funds (Scotland) Act 2015 is an example of such innovation. This Act made the Scottish Public Services Ombudsman responsible for reviewing welfare fund decisions made by local authorities, a service normally considered to belong in the tribunal system. Further, the Public Services Reform (Scotland) Act 2010 established the Scottish Public Services Ombudsman as a complaint standards authority, a function normally retained in the regulatory sector, if provided at all. Meanwhile, in Northern Ireland, not only has the integrated approach towards ombudsmanry been expanded across most of the public sector, but the complaint standards authority model has been borrowed from Scotland, demonstrating the learning potential inherent in the devolution enterprise as multiple platforms for experimentation are created. Similarly, the Northern Ireland Ombudsman was the first to be granted a power to launch

[104] Northern Ireland Public Service Ombudsman and Northern Ireland Human Rights Commission, *Human Rights Manual* (2016).

[105] Examples include The Regulatory Reform (Collaboration etc between Ombudsmen) Order 2007 and the Local Government and Public Involvement in Health Act 2007.

[106] See, eg the Public Services Ombudsman (Northern Ireland) Act 2016 and the Public Services Ombudsman (Wales) Act 2019.

[107] The Public Services Ombudsman (Northern Ireland) Act 2016 was piloted through the Assembly by the Committee for the Office of the First Minister and deputy First Minister as a non-executive Bill. Likewise, in Wales it was the Finance Committee that introduced the Public Services Ombudsman Bill, and the Equality, Local Government and Communities Committee that piloted the Bill through the Assembly.

inquiries into administrative practice even in the absence of a complaint, again a practice that has been previously rejected in the UK on the basis that it crosses over into a regulatory function.[108] In Wales, additional legislative ombudsman reform has recently been passed mirroring developments in Northern Ireland, and in Scotland the ombudsman has been given a new role as the Independent National Whistleblowing Officer for the NHS.[109] All these developments stand in stark contrast to the glacial response to ombudsman reform in Whitehall, where a relatively timid effort at legislative reform pushed by various branches of government has regularly run into the sand due to a combination of institutional resistance and the challenge of finding legislative time.[110] What has possibly evolved in the ombudsman sector, therefore, is an example of the experimental potential in devolution.

Constitutional lawyers have been wrestling with the implications of devolution during the New Labour years and afterwards. The new territorial constitution and the public law tangles it has wrought are underpinned by rapid developments in devolved administrative justice. At the present time, it is clear this is by far the most significant New Labour administrative justice reform. We are only just beginning to understand the implications, both within devolved administration and at a UK-wide level.

V. CONCLUSION

This chapter has sought to add layers to the standard account of New Labour's administrative justice legacy, including by challenging some aspects of it, adding depth and suggesting new dimensions. Overall, the analysis presented here suggests we should be more positive about New Labour's contribution to administrative justice than some of the earlier commentaries on the subject imply. Ten years on, we cannot ignore the dramatic scale of change to administrative justice imposed by governments that have followed. However, if we focus on certain institutional structures of the New Labour administrative justice system and certain policies that have been implemented, we can see that New Labour did have a lasting and significant influence on the way that administrative justice has evolved. In one area examined here in particular, devolution, the legacy looks set to be one of radical and long-lasting institutional change. Soft influences, such as a continued drive for user-friendly processes and system-level oversight,

[108] Cabinet Office, *A Public Service Ombudsman: Government Response to Consultation* (December 2015) 17–18.

[109] The Public Services Reform Scottish Public Services Ombudsman (Healthcare Whistleblowing) Order 2020.

[110] For the latest example, see Cabinet Office, *Draft Public Services Ombudsman Bill 2016* (Cm 9734, 2016).

also maintain traction. Other examples of the lasting influence of New Labour on administrative justice not considered here (but considered elsewhere in this book) also form important parts of the same legacy, such as the enactment of the Freedom of Information Act 2000 and the Human Rights Act 1998. This is an important and influential legacy. It deserves further consideration by public law scholars as much as the constitutional legacy of New Labour, of which it is also a critical part.

14

Referendums and New Labour's Constitutional Reforms

LEAH TRUEBLOOD

I. INTRODUCTION

NEW LABOUR'S USE of referendums was a microcosm of their project of constitutional reform as a whole: radical in some ways and conservative in others, piecemeal, plausible in theory, but with serious unintended consequences. With their 1997 manifesto, New Labour was offering a marked approach with the past.[1] Referendums were central to key New Labour reforms such as devolution and European integration; they played both political and legal roles in helping to achieve these reforms. It was not only New Labour's decisions to hold referendums that were important, their decisions not to hold referendums were crucial too. Their decision not to hold a referendum on the Lisbon Treaty, despite promising to do so,[2] was as important for the current status of referendums in the UK as any decision about referendums they did take. This decision was crucial because it helped lay the foundation for the referendum on EU membership in 2016, one of the most significant post-war events in the UK. This chapter will argue that New Labour's legacy on referendums is principally that of compounding confusion. The status of referendums in the UK's constitutional arrangements was confused before New Labour, but the piecemeal approach taken by New Labour exacerbated this. Some piecemeal evolution may be inevitable in an uncodified constitution. Nevertheless, New Labour's actions both politically and through legislation were not consistent enough to provide clarity about the role of referendums in the UK. The use of referendums by New Labour gave rise to some elements of a constitutional

[1] 'Why for instance did the Labour Party change its name to "New Labour?" According to one of its key advisors, "Blair knew that only by contrasting new Labour with old labour explicitly would the electorate believe that Labour had changed and could be trusted"': N Fairclough, *New Labour, New Language?* (Routledge, 2000) vii.

[2] J-C Piris, *The Lisbon Treaty: A Legal and Political Analysis* (Cambridge University Press, 2010) 50.

convention that referendums are required for certain types of constitutional change. The difficulty is that while New Labour's actions created at least some elements of a constitutional convention, their actions were not consistent enough to determine what the content of that convention was. Put differently: New Labour's decisions created a situation where referendums were arguably required politically for some constitutional changes, and required legally for others, without clarifying *how* referendums should be used either legally or politically. The problem with this approach is that not all uses of referendums are the same, and they are not all created equal. By reintroducing referendums after a hiatus since the 1970s, and then neither through consistent action nor overarching legislation clarifying how referendums should be used, New Labour must bear some responsibility for the failures of the unprincipled use of referendums in the UK today: including the Brexit referendum.

This chapter falls into three parts. It first explains the role of referendums before New Labour and the tensions underlying their use in the UK. It then shows how New Labour used referendums, before turning to why the New Labour approach compounded confusion. It considers in particular the question of whether New Labour's approach to referendums gave rise to at least some of the elements of a constitutional convention. The third and final section explains the use of referendums post-New Labour and shows how decisions of that era shape the unprincipled use of referendums today.

II. REFERENDUMS BEFORE NEW LABOUR

Debates about the proper role of referendums in the process of constitutional change long preceded New Labour. As Bogdanor explains, the debate about the role of referendums goes back to the Great Reform Acts and the question of how democracy would work in the wake of universal suffrage. Bogdanor says the question was: how were the 'people' – the newly enfranchised electorate – to exercise their power: solely through representative institutions or through the machinery of direct democracy?[3] While the possibility of referendums was entertained on issues such as membership of the League of Nations, women's suffrage and tariff reform,[4] the use of referendums only began in earnest in the 1970s.[5] A referendum was held in 1973 in Northern Ireland, where the electorate (or those who did not boycott the process[6]) voted to remain part of the UK. The first UK-wide referendum in 1975 endorsed continued membership of the

[3] V Bogdanor, *The People and the Party System* (Cambridge University Press, 1981) 11.

[4] ibid 33–35.

[5] 'Although there was prior experience, such as the Scottish referendum on prohibition in 1920 … and local polls in Wales on the Sunday opening of pubs during the 1960s … the modern history of referendums in the UK begin(s) in 1973': House of Lords Constitution Committee, *Referendums in the United Kingdom*,12th Report of Session 2009–10, 7.

[6] 'Turnout for "no" was 1.1% (the poll was subject to a widespread boycott by the Nationalist community)': ibid 9.

European Economic Community (EEC). Referendums were also held concerning devolution in Wales and Scotland in 1979,[7] and these proposals were rejected.[8]

The three uses of referendums in the UK in the 1970s had a unifying logic. The issues at stake – secession, European integration and devolution – fall into a similar category. The outlines of a set of constitutional changes that required referendums were beginning to come into focus. All of these questions would eventually be classified by the House of Lords Constitution Committee as 'fundamental constitutional issues', although the Committee was reticent enumerate that list exhaustively. The Committee said:

> We do not believe that it is possible to provide a precise definition of what constitutes a 'fundamental constitutional issue'. Nonetheless, we would consider to fall within this definition any proposals: To abolish the Monarchy; To leave the European Union; For any of the nations of the UK to secede from the Union; To abolish either House of Parliament; To change the electoral system for the House of Commons; To adopt a written constitution; and to change the UK's system of currency. This is not a definitive list of fundamental constitutional issues, nor is it intended to be.[9]

Articulating the underlying logic to this category is deceptively difficult. The Committee considered a wide range of suggestions[10] of what questions should be put to a referendum, including: 'if the structure and rules of politics are to be changed',[11] the 'highest issues of constitutional principle'[12] and those changes that make 'significant, encompassing, and lasting change in the formal and general rules and rights which locate political authority'.[13] The bottom line is that it is difficult to draw sharp lines around the category of 'fundamental constitutional issue', but after the 1970s some clear-cut cases were beginning to emerge.

The difficulty is that while the three referendums in the 1970s considered similar types of constitutional questions, the forms of the referendum questions were very different. This is important because the structure of referendum questions is illustrative of what role a referendum is taken to be playing in the process of constitutional change. The three referendum questions suggest very different approaches to referendums in the UK. The 1973 referendum asked a question about the status quo;[14] the 1975 question was put at the end of a renegotiation;[15] and the 1979 referendum put forward a series of proposals

[7] 'Devolution did not proceed as the threshold requirement that not less than 40 per cent of the total electorate had to vote "yes" for devolution was not met – only 32.8 per cent voted "yes"': ibid. 6.

[8] For an overview of the questions put, and turnout in, referendums in the UK, see ibid 9–10.

[9] ibid 93.

[10] A summary of the proposals may be found at ibid 23.

[11] Memorandum by Peter Browning, ibid 133.

[12] Memorandum by Stephen Tierney, ibid 49.

[13] Memorandum by Michael Saward, ibid 15.

[14] 'Do you want Northern Ireland to remain part of the United Kingdom? Or Do you want Northern Ireland to be joined with the Republic of Ireland outside the United Kingdom?'

[15] 'Do you think that the United Kingdom should stay in the European Community (the Common Market)?'

for reform.[16] The academic literature on referendums outlines different taxonomies to carve up and label these different types of referendum questions.[17] A familiar distinction in these taxonomies is: are referendums devices of veto or are they devices of popular initiative? Put differently, should referendums initiate or conclude processes of constitutional change? This can be seen most clearly in the contrast between the referendums in 1973 and 1979. The former was an open-ended question about the status quo. The latter performed an approval function for fully developed proposals. The 1975 referendum sits uncomfortably between these types of referendums because voters were being asked to affirm membership of ECC, not to enter into it. The renegotiated settlement with the EU was also central to the referendum,[18] and some voters saw themselves as approving those reforms whereas other voters understood the point of the referendum to be something else entirely.[19] This distinction between referendums as beginning and concluding processes of constitutional change is of paramount importance. The distinction is important both practically and normatively, and the practical and normative implications of this distinction are connected. The distinction matters practically because not all uses of referendums are created equal. There are some roles that referendums are better placed to achieve than others. Referendums work better when used post-legislatively because greater clarity is provided to voters about what they are voting on, to legislators about what voters' preferences are and to the executive about how to execute proposals for reforms. UCL's 2018 Independent Commission on Referendums (ICR) offers a five-part rationale for post-legislative referendums. Post-legislative referendums offer (i) a closer connection between votes and the outcomes of those votes, (ii) clarity for elected representatives and (iii) higher feasibility of proposals put to a vote; (iv) the pre-legislative process may raise public awareness; and (v) civil servants can prepare for outcomes.[20] In making a case for post-legislative rather than pre-legislative referendums, I argued to the ICR:

> Votes in referendums are very well placed to tell us what voters do not want. Given the variety of views that voters have when they vote, referendums are not well placed to articulate what voters do want out of a proposal for constitutional reform.

[16] 'Do you want the provisions of the Scotland/Wales Act 1978 to be put into effect?'

[17] Gallager and Uleri, for instance, call this the difference between law-initiating and law-controlling referendums. M Gallager and P Uleri, *The Referendum Experience in Europe* (Macmillan, 1996) 4. The UK's Independent Commission on Referendums makes the same point through the labels pre- and post-legislative referendums: *Report of the Independent Commission on Referendums* (Constitution Unit, 2018) www.ucl.ac.uk/constitution-unit/publications/tabs/unit-publications/182_-_Independent_Commission_on_Referendums.

[18] In making a case for EEC membership, for instance, the government argued 'The other members of the European Community want us to stay in. That is why they have been flexible in the recent re-negotiations and so made possible the improved terms which have converted many former doubters': V Miller, 'The 1974–75 UK Renegotiation of EEC Membership and Referendum' http://researchbriefings.parliament.uk/ResearchBriefing/Summary/CBP-7253.

[19] The meaning of the vote in the EEC referendum was deeply contested: R Saunders, *Yes to Europe!: The 1975 Referendum and Seventies Britain* (Cambridge University Press, 2018) ch 4.

[20] Independent Commission on Referendums (n 18) 85.

> When referendums begin processes for reform they are too blunt an instrument to aggregate political will about what those reforms should include.[21]

The structure of referendum questions not only makes a difference for the role referendums play in the process of constitutional change practically; it also reflects normative arguments about what role referendums are playing too. The different structures of referendum questions reflect different accounts of the relationship between popular sovereignty and parliamentary sovereignty. What is the role for voters in the process of constitutional change, and what are they being asked to do? Are referendums free-standing expressions of popular sovereignty, as suggested by the 1973 referendum, or are they small 'c' conservative limits on the actions of representatives and approval mechanisms, as was the case in 1979? The use of referendums in the New Labour era did nothing to address this uncertainty about what exactly the role of referendums was for and how they should be used.

While both practically and philosophically the case for referendums as post-legislative processes of approval is the better one, reality will complicate this general rule. There are certain cases, secession referendums being the clearest example, where referendums may need to begin a process of constitutional change with the specifics of proposals for reform to be determined later. The Independent Commission on Referendums accepted this. Its support for post-legislative referendums had qualifications, and it acknowledged that some element of flexibility regarding referendums is required in a political constitution.[22] But even in circumstances where referendums initiate constitutional reforms, the ICR argued, it is important to hold a post-legislative referendum too. This is to ensure accountability and that the ultimate content of constitutional reforms matches voters' intentions in initiating a process of reform through a referendum.[23] Crucially, though, it must be clear from the outset how referendums will be used throughout the process of reform. This clarity upfront is necessary in order for uses of referendums to be perceived as legitimate, rather than changing the rules of the game at half-time.[24]

The purpose of referendums is politically, and perhaps even legally, important in determining the significance of referendums and the meaning of voters' directions to representatives. What exactly is a referendum instructing representatives to do?[25] The question of the purpose of referendums in the UK's constitutional arrangements was not answered by the three referendums pre-New Labour. Coming into the New Labour era, the foundation for the use of referendums in the UK was shaky. While the outlines of what sort of questions should be put

[21] ibid 6.20.
[22] ibid 6.31.
[23] ibid 6.33.
[24] ibid 6.41.
[25] This can be seen in the confusion regarding how to implement the 2016 referendum, and Prime Minister Theresa May's iconic phrase 'Brexit means Brexit'.

to a referendum had emerged, it was not clear how or why referendums should be used. New Labour reintroduced referendums without answering these questions, and not answering these questions deepened underlying instability.

III. REFERENDUMS UNDER NEW LABOUR

New Labour used referendums a great deal, and they began using them right away. They kept their manifesto commitments to hold a series of referendums within months of taking office. Referendums were held on proposals for Scottish and Welsh devolution in September 1997 and shortly thereafter, in May 1998, Londoners voted for the establishment of a Greater London Authority. Later that month, a referendum was held in Northern Ireland (as well as the Republic of Ireland) to ratify the Belfast Agreement.[26] What connects these early referendums is that they were small 'c' conservative uses of referendums where voters were asked to weigh in on proposals put forward by the government, albeit different types of proposals at different stages of development.[27] This relatively consistent use of referendums would not last, however. Consider first the ways in which New Labour proposed to use referendums in their 1997 manifesto, before turning to the many different ways New Labour ended up using referendums throughout their tenure in office.

A. Referendums and Reforms

The 1997 New Labour manifesto mentions referendums 11 times. The manifesto advocated for the use of referendums in a wide variety of ways and on a range of subjects. It began with electoral reform, saying: 'We are committed to a referendum on the voting system for the House of Commons. An independent commission on voting systems will be appointed early to recommend a proportional alternative to the first-past-the-post system.'[28]

A referendum was proposed as one of the prerequisites for the UK joining the euro: 'there are three pre-conditions which would have to be satisfied before Britain could join during the next Parliament: first, the Cabinet would have to agree; then Parliament; and finally the people would have to say "Yes" in a referendum.'[29]

[26] For a summary of the specific questions and turnout in these various referendums see House of Lords Constitution Committee (n 5) 7–8.

[27] The proposals for the Greater London Authority, for instance, were provisional compared to the exhaustive negotiations that preceded the referendum on command paper 3883 (the Belfast Agreement).

[28] '1997 Labour Party Manifesto – LABOURMANIFESTO.COM' http://labourmanifesto.com/1997/1997-labour-manifesto.shtml.

[29] ibid.

The New Labour manifesto also outlined the role of referendums with respect to their proposals for devolution:

> As soon as possible after the election, we will enact legislation to allow the people of Scotland and Wales to vote in separate referendums on our proposals, which will be set out in white papers. These referendums will take place not later than the autumn of 1997. A simple majority of those voting in each referendum will be the majority required. *Popular endorsement will strengthen the legitimacy of our proposals and speed their passage through Parliament* (emphasis added).[30]

The rationale for referendums outlined in this passage is very important. Here, the manifesto is not suggesting that referendums are required for devolution, but rather that a referendum will (i) strengthen the legitimacy of proposals in order to (ii) get the proposals through Parliament more quickly. The idea behind this manifesto commitment seems to be that popular support for proposals in a referendum lends them legitimacy, and so limits the opposition to passing reforms in Parliament. Referendums are treated here as a tool with a specific purpose that can help to achieve the objective of reform. The key role referendums play is in 'endorsing' reforms. The role of referendums as devices of endorsement can be seen throughout the manifesto, but particularly with respect to devolution. The manifesto goes onto say:

> For Scotland we propose the creation of a parliament with law-making powers, firmly based on the agreement reached in the Scottish Constitutional Convention, including defined and limited financial powers to vary revenue and elected by an additional member system. *In the Scottish referendum we will seek separate endorsement of the proposal to create a parliament, and of the proposal to give it defined and limited financial powers to vary revenue.* Following majorities in the referendums, we will introduce in the first year of the Parliament legislation on the substantive devolution proposals outlined in our white papers (emphasis added).[31]

Here again, the manifesto speaks of endorsement of proposals as important, albeit not constitutionally or legally necessary, for devolution. The passage above stresses that the purpose of securing endorsements is to assess demand for reform. This can be seen too in the wording of the promise to hold a referendum on proposals for the Greater London Authority.

> London is the only Western capital without an elected city government. Following a referendum to *confirm popular demand*, there will be a new deal for London, with a strategic authority and a mayor, each directly elected. Both will speak up for the needs of the city and plan its future. They will not duplicate the work of the boroughs, but take responsibility for London-wide issues – economic regeneration, planning, policing, transport and environmental protection (emphasis added).[32]

[30] ibid.
[31] ibid.
[32] ibid.

This passage from the manifesto clarifies that the role of endorsement is to assess the public's support for proposals. Further, New Labour proposes that this assessment proceeds on a piecemeal basis.

> Demand for directly elected regional government so varies across England that it would be wrong to impose a uniform system. In time we will introduce legislation to allow the people, region by region, to decide in a referendum whether they want directly elected regional government.

This role of referendums in creating a patchwork of different approaches to devolution across the UK generally reflects what Elliott calls devolution on a 'supply and demand' basis.[33] Referendums, especially since New Labour, have been a key mechanism by which that demand has been established, and has resulted in asymmetries where such a demand is not present (as with the Northeast Regional Assembly in 2004). In this way, referendums have been key to creating the patchwork of devolution agreements that characterises the UK's constitutional arrangements today.[34]

At the end of their proposals on devolution and the Greater London Authority, the New Labour manifesto emphasises that 'London-wide responsibility for its own government is urgently required. *We will make it happen*'.[35] This strong wording underlines three general features of New Labour's manifesto reforms about the constitution: first, the 'urgency' with which reforms are required; second, the need to catch up with constitutional arrangements around the world; and third, New Labour's ability to make changes that have not been possible before. This part of the manifesto stresses that New Labour has both the ability and the commitment to make constitutional changes that are long overdue. Referendums are a democratic process that reinforces all of these goals and support this overall project. Indeed, as Coates et al argue, particularly in this early period 'On big issues, referenda were [Prime Minister Blair's] chosen mechanism'.[36] They were a marked departure from the status quo as a method of constitutional change, and so their use underlined the distinctiveness of the New Labour project. Referendums were also ways of at least attempting to circumvent political deadlock and establish modes of thinking by bringing another actor – voters – into the reform processes. So, in addition to being a method to achieve proposals for reform, the use of referendums in the New Labour manifesto performed a higher-order role too. The radical nature of the New Labour

[33] 'This asymmetry reflects what might be considered a demand-and-supply model, according to which different parts of the country are accorded a degree of autonomy that reflects what is desired': Professor Mark Elliott in House of Lords Constitution Committee, *The Union and Devolution*, 10th Report of Session 2015–16, 144.

[34] C Jeffery, 'Devolution in the United Kingdom: Problems of a Piecemeal Approach to Constitutional Change' (2009) 39 *Publius: The Journal of Federalism* 289, 291.

[35] '1997 Labour Party Manifesto – LABOURMANIFESTO.COM' (n 29).

[36] And Parliament had the status of a 'focus group'. D Coates, P Lawler and P Augustine Lawler, *New Labour in Power* (Manchester University Press, 2000) 89.

agenda and its attempt to modernise the British constitution provide a clean break with the past. Throughout their tenure, New Labour would use referendums in a wide range of ways in support of this overall project. Some were more successful than others; some of the highs and lows of New Labour's uses of referendums are now consider.

B. Belfast Agreement 1998

Some of the uses of referendums under the New Labour government were triumphs. The referendum on the Belfast Agreement in 1998 set the gold standard for the use of referendums not only in the UK, but around the world. The 1998 referendum was an opportunity to affirm or reject the results of the peace process and the compromises embedded within it. The referendum on the Belfast Agreement in 1998 was passed by 71.12 per cent of voters in Northern Ireland and 94.39 per cent in the Republic of Ireland.[37] The academic consensus is that this referendum was a great success.[38] It did not treat the vote as the beginning and the end of the referendum process, as was the case in the earlier Irish border poll vote in 1973.[39] By definition, the process was consociational rather than majoritarian,[40] finding compromises through a power-sharing agreement. In the peace process itself, eight different public opinion polls were commissioned, which meant the content of the peace agreement put to a referendum was continuously shaped by the views of the public.[41] Further, feedback was sought from a wide variety of civil society actors on the agreement. The process engaged not only elites and members of the public, but 'non-traditional members of the elite' as well.[42] Finally, the Civic Forum for Northern Ireland was established to help maintain the spirit of collaboration and compromise after the peace process and

[37] House of Lords Constitution Committee (n 5) 10.

[38] C Irwin, *The People's Peace Process in Northern Ireland* (Palgrave Macmillan, 2002); S Tierney, *Constitutional Referendums: The Theory and Practice of Republican Deliberation* (Oxford University Press, 2012) 251; K McEvoy and J Morison, 'Beyond the "Constitutional Moment": Law, Transition, and Peacemaking in Northern Ireland' (2003) 26 *Fordham International Law Journal* 960.

[39] A letter to *The Times* in 1973 expressed the concern that without tying the vote to a process of consultation or reform, the process would become a straightforward sectarian head count, and that is exactly what happened: *The Times* (16 January 1973).

[40] J McGarry and B O'Leary, 'Consociational Theory, Northern Ireland's Conflict, and Its Agreement Part I: What Consociationalists Can Learn from Northern Ireland' (2006) 41 *Government and Opposition* 43.

[41] 'This involved in-depth interviews with party negotiators, the testing of their proposals by public opinion survey and the publication of the results of these polls in the popular press, making the process transparent, engaging elites and ordinary citizens in a genuine dialogue, and allowing politicians on both sides of the conflict to map out areas of compromise and common ground': Tierney, *Constitutional Referendums* (2012) 251.

[42] D Birrell and A Williamson, 'The Voluntary-Community Sector and Political Development in Northern Ireland Since 1972' [2001] *Voluntas: International Journal of Voluntary and Non-Profit Organizations* 205, 214.

referendum were over.[43] These efforts bore fruit in the form of an imperfect but nevertheless enduring agreement. The political circumstances that informed the referendum on the Belfast Agreement were fraught and the stakes were high, so great care was taken in constructing and executing the referendum process. When the stakes were lower in other referendums, New Labour paid far less attention to the quality of the consultation and referendum process itself.

C. Devolution and the Referendum on the North East Regional Assembly

Success in referendums may be measured on multiple axes. That the proposal for a North East Regional Assembly did not pass did not itself make the referendum a failure. A referendum may still be a success if it presents a proposal for reform that some voters prefer but a majority ultimately reject. The low turnout in the Northeast Regional Assembly referendum and the extremely low level of support for the proposed reforms[44] suggest that this referendum was not the productive result of a carefully crafted consultation process. Further, the reasons that support for the North East Regional Assembly was so low also reflect the lack of thought that went into the consultation, reform and referendum processes. There were a wide range of basic problems with the referendum, including its timing and the all-postal-vote submission rate.[45] The referendum was held at a point when both the local and the national Labour Party were very unpopular, and yet the proposals were pitched as New Labour rather than cross-party initiatives. Voters saw this referendum as an opportunity to give Tony Blair 'a bloody nose'.[46] The proposals for the Northeast Regional Assembly were not the result of sustained, broad and deep consultation, as was the case with respect to the Belfast Agreement. The proposals put to a referendum overlooked fundamental disagreements within the North East itself. They tried to impose a political identity from above and, as Knock explains, 'Teeside … was not keen on what some thought would be a "Geordie Parliament"'.[47] These underlying failings with the timing and process of the referendums process, combined with the unappealing content of the proposed reforms themselves, meant that the quality of debate in the referendum was very low. The rationale for the North East Regional Assembly was to increase representation, but the 'No' campaign easily dismissed this as just more bureaucracy and politicians. The campaign against the assembly found a big white elephant balloon which they took to all of their

[43] ibid 214; Tierney (n 38) 252.

[44] Turnout in this referendum was 47.1%, 77.9% of which disagreed with the idea of a Northeast regional assembly. House of Lords Constitution Committee (n 5) 10.

[45] K Shaw and F Robinson, 'The End of the Beginning?: Taking Forward Local Democratic Renewal in the Post-Referendum North East' (2007) 22 *Local Economy* 243, 249.

[46] K Knock, 'The North East Referendum: Lessons Learned' (2006) 59 *Parliamentary Affairs* 282, 291.

[47] ibid.

campaign events.[48] In interviews conducted after the referendum, some voters indicated that they did not support the proposals for reform because they sensed New Labour only half-heartedly supported the reforms themselves.[49] Shaw and Robinson say 'the timing of the referendum, late in the Parliament suggested that the Government was not fully committed to it' (and, indeed, some parts of the government were not).[50] This suggests that voters can sense apathetic efforts at reform through referendums, and then they themselves respond in kind.

The result in the 2004 referendum on a North East Regional Assembly was significant in itself, but it also had important spin-off effects. This was meant to be the referendum which would lead to further referendums in the Yorkshire and Humber regions, and to regional devolution as an aim of the New Labour government in general.[51] The Northeast Regional Assembly referendum demonstrates, and foretells, a lesson that governments (not only New Labour) have learned the hard way. A referendum is not a magic wand. It cannot create political will where none exists either among the public or in government. A referendum does not take place in a political vacuum. It will be shaped by its political participants.[52] A good referendum is the icing on a cake of a much longer process of public consultation achieving reform, where voters are already invested in the outcome.[53]

D. European Integration: Acts and Omissions

While a referendum was never held on the euro as outlined in the 1997 manifesto (the euro did not pass the five economic tests identified by the government),[54] European integration is central to New Labour's legacy on referendums. Indeed, part of New Labour's legacy on referendums was not a referendum it held, but rather one that it decided not to hold:[55] on the Lisbon Treaty. New Labour promised to hold a referendum on the Constitutional Treaty, but then argued that the Lisbon Treaty outlined a different vision of European integration, so a

[48] ibid 290.

[49] Shaw and Robinson, 'The End of the Beginning?' (2007) 249.

[50] ibid.

[51] ibid 244.

[52] Indeed, referendums are inevitably, at least in part, a verdict on the representatives who advocate for particular results: M Walker, *The Strategic Use of Referendums: Power, Legitimacy, and Democracy* (Springer, 2003).

[53] The referendum result also reflected deep disenchantment with politicians, democracy and even the European Union (the Assembly was cast as a European plot). This also foretold the result in the 2016 Brexit referendum. Shaw and Robinson (n 46) 247.

[54] A Mullen and B Burkitt, 'European Integration and the Battle for British Hearts and Minds: New Labour and the Euro' (2003) 74 *The Political Quarterly* 322.

[55] Of course, this is not specifically a New Labour problem; the question of whether to hold a referendum afflicted John Major too regarding the Maastricht Treaty. House of Lords Constitution Committee (n 5). D Baker, A Gamble and S Ludlam, 'The Parliamentary Siege of Maastricht 1993: Conservative Divisions and British Ratification' (1994) 47 *Parliamentary Affairs* 37.

referendum was not required. This decision was legally challenged, and in *R (on the Application of Wheeler) v The Office of the Prime Minister*[56] it was argued that the promise to hold a referendum on the Constitutional Treaty created a legitimate expectation that there would be one on the Lisbon Treaty too. The court held that a referendum was not required to ratify the treaty, concluding: 'There was nothing in the claimant's case to cast doubt on the lawfulness of ratifying the Lisbon Treaty without a referendum.'[57] Nevertheless, *Wheeler* demonstrates that in the latter years of the New Labour era the potential for a referendum was not only a tool that the government could use, it was also a tool that could be used against the government as well.

New Labour's decision to not hold a referendum on the Lisbon Treaty continues to resonate today. Not using the referendum as a device of ratification to approve the Lisbon Treaty meant it never received the broad public support that referendums can demonstrate. This created an unresolved political problem both in the UK in general and especially for the Conservative Party in particular.[58] Further, because referendums were not used as a device of approval on the Lisbon Treaty, it potentially led to confusion on what exactly the meaning of the 2016 referendum on the UK's membership of the EU was. The significant degree of European integration since the original referendum in 1975, without further ratifying referendums on additional treaties, created the possibility of a legal and political crisis. There might have been specific stages in the process of European integration, for instance the Maastricht and Lisbon treaties, that a majority of voters found objectionable.[59] New Labour were not the only government who declined to use referendums to approve further European integration, but their decision to not hold a referendum on the Lisbon Treaty (despite promising to do so on the Constitution Treaty) reflects the ad hoc uses of referendums in the UK more broadly. Had there been a referendum on the Maastricht or Lisbon Treaty, it is possible there would still have been an in/out referendum on the status quo in 2016, but this seems far less likely. Had referendums been used consistently as an ad hoc process of ratification, then there would have been a case, as section 6 the European Union Act 2011 suggested, of only holding referendums on further integration.[60] Ratifying referendums have a clearer structure. They isolate one aspect of European integration, rather than trying to unpick a range of potential relationships in a binary way. The challenges of the Brexit referendum and its aftermath

[56] [2008] EWHC 1409.

[57] ibid [59] (Richards LJ).

[58] Although, of course, a referendum alone would never have solved the underlying problems, T Oliver, 'To Be or Not to Be in Europe: Is That the Question? Britain's European Question and an in/out Referendum' (2015) 91 *International Affairs* 77.

[59] It seems at least plausible, given that they affirmed EEC membership in 1975, that at some point in the integration process a majority of voters would become disenchanted. Or it might have been that different generations had different views of European integration.

[60] European Union Act 2011, s 6, since repealed by the European Union (Withdrawal) Act 2018.

demonstrate how difficult it is to disambiguate a range of relationships with the EU from a binary choice. The ineffective all-or-nothing structure of the Brexit referendum was, at least in part, a result of New Labour's decision not to hold a ratifying referendum on the Lisbon Treaty. Had New Labour held this referendum, it would have begun to establish a consistent role for referendums as approving stages of European integration – a role that as a democratic process they are far better placed to play.

Referendums are essential to understanding the New Labour era. They were a constant presence in the 1997 manifesto, emphasising the clean constitutional break with the past that New Labour was offering. Especially early on, they were Prime Minister Tony Blair's preferred method of reform.[61] New Labour not only reintroduced referendums after an 18-year hiatus, three significant referendums were held within their first year of taking office. This underlined the ambition of their reforms. The use of referendums continued throughout their tenure, but in later years decisions to hold referendums (or not hold them) were confused and half-hearted. New Labour's legacy on referendums is not confined only to the referendums they held (and did not hold), however. The current law governing the use of referendums was passed by New Labour. The legal framework passed by New Labour was skeletal, outlining only the administrative requirements of referendums. The skeletal infrastructure created by New Labour was insufficient to address the constitutional questions arising from the reintroduction of referendums. New Labour continued to leave unanswered the questions of how and why referendums should be used.

E. New Labour and the Political Parties, Elections and Referendums Act 2000

Not all uses of referendums are the same, and they are not all created equal. As argued above, referendums are better placed to act as small 'c' conservative devices as 'The People's Veto'.[62] This is not the way that referendums are always used, however, and New Labour did not outline a model for their use. As can be seen in the discussion of manifesto commitments above, New Labour had some core rationales for the use of referendums (endorsement, asserting voters demand for reforms, securing legitimacy), but these ideas alone do not amount to consistent constitutional principles, and they allow for the possibility that referendums may be used in different ways. New Labour had an opportunity to provide clarity on at least some of these questions when they created the legal framework that governs the use of referendums. New Labour created the current infrastructure for referendums through the Political Parties, Elections and Referendums Act 2000 (PPERA). This Act was passed by, and in response

[61] Coates et al, *New Labour in Power* (2000) 89.

[62] AV Dicey (RE Michener ed), *Introduction to the Study of the Law of the Constitution*, 8th revised edn (Liberty Fund, 1982) cviii.

to, the findings of the Neill Report.[63] The aim of the PPERA and the objective of the report that informed it were to ensure fairness in both elections and referendums in the UK. To that end, one of the main purposes of the Act was to establish the Electoral Commission.[64] The PPERA governs the execution and financing of referendums. It outlines especially the role of the Electoral Commission with respect to referendums. This is an administrative Act about the mechanics of conducting referendums. It neither stipulates what sorts of questions should be put to a referendum nor what role referendums should play in the process of constitutional change. Admittedly, the principal aim of passing the PPERA was to consider the funding of political parties and to level the playing field in British democracy. Nevertheless, in passing this Act, New Labour had an opportunity to go a bit further. The law could have required not only enabling legislation for referendums,[65] but greater clarity from that enabling legislation about what the legal impact of a referendum would be.[66] Further, it is still possible to maintain flexibility and allow for different types of enabling legislation, while still requiring that Parliament articulate proposals for reform before initiating a referendum. It is enough that proposed legislation or reforms that are part of the enabling legislation could exist in outline or even lay out a consultation process. It might even be enough to identify the headings of proposed legislation to be developed later. The bottom line is that New Labour's infrastructure for referendums did not identify a rationale for their use or establish how they should be used. This continued to make it possible for referendums to be used by governments when it best suited them, rather than on the basis of constitutional principle. New Labour was not the only government to decline to provide substantive guidance for the use of referendums in the UK, but (i) passing the PPERA was one of the best opportunities to least partly address some of these questions and (ii) this declination to clarify the role and purpose for referendums in the UK was part of the foundations of the most serious political crisis in the post-war period; the lack of thought and care taken with regard to the Brexit referendum of 2016.

[63] Committee on Standards in Public Life, Fifth Report, *The Funding of Political Parties in the United Kingdom* (Cm 4057-I, 1998).

[64] Political Parties, Elections and Referendums Act 2000, s 1(1).

[65] '"Referendum" means a referendum or other poll held, in pursuance of any provision made by or under an Act of Parliament, on one or more questions specified in or in accordance with any such provision': PPERA, s 101(2)a.

[66] In the case of the Alternative Vote referendum, s 8 of the Parliamentary Constituencies and Voting Act 2011 outlined two possible paths for the legislation, depending on the results of the popular vote. If there was a majority of votes in the referendum for the proposed changes, then the Secretary of State was to introduce an order bringing the changes in legislation into force. If there was a majority of votes against the changes, then the Secretary of State was to bring an order repealing it. The enabling legislation for the Brexit referendum, by contrast (the European Union Referendum Act 2015), made no such provisions for the outcome of the vote.

F. Referendums after New Labour

The use of referendums often begets the use of more referendums.[67] The reintroduction of referendums under New Labour after an 18-year hiatus precipitated further use of referendums under the Coalition government, with referendums held on Electoral Reform in 2011, Scottish Independence in 2014 and the UK's membership of the EU in 2016. These uses of referendums reflect continuations of the New Labour legacy. New Labour promised a referendum on the electoral system in 1997 but never delivered.[68] The referendum on Scottish independence reflected a continuation of the use of referendums in devolution and secession referendums which can be traced back to the 1970s and was reaffirmed under New Labour. The two referendums under the Coalition on electoral reform and Scottish Independence were very different processes, however, in part reflecting the fundamentally different subject matters. The referendum on electoral reform was essentially post-legislative, where a majority vote in a referendum would have triggered the creation of law.[69] On the other hand, the Scottish referendum was much closer to a pre-legislative referendum,[70] although there was a comprehensive White Paper.[71] This is to say: the direction of trajectory set by New Labour continued under the Coalition government. The category of questions to be put to a referendum, established in the 1970s, continued, but it continued to be unclear how and why referendums should be used. As argued above, the most recent referendum on the UK's membership of the EU in 2016 is a clear example of the underlying confusion regarding the use of referendums in the UK. This all says that New Labour's approach to referendums, and the underlying confusion about how they should be used, continued under subsequent Coalition and Conservative governments. New Labour set the direction of trajectory regarding referendums that continues to this day.

IV. AN INCHOATE CONSTITUTIONAL CONVENTION?

The general view is that there are no constitutional conventions regarding referendums in the UK.[72] This may slowly be beginning to change. Phillipson now argues, for instance, that it is time to take seriously the idea that the results of a

[67] 'Usage tends to beget further referendums': S Tierney, 'Europe Is Entering the "Age of the Referendum", but There Is Nothing to Fear for European Democracy If Referendums Are Properly Regulated' (*Democratic Audit Blog*, 22 October 2014) 3.

[68] Coates et al (n 36) 90–91.

[69] Parliamentary Voting and Constituencies Act 2011.

[70] In the UK, the difference between pre- and post-legislative referendums is a matter of degree rather than kind.

[71] Scottish Government, *Scotland's Future: Your Guide to An Independent Scotland* (2013) http://www.gov.scot/resource/0043/00439021.pdf.

[72] The possibility of such conventions is not considered either in the House of Lords' Constitution Committee Reports on Referendums in 2009 or Constitutional Change in 2011.

referendum will be adhered to as a constitutional convention.[73] Referendums are also legally required for certain types of constitutional change, including those brought by the Wales Act 2017,[74] the Scotland Act 2016[75] the European Union Act 2011[76] and the Northern Ireland Act 1998.[77] In evaluating New Labour's legacy on referendums, it is necessary to consider not only the requirements for referendums within the four corners of legislation, but also whether there are constitutional conventions around different elements of their use. Jennings lays out a three-part test to determine if a practice qualifies as a constitutional convention:

> First, are there precedents for the Convention? Secondly, did the actors believe they were bound by a rule? And; finally, is there a reason for the rule? A single precedent with a good reason may be enough to establish the rule. A whole string of precedents without such a reason will be of no avail, unless it is perfectly certain that the persons concerned regarding them as bound by it.[78]

Consider each element of Jennings's criteria in turn. First, precedents: the use of referendums in the 1970s began to establish the precedents for the constitutional convention. As argued above, the three first nationwide referendums began to carve out a category of 'fundamental constitutional change' for which referendums were arguably necessary. Second, the question of whether actors felt bound by a rule: given the absence of previous referendums as precedents, it is difficult to say that constitutional actors in the 1970s were 'bound' by a rule that referendums were required. Indeed, there was no referendum concerning entry into the Common Market in 1973; the decision to hold one in 1975 was a tactical one to affirm existing membership and to address disagreements in the Labour Party.[79] Likewise, particularly at the beginning of their tenure in 1997, it does not seem that New Labour considered themselves *bound* to hold referendums.

[73] 'This paper therefore contends that if the UK is to continue using referendums – which seems likely – it is time to consider whether a convention should now be recognised to the effect that parliament and government will abide by the results of referendums': G Phillipson, 'Brexit, Prerogative and the Courts: Why Did Political Constitutionalists Support the Government Side in Miller?' (2018) 36 *University of Queensland Law Journal* 311, 324.

[74] '[I]t is declared that the Assembly and the Welsh Government are not to be abolished except on the basis of a decision of the people of Wales voting in a referendum': Wales Act 2017, s 1(3).

[75] '[T]he Scottish Parliament and the Scottish Government are not to be abolished except on the basis of a decision of the people of Scotland voting in a referendum': Scotland Act 2016, s 63A(3).

[76] Section 6 required a referendum on further European integration, but this has been repealed by the European Union (Withdrawal) Act 2018.

[77] 'It is hereby declared that Northern Ireland in its entirety remains part of the United Kingdom and shall not cease to be so without the consent of a majority of the people of Northern Ireland voting in a poll held for the purposes of this section in accordance with Schedule 1. (2) But if the wish expressed by a majority in such a poll is that Northern Ireland should cease to be part of the United Kingdom and form part of a united Ireland, the Secretary of State shall lay before Parliament such proposals to give effect to that wish as may be agreed between Her Majesty's Government in the United Kingdom and the Government of Ireland': Northern Ireland Act 1998, s 1, (1)–(2).

[78] I Jennings, *The Law and the Constitution*, 5th edn (University of London Press, 1959) 136.

[79] Saunders, *Yes to Europe!* (2018) ch 2.

The 1997 manifesto outlines a series of functional roles for referendums, such as securing endorsements in order to speed the passage of proposals through Parliament. The manifesto did not say that referendums *must* be held; rather, it said that they *should* be held. This approach changed through the New Labour era, and even during Tony Blair's premiership. When Prime Minister Tony Blair promised to hold a referendum on the Lisbon Treaty, he said 'We will put it [the constitution] to the British people in a referendum and campaign wholeheartedly for a Yes vote', but then later concluded 'No. If it's not a constitutional treaty, so that it alters the basic relationship between Europe and the member states, then there isn't the same case for a referendum.'[80] The distinction that Blair draws between the two treaties suggests that there are certain categories of constitutional change which 'alter the relationship between Europe and the member states'. As the Lisbon Treaty, Blair argued, did not alter this relationship, no referendum was required.

This is connected to the third of Jennings's criteria: is there a reason for the rule? This question is more challenging. As argued above, governments have not yet answered the question of 'why' referendums are necessary in the UK. What are referendums for? Are referendums for approving constitutional changes? Or are referendums an opportunity for voters to have their say directly as expressions of popular sovereignty, and to begin processes of constitutional change? Admittedly, the root of these two alternatives is the same idea: the purpose of a referendum is to involve voters in the process of constitutional change. That *might* be enough of a reason for a constitutional convention, but it is a broad reason and (if it is a constitutional convention at all) it is a loose one. I have argued here that the former view of referendums as approving constitutional changes is the better one, but this has not yet emerged as the rationale for referendums in the UK. Nor has the alternative view clearly coalesced. Consequently, New Labour placed the UK on the road to developing constitutional conventions regarding the use of referendums, but those conventions – and their meaning – are in a state of flux. In sum: by the end of the New Labour era, elements of Jennings's criteria of constitutional conventions are present in a way they were not before 1997. Towards the end of the New Labour era, there were (i) a set of precedents going back to 1975, (ii) political actors promising or obligating themselves to hold referendums under certain circumstances and (iii) the beginnings of a general rationale for referendums, which is continuing to evolve today.

One final note about New Labour's legacy on constitutional conventions regarding referendums. Referendums are distinctive processes in that they are opportunities for broad involvement in the process of constitutional change. They include voters in the way that other methods of constitutional change do not. This is to say: it is important to see conventions both as top-down and

[80] Piris, *The Lisbon Treaty* (2010) 50.

bottom-up.[81] As familiarity with referendums increased in the New Labour era, expectations changed among both representatives and the electorate about the role of referendums in the process of constitutional change. Inchoate and inconsistent expectations are central to New Labour's legacy on referendums. While it may not be the case that fully fledged constitutional conventions have developed for the use of referendums in the UK with respect to constitutional change, the expectations about the necessity of referendums of both representatives and the public have changed since 1997, and this is not confined to referendums required by law.

V. CONCLUSION

New Labour was not the only government to take an ad hoc[82] approach to referendums, but both through inaction and action they left a piecemeal legacy about the role of referendums in the UK. New Labour reintroduced referendums after an 18-year hiatus without clarifying how they should be used, and in doing so exacerbated long-standing tensions about the role of referendums in British parliamentary democracy. I have suggested above that the small 'c' conservative, post-legislative role of referendums is the better view in the UK's constitutional context, but even more important than how referendums are used is that they are used consistently. The Political Parties, Elections and Referendums Act 2000 was an opportunity to provide a greater degree of consistency, but the Act provides only an administrative skeleton rather than substantive guidance. In passing the Act, New Labour had the best opportunity in a generation to clarify how referendums should be used. The New Labour legacy on referendums has some triumphs, such as the referendum on the Belfast Agreement in 1998, but its record of success is mixed. Referendums were used consistently enough to begin to give rise to some elements of a constitutional convention, but not so much as to make that use inarguable or to clarify how or why they should be used. This omission is perhaps understandable, but it also helped make the crises around the Brexit referendum possible.

What does the future hold for the uses of referendums in the UK 20 years on from New Labour? Dicey warned that: 'I am quite certain that, once established, the Referendum would not be got rid of by anything short of revolution.'[83] It is always dangerous to disagree with Dicey, but I am not sure Dicey is necessarily

[81] A Perry and A Tucker, 'Top-Down Constitutional Conventions' (2018) 81 *MLR* 765.

[82] 'In particular, we regret the *ad hoc* manner in which referendums have been used, often as a tactical device, by the government of the day. Referendums may become a part of the UK's political and constitutional practice. Where possible, cross-party agreement should be sought as to the circumstances in which it is appropriate for referendums to be used': House of Lords Constitution Committee (n 5) 209.

[83] Dicey to Leo Maxse, 2 February 1894 (Maxse Papers). Cited in M Qvortrup, 'AV Dicey: The Referendum as The People's Veto' (1999) 20 *History of Political Thought* 531, 545.

right about this. After the three referendums in the 1970s, I think there was a chance that referendums might have just faded away in the UK. It is at least arguable that the government's position on the Maastricht referendums[84] – that referendums are not required in the UK's constitutional arrangements – could have remained the prevailing view.[85] After New Labour, there are at least some elements of a constitutional convention *for* their use but not *about* their use. The possibility of their use will now be in the political background of all major constitutional changes, and their use is (currently) legally required for key constitutional reforms. This is the difficulty with New Labour's legacy on referendums: they reintroduced the referendum without providing it with a principled foundation, and there is no getting rid of referendums now.

[84] 'The government states its position, in terms that deserve to find a place in textbooks on the constitution, in the mass circulation of a booklet it published last December to mark the British presidency. It offers this answer to a question "Why can't we have a referendum like the Danes, the Irish and the French?" The British system is a parliamentary democracy: the Government are accountable to Parliament and Parliament is accountable to the electorate. The House of Commons approved the negotiating position pre-Maastricht and the results afterwards. It has also given a second reading, after the election, to the Bill which would enable the Government to ratify the Treaty. Parliament will have a thorough and detailed discussion of the Bill in Committee stage. The government believe that is the right way to proceed in a parliamentary democracy': Baker et al, 'The Parliamentary Siege of Maastricht 1993' (1994) 48.

[85] Although referendums have always been closely tied to European integration, so as long as there were moves towards European integration, referendums would have likely been a political consideration, at least for a minority of voters. The Referendum Party received 2.7% of the vote in the 1997 general election. For more on the Referendum Party, see I McAllister and DT Studlar, 'Conservative Euroscepticism and the Referendum Party in the 1997 British General Election' (2000) 6 *Party Politics* 359.

15

Neoliberalism, Labour Law and New Labour's Turn to Constitutionalism

ROBERT KNOX[1]

I. INTRODUCTION

IN HIS 1975 introduction to *The Red Paper on Scotland*, a young Gordon Brown addressed, in bold and radical terms, the challenge that the Scottish National Party (SNP) posed to the labour movement. According to Brown, 'the rise of modern Scottish nationalism is less an assertion of Scotland's permanence as a nation than a response to Scotland's uneven development'.[2] For Brown, Scottish nationalism could not simply be read as a 'purely' constitutional question. Instead, this 'constitutional' moment resulted from the 'the gap between people's experiences as part of an increasingly demoralised Great Britain and their (oil-fired) expectations at a Scottish level'.[3]

This deeper economic malaise meant that neither the solutions of the SNP nor those of a conservative Scottish Labour could address Scotland's real issues. Instead, it was necessary to 'transcend that false and sterile antithesis which has been manufactured between the nationalism of the SNP and the anti-nationalism of the Unionist parties' and inquire into the questions of 'private power' and 'social control' which underlay Scottish capitalism.[4]

Such a project would have to 'start from where people are, the realities of day-to-day living, extremes of wealth and poverty, unequal opportunities at work, in housing, health, education and community living generally'.[5] A crucial

[1] Many thanks to Rory MacQueen for comments on drafts of this chapter.

[2] G Brown, 'Introduction: The Socialist Challenge' in G Brown (ed), *The Red Paper on Scotland*, 1st edn (EUSPB, 1975) 8.

[3] ibid.

[4] ibid.

[5] ibid 9.

element of this project would thus be the building of a planned economy, in which the commanding heights of the economy were brought under social control. Yet Brown went further than this. A planned economy would not be able to address the 'demands by trade unionists for real control over the decisions affecting their livelihood'.[6] Such demands were, in Brown's telling, a key driver of the rise of the SNP's rhetoric of self-determination. Accordingly, to meet the 'constitutional' challenge posed by the SNP, it would be necessary to promote 'workers' self-management and the prioritising of social needs set by the communities themselves'.[7]

In *Red Paper*, therefore, Gordon Brown forged a distinctly radical approach to the UK's constitution. Faced with the constitutional challenge of the UK's makeup, Brown sought not to confront it on its own terms; instead, he rooted this constitutional demand in the wider economic logic of British capitalism. At the same time, he did not simply abandon the political issues driving this constitutional crisis; rather, he sought to situate them within the broader narrative of people seeking control over their own existence under conditions of capitalist alienation.

It is striking to compare this constitutional vision to that which was actually implemented during Brown's tenure. In sharp contrast to the radical political-economic programme of *Red Paper*, New Labour's vision was impeccably liberal. Whilst some of their constitutional changes represented a break with constitutional orthodoxy, none were linked to a more fundamental challenge to British capitalism.

What can account for this disjuncture? One simple explanation is the ravages of time. Brown was a young radical in the 1970s, and by the time the New Labour government was elected he had either – according to one's political preference – sold out this youthful radicalism or outgrown it. Whilst there is certainly something to this argument, it is ultimately unsatisfactory. Even if Brown himself changed, why did the wider labour movement change in the same way?

Explanations in this vein have not been forthcoming. Most accounts treat New Labour's constitutional reforms as contingent or accidental, rooting them in the personalities of Blair and Brown.[8] More convincing accounts view them through the lens of purely tactical political considerations, particularly as regards the impact of the Social Democratic Party on Labour and through the internal dynamics of the Labour Party, tracing how constitutional reform interacted with wider politics factions within it.[9] Even the most sophisticated of

[6] ibid 15.

[7] ibid 18.

[8] See, eg M Flinders, 'New Labour and the Constitution' in S Ludlam and MJ Smith (eds), *Governing as New Labour: Policy and Politics Under Blair* (Macmillan International Higher Education, 2017) 126; P Norton, 'Tony Blair and The Constitution' (2007) 2 *British Politics* 269.

[9] M Evans, 'New Labour and the Rise of the New Constitutionalism' in M Beech and S Lee (eds), *Ten Years of New Labour* (Palgrave Macmillan UK, 2008).

these accounts have difficulty in explaining why the broader labour movement went along with New Labour's constitutional reform.

This chapter argues that in order to understand New Labour's constitutionalism, it is necessary to situate it within a broader understanding of the changing relationship between the labour movement, capitalism and the British state; crucial in this relationship were the changing fortunes of labour law. The chapter demonstrates that the historical labour movement's orientation was best understood as an 'anti-juridical constitutionalism', in which the aim was to insulate collective deliberative processes from the intervention of elite elements of the state. This was a result of the experience of the labour movement's legal confrontation with an activist state and – crucially – judiciary.

The chapter then demonstrates how the 1945 Labour government took this anti-juridical approach and institutionalised it at the level of the state, in a constitutional settlement. In this settlement, the state directly socialised areas of previously 'private' life, and the trade union movement – through labour law – was able to become a constitutional actor, governing much of people's day-to-day lives. However, that settlement was built on a particular material foundation that obtained during the post-war period. When these conditions broke down, the Conservative Party set about dismantling that settlement: this was crucially achieved through legal changes which centralised state power and undercut the labour movement's governance function.

When New Labour took power in 1997, it did so in a situation of the material and ideological collapse of anti-juridical constitutionalism. The chapter shows how such changed conditions fundamentally shaped New Labour's constitutional agenda, with New Labour adopting a fundamentally neoliberal framework whilst attempting to satisfy the material needs of its social base.

II. THE TWO SOULS OF LABOUR CONSTITUTIONALISM

In Brown's Introduction to *Red Paper* we can detect two distinct 'constitutional' aspects. The first is a refusal to address 'constitutional' issues on their own terms. Where the SNP sought to define Scottish independence as a purely constitutional problem, Brown wished to reframe the issue as one of the development of British capitalism. The second aspect argues that the 'constitutional' framing of particular issues does not sufficiently capture the real sources of power and control in most people's lives; instead, we must focus on increasing democracy in the workplace and local communities. The first aspect, then, essentially argues that 'constitutional' politics displace the real political-economic forces at play. The second aspect argues that the legitimate range of 'constitutional' thought needs to extend beyond the 'high politics' of the state.

Although couched in a radical idiom, Brown's argument reflects the predominant mode of constitutional thought within the labour movement. In *Constitution-Making and The Labour Party*, Mark Evans identifies two 'dominant traditions' within the British labour movement's thinking on constitutionalism: Fabianism and syndicalism. The Fabian tradition represents 'the favoured mode of governance of the British political tradition; strong, decisive and responsible government' in which 'the existing institutions of the British state could be used as a socialist apparatus for social and political engineering'.[10] At the core of Fabianism was the belief that socialism 'was to be advanced by an electoral majority representing a unified economic interest installing a party in office to carry out its wishes by passing appropriate legislation'.[11] Accordingly, for Fabians, parliamentary sovereignty is the supreme political principle. Fabianism has thus traditionally resisted all forms of constitutional reform which undermine the sovereignty of Parliament.[12]

Although Evans describes Fabianism as a 'leadership project' within the Labour Party, it had a much broader currency within the British labour movement. To take one striking example, the Communist Party of Great Britain, in its 1951 programme 'The British Road to Socialism' – allegedly approved by Stalin himself[13] – stated its aim as being to 'restore to the British Parliament its exclusive sovereign right to control the country's financial, economic and military policy'. The strategy for achieving such a victory rested on 'returning a majority to Parliament which represents the interests of all working people'.[14]

By contrast, Evans argues that the syndicalist tradition 'has largely been informed by dissatisfaction with both Labour's parliamentary leadership and the … centralized, sovereign state'.[15] This syndicalist tradition focuses its attention on the workplace, emphasising the importance of direct, militant trade union action in transforming the basic conditions of existence for working people. Its aim is to achieve change outside of the structures of Parliament.

In Evans's account, these two traditions represent distinct alternatives within the labour movement. Brown's Introduction complicates this opposition, encompassing both a strong sovereign Parliament and workers' control. Moreover, Evans elides the profound constitutional similarities between these two positions. What both 'Fabianism' and 'syndicalism' have in common is a refusal to foreground 'constitutional' critique. For the former, constitutional questions are secondary to broader political transformation; for the latter, 'constitutional' questions miss the more important issues at play.

[10] M Evans, *Constitution-Making and the Labour Party* (Palgrave Macmillan, 2003) 19.

[11] A Wright, 'British Socialists and the British Constitution' (1990) 43 *Parliamentary Affairs* 322, 335.

[12] Evans, *Constitution-Making and the Labour Party* (2003) 20.

[13] J McIlroy, 'Another Look at EP Thompson and British Communism, 1937–1955' (2017) 58 *Labor History* 506, 521.

[14] 'CPGB: The British Road to Socialism (1951)' www.marxists.org/history/international/comintern/sections/britain/brs/1951/51.htm.

[15] Evans (n 10) 20.

III. AN ANTI-JURIDICAL CONSTITUTIONALISM?

For many analysts of the British labour movement, this refusal to directly foreground constitutional questions was evidence of a fundamental satisfaction with the constitutional order.[16] Tom Nairn, for instance, argues that 'After the defeat of Chartism in the 1840s, a general acceptance of the endlessly liberal and adaptable nature of the United Kingdom state came to inform left-wing parties and most other movements'.[17] For Nairn, this was evidence of a broader problem with the socialist movement, rooted in:

> [T]he idea that constitutional politics and ideas are essentially secondary or 'superstructural' ... That is, they may be 'a good thing' but they are never urgent enough to tackle now. They are not necessary conditions of successful social, economic and cultural or other policies.[18]

Nairn's description of the labour movement's view of constitutional politics as superstructural grasps something important. However, he also misses a vital point. Whilst he is certainly right to flag up the Chartists as one of the highpoints of the labour movement's engagement with 'constitutional' questions, the same spirit was present within the Labour Party itself. The core goal of the Chartists was the expansion of the franchise, with the eventual aim of universal (male) suffrage. Yet this goal was also taken up – unevenly – by the British labour movement after Chartism.[19] In particular, the Fabian tradition had a vested interested in arguing for a wider democratic franchise. Insofar as the franchise could be widened to include more and more workers, the reasoning went, the likelihood of a socialist government would increase.

In this respect, the 'superstructural' view of the British constitution did not necessarily betoken an abandonment of constitutional issues. Rather, it conditioned the way in which the labour movement was to approach them. For all wings of the labour movement, the crucial issue was focused on widening the franchise. For Fabians, with their focus on building a socialist Parliament, the emphasis was placed upon removing, or blocking, any limitations on Parliament's 'democratic' ability to act. For syndicalists, the aim was to secure changes which would give workers the widest freedom of action at the 'local' level.

In a sense, then, we can detect a 'constitutional' theme common to both the 'Fabian' and 'syndicalist' traditions: namely, their commitment to strengthening the collective, democratic elements of the British state. Crucially, in both cases, what this tended to resolve into was expanding the number of subjects

[16] Wright, 'British Socialists and the British Constitution' (1990).

[17] T Nairn, *Gordon Brown: 'Bard of Britishness'* (Institute of Welsh Affairs, 2006) 19.

[18] ibid.

[19] P Thane, 'Women in the Labour Party and Women's Suffrage' in M Boussahba-Bravard (ed), *Suffrage Outside Suffragism: Women's Vote in Britain, 1880–1914* (Palgrave Macmillan UK, 2007); C Wrigley, 'The Labour Party and the Impact of the 1918 Reform Act' (2018) 37 *Parliamentary History* 64.

who could participate in such democratic processes and removing limitations placed upon the outcomes of these processes. Widening democracy was about limiting the power of unaccountable or elite bodies and individuals – such as the judiciary or the civil service – to interfere in democratic processes.

Crucially, then, it cannot simply be said that 'constitutional' questions were ignored by the British labour movement. Rather, it held to what we can characterise as an 'anti-juridical constitutionalism'. In such a vision, the aim was to protect collective social control from externally imposed intervention, including the intervention of the judiciary. This, of course, meant that the avenues of liberal constitutionalism – particularly Bills of Rights – could not be part of the labour movement's vision.

Viewed in this way, we can see what a radical break New Labour represented with the older traditions of the labour movement. This is perhaps most obvious in the fate of Clause IV of the Labour Party constitution. Clause IV was infamously amended in 1995.[20] Accounts of this amendment have generally emphasised the shift from the language of 'common ownership' to a more amorphous language of 'common endeavour'. Yet alongside this we can also detect a fundamental constitutional transformation. In the original draft, written by the Fabian Sidney Webb in 1917,[21] the Labour Party was committed to 'the best obtainable system of popular administration and control of each industry or service', that is to say, it was committed to the extension of popular and democratic control over the economy. In this version of Clause IV there was no mention of rights. By contrast, the 1995 version of Clause IV explicitly makes reference to a situation 'where the rights we enjoy reflect the duties we owe'.

What is marked in this revised version of Clause IV is that it directly foregrounds a more liberal constitutionalist understanding. This was reflective of New Labour's broader commitment to constitutional ideas. In an unprecedented move, New Labour presented constitutional issues as a distinct set of problems that needed to be considered in their own right. In order to understand this transformation, it is necessary to map the shifting material and legal context in which the labour movement's anti-juridical constitutionalism developed and solidified.

IV. CONSTITUTIONALISING LABOUR

A. Labour Law as Subject-Producing

It is only possible to understand the 'anti-juridical constitutionalism' of the labour movement by charting its historical relationship to the state. In this

[20] P Riddell, 'The End of Clause IV, 1994–95' (1997) 11 *Contemporary British History* 24.
[21] R Hattersley, 'Is Equality Outdated?' (2006) 77 *The Political Quarterly* 3, 3.

respect, an understanding of the history of labour law is crucial. As Kay and Mott note, labour law is deeply constitutional. It was only 'through the law of labour … that the working class has been brought into the state and its sphere of right'.[22] This was true both on the individual level and, more profoundly, on the collective level.

As is well known, it was not until the 1918 Representation of the People Act that the property qualification was abolished for men in Britain. The 1918 Act was itself was the culmination of a series of reforms beginning in 1832 with the first Representation of the People Act, and the Chartist movement that sought to push the 1832 Act in a more radical direction. Prior to this period, political rights had been directly tied to the ownership of property. As such, the working class were effectively excluded from the political realm.

In this context, the legal regulation of labour took on a particular significance. In this sphere, each individual contracted as a free person, who is 'equal before the law',[23] with workers and capitalists recognising each other as formal equals. In the absence of political rights, the labour contract was one of the few mechanisms by which members of the working class were recognised as legal subjects. Insofar as the state interested itself in the legal process, this was arguably the major 'constitutional' contract that it made with the working class.

What was true on the individual level was true a fortiori collectively. For Kay and Mott, it was only when the state began to understand the position of labour collectively that real constitutional effects were achieved. They argue that 'sequence of legislation defining both labour organisations and their space in law, was the formation of the legal subjectivity of labour by the state'.[24] In this way, labour law offers a key insight into the understanding of the formation of the British state, since:

> The recognition of the proletariat as the class subject of a general force marked a decisive moment in the development of the state and a clear break from the feudal past. Right was extended to all, and all discontinuities were overcome as the state addressed itself to all classes of society on the same terms. In a sense one can take this moment of the full legal recognition of working-class subjectivity as the completion of the development of the state into a unitary state.[25]

On this reading, there is a twofold constitutional significance to the role of labour law. On the one hand, it had a crucial 'constitutional' effect on the shape of the British state. On the other hand, it also fundamentally shaped the character of the labour movement and the labour movement's relationship to the state.

[22] G Kay and J Mott, *Political Order and the Law of Labour* (Palgrave Macmillan, 1982) 119.
[23] K Marx, *Capital: A Critique of Political Economy* (Penguin, 1990) 280.
[24] Kay and Mott, *Political Order and the Law of Labour* (1982) 117.
[25] ibid.

B. Law, Judiciary and the Labour Movement

The first attempt to regulate the role of labour within the British context occurred in the aftermath of the Black Death.[26] Owing to the vast numbers of people who died during that outbreak, the supply of labour became scarce, giving labourers a greater bargaining power. In response to this, the King and Parliament passed several Ordinances and Acts designed to restrict the bargaining power of labour and regulate wages. The most famous of these was the Statute of Labourers, which set maximum wages and forbade the withdrawal of labour.[27]

The Statute of Labourers set the tenor for the manner of regulation taken in Britain prior to the Industrial Revolution. The aim was to restrain the bargaining power of workers as much as possible, and to significantly limit – or forbid – their ability to organise. This was achieved in a fragmentary manner, across a long historical period, and culminated in the passing of the Combination Acts (1799–1800), which definitively outlawed the organisation of workers in 'combinations'.[28]

Crucially, the legal restrictions on trade union activity were not simply achieved through legislative means. As Trevor Coling has argued, the common law has an 'almost inherent hostility to the encroachment of collective power on individual liberties'.[29] This hostility has meant that the judiciary has played a key role in the restriction of trade union activity. In the most direct sense, the courts have always argued that industrial action generates liability for breaches of contract law. As a result of such breaches, those participating in industrial action can be subject to dismissal from employment, and an employer might obtain an injunction to prevent the breach from taking place.

Judicial interventions took on a great deal of importance in the mid-1800s. In 1824, the legislative ban on trade unions was repealed.[30] In response to this, English judges created a series of legal 'innovations' to circumvent legislation and restrict the ability of the labour movement to organise. In 1853, in the case of *Lumley v Gye*, the courts created the tort of 'inducing breach of contract', which held that if a third party interferes with the contract between two parties, the wronged party could claim damages from the third party.[31] Since industrial

[26] FC Setaro, 'The Legal Genesis of Labor Unions' (1938) 72 *United States Law Review* 514, 514–15.

[27] GW Keeton, 'The Background of the Trades Disputes Act, 1906' (1946) 1 *Industrial Law Review* 33, 33–34.

[28] EP Thompson, *The Making of the English Working Class* (Vintage 1966) 506.

[29] T Colling, 'Court in a Trap? Legal Mobilisation by Trade Unions in the United Kingdom' (2009) Warwick Papers in Industrial Relations No 91, 6.

[30] R Lewis, 'The Historical Development of Labour Law' (1976) 14 *British Journal of Industrial Relations* 1, 3.

[31] D Howarth, 'Against Lumley v Gye' (2005) 68 *MLR* 195.

action will – in a direct and indirect manner – almost always cause further breaches of contract, it will inevitably fall foul of this.

Alongside these direct attacks on the ability to take industrial action, the courts made it difficult for trade unions to function as collectives. Under the 'restraint of trade' doctrine, the courts held that any contractual agreement aimed at restricting competition would be unenforceable at common law. For the courts, trade unions – by binding workers together collectively – were covered by this doctrine.[32] As such, 'agreements between the members and those between the Union and its officers were illegal' and courts 'refused to give any protection to the considerable funds which the unions had accumulated'.[33] This made it almost impossible for trade unions to operate as large, coherent, collective bodies.

Accordingly, it was not simply enough to remove the direct legislative restrictions placed upon trade union organising. Instead, the labour movement increasingly pushed for parliamentary intervention to protect their activity from judicial restraints. Throughout the 1870s, pressure from the growing power of the labour movement combined with liberal sentiment resulted in the passing of a number of statutes that excluded unions from the restraint of trade doctrine[34] and immunised them from the criminal conspiracy insofar as 'an act or combination by two or more persons to do or procure any act in contemplation or furtherance of a trade dispute between employers and workmen'.[35]

In response to this, the judiciary intensified their campaign against organised labour and industrial action. The prominence of tortious liability for inducing a breach of contract rose, and added to it were a series of tortious liabilities around 'conspiracy' (replacing the newly repealed criminal liabilities).[36] Most infamously, in 1901 the House of Lords, in *Taff Vale Railway Co v Amalgamated Society of Railway Servants*, ruled that a trade union could be sued directly in tort, as distinct from its officers, for the losses occasioned by industrial action.[37] This decision directly contradicted the 1871 Act, which expressly stated trade unions could not be an incorporated association.[38] *Taff Vale* 'destroyed the main advantage to unions of their legal status of unincorporated associations and it meant that many trade unions could be made liable to pay heavy damages and costs'.[39]

These developments exerted a fundamental influence on the labour movement. Whilst it had up to that point been largely concerned with relatively

[32] A Hodge, 'The Curious History of Trade Union Law' (2012) 4 *Denning Law Journal* 92, 97–98.
[33] O Kahn-Freund, 'The Illegality of A Trade Union' (1944) 7 *MLR* 192, 193.
[34] ibid 195.
[35] S Deakin and F Wilkinson, 'The Evolution of Collective Laissez-Faire' [2004] *Historical Studies in Industrial Relations* 1, 6.
[36] Lewis, 'The Historical Development of Labour Law' (1976) 4.
[37] [1901] AC 426.
[38] Keeton, 'The Background of the Trades Disputes Act, 1906' (1946) 38.
[39] Lewis (n 30) 4.

narrow industrial issues, in the late 1890s it 'moved decisively towards independent labour representation in Parliament'.[40] The *Taff Vale* case played an absolutely crucial role in accelerating this process, as it convinced the trade union movement that without strong political representation, the judiciary would continually undermine their actions.[41] The result of this was the creation of the Labour Representation Committee and – eventually – the Labour Party itself. In the 1906 general election, the Labour Representation Committee won 29 seats (as opposed to two at the previous election). At the same time, trade unionists actively lobbied Liberals candidates to protect trade unions and industrial action from the judiciary.

The result of these developments was the passing of the landmark Trade Disputes Act 1906. Building on the legislation of the 1870s, the Act provided trade unions with immunity from being sued in tort (thus reversing *Taff Vale*), and provided individuals with immunity from liability in tort insofar as their actions were 'in contemplation or in furtherance of a trade dispute'. This became known as the 'Golden Formula' in UK labour law, and created the basis for the subsequent legal settlement.

This legal settlement was famously dubbed by Otto Kahn-Freud as 'collective laissez-faire',[42] and has also been called 'legal abstentionism'.[43] The British labour movement very explicitly did not seek to achieve a set of legally binding rights around pay, working conditions etc. Whilst there were moves to achieve a minimum floor of these protections, the major regulation of the terms and conditions of the working day was to be achieved through collective bargaining, backed up by threat of industrial action. In such a model, the role of the law was to exclude any interference by the courts in the workplace through providing immunities subject to the 'Golden Formula', and to restrain moves by Parliament to intervene directly within that relationship.

Here, then, we can see the roots of the anti-juridical constitutionalism of the labour movement. Its formative experiences with the state highlighted the need to protect itself from both legislative and judicial intervention. In order to achieve this, it was necessary to build a strong force within Parliament, which had the power to restrain the judiciary. Given the historical experience of an activist judiciary in intervening against the labour movement, expanding that judiciary's power through the provision of legally binding individual rights was entirely off the cards. The formative 'constitutional' experience for the labour movement was directed against an activist judiciary.

This also indicates the fundamental unity of Evans's two wings of Labour's constitutionalism: the 'syndicalism' of collective bargaining – and the associated

[40] C Wrigley, 'Trade Unionists and the Labour Party in Britain: The Bedrock of Success' (2009) 15 *Revue Française de Civilisation Britannique. French Journal of British Studies* 59, 61.
[41] ibid.
[42] Deakin and Wilkinson, 'The Evolution of Collective Laissez-Faire' (2004).
[43] Hodge, 'The Curious History of Trade Union Law' (2012).

power of the trade unions – could only be achieved through an expansive Parliament which could prevent the judiciary from interfering with the labour movement. At the same time, the 'Fabian' ambition of a sovereign Parliament was dependent upon the power of organised labour in the form of the trade unions that constituted the Labour Party and provided it with both material support and industrial might. We can trace the core elements of the labour movement's anti-juridical constitutionalism to its confrontation over issues of industrial action.

V. CONSTITUTIONAL SETTLEMENTS

A. The Plot against Localism

Despite the political advances made by the Labour Party prior to the First World War, they had not managed to attain government power on a national level. However, the Labour Party made advances on a more local level. Absent taking power in central government, the Labour Party experimented with forms of 'municipal socialism'. Most famously in the London borough of Poplar, the Labour Party won 39 out of 40 possible seats.[44]

In the 1920s, the Poplar Borough Council embarked on an ambitious programme of local reform involving the provision of a generous minimum wage for council workers that was equal between men and women. These reforms attracted the ire of both central government and the judiciary. In 1925, the District Auditor – a centrally appointed authority whose job it was to check the financial records of local government – found that Poplar's wages were in excess of the market value, and surcharged the councillors £5000, alleging that wages were not in fact wages but gratuities.[45]

The councillors sought to appeal this decision, which eventually went to the House of Lords. There, in the case of *Roberts v Hopwood*, the judges upheld the District Auditor's decision. The ruling was seen by the labour movement of further evidence of the judiciary's hostility to the labour movement, and was particularly pilloried by George Lansbury, who had previously been a Poplar councillor and became Labour leader in 1932. This conviction was fuelled by the words of the judges, who explicitly stated this hostility. Most infamously, Lord Atkinson found that the Council had acted ultra vires, by taking into account irrelevant considerations, bluntly stating:

> The council would, in my view, fail in their duty if, in administering funds which did not belong to their members alone, they put aside all these aids to the ascertainment of what was just and reasonable remuneration to give for the services rendered to

[44] P Fennell, 'Roberts v Hopwood: The Rule against Socialism' (1986) 13 *Journal of Law and Society* 401, 403.
[45] ibid 402.

> them, and allowed themselves to be guided in preference by some eccentric principles of socialistic philanthropy, or by a feminist ambition to secure the equality of the sexes in the matter of wages in the world of labour.[46]

If *Roberts v Hopwood* marked the death knell of Labour's experiment with municipal socialism, then the 1926 General Strike strengthened Labour's resolve to insulate industrial action. The General Strike represented the trade union movement's first attempt to significantly flex its industrial muscles. Concerned with the deteriorating wages in the coal mining industry, the Trades Union Congress (TUC) called for a general strike.

Despite opposition from the Labour Party – which had begun to position itself as a 'party of government' – the TUC managed to mobilise around 1.7 million workers. The strike was ultimately ineffective. Despite this, there were judicial interventions in respect of the strike. In particular, the National Sailors' and Firemen's Union sought an injunction against one of its branch officials, who was agitating members to join the strike. Justice Ashbury, in the Chancery Division, awarded the injunction, finding that a trade dispute could not exist between a union and the government, meaning the action would not be protected by the Trade Disputes Act 1906, leaving the union liable for damages.

Although this judgment did not have much impact in and of itself, it signalled the continued willingness of the judiciary to thwart industrial action. Perhaps more importantly, it prefigured the legislative changes which would come about after the failure of the General Strike. In 1927, the Conservative government passed the Trades Disputes and Trades Union Act, which explicitly excluded 'political strikes' and secondary action (ie industrial action in support of striking workers from outside of one's own workplace) from the scope of a 'trade dispute'.

B. The Post-war Settlement

When the Attlee government came to power in 1945, it did so in the shadow of these events. It has been frequently remarked that, despite the sweeping changes that this government made in the social, economic and political arenas, the 1945 Labour government largely left the British constitutional order untouched.[47] There is a sense in which this was true. Under the Attlee government there was no radical shake up of the monarchy or the House of Lords, and no decisive moves were made against the judiciary.

[46] [1925] AC 578, 594.

[47] J Bew, *Clement Attlee: The Man Who Made Modern Britain* (Oxford University Press, 2017) 389.

In part, this was driven by the conservativism of the Labour Party. In the post-war context, Labour was at pains to distinguish itself from the communist movement and insisted upon the use of 'constitutional' and 'democratic' measures to achieve socialism. However, to rely solely on this explanation misses the fact that Labour's stance was also a continuation of the deeper constitutional trends in the labour movement outlined previously.

Viewed in the light of Labour's anti-juridical constitutionalism, we can begin to understand the substantive nature of Attlee's constitutional politics. Whilst the Attlee government was conservative insofar as it did not, for instance, radically transform the judiciary, the monarchy or the House of Lords, it nonetheless produced a distinctive constitutional settlement. This constitutional settlement did not attack those institutions of the British state directly; rather, it limited the ability of the institutions to intervene in those areas in which the labour movement had a stake.

On the one hand, this involved the strengthening of the 'Westminster model' and of parliamentary sovereignty. One of the key achievements of the Attlee government was the implementation of a Keynesian-style economic programme. This involved the nationalisation of key industries, a commitment to the achievement of full employment, state-provided benefits for the unemployed and the creation of a National Health Service.[48] All of these developments were driven through a centralised state apparatus under the control of a Labour majority. In this way, the social programme of the Attlee government resonated strongly with the Fabian tradition's need to protect the sovereignty of Parliament.

As Danny Nicol notes, in 1937 Attlee himself had 'emphasized the need to face down the House of Lords in the likely event that it would try to frustrate Labour's policies by using its delaying power'.[49] In practice, a head on confrontation never came, since

> the bulk of Labour's program met no serious resistance from their Lordships. Indeed it was only towards the end of Labour's term, when the Party was having difficulty with its legislation to take over the steel industry, that the government introduced legislation to curb the Lords. The immediate inspiration for the Parliament Bill 1949, which reduced their Lordships' power of delay from two years to one, was as a preemptive measure to get the Steel Bill through.[50]

However, as the foregoing analysis has shown, the labour movement was not simply committed to nationalisation, there was an also an overriding concern about how workplaces would be governed, as embedded in the tradition of syndicalism. A common radical criticism of the 1945 Labour government was its timidity in this regard; whilst key industries were nationalised, they largely

[48] A Cairncross, *Years of Recovery: British Economic Policy 1945–51* (Routledge, 2013); J Tomlinson, 'Mr Attlee's Supply Side Socialism' (1993) 46 *Economic History Review* 1.

[49] D Nicol, 'Progressive Eras, Periods of Reaction, and Constitutional Change' (2014) 15 *German Law Journal* 437, 448.

[50] ibid.

retained older management structures, and there was no comprehensive plan of workers' control or a broader democratisation agenda.[51]

Such a criticism, whilst accurate, misses the deeper constitutional significance of collective laissez-faire. In the post-war period, in much of the advanced capitalist world, social democratic parties sought constitutional and rights-based guarantees for workers. The same could not be said in the British context (and other common law countries). In line with the historical experience of the labour movement in Britain, the majority of workplaces – which in practice meant the majority of people's lives – were to be governed by the collective power of labour (and the exclusion of the judiciary).

The Attlee government took the developments of the inter-war period and significantly expanded them. The 1946 Trades Unions and Trades Disputes Act repealed the 1927 Act, removing the restrictions on the definition of a 'trade dispute'. Specifically, secondary industrial action – industrial action directed against an employer other than one's own – in support of other striking workers was to be protected under the 'Golden Formula'. Importantly, 'political strikes' were, following this repeal, not explicitly excluded from the definition of a 'trade dispute'.

The increased protections for trade unions from judicial intervention gave them a strong ability to project their industrial power. Recalcitrant employers would not simply face the possibly of their own workers taking industrial action, but workers in other industries too. This, combined with the support from the government, pushed employers towards concluding collective agreements with trade unions in order to set wages, pay and conditions in their workplaces. By 1950, around 70 per cent of UK workplaces were covered by such a collective agreement, rising to a high of around 82 per cent in 1979.[52]

C. Collective Laissez-Faire as Constitutional Settlement

For a traditional constitutional lawyer, the developments outlined above might not be understood as any kind of 'constitutional' settlement. Yet, as Nicol notes, when thinking about the 1945 government we need to broaden our understanding of what we mean by 'constitutional'. For Nicol, if 'we interpret constitutional reform as embracing all durable … alterations to the system of government', we can also interpret the nationalisation agenda – which fundamentally transformed the role of government and Parliament – as constitutional.[53]

[51] RA Dahl, 'Worker's Control of Industry and the British Labor Party' (1947) 41 *American Political Science Review* 875.

[52] Ö Onaran, A Guschanski, J Meadway and A Martin, 'Working for the Economy: The Economic Case for Trade Unions' (2015) Greenwich Political Economy Research Centre Policy Brief No PB05-2015, 16.

[53] Nicol, 'Progressive Eras, Periods of Reaction, and Constitutional Change' (2014) 448–49.

What was true of nationalisation was also true of collective laissez-faire. On the one hand, collective laissez-faire was constitutionally significant for what it was *not*. Collective laissez-faire directly embodied the labour movement's profound distrust of judicial intervention. As such, collective laissez-faire represented a direct alternative to a model based on the provision of positive individual rights and protections.

Insofar as collective laissez-faire was an alternative to a positive, rights-based framework, it was also productive of a particular constitutional settlement. As previously noted, prior to the 1980s, collective agreements regulated between 70 and 80 per cent of the workforce. They covered issues around wages, working hours, pensions, working conditions and questions of governance. As such, they were an absolutely essential part of the welfare state: Parliament delivered higher-level political transformations and legislated certain minimum standards, but it was the trade unions – through their collective economic power – that fleshed out the majority of the substance of living conditions.

Harry Arthurs, writing in the Canadian context, characterised this as a form of 'industrial citizenship'.[54] For Arthurs, collective bargaining agreements impacted significantly upon people's various rights; given how much time people spend in the workplace, such rights did not simply include pay and conditions, but also extended to issues of speech and political action. Indeed, Arthurs characterised these workplaces as a 'state within a state'.[55] We need not go as far as Arthurs to understand the fact that the extension of collective laissez-fare had a profound constitutional impact. In essence, it enabled trade unions a significant stake in the governance of the UK; under this arrangement trade unions became constitutional actors.

The unions' role as constitutional actors did not simply extend to their governance function. Although the unions had no formal power to enact positive political transformations, the legal regime around collective laissez-faire granted them a great deal of negative constitutional power. The 1946 Act, and subsequent legislation, defined a 'trade dispute' extremely widely. This gave trade unions the possibility of taking industrial action in such a way as to forestall significant constitutional change, enabling them to block 'proposals for worsening their own legal status'.[56]

The starkest example of this power was in relation to the 1971 Industrial Relations Act. That Act was designed to enable more direct legal and judicial intervention into the employment relationship, which would limit the protection of industrial action and create a new National Industrial Relations Court (NIRC).

[54] HW Arthurs, 'Developing Industrial Citizenship: A Challenge for Canada's Second Century' (1967) 45 *Canadian Bar Review* 786.

[55] ibid 767.

[56] H Collins, 'Review of Trade Unions and the Government by VL Allen' (1961) 1 *New Left Review* 71.

Obviously such developments were inimical to the labour movement's anti-juridical constitutionalism. Rather than just rely on the Labour Party to fight these changes at the legislative level, the trade unions used their position to fight the law directly. Initially, the TUC engaged in a campaign of non-registration. In 1972, matters escalated as more radical union members refused to obey an injunction from the NIRC to cease picketing. Five shop stewards were arrested and jailed for contempt of court, sparking mass union-backed protests, a series of rolling strikes in support and the TUC calling for a national strike. This pressure created a *constitutional crisis*, with the Court of Appeal overturning the convictions and the Industrial Relations Act essentially being scrapped.[57] Underscoring the constitutional role of trade unions in this period, in its February 1974 election campaign – triggered in response to a rising wave of industrial action – the Conservative Party infamously posed the question: 'Who governs Britain?'

Despite appearances, therefore, the 1945 Labour government created a distinct constitutional moment, organised around its anti-juridical constitutionalism. It oversaw a consolidation of the principle of parliamentary sovereignty. It extended the power of Parliament to legislate into a host of previously 'private' economic activity, and ensured that such legislation was protected from judicial intervention. Simultaneously with this, it created a situation in which much of the day-to-day governance of social life was achieved through the collective activity of trade unions, whose power to engage in industrial action was legally protected from external intervention. This wide range of permitted industrial action also meant that trade unions could put their 'economic' power to political uses: industrial action was not simply confined to narrow pay disputes. As such, trade unions were meaningful constitutional actors.

The net effect of this was to create a certain 'division of labour' within the labour movement. In this division, the role of the Labour Party was not to create detailed legislation on substantive issues – from wages to rights etc – but rather to take high-level political decisions around nationalisation and social welfare and to maintain the legal regimes which enabled unions to exist as constitutional actors. In this role, the Labour Party was not simply financially supported by trade unions, but backed up by their economic and political power.

What is remarkable about this situation was that it represented a constitutional settlement; it was accepted not only by the Labour Party, but also – to a degree – by the Conservative Party. As many have noted, the 1945 Labour Party managed to achieved a political and economic 'consensus'. All of the major British political parties accepted the necessity of state intervention in the

[57] L Panitch, *Social Democracy and Industrial Militancy: The Labour Party, the Trade Unions and Incomes Policy, 1945–1974*, 1st edn (Cambridge University Press, 1976).

economy, the goal of full employment and the existence of the welfare state. As Nicol notes, this economic consensus was matched by a constitutional consensus.[58]

In the case of Labour's Fabianism, this was not wholly surprising, as both parties supported 'parliamentary sovereignty, the first-past-the-post electoral system, and a powerful unitary government' for their own reasons.[59] What is more surprising is the degree to which the syndicalism of the Labour Party was also a consensus position. Until 1971, with the Industrial Relations Act, the Conservative Party essentially accepted – however begrudgingly – the constitutional role of trade unions. Even after the struggles in 1971, in its October 1974 manifesto, the Conservative Party accepted an extensive constitutional role for organised labour. Whilst the Party's manifesto noted that trade unions 'are not the government of the country', it granted that they were 'an important estate of the realm'[60] with which close cooperation was necessary, and sought the help of unions not just in relation to pay, but in the design of the industrial relations architecture and even race relations.[61]

D. A Note on Supranationalism

One question that continually haunted Labour's anti-juridical constitutionalism during this period was its relationship to supranational bodies – most obviously in the form of the European Convention on Human Rights (ECHR) and the (then) European Communities. On the one hand, given the relatively conservative, Atlanticist and anti-communist orientation of the Labour Party, it was committed to such supranational projects. On the other hand, they ran directly against its anti-juridical constitutionalism.

This was a very direct issue in the case of the ECHR, where the Attlee government 'believed that human rights were for export only', seeing them as a possible 'propaganda tool against the Soviets'.[62] At the same time, the Attlee government believed that the ECHR might undercut parliamentary sovereignty, and serve as a project by which the Conservative Party could undermine the achievements of social democracy.[63] This equivocal stance translated into the Labour Party reluctantly signing the ECHR, but refusing to 'recognize the jurisdiction of a European Court of Human Rights or the right of individuals to lodge claims

[58] Nicol (n 49) 450.

[59] ibid.

[60] I Dale (ed), *Conservative Party General Election Manifestos, 1900–1997*, 1st edn (Routledge, 2013) 231.

[61] ibid 245.

[62] M Duranti, *The Conservative Human Rights Revolution: European Identity, Transnational Politics, and the Origins of the European Convention* (Oxford University Press, 2017) 226.

[63] ibid 228–29.

regarding violations of the European Convention' and failing to 'incorporate the ECHR into domestic legislation'.[64]

Similar considerations played out in relation to the European Communities. In the 1950s, the Labour government refused to enter into the European Coal and Steel Community, with Attlee arguing it would involve handing over control of the British economy to an undemocratic and unrepresentative body.[65] This continued into the 1960s, when many within the Labour Party – most famously Hugh Gaitskell – argued that the European Economic Community would lead to a political union, and thus reduce Britain's economic and political sovereignty.[66] Crucially, this was in response to the Conservative government's rejected application for European Economic Community (EEC) membership in 1961.[67] Under Harold Wilson, with fears that Britain could be outcompeted by an emerging European bloc, Labour moved to a position of accepting accession in principle, on the basis of achieving a 'good deal'.

When the Conservatives took Britain into the EEC in 1972, Labour criticised the terms, and pledged a referendum in their election manifesto. In 1975, prior to the referendum, the Labour Party membership, MPs and affiliated unions overwhelmingly voted – at a special conference – to leave the EEC.[68] Accordingly, in the 1975 referendum, Labour was officially neutral on the question of EEC membership. Throughout the 1970s and 1980s, with Labour's left in a position of power, the Party's position was to leave the EEC, a position that made its way into the 1983 manifesto.

Crucially, then, anti-juridical constitutionalism meant the Labour Party, and the broader labour movement, was at best ambivalent about membership in supranational bodies. Where circumstance and political necessity did force membership, this tended to be met with manoeuvres to limit the power of these external bodies.

VI. A NEOLIBERAL CONSTITUTIONALISM?

A. Class Politics

It would be a mistake to imagine that the post-1945 constitutional consensus was a seamless situation produced by the Labour Party's superior ideas. As is clear from the 1970s onwards, the consensus did not sit easy with the

[64] ibid 252.

[65] R Davis, 'Euroscepticism and Opposition to British Entry into the EEC, 1955–75' (2017) 22 *Revue Française de Civilisation Britannique. French Journal of British Studies* 6–7.

[66] ibid 8.

[67] S George and D Haythorne, 'The British Labour Party' in J Gaffney (ed), *Political Parties and the European Union* (Routledge, 1996) 110.

[68] C Georgiou, 'British Capitalism and European Unification, from Ottawa to the Brexit Referendum' (2017) 25 *Historical Materialism* 90, 101.

Conservative Party, which ultimately harboured ambitions to dethrone the trade union movement from its constitutional role. Instead, the post-1945 settlement rested on a confluence of material factors. This economic and political situation has variously been known as the post-war consensus, embedded liberalism and Fordism.[69]

The Second World War had marked a sea change in the global economic order. Mobilisations during the war had normalised state intervention in the economy. At the same time, the perceived rootedness of the war in the economic turbulence of the 1930s led to a determination on the part of the major capitalist powers to regulate economic affairs at an international level, through the Bretton Woods Institutions.[70]

To this context was added a high level of dissatisfaction with the state of life on the part of the working classes in the advanced capitalist world, and a greater and more organised labour movement. The prominence of the Soviet bloc during the war, its expansion into Europe and the strength of the European communist movement all meant that capitalism itself was plausibly under threat. In order to hold onto social peace, the European capitalist class had to 'extend and renew its social franchise' and agree to supervision 'by an interventionist state committed to disciplining the market for planning and redistribution'.[71] The position of the advanced capitalist countries within the global imperial order meant that their profit rates could be maintained even with these domestic 'sacrifices'. The post-1945 constitutional order was thus founded on a delicate balance of the coercive power of organised labour and a material context which meant that capital was willing to compromise on a range of issues.

B. The Assault on Labour

The post-war economic and political settlement would only last as long as the capitalist class and its representatives felt that trade-off between 'social peace' and profitability was advantageous. By the 1970s, the settlement was breaking down. A series of international developments had driven down global profit rates.[72] Yet this economic slowdown was not matched by deflation; rather, inflation was on the rise, increasing the cost of living, which generated discontent.

[69] D Fraser, 'The Postwar Consensus: A Debate Not Long Enough?' (2000) 53 *Parliamentary Affairs* 347; N Pizzolato, 'The Making and Unmaking of Fordism' in N Pizzolato (ed), *Challenging Global Capitalism: Labor Migration, Radical Struggle, and Urban Change in Detroit and Turin* (Palgrave Macmillan US, 2013); JG Ruggie, 'International Regimes, Transactions, and Change: Embedded Liberalism in the Postwar Economic Order' (1982) 36 *International Organization* 379.

[70] A Lang, *World Trade Law after Neoliberalism : Reimagining the Global Economic Order*/ (Oxford University Press, 2011) 40.

[71] W Streeck, *Buying Time: The Delayed Crisis of Democratic Capitalism*, 2nd revised edn (Verso, 2017) 24–25.

[72] D Harvey, *A Brief History of Neoliberalism* (Oxford University Press, 2005) 12, 57–58.

Consequently, the 'social peace' promised by the post-war settlement was no longer holding, with sustained industrial action on the rise at the same time as profits fell.

As the material conditions that sustained the post-war compromise began to sour, the advanced capitalist countries began to polarise. The forces of the organised working class and the left sought to deepen social control over the economy, and fought for higher wages and better working conditions. By contrast, capital and its representatives sought to break the power of organised labour and find new opportunities for capitalist accumulation.[73]

During the 1970s in Britain, these battles played out through a series of heightened class struggles. The Labour government was elected in October 1974 on the promise of reigning in trade union demands. Yet the government failed to do so, with the economic crisis worsening to the point that in 1976 Labour was forced to request an emergency loan from the International Monetary Fund (IMF). This culminated in the 'Winter of Discontent', when in the winter of 1978–79 public sector workers took sustained industrial action against a 5 per cent wage cap.[74]

It was against this background that the Conservative Party – under Margaret Thatcher – won the 1979 general election. The Thatcher government moved quickly to defeat the power of organised labour and radically reduce the role of the state in the economy. Thatcher's government oversaw the defeat of major trade unions – particularly the National Union of Mineworkers and the print and media unions – and the privatisation of much of Britain's nationalised industry. If the 1945 Labour government had inaugurated a consensus in Britain, the 1979 Conservative government set about dismantling it.

Of course, the breakdown of this consensus was not confined to Britain alone. The 1979 Conservative government has come to be understood as a harbinger of a wider political-economic global transformation, in which Keynesianism was dismantled to make way for what has subsequently been dubbed 'neoliberalism'. The neoliberal moment was a combination of a set of consciously cultivated ideas and a wider set of political-economic transformations. Neoliberalism was a '*political* project to re-establish the conditions for capital accumulation and to restore the power of economic elites'.[75] In the process through which these conditions were re-established, policy-makers drew on a body of ideas developed by a series of figures – such as Hayek, von Mises and Friedman – in which 'human well-being can best be advanced by liberating individual entrepreneurial freedoms and skills within an institutional framework characterized by strong private property rights, free markets, and

[73] ibid 19.

[74] C Howell and M Vale, 'Family or Just Good Friends? The Changing Labour Party–Trade Union Relationship in Britain since 1979' (1992) 22 *International Journal of Political Economy* 17, 23.

[75] Harvey, *A Brief History of Neoliberalism* (2005) 19.

free trade'.[76] Accordingly, neoliberalism did not simply involve privatisation and deregulation, but wider and more far-reaching transformations.[77]

C. Neoliberal Legalities?

For the classical theorists of neoliberalism, law – and in particular constitutional law – was extremely important.[78] This was true on an obvious level, insofar as law was needed to protect private property, but the commitment to law went beyond this. One of the overriding concerns for neoliberal thinkers was how to insulate the sphere of the 'economic' from popular and social control.[79] Law and legal institutions were the perfect way to achieve this: insofar as a market rationality could be protected by law – and indeed constitutionalised – it could be taken out of the sphere of ordinary political contestation.[80] These neoliberal ideas were very much realised in practice.[81] International legal institutions such as the IMF and the World Bank[82] and regimes such as investment law[83] played a key role in birthing and consolidating neoliberalism.

What was true internationally was also true domestically. For Thatcher herself, there was an indissoluble link between law, 'liberty' and the 'free market'. In a 1981 speech delivered at Georgetown University, she argued that the 'vast expansion of individual liberty, under a common law, has been one of the most remarkable developments of Western man'. This liberty was guaranteed by 'a rule of law which protects personal rights against the arbitrary actions of political authority' and 'economic freedom' which represented 'the foundation upon which the unparalleled prosperity of the West is built'. Such economic freedom 'requires a system of law that identifies and safeguards the right to property and the right to enter into contractual arrangements'.

For Thatcher, the post-1945 settlement had fundamentally broken this delicate balance between law and economic freedom. Under the settlement, the 'reach of government [had] far exceeded' its legitimate role, with governments pursuing 'policies of extensive and detailed intervention far beyond

[76] ibid 2.

[77] P Dardot and C Laval (G Elliot tr), *The New Way of the World: On Neoliberal Society* (Verso Books, 2014).

[78] FA Hayek, *The Constitution of Liberty*, 1st edn (Routledge, 2006).

[79] Q Slobodian, *Globalists: The End of Empire and the Birth of Neoliberalism* (Harvard University Press, 2018).

[80] R Knox, 'Against Law-Sterity' (2018) 6 *Salvage* 49.

[81] For a comprehensive account of the contexts in which this took place, see H Brabazon (ed), *Neoliberal Legality: Understanding the Role of Law in the Neoliberal Project*, 1st edn (Routledge, 2016).

[82] T Krever, 'Quantifying Law: Legal Indicator Projects and the Reproduction of Neoliberal Common Sense' (2013) 34 *Third World Quarterly* 131.

[83] N Tzouvala, 'The Ordo-Liberal Origins of Modern International Investment Law: Constructing Competition on a Global Scale' in JD Haskell and A Rasulov (eds), *New Voices and New Perspectives in International Economic Law* (Springer International Publishing, 2020).

those one would expect to find in a free society'. As such, 'Restoring economic freedoms to Britain was one of the great tasks which the [Conservative] Government set itself'.[84]

Thatcher's vision here was a constitutional one, reflecting on the scope of government and the role that law – and the judiciary – ought to play in social life. The vision was not, as some would have it, simply one of 'deregulation', but one in which the role of the law was to actively create and protect 'liberty' and 'economic' freedom.

D. The Conservative's Radical Constitutionalism

There is a seeming continuity between the 1945 Labour government and the 1979 Conservative government on the issue of parliamentary sovereignty. Like Labour, the 1979 Conservative government used its parliamentary majority to enact sweeping change. However, what the Conservative government did with sovereignty had wide-ranging constitutional consequences that were diametrically opposed to those of the 1945 Labour government.

The most obvious way in which this occurred was through privatisations. If the 1945 Labour government had achieved a constitutional shift through radically widening the sense of what realms could be the subject of public control, the Conservative government set about reducing this scope. The transference of formerly public enterprises into private hands was a profound shift of power and governance in the British economy. However, such widespread change did not simply happen through withdrawing state power. Instead, neoliberalism required the *intensification* of centralised state power. Two key areas in which this took place – and which were of great importance to the Labour movement – were in local government and within the workplace itself.

As Loughlin has noted, the Conservative government 'was committed not only to a general reduction in public expenditure but in particular to cutting back expenditure on such services as education, housing and social services'.[85] Many of these expenditures were in fact controlled by local authorities. Accordingly, one of the key moves of the Conservative government was to reduce the discretion of local authorities as much as possible, and to 'incentivise' them to outsource and privatise services. This was achieved through a series of legal changes to how funding would be allocated to local government.

In 1980, the government passed the Local Government Finance Act. Under the Act, a centrally appointed government body was tasked with calculating the cost of services a local authority needed to provide, as well as the total

[84] Margaret Thatcher, speech at Georgetown University, 27 February 1981 www.margaretthatcher.org/document/104580.

[85] M Loughlin, *Legality and Locality: The Role of Law in Central-Local Government Relations* (Clarendon Press, 1996) 88.

resources theoretically available to the local authority. If a local authority's spending exceeded the cost of services, it would not be fully compensated by the central government. In response to this, however, many local authorities instead chose to increase rates (local taxes) and thus maintain their level of service. The Conservative government then made an even greater set of centralising moves. In particular, under the 1984 Rates Act, the government was able to set a limit for the level at which local authorities could set the rates, with any going above it being 'designated' by the Secretary of State, who could freeze the rate.[86]

The latter changes were a direct response to the resurgence of municipal socialism. In the face of a powerful Conservative government, radical Labour councils pursued programmes of increased spending and local taxation. The two most prominent examples of this were the Great London Council (GLC), under Ken Livingstone,[87] and the Liverpool City Council, which in the 1980s was under the control of the radical Militant Tendency within the Labour Party.[88] The fate of both of these bodies neatly illustrates the new constitutional settlement that was created in the 1980s.

Liverpool City Council took direct action against local government cuts. In 1983, the Council set an illegal deficit budget, gambling that the central government would not actually follow through on its threats. This initially worked, with the Council securing concessions from the central government. This inspired a wider campaign amongst left-wing Labour councils. When, in 1984, a number of these councils were designated for rate capping, some responded by setting illegal budgets and some, including Liverpool, by refusing to set a budget at all. In response, the central government held an extraordinary audit of Liverpool City Council, which found that the Council's failure to set a rate had cost the Council over £100,000 and found the councillors personally liable for the sum. Since the losses were so high, the councillors were legally disqualified from holding office.[89]

The GLC made great use of the discretion afforded to it through pre-existing laws. Through its discretionary funding, it distributed money to community groups, particularly women's groups, racial minorities and LGBTQ groups.[90] It also sought to mitigate the impact of wider cuts. Most famously, the GLC implemented a 30 per cent reduction in prices on the London Underground through its 'Fare's Fair' scheme, funded by increasing local government rates

[86] ibid.

[87] A Cochrane, 'What's in a Strategy? The London Industrial Strategy and Municipal Socialism' (1986) 10 *Capital & Class* 187.

[88] J Ball, '"Militant Liverpool" as Liverpool Exceptionalism: The Rise, Fall and Character of the City Council, 1983–1987' (2017) 166 *Transactions of the Historic Society of Lancashire and Cheshire* 145.

[89] Loughlin, *Legality and Locality* (1996) 185–202.

[90] G Eley, *Forging Democracy: The History of the Left in Europe, 1850–2000* (Oxford University Press, 2002) 460.

in London by 5 per cent.[91] These measures were combatted through the reassertion of centralised state power. In 1986, the GLC and other metropolitan county councils were abolished and in 1988 section 28 of the Local Government Act 1988 forbade local authorities from supporting or promoting LGBTQ groups financially.

This increased centralisation of power was matched by an increased extension of judicial power. In response to the Fare's Fair scheme, Bromley Borough Council – controlled by the Conservative Party – sought judicial review of the scheme, which eventually reached the House of Lords. There, in a case reminiscent of *Roberts v Hopwood* – indeed, explicitly citing that case – the House of Lords found the scheme was ultra vires since the scheme ran contrary to 'ordinary business principles'.[92]

This combination of legislative and judicial intervention was strongest in relation to the trade union movement. At the core of the 1945 constitutional consensus had been the carving out of the workplace as a space governed by the collective power of the union movement. This was achieved through insulating collective bargaining as much as possible from external (especially judicial) intervention. Such a situation was wholly incompatible with the neoliberal transformations pursued by the Conservative government. The trade union movement was a staunch defender of the post-war settlement, and was strong within the nationalised industries. As such, trade unions attempted to use their industrial power to resist these transformations.[93] More importantly, collective laissez-faire was an existential problem for the Conservatives. Insofar as neoliberalism was a project to restore class power and the 'freedom' of the market, it was not possible to grant collective organisations of workers such wide-ranging governing powers.

The Conservatives attacked collective laissez-faire with alacrity. The central initial move, achieved in a number of Acts of Parliament over the 1980s, was to limit the circumstances in which industrial action would be protected from liability. Secondary action was quickly removed from the Golden Formula,[94] workers were narrowly defined to be those directly employed[95] and a trade dispute was understood as narrowly referring to terms and conditions.[96]

Alongside narrowing the range of protection for industrial action, legislation moved towards intervening directly within the internal organisation of trade unions. Legislation restored the *Taff Vale* rules relating to liability for industrial action, and assigned unions legal liability for *any industrial action taken by their members* unless the union repudiated the action, and thus disowned those members.[97] Infamously, in 1984, the Trade Union Act required that industrial

[91] Loughlin (n 85) 231–37.
[92] *Bromley LBC v Greater London Council* [1983] 1 AC 768.
[93] S Milne, *The Enemy Within: The Secret War Against the Miners* (Verso Books, 2014).
[94] Employment Act 1980, s 17.
[95] Employment Act 1982, s 18(6).
[96] Employment Act 1982, s 18(2).
[97] Employment Act 1982, s 15.

actions would only be protected if they had been affirmed by a majority vote in a ballot.

Finally, concerted action was taken against the closed shop. Initially, this was achieved through allowing workers who had been dismissed for not being a member of a trade union to claim damages unless 80 per cent of the workplace voted for the closed shop.[98] However, over the course of the late 1980s and early 1990s, this had been extended, with workers being 'protected' from dismissal if they were not members of a trade union.[99] In this way, the closed shop was couched in terms of the rights of the individual against both their employer and the trade union. Here, the Conservative government's argument was supported by the European Court of Human Rights, which has understood freedom of association to include a right to negative association – ie the right to not join a trade union.[100]

These transformations – only achieved after years of sustained class struggle with the labour movement – tore out the heart of collective laissez-faire. The judiciary, which had been largely excluded under the post-1945 settlement, was now empowered to intervene in industrial disputes. Judicial interventions would be possible in a wider range of instances – since the range of protected action had contracted significantly – and extended to the internal functioning of trade unions. At the same time, the effectiveness of industrial action was lessened considerably, with unions only able to take action for a narrow range of reasons and after engaging in complicated balloting procedures.

E. The Neoliberal Settlement

The 1945 Labour government managed to introduce a series of constitutional transformations which generalised the labour movement's anti-juridical constitutionalism to a national level. The power of Parliament was buttressed and protected, and extended to bring new spheres of 'private' life under social control. Simultaneously, swathes of social life were to be governed through the collective organisations of workers, through the system of collective laissez-faire.

By 1992, this had been completely reversed. The Conservative government had relied upon and extended the power of a sovereign Parliament. However, it had used that power to remove much of the economy from social oversight and subject it to the 'discipline' of the market. This was buttressed by a series of manoeuvres designed to force other bodies – particularly local government – into

[98] Employment Act 1980, s 7(3).
[99] Employment Act 1990, s 1.
[100] See R Knox, 'A Marxist Approach to RMT v the United Kingdom' in D Gonzalez-Salzberg and L Hodson (eds), *Research Methods for International Human Rights Law; Beyond the Traditional Paradigm* (Routledge, 2019).

adopting privatisation. A key element in this was the reinsertion of the judiciary into such spheres. Simultaneously with this, Conservative legal transformations had undercut the ability of trade unions to act as constitutional actors. The range of industrial action was sufficiently narrowed that unions could no longer project their power beyond their own workplaces. As such, the unions could no longer perform the governance role which they had exercised under the post-1945 settlement.

VII. RECONSTITUTING NEOLIBERALISM?

In his 2011 book *From Rebellion to Reform in Bolivia*, Jeffery Webber argues that, despite its radical appearance, the then-government of Bolivia led by Evo Morales represented a form of 'reconstituted neoliberalism'.[101] For Webber, although the Morales period saw political transformations and advances, its 'policy and the class interests it served' signalled a 'significant degree of continuity with the inherited neoliberal model'.[102] Similar accusations were repeatedly levelled against New Labour, who, once in power, preserved many of the changes wrought under the Conservative governments. Eric Hobsbawm for instance – whose writings in *Marxism Today* provided some of the intellectual justification for New Labour's pivot from traditional class politics[103] – dubbed New Labour 'Thatcherism in trousers'.[104]

When Labour was elected in 1997, there was no wave of renationalisations, no restoration of collective bargaining and no realignment on foreign policy; indeed, a core part of New Labour's electoral pitch was the promise to stick to Conservative spending plans.[105] This, in part, helps explain New Labour's departure from anti-juridical constitutionalism. Insofar as New Labour adopted Thatcher's neoliberal settlement, they also internalised Thatcher's constitutionalism.

In this way, New Labour's 'reconstituted neoliberalism' was arguably accompanied by a reconstituted neoliberal constitutionalism. This offers us a negative explanation for New Labour's constitutionalism – that is to say, it provides an explanation for why New Labour did not attempt to recreate the post-1945 constitutional consensus. However, it cannot fully explain the positive elements of New Labour's constitutionalism – that is to say, why New Labour made a turn towards specific constitutional mechanisms. Equally importantly, this position requires further explanation as to why New Labour made the decision to

[101] JR Webber, *From Rebellion to Reform in Bolivia: Class Struggle, Indigenous Liberation, and the Politics of Evo Morales* (Haymarket Books, 2011) 4.

[102] ibid.

[103] H Pimlott, 'From "Old Left" to "New Labour"? Eric Hobsbawm and the Rhetoric of "Realistic Marxism"' (2005) 56 *Labour/Le Travail* 175.

[104] E Hobsbawm, 'The Death of Neo-Liberalism' [1998] *Marxism Today* 4, 4.

[105] W Keegan, *The Prudence of Mr. Gordon Brown* (Wiley, 2004) 250–51.

cleave so closely to Thatcherism and why the wider labour movement either acquiesced to this or was unable to prevent it.

A. The New Social Movements and the End of Anti-juridical Constitutionalism

Towards the end of the 1970s, there was a great deal of concern about the state of the labour movement. In 1978, on the eve of Thatcher's coming electoral dominance, Eric Hobsbawm gave a famous speech, 'The Forward March of Labour Halted', which was later published in *Marxism Today*, the Communist Party of Great Britain's theoretical magazine.

In that article, Hobsbawm argued that the British labour movement had fundamentally changed. According to Hobsbawm, the entrance of women and ethnic minorities into the workforce, as well as the increased number of white-collar, 'middle class' and public sector workers, had led to a sectionalisation and stratification of the working class.[106] In the place of an older, more homogeneous, working-class subject – around which much of the politics of the labour movement was built – was a more fractious grouping. In such a situation, Hobsbawm argued, traditional trade union economism 'may at times actually set workers against each other rather than establish wider patterns of solidarity',[107] and this was particularly the case in the nationalised sectors, where the power of industrial action was 'not in the amount of loss they can cause to the employer, but in the inconvenience they can cause to the public, i.e. to other workers'.[108]

The worries that Hobsbawm first expressed on the eve of the Conservative government became more strongly felt over the course of the 1980s. It was argued that 'Thatcherism' expressed something different from previous Conservative governments, and that this Thatcherism was both responding to significant changes in the social terrain and reshaping society in its wake. As Stuart Hall noted, Thatcherism 'succeeded on the back of a deep and profound disillusionment among ordinary people with the very form of social democratic "statism"' in which 'a centralised bureaucracy … was substantively outside their control'.[109]

Crucially, then, the theorists of *Marxism Today* understood two distinct challenges confronting the labour movement, both linked to a growing 'individualism'. On the one hand, there was the growth in 'identity politics', in part signalled through the growing gender and racial diversity in the workforce, but also through the increasing importance of feminist, anti-racist and LGBTQ

[106] E Hobsbawm, 'The Forward March of Labour Halted?' (1978) 22 *Marxism Today* 279, 283–84.
[107] ibid 286.
[108] ibid 285.
[109] S Hall, 'Thatcherism: A New Stage?' (1980) 24 *Marxism Today* 26, 27.

movements. On the other hand, there was a growing disdain with the monolithic and centralised state. The net result of this was an understanding that the older traditions of the labour movement would need to change.

Such positions went beyond the confines of the intellectuals of the Communist Party (although these intellectuals were influential in their own right, with Hobsbawm known as 'Kinnock's favourite Marxist'[110]) and corresponded to a broader sense that the labour movement would need to adapt to meet these new challenges. What is interesting is that – at least initially – these changes were attempted within the existing framework of the labour movement's anti-juridical constitutionalism. Particularly important here were the experiments in municipal socialism, especially those carried out by the GLC. The GLC was very much focused on empowering grassroots, local organisations, by providing space and finances: these groups were particularly focused around ethnic minorities[111] and LGBTQ groups.[112]

Similarly, the labour movement had – to some degree – attempted to broaden its political coalitions with oppressed groups. Trade unions, the Labour Party, the Communist Party and other radical left wing groups all co-organised anti-fascist work under the umbrella of the Anti-Nazi League.[113] From the mid-1970s onwards, under pressure from black workers – particularly the 1976–78 Grunwick strike – the TUC also broadened its commitment to anti-racism.[114] At the same time, in the resistance to the attacks of the Conservative government on trade unions, solidarity efforts were formed – most famously Lesbians and Gays Support the Miners – which resulted in trade union support for those causes.[115]

Accordingly, during the earlier period of resistance to neoliberalism in Britain, an attempt was made to respond to the changing social conditions within the context of anti-juridical constitutionalism. The idea was that through a deepening and radicalisation of the post-1945 constitutional consensus, it might be possible to arrive at a transformed labour movement. However, as noted in relation to municipal socialism, the Thatcher government pushed back hard against this. By passing section 28, limiting central government funding, capping rates and – sometimes – abolishing troublesome local bodies, the Conservative government cut off the attempt to adapt anti-juridical constitutionalism to the

[110] BD Palmer, *Marxism and Historical Practice, Vol II. Interventions and Appreciations* (Brill, 2015) 247.

[111] H Ouseley, 'Resisting Institutional Change' in W Ball and J Solomos (eds), *Race and Local Politics* (Palgrave Macmillan UK, 1990).

[112] J Vincent, *LGBT People and the UK Cultural Sector: The Response of Libraries, Museums, Archives and Heritage since 1950* (Routledge, 2016) 36.

[113] N Copsey, *Anti-Fascism in Britain* (Palgrave Macmillan UK, 2000) 115–52.

[114] S Virdee, 'Racism and Resistance in British Trade Unions, 1948–79' in P Alexander and R Halpern (eds), *Racializing Class,Classifying Race: Labour and Difference in Britain, the USA and Africa* (Palgrave Macmillan UK, 2000) 140–45.

[115] P Purton, *Champions of Equality: Trade Unions and LGBT Rights in Britain* (Lawrence & Wishart, 2017) 54–84.

new terrain. Similarly, in radically narrowing the range of protected industrial action, the ability of trade unions to articulate the demands of oppressed groups was compromised. It would be legally impossible to take solidarity action in support of oppressed groups, or to directly use economic power to support them.

These legal changes were not the sole driving force in the retreat of the labour movement, but they played a crucial role in shaping the terrain within which the great social struggles occurred. By 1985, and the end of the miners' strike, the social basis for the labour movement's constitutional settlement was thoroughly defeated. A similar pattern played out across the Labour Party itself. Labour's 1983 manifesto was the last attempt to defend and extend the post-1945 settlement. It essentially called for the reinstatement and radicalisation of said settlement – promising extensive renationalisation, the restoration of collective bargaining and an expansion of the power of local government. Labour was defeated in that election, with the right of the Party blaming the manifesto for the defeat.

The net result of all of these developments was a conviction across the labour movement that Britain had entered – in *Marxism Today*'s phrasing – 'New Times'. As the editors put it in 1988, Thatcherism embodied a 'sense of New Times, of living in a new era'; where the left remained 'profoundly wedded to the past, to 1945, to the old social-democratic order', the right appeared 'modern, radical, innovative and brimming with confidence and ideas about the future'. Specifically, in these 'New Times':

> Our world is being remade. Mass production, the mass consumer, the big city, big-brother state, the sprawling housing estate, and the nation-state are in decline: flexibility, diversity, differentiation, mobility, communication, decentralisation and internationalisation are in the ascendant. In the process our own identities, our sense of self, our own subjectivities are being transformed. We are in transition to a new era.[116]

In the wake of the successive defeats of the labour movement, it was understood that the old settlement – including its constitutional order – was dead. In its 1987 and 1992 manifestos, the Labour Party removed any mention of renationalisation and the restoration of collective bargaining.[117] At the same time, absent this anti-juridical constitutional framework, issues of 'identity' – of race, gender and sexuality – were now understood as matters concerning individuals and accordingly best dealt with through the framework of individual rights.

Taken together, these developments engendered a shift in the labour movement's constitutional outlook. Anti-juridical constitutionalism ultimately depended on a model in which collective action – in the form of the state and trade unions – could secure a host of benefits. Yet this collective action was

[116] 'New Times' (1988) 32 *Marxism Today* 1, 1.

[117] I Dale and D Kavanagh, *Labour Party General Election Manifestos 1900–1997 (Volume Two)*, 1st edn (Routledge, 2007) 306, 323.

no longer on the table. Accordingly, the labour movement turned more towards traditional liberal constitutionalism – in particular, conceptions of rights: oppressed groups, as well as workers more generally, could be best protected through the provision of legally binding rights enforced by the judiciary.

The most obvious evidence of this shift was in the rise of Charter 88, an organisation dedicated to securing Britain a written constitution. Charter 88 was highly influential, boasting signatures of several figures from the Marxist (Stuart Hall, Eric Hobsbawm,[118] Ralph Miliband[119]) and social democratic (Will Hutton, David Marquand[120]) left. Whilst Charter 88 met with some hostility from the Labour Party, it did signal the changed conception of constitutional issues on the left and within the labour movement. Thus, the 1992 Labour manifesto, alongside sidelining the key elements of the post-1945 settlement, noted that at the core of the Labour Party's 'convictions is belief in individual liberty' with a focus on 'the rights of the individual'.[121] Under John Smith, the Labour Party 'seemingly embraced Charter's overarching constitutional vision'.[122] Finally, in 1997, Tony Blair stated that he 'subscribe[d] to the vast bulk of Charter 88'.[123]

B. New Labour and Neoliberalism

When New Labour was elected, therefore, it found itself in a very specific moment. The labour movement's historical anti-juridical constitutionalism was based upon a situation in which the collective organisations of the working class could guarantee benefits and protections for the wider working class. However, by 1997, this situation was distant. On the one hand, the offensives of the Conservative governments had created a new legal situation in which the bastions of labour – both in the unions and in local government – were hemmed in by a web of legal restrictions. On the other hand, the long years of Conservative governments had resulted in profound social and political defeats. Alongside these facts – and in part because of them – the wider left and labour movement had grown convinced that anti-juridical constitutionalism was unable to deal with a number of crucially important issues around race, gender and sexuality, and that 'rights' would need to be taken more seriously.

[118] M Hall, *Political Traditions and UK Politics* (Springer, 2011) 192.

[119] R Blackburn, 'Ralph Miliband 1924–1994' [1994] *New Left Review* 15, 21.

[120] D Erdos, 'Charter 88 and the Constitutional Reform Movement: A Retrospective' (2009) 62 *Parliamentary Affairs* 537, 541–47.

[121] Dale and Kavanagh, *Labour Party General Election Manifestos 1900–1997 (Volume Two)* (2007) 316.

[122] Erdos, 'Charter 88 and the Constitutional Reform Movement' (2009) 542.

[123] 'Redesigning Britain's Constitution' *The Economist* (30 October 1997) www.economist.com/britain/1997/10/30/redesigning-britains-constitution.

Of course, even in such a situation New Labour might – hypothetically – have elected to attempt to restore the old settlement: the Labour Party had a huge majority and a great deal of good will. Here, however, it is worth recalling that the post-war settlement – and its attendant constitutional regime – was premised on high rates of global profit and sufficient levels of class struggle that capital was willing to forsake profits in exchange for social peace. In 1997, with the defeat of global communism, the crushing of organised labour and the 'end of history',[124] any attempt to reinstate the post-war settlement would have necessitated an unprecedented level of social confrontation.

Adding to this situation, the Conservatives' constitutional transformation had also fundamentally undermined the division of labour between the Labour Party and the trade union movement. Under the post-1945 consensus, the role of trade unions as constitutional actors created a symbiotic relationship between the two. The Labour Party used its parliamentary power to protect freedom of action for the trade unions and, in return, the trade union movement used its industrial power to support the Labour Party. But the transformations that had occurred under the Conservative governments meant that the trade union movement could no longer carry out that function, confined as it was to a more narrow 'economic-corporate' focus.[125] In such a situation, whilst the trade unions continued to influence the Labour Party through funding, and their institutional position within the Party, their relationship to it had changed, with the Party becoming much more dominant.

All of this taken together helps explain why New Labour essentially preserved Thatcher's constitutional transformations, thus concretising them as a constitutional settlement. Despite this, it would be a mistake to describe New Labour as simply 'adopting' neoliberalism. Insofar as we can characterise the New Labour period as one of 'reconstituted neoliberalism', the specific form that this reconstitution took is vital.

C. New Labour's Constitutionalism

At the dawn of the New Labour era, there was much talk about the politics of a 'third way', in which social democratic objectives were to be combined with a commitment to 'modernisation', markets and efficiency.[126] What this meant in practice was that, as Jamie Peck notes, New Labour's politics were essentially a 'hybrid neoliberalism and a recalibrated form of social democracy'.[127] Stuart Hall perhaps captured this dynamic best, understanding New Labour

[124] F Fukuyama, *The End of History and the Last Man* (Penguin, 1993).

[125] R Knox, 'Law, Neoliberalism and the Constitution of Political Subjectivity: The Case of Organised Labour' in Brabazon, *Neoliberal Legality* (2016).

[126] A Giddens, *The Third Way: The Renewal of Social Democracy*, reprint edn (Polity, 1998).

[127] J Peck, *Constructions of Neoliberal Reason* (Oxford University Press, 2010) xvi.

as a 'social democratic government trying to govern in a neo-liberal direction, while maintaining its traditional working-class and public sector middle-class support, with all the compromises and confusions that entails'.[128]

This, then, is how we best explain New Labour's constitutionalism. It represented the attempt to enact historically social-democratic objectives within a neoliberal constitutional settlement.

New Labour sought to 'modernise' the British state – making it both more transparent and more democratic. This was achieved in numerous areas: from prerogative reform to the Freedom of Information Acts, House of Lords reform and judicial reform. In a sense, none of these manoeuvres represent a radical break with the history of the labour movement: all were essentially aimed at making political processes less alienated from the general public, in a continuation of the aims of Chartism. However, what is markedly different was New Labour's need to foreground these reforms as a programme. In the post-1945 context, such reforms were ultimately seen as unnecessary: rather than directly take on the organisation of the British state, they chose to sideline it. In the absence of the social forces and legal frameworks which had sustained this, however, such an approach was no longer tenable, and so constitutional 'reform' would have to become a direct objective of the Labour government.

In this way, then, New Labour's 'double shuffle' produced a peculiar form of constitutionalism. The older social democratic goals had to be achieved, in part, through frameworks that were compatible with the broader changes wrought by neoliberalism. This entailed a clear break with the labour movement's anti-juridical constitutionalism. The clearest example of this was in the field of individual rights. Whilst New Labour held on to its traditional Fabianism, this was accompanied by a newfound faith in the ability of rights – and the judiciary – to protect individuals. This is most obviously the case with the passing of the Human Rights Act 1998. Yet, the New Labour project also oversaw an expansion of rights relating to equality – in terms of gender, race and sexuality – and moves towards institutionalising these concerns at various points within the state.

It is telling that for those constitutional lawyers with commitments to Labour's anti-juridical constitutionalism, this was an object of hostility.[129] The Human Rights Act in particular, whilst couched so as to not undermine parliamentary sovereignty, nonetheless significantly empowered the judiciary. In a sense, though, this was precisely the point. In the absence of the structures that underpinned anti-juridical constitutionalism, a focus on individual rights and

[128] S Hall, 'New Labour's Double-Shuffle' (2005) 27 *Review of Education, Pedagogy, and Cultural Studies* 319, 323–24.

[129] KD Ewing, 'The Human Rights Act and Parliamentary Democracy' (1999) 62 *MLR* 79; T Campbell, KD Ewing and A Tomkins, *The Legal Protection of Human Rights: Sceptical Essays* (Oxford University Press, 2011).

the concomitant expansion of power of the judiciary was the only viable way to secure certain protections.

This position also explains another important constitutional issue: New Labour's – and the broader labour movement's – much more wholehearted commitment to supranational legal institutions. As previously noted, the labour movement's anti-juridical constitutionalism occasioned, at best, an ambivalent relationship to such institutions. In passing the Human Rights Act and thoroughly embracing the EU, New Labour represented a huge break by endorsing mechanisms through which elite and external bodies could intervene in collective processes

However, absent a viable framework of something like collective laissez-faire, the very isolation of these bodies proved an advantage. If the labour movement is – legally and politically – unable to secure benefits for workers themselves, then the creation of rights enforced by distant bodies suddenly becomes hugely important, since it will insulate such protections from the whims of Conservative governments. In the case of the EU, a key turning point was in September 1988, when Jacques Delors – then President of the Commission of the European Communities – delivered a speech outlining the future of 'social Europe', in which the development of the internal market was linked to the development of internal protections and rights in the labour market.[130]

In the same year, following a left-wing challenge for the Labour leadership from Tony Benn, Neil Kinnock – at a speech in Blackpool – explicitly referenced Delors's vision of social Europe, arguing that social Europe had the 'highest standards of working conditions and workers' rights right across that single market'.[131] Such an attitude fundamentally conditioned New Labour's – and the broader trade union movement's – embrace of much of the constitutional architecture of the EU. In the absence of a collective laissez-faire, the raft of Europe-mandated rights and protections – on equal pay, on working time, on discrimination, etc – represented a tangible form of protection.

Similar considerations underlay New Labour's devolution agenda. The Labour Party had traditionally viewed the devolution agenda as a distraction from achieving real social change. The typical response – in more or less radical ways – was to argue for a strengthening of local control at the level of the workplace, and to push for forms of municipal socialism. Yet New Labour had committed itself to the Conservative spending frameworks of balanced budgets at a local level, and was unwilling and unable to restore collective laissez-faire. Accordingly, with both avenues shut down, some form of devolution was now

[130] J Delors, '"1992: The Social Dimension", address to the Trades Union Congress, Bournemouth, 8 September 1988' (European Commission, September 1988) https://ec.europa.eu/commission/presscorner/detail/en/SPEECH_88_66.

[131] N Kinnock, 'Leader's Speech, Blackpool 1988' (1988) www.britishpoliticalspeech.org/speech-archive.htm?speech=194.

the only plausible way in which demands for self-determination could be met by the labour movement.

What we can thus see is that New Labour's major reforms had a specific material and historical basis. They were attempts to cater to a social-democratic base whilst accepting the end of anti-juridical constitutionalism. This also helps to explain why New Labour's reforms were ultimately so uneven. Many commentators have complained that New Labour's constitutional reforms seemed incomplete and without a coherent objective. Yet what seems irrational from the perspective of liberal constitutionalism can be better understood when we situate New Labour within this context. The awkward fit between social democratic objectives and neoliberal means was never a recipe for a seamless constitutional vision; rather, it produced flurries of activity where these were needed to fulfil those objectives and a comparative neglect of other areas.

VIII. CONCLUSION

This chapter has attempted to map out a difficult historical question: how and why did New Labour make such a radical break with the labour movement's previous 'constitutionalism'? It argued that we can only understand this through an account of the deep historical origins of the labour movement's traditional antipathy towards 'constitutional' reform, which in turn means paying close attention to labour law. It was in the form of labour law that the labour movement first encountered the British state and the wider state apparatus. What this experience taught the labour movement was that the most effective way to protect its ability to organise was not through the creation of constitutional protections, but rather by excluding the power of the law. As such, two principles undergirded the labour movement's 'constitutional' positions: Fabianism, in which a strong democratic legislature could extend social control over the 'private' sphere and insulate key areas of life from judicial intervention; and syndicalism, in which the labour movement emphasised the importance of local action in the workplace and in local government. This came together in an anti-juridical constitutionalism.

This attitude of the British labour movement became institutionalised in the British state following the election of the 1945 Attlee government. That government did not issue sweeping constitutional changes, but rather extended the power of the state through nationalisation, and carved out a huge role for governance on the part of the unions through collective laissez-faire. Crucially, this settlement was based on a confluence of material factors, which enabled a compromise between labour and capital. However, with the crises of the 1970s, this compromise became the subject of intense political battles, in which the representatives of capital sought to claw back the institutionalised gains of the labour movement.

Accordingly, with the election of Margaret Thatcher, that settlement was attacked directly, with a raft of legal changes designed to prevent organised labour from exercising power outside of the narrowest economic circumstances. This was accompanied by a brutal assault on the bastions of organised labour, virtually exhausting them as a social force. In this context, the anti-juridical constitutionalism of the labour movement was shaken. Absent organised social forces, and a legal framework within which they could project their power, anti-juridical constitutionalism seemed unable to protect the working class. At the same time, the growth of other liberation movements – based around gender, race and sexuality – challenged narrow notions of class solidarity.

The net result of this was that when New Labour came to power in 1997 it did so in the context of the material and ideological collapse of anti-juridical constitutionalism. Absent a constitutional alternative, New Labour essentially accepted the Conservative constitutional settlement and sought to advance reforms that would benefit its own social base. This produced the somewhat uneven set of New Labour constitutional reforms.

Given all this, the question remains what ought a constitutional agenda look like for the labour movement. This chapter has attempted to argue that reducing New Labour's constitutional reforms to sheer voluntarism misses the deeper social transformations at work. At the same time, however, New Labour were not wholly constrained in their choices; the wholesale adoption of a neoliberal framework was by no means a necessity. More importantly, decades later, with neoliberalism subject to challenge and Britain embroiled in a series of political and constitutional crises, any possible necessity has long since passed.

This does not mean that a return to the 1945 settlement is possible, or even desirable. The 1945 settlement was based on an extraordinary set of material conditions. Given Britain's declining position in the global division of labour, a return to sufficiently high profit rates is almost impossible, and despite renewed opposition to global neoliberalism, the world conjuncture is hardly revolutionary. As such, a return to the 1945 settlement would require a level of social conflict unseen in Britain. Equally, a return to this settlement in its traditional form would do nothing to address the very real concerns of the feminist, anti-racist and LGBTQ movements.

The basic impulse at the heart of anti-juridical constitutionalism was a certain distrust of the ability and willingness of the institutions of the British state to represent and protect the interests of labour. The aim, therefore, was to as much as possible bring the economy under democratic control, and protect certain areas of governance from the more elitist elements of the state.

The 1945 settlement, in part because of the conservatism of the Labour government, never decisively confronted the state. Because so many of that government's changes were – seemingly – accepted by the Conservative Party and capital, the need to fundamentally restructure Britain's state institutions was not felt. The power of Parliament was understood as the major buttress against the wider elite state institutions, and there was an implicit assumption that a working-class majority would consistently deliver Labour governments. Where Conservative governments did come to power, the force of the labour movement would be sufficient to prevent any major changes.

What this ultimately underestimated was how fragile these developments were. The Conservative legislative assault was able to undermine the resistance through utilising the power of the centralising state. It is here that, following Evans, Fabianism and syndicalism might be said to be in tension. Whilst a Fabian orientation was essential to securing the freedom to organise, it also left that freedom uniquely vulnerable to the election of a determined Conservative government. At the same time, the most effective forms of resistance to neoliberalism in Britain – the trade union movement and local government – operated at the non-central state level. The challenge for the labour movement, then, is how to create and embed legal frameworks that can defend this capacity.

A first step here must be an emphasis on the wider democratisation of the British state. The gamble of the 1945 government was that this could be avoided through legislative insulation, but this proved to be false. Such democratisation needs to be extended beyond Parliament and into those more secretive and elite elements of the British state. A second crucial concern here is local government. Local governments were some of the staunchest sites of resistance to the establishment of neoliberalism, and some of the prime targets for its implementation. Both a significant expansion of power of local government, providing them with autonomy, and the empowerment of grassroots organisations would be central here.

Finally, this chapter has insisted that the 'constitutional' sphere must be understood as being wider than high politics. The position of labour – as embodied in labour law – plays a crucial role in creating Britain's constitutional settlement. As such, any project of labour constitutionalism will need to reorient itself on the question of collective bargaining, and the possible political and constitutional role of organised labour, as well as its relation to other oppressed groups. As others have argued, this will also necessarily involve reconceptualising structures of ownership within the capitalist economy. The workers' control promised by a young Gordon Brown is one effective way to buttress a new constitutional settlement.

It is clear here that such measures break the mould of liberal constitutionalism. It is in this way that they are intrinsically linked with the older traditions of the labour movement. The point was never to focus on constitutional questions on 'their own terms', but rather to consider their relationship to wider political and economic processes. By opening spaces for organising, inviting participation within broader state apparatuses and encouraging direct political mobilisation, such 'constitutional' changes would also serve a key role in reconstituting the organised working class – in all its diversity – as a combative political subject.

16

The Legacy of the New Labour Constitution and the Future of Labour Constitutionalism

MICHAEL GORDON AND ADAM TUCKER

After years in the wilderness, the New Labour government was elected in 1997 on a manifesto of unprecedented constitutional ambition and delivered a set of reforms which fundamentally changed the UK constitution. That 1997 election manifesto promised devolution, the Human Rights Act, reform of the House of Lords, elected city mayors, freedom of information, electoral reform, modernisation of the House of Commons, party funding reform, reinvigoration of local government and more. Other major reforms – including the creation of the Supreme Court – were subsequently added to the agenda. And while not all of those initial aspirations were realised, it was a defining period in the development of the modern UK constitution. This period of constitutional change continues to give rise to a series of questions and controversies about the nature of the contemporary UK constitution and the significance of the changes instigated by New Labour. While this book cannot answer all of those questions nor settle those controversies, the aim of the contributions to this volume – especially when read alongside each other – has been to bring some of them into much sharper relief.

Twenty years did not used to be a long time in UK constitutional law (not even when the conference at which this book originated was originally conceived). But the succession of constitutional controversies provoked by the process of the UK's withdrawal from the EU has made the New Labour reforms seem like a more distant feature of our constitutional history, and their outcome like a relatively well-established part of our constitutional architecture. The New Labour constitution has provided the backdrop – or at least the skeleton of the backdrop – against which more recent controversies have unfolded. It may, of course, turn out to be the case that Brexit and its aftermath prompt an unravelling of the New Labour constitution, or a regression to a prior constitutional mean. Yet equally, the resilience of the comprehensive constitutional reshaping conducted by New Labour should not be underestimated. And, at the very least, the New Labour programme of reform can be seen to have produced a phase of UK constitutional history which provided the essential baseline for the post-EU period to come.

Against the backdrop of the complex legacies of the New Labour constitution identified and analysed in the preceding chapters of this book, in this chapter our aim is to reflect on some more overarching features of the reform programme, in order to assess its contemporary significance and its implications for the future trajectory of UK constitutional change. It is inevitably contentious that a constitution which has deep historical roots, has evolved slowly, and only when absolutely necessary, can now be characterised as 'the New Labour constitution' on the basis of a thirteen year period in government.[1] Yet in establishing a new approach to thinking about and engaging with the constitution, and in changing so many substantive aspects of the system of government, the New Labour years can be seen as a decisive modern moment in the UK's constitutional development. Consequently, it is important not only to understand the impact of specific reforms in distinct areas of activity, but to evaluate the impact on the overarching shape, structure and characteristics of the UK constitution.

In the sections that follow, first we consider the process of reform. In particular, we assess the extent to which New Labour changed the UK's methodology of constitutional reform, in adopting an approach which, while lacking any overarching programmatic coherence, was expansive and proactive. Second, we consider the substance of the New Labour constitution. Our specific focus is on whether the 1997–2010 era of reform has produced a distinctively 'Labour' constitutional settlement, and the extent to which this piecemeal programme of reform is nonetheless underpinned by significant interdependencies. Third, we consider the legacy of New Labour's constitutional project. We evaluate the resilience of the constitutional settlement established under the Blair and Brown governments, some of which is the subject of ongoing political contestation. We discuss whether the change in the methodology of reform has also changed our consciousness of the constitution more broadly. Finally, and as necessitated by our preceding analysis of the New Labour constitution, we explore the parameters of a framework for future (Labour) constitutional reform.

Overall, across this chapter we argue that the New Labour era of reform was a crucial period for the development of the UK constitution. Between 1997 and 2010, New Labour established a significantly altered constitutional framework in which major political shifts have occurred, from Brexit to the extension and embedding of devolution and to the change in power of the courts. New Labour changed some – but certainly not all – of the key institutions and norms of the UK's legal and political system, but also changed attitudes to the constitution

[1] See the Introduction to this volume.

itself. It is in that sense that the modern UK constitution is the New Labour constitution. Yet New Labour's constitutional creation was also far from comprehensive, many aspects of it remain controversial and some of its key components are the targets of further reform. How much of the substance of the New Labour constitution will endure is difficult to predict, and a long period of stasis seems unlikely. Yet, the reforming ethos which New Labour instilled into UK constitutional activity has been crucial to generating the current political counterreaction, and we outline a revised approach to Labour constitutionalism which will be required beyond that.

I. PROCESS AND THE NEW LABOUR REFORM PROGRAMME

While the UK is famous for the flexibility of its uncodified constitution, organised around the doctrine of the sovereignty of the UK Parliament, in some respects this flexibility is more theoretical than actual. The flexibility of the UK constitution in theory was traditionally constrained by a conservative, if not outright complacent, attitude to whether that flexibility actually ought to be exploited to change anything. As Rodney Brazier has argued, the standard methodology of constitutional reform in the UK was 'reactive' and 'ad hoc'[2] – in other words, the UK constitution worked very well and required no attention, until it did not. At which point, often prompted by major external events 'such as a political scandal or national disquiet',[3] reform would be implemented, and the smooth operation of the constitution would resume. To reverse the usual order of the phrase, if it did not require fixing, it was not broken.

The approach of New Labour challenged this traditional method, at least to some extent, for the New Labour constitutional reform programme was, in large part, the product of a proactive, rather than a reactive, approach to legal and political change. It was planned in detail during Labour's period in opposition, notably under the leadership of John Smith and then Tony Blair.[4] It was also an agenda which was developed in collaboration with the Liberal Democrats, reflecting Labour's attempt to build some kind of cross-party support for these plans, while also securing the support of a potential coalition partner in government if (despite its considerable lead in the polls) it had failed to win an absolute majority in the House of Commons. Prior to the 1997 general election, the two parties set up a Joint Consultative Committee on Constitutional Reform, producing a report in March 1997 which would 'form the basis of a New Labour

[2] R Brazier, 'New Labour, New Constitution?' (1998) 49 *Northern Ireland Legal Quarterly* 1, 7; see also ch 2 in this volume.

[3] ibid 7.

[4] See R Blackburn and R Plant, 'Introduction' in Blackburn and Plant (eds), *Constitutional Reform: The Labour Government's Constitutional Reform Agenda* (Longman, 1999).

Government's constitutional policies'.[5] Once in office, Labour's 1997 landslide majority of 179 seats meant that the support of the Liberal Democrats was not necessary to sustain a government or the reform programme. Yet a Joint Consultative Cabinet Committee focused primarily on the constitution was created with five seats for Liberal Democrats, to supplement the six seats for Labour ministers.[6] This cabinet committee lasted until 2001, when it was suspended and then abolished after Charles Kennedy replaced Paddy Ashdown as Leader of the Liberal Democrats.[7]

The New Labour approach therefore took the constitution as something which could, in a number of ways, be positively and deliberately changed to improve its operation. To describe this as a shift to proactive constitutional reform does not mean there were no other driving factors, beyond a desire to enhance the UK's system of government. This renewed focus on constitutional reform was still in part a reaction to Labour's years in the political wilderness, when the Conservative party, especially between 1979 and 1990 under the leadership of Margaret Thatcher, had demonstrated the uninhibited scope of the power possessed by a majority government to disassemble the state. Yet the Labour constitutional reform agenda that Thatcher's attack on welfare and public ownership prompted was an entirely general response aimed at diluting and dispersing state power, which accepted rather than challenged the 'Competition State' which the Conservatives had created.[8] In that sense, New Labour's reform programme either transcended the immediate circumstances of the UK's political system after Thatcherism or failed to address the real challenge to the state – or indeed both. However, as Evans argues, a proactive series of reforms of this scale and extent did 'represent a historic challenge to both the British political tradition and Labour Party orthodoxy'.[9]

In other respects, New Labour's approach to constitutional reform was less of a break with the dominant method. Despite the readiness with which we – and others – refer to the reforms enacted by the New Labour governments as a 'programme' of reform, it is a famous and enduringly striking feature of the project that it was not programmatic in a significant way. In fact, it was both conceived and delivered in piecemeal form. In this respect, therefore, New Labour made little departure from the traditional ad hoc approach to constitutional reform which long preceded its arrival in office.[10]

[5] Brazier, 'New Labour, New Constitution?' (1998) 8.

[6] ibid 16–17. This Joint Cabinet Committee was suspended in 2001 after Charles Kennedy replaced Paddy Ashdown as Leader of the Liberal Democrats.

[7] 'Lib–Lab Committee Disbanded' *BBC News* (20 September 2001) http://news.bbc.co.uk/1/hi/uk_politics/1554194.stm.

[8] M Evans, *Constitution-Making and the Labour Party* (Palgrave Macmillan, 2003) ch 3.

[9] ibid 98.

[10] As Lord Falconer argued at the time, 'If we wait for a big vision of the constitutional jigsaw before we move forward, we will never move at all'; 'What is Labour doing to the constitution?' *Prospect* (20 May 2004) www.prospectmagazine.co.uk/magazine/whatislabourdoingtotheconstitution.

It was not designed as a coherent programme. The bulk of the constitutional promises made in the 1997 manifesto came under the rubric (itself the ninth of the 10 promises around which the manifesto was organised) of 'cleaning up politics'. And it is clear that – like the matters listed under each of the 10 promises – the various strands in that aspect of the manifesto were linked merely thematically rather than programmatically. The creation of the Supreme Court never featured in a manifesto. It was first formally proposed in a Consultation Paper produced by the Department for Constitutional Affairs in 2003, which characterised the change as 'part of the Government's continuing drive to modernise the constitution and the legal system'.[11] Whilst that characterisation alluded to the rest of the set of reforms by then underway, the White Paper made no further attempt to integrate into them the creation of a Supreme Court. And it is noteworthy that even that allusion was equivocal as to whether the creation of a Supreme Court was properly understood as a change to the constitution or to the legal system. The various strands of what became New Labour's constitution were introduced and promised as standalone reforms, united (if at all) only by reference to the vague and shallow principles of cleaning up and modernisation.

It was also not delivered as a coherent programme. Each particular measure had a specific government department tasked with ensuring its enactment.[12] This 'fragmentation of responsibility'[13] reflected an underlying belief that the reforms were seen as separate means of making changes to distinct parts of the system of government. Individual reforms were each generally enacted in their own statute – including the devolution settlements for Scotland, Wales and Northern Ireland, which were notable also for their initial asymmetry.[14] The passage and the coming into force of these various statutes was spread over a considerable time, following an uneven '"stop–go" cycle' which saw more stop and less go as New Labour's time in government went on.[15]

[11] Department for Constitutional Affairs, *Constitutional Reform: A Supreme Court for the United Kingdom* (CP 11/03, 2003).

[12] R Hazell, 'Reinventing the Constitution: Can the State Survive?' [1999] *PL* 84, 100: 'The lead is currently divided between eight Whitehall departments: the Home Office, Scottish Office, Welsh Office, Northern Ireland Office, Department of the Environment, Transport and the Regions, Foreign Office, Lord Chancellor's Department and the Cabinet Office.' The creation of the Department for Constitutional Affairs in 2003 provided a degree of institutional unity, but this was short lived, as the Department was replaced by the Ministry of Justice in 2007.

[13] ibid.

[14] While still an important feature of the UK's devolution arrangements, to some extent that asymmetry is now receding; for example, the Government of Wales Act 2006 went beyond the initial 1998 Act in establishing a system of primary legislative power which brought Wales into greater alignment with Scotland and Northern Ireland. That trajectory has continued with the enactment of the Wales Act 2017, which creates a reserved rather than conferred powers model for Wales, again bringing those structures into greater (but certainly not complete) alignment with the Scottish and Northern Irish models, which themselves differ in key respects.

[15] Evans, *Constitution-Making and the Labour Party* (2003) 93. Compare the 12 constitutional Bills introduced in the 1997/98 parliamentary session with the two constitutional Bills introduced in 2009/10, producing the Constitutional Reform and Governance Act 2010 and the (incredibly short) Northern Ireland Assembly Members Act 2010.

In short, there was no attempt at casting the reforms as a single programme through simultaneity, and no attempt to rationalise them as adding up to more than their constituent parts.[16]

Although this body of legislation contributed a substantial new mass of written sources to the constitution, it was at no time delivered as a codification or part-codification project (even by stealth). Despite some claims that New Labour had established an 'incipient codified constitution',[17] the closest it actually came to exploring codification was towards the end of its era of reform in 2007, when the new Prime Minister, Gordon Brown, launched his consultation project *The Governance of Britain*. Brown's paper suggested that it 'might in time lead to a concordat between the executive and Parliament or a written constitution',[18] yet no serious attempt to deliver this ever followed. Indeed, despite his palpable enthusiasm for constitutional reform – which far exceeded that of his predecessor Tony Blair – Brown's key legislative contribution to the New Labour constitution was underwhelming and lacking clear focus. His Constitutional Reform and Governance Act 2010 was rushed through in the parliamentary 'wash up' before the 2010 general election, and while putting the Civil Service and Parliament's role in relation to treaties on a statutory footing, the Act was shorn of the radicalism Brown had sought when exploring the possibility of codifying the portfolio of royal prerogative powers exercised by the monarch on ministerial advice.[19] And for all its significance, even that original proposal would in many respects still have been another standalone reform.

Gordon Brown's flirtation with codification did set in train the process which, in 2011, saw the creation of a *Cabinet Manual*, but only after New Labour had been displaced by the Conservative–Liberal Democrat Coalition government. The *Cabinet Manual* did provide a broad overview of many key constitutional rules, functions and relationships, and could – at least in part – have helped to lay the ground for a subsequent codification exercise. Yet, in reality, it is an executive-focused and executive-produced document, which was 'not intended to be legally binding or to set issues in stone'.[20] In that sense, both in its belated publication and its narrow presentation of the constitution from the viewpoint of only the government, the *Cabinet Manual* was not systematically integrated into the New Labour reform programme, and therefore provides a further indication of the piecemeal tendencies of this era of constitutional change.

[16] See also Gee, ch 5 in this volume, on the 'lack of a coherent strategic vision at the very heart' of New Labour, p 90; and Masterman, ch 10 in this volume, '[the project] was not informed by any overarching constitutional vision', p 196.

[17] V Bogdanor, 'Our New Constitution' [2004] *Law Quarterly Review* 242, 259.

[18] *The Governance of Britain* (Cm 7170, 2007) [212].

[19] See *The Governance of Britain: Review of the Executive Royal Prerogative Powers: Final Report* (Ministry of Justice, 2009).

[20] *Cabinet Manual* (2011) Preface by Sir Gus O'Donnell, iv.

The process, then, was proactive, but remained piecemeal.[21] The piecemeal nature of the reform process was also exacerbated by the importance of personalities in the process: the priority accorded to any given aspect of the reform programme varied according to the extent to which senior figures in New Labour were committed to it.[22] So not only were reforms delivered individually, severed from each other both in time and in substance, but the construction of the New Labour constitution was often guided not by principle or substantive priority, but rather by the (potentially arbitrary) preferences of key actors in the political process more widely.

But what of the substance? Is the substance of the New Labour constitution merely an assemblage of unsystematic alterations to the constitution? Or does it have any overall coherence despite its piecemeal origins?

II. THE SUBSTANCE OF THE NEW LABOUR CONSTITUTION

The previously published literature on the New Labour constitution defended an astonishing variety of views on the range and significance of its substantive impact. At one end of the spectrum, Peter Dorey was sceptical. Whilst acknowledging that the programme 'went further than any ... reforms pursued by previous Labour governments', he nevertheless dismissed its outcome as 'highly conservative', and characterised it as 'sustain[ing] traditional and long-standing features of the British political system'. At the other end of the spectrum, Vernon Bogdanor concluded (in the title of his book on the topic) that the New Labour project had yielded a 'new British constitution', in the sense that it 'had the effect of replacing one constitution with a new constitution'.[23] In his seminal *The Third Way*, Giddens cast the New Labour reforms as a fundamental shift in our constitutional arrangements, 'a process of deepening and widening democracy', whereas Sir John Baker argued that New Labour had 'simply' downgraded the constitution into just another normal policy area, 'on a par with immigration, defence procurement, or the health service, to be managed on a routine basis as an act of governmental power'.[24]

The essays in this collection tend to continue rather than settle this tradition of disagreement.[25] But these debates can usefully be organised around

[21] See also Wheatle, ch 4 in this volume, who treats the piecemeal nature of the process as part of the very nature of (what she labels) legislative constitutionalism, p 64.

[22] For example, the regionalism agenda was driven by the personal enthusiasm of John Prescott, freedom of information legislation was championed in particular by Derry Irvine, and the abolition of the role of Lord Chancellor was a personal project of Tony Blair. See also chs 1 (Falconer), 2 (Brazier), 8 (Worthy) and 9 (Thompson) in this volume.

[23] P Dorey, *The Labour Party and Constitutional Reform: A History of Conservativism* (Palgrave, 2008), 1; V. Bogdanor, *The New British Constitution* (Hart, 2009), 1.

[24] A Giddens, *The Third Way: The Renewal of Social Democracy* (Polity, 1998) 69; J Baker, 'The Unwritten Constitution of the United Kingdom' (2013) 15 *Ecclesiastical Law Journal* 4, 9.

[25] Notably chs 1 (Falconer), 3 (Tyrrell), 10 (Masterman) and 15 (Knox) in this volume.

two important underlying themes. First, what was distinctively *Labour* about the New Labour constitution? And secondly, to what extent can the content of the New Labour project be understood collectively as a coherent package of constitutional reform?

First, there are (at least) two senses in which a Labour constitution might usefully be thought of as distinctively 'Labour'. It might be 'Labour' in a pure (or literal) sense, such that the 'Labourness' of the New Labour constitution would turn on the extent to which it reoriented the UK's system of government around the pursuit and protection of the interests of workers – either institutionally (say, by securing or entrenching the institutional position of trade unions) or substantively (say, by securing special protection for labour rights via entrenchment, or by giving greater domestic prominence or priority to the UK's relevant international commitments, such as international labour standards set by the International Labour Organization). As Knox shows, the New Labour constitution is not – and indeed makes no real claim to be – a Labour constitution in this sense.[26]

It may still, however, have an intelligible claim to being a distinctively *New Labour* constitution – Labour, that is, in a looser, less literal sense, but one which aligns more closely with the orientation of the Labour Party during its period in government. Tony Blair's famous reform of Clause 4 of the Labour Rule Book diluted the party's commitment to the connection between work and political justice and instead gave greater prominence to the ambition of creating 'a community in which power … [is] in the hand of the many not the few', an idea which also permeated the party's 1997 general election manifesto.[27] It might make more sense to assess the Labourness or even the New Labourness of the New Labour constitution in that sense, by asking about the extent to which the programme delivers on the promise to distribute power from the few to the many, as a decentralising project organised around this newly prominent foundational value of the Labour Party.[28]

Yet this turn to constitutionalism for the Labour Party was also intimately connected to the reorientation which resulted in New Labour itself. The programme of liberal constitutional reform implemented so significantly by New Labour was itself the product of a shift away from Labour's more traditional constitutional minimalism. The old approach was based on accepting the utility of the doctrine of parliamentary sovereignty to enable a strong government, elected on a popular mandate, to deliver a radical programme

[26] See further Knox, ch 15 in this volume. For example, although New Labour enacted the National Minimum Wage Act 1998, its legislative reforms to restore the position of trade unions which had been comprehensively disempowered under successive Conservative governments were limited in effect; see T Novitz, 'A Revised Role for Trade Unions as Designed by New Labour: The Representation Pyramid and 'Partnership'' (2002) 29 *Journal of Law and Society* 487.

[27] Labour Rule Book. 1997 Manifesto.

[28] See chs 3 (Tyrrell), 8 (Worthy), 10 (Masterman) and 14 (Trueblood) in this volume.

of socialist change.[29] The unlimited law-making power of the UK Parliament would be an instrument for fundamental political, economic and social reform, free of any judicially enforced constitutional limits, while also offering the potential to challenge any other vested interests (most obviously in the unelected House of Lords) which sought to obstruct that change.[30] It was this basic socialist approach to the constitution which was both challenged and complicated by New Labour's programme of liberal constitutional reform.[31] But whether the effect was direct or incidental, this shift in constitutional strategy ran alongside a broader dilution of socialism and its replacement by the social democratic centralism of the 'third way', which equally rejected the New Right and the Old Left. As such, the fact that this was a distinctively New Labour brand of constitutionalism is significant, because it leaves open the question of what a more traditional Labour constitutionalism might in future become.

Secondly, how coherent was the reform project? The piecemeal way in which the project was developed might seem to undermine its potential to make sense as a single, coherent project in its own right. But this is tempered by significant elements of interdependency between the various elements of the reform programme, an underpinning with the potential to lend the whole greater coherence than its piecemeal origins might seem to promise. In particular, whilst the Human Rights Act was treated in the manifesto and in Parliament as a standalone reform, the European Convention on Human Rights (ECHR) is also tightly woven into the devolution settlements.[32] The additional powers allocated to the courts under the Human Rights Act 1998 (HRA) contribute to the justification for the creation of an institutionally independent Supreme Court, and the fact that this court acquired jurisdiction over devolution issues from the Judicial Committee of the Privy Council integrates devolution questions more decisively into the UK's core body of constitutional law.

Similarly, other elements of the New Labour programme (and again, in particular, the devolution settlements) presupposed the UK's continuing membership of the EU. This interdependence was a significant source of difficulty in the Brexit process. The repatriation of powers from the EU gave rise to tension around the awkward questions of whether those competencies properly belong in Westminster or with the devolved administrations, which required

[29] See, eg RS Cripps, *Can Socialism Come by Constitutional Methods?* (Socialist League, 1933).

[30] See, eg the Parliament Act 1949, enacted under the Labour government of Clement Attlee, which amended the Parliament Act 1911 to further reduce the veto power wielded by a House of Lords which was at that time dominated by Conservative peers.

[31] See, eg A Wright, 'British Socialists and the British Constitution' [1990] *Parliamentary Affairs* 322.

[32] Indeed, it is striking that the analysis which leads Dorey to his sceptical conclusions on the project as a whole neglects the Human Rights Act: Dorey, *The Labour Party and Constitutional Reform* (2008).

answering through the painstaking development, one policy area at a time, of common frameworks.[33] And the withdrawal from the EU single market led to the project to construct a replacement – for the first time, overarching 'internal market' legislation for the UK.[34]

In one sense, these interdependencies illustrate the way that the New Labour constitution has come to hang together despite its piecemeal origins – it may have obtained a systemic character, to some degree, even if it was not designed in this way from the outset.[35] Yet in another sense, it is also notable that a central part of this interdependency was the UK's membership of the EU, which long predates New Labour's reform programme. If it was EU membership which gave greater coherence to the New Labour project, then it may be that Brexit makes that constitutional framework more vulnerable to being unravelled – for example, by prompting change to the devolution arrangements as the UK government seizes control of powers returning from the EU, which would otherwise fall within existing areas of devolved competence.[36] An important consequence of the partial interdependency of New Labour's constitution may therefore be that reform which corrodes one of those foundations can thereby undercut the coherence of the New Labour constitution as a whole – for example, if a British Bill of Rights was to replace the HRA and depart from ECHR standards at UK level, it is far from clear how such a dilution in rights standards could be reflected in the devolution statutes.

The substance of the New Labour constitution is therefore somewhat contradictory – it may not have been a traditionally 'Labour' programme of reform, but it has produced a distinctively 'New Labour' constitution. And it may not have been a coherent body of constitutional change, but it is based on substantive interdependencies which continue to shape its operation. With its status and content a complex and uncertain matter, we therefore turn to consider the potential legacy of the New Labour constitution.

III. THE LEGACY OF THE NEW LABOUR CONSTITUTION

The chapters in this collection invite reflection on the overall legacy of the New Labour constitution. In this section, we explore how the resilience of the New Labour constitution has led to it setting the background conditions for politics, often in ways which have been – for now at least – widely accepted across the political spectrum, beyond the New Labour era, across Coalition, minority- and now majority-Conservative administrations. These background

[33] https://www.gov.uk/government/collections/uk-common-frameworks.

[34] United Kingdom Internal Market Act 2020.

[35] See also Tyrrell on the argument that Freedom of Information and House of Lords reform were seen as necessary supports for human rights protections in the absence of the possibility of entrenchment: Tyrrell, ch 3 in this volume, pp 44–5.

[36] See EU (Withdrawal) Act 2018, s 12.

conditions include a sustained tension between juridification, which is a prominent feature of the New Labour constitution, and the preservation of political avenues of constitutional accountability, which occupied a more secondary role in that programme. The relative stability of this New Labour model also means that it has effectively embedded, or at least put in a privileged position, one particular conception of what counts as constitutional – or even as constitutionalism – in the UK tradition, even as the substance of the project is becoming the subject of renewed political contestation.

The changes made by New Labour still resonate today. They set the scene for both everyday government and future initiatives in constitutional reform. The New Labour constitution has been the backdrop for the MPs' expenses crisis, the Coalition government, austerity, the Scottish independence referendum, the EU referendum and its aftermath and, most recently, the state response to the COVID-19 pandemic. So a crucial part of the legacy of the New Labour reforms is the extent to which they equipped the UK with appropriate institutional arrangements for the navigation of each of these political projects and constitutional challenges.

The MPs' expenses crisis, which started in 2009 but generated a massive challenge to the UK's political class extending well beyond New Labour and into the next decade, was triggered by the pursuit of information under the Freedom of Information Act 2000.[37] The Coalition government was formed in accordance with a process established in a (then draft) chapter of the *Cabinet Manual* which emerged from New Labour's Governance of Britain proposals,[38] and that coalition was (at least in part) made possible by a commitment to pursue a referendum on voting reform which New Labour had promised and then abandoned.[39] The 2014 Scottish independence referendum was a direct result of the SNP's success in taking control of the Scottish Parliament created by New Labour, winning an outright majority in the 2011 elections despite the mixed member proportional voting system making single party government theoretically difficult to achieve. The EU referendum was the culmination of a process of bringing referendums into the constitutional mainstream which accelerated during the New Labour era.[40] The drive for an EU referendum in particular was intensified by Labour's unwillingness to extend its 2005 manifesto commitment to hold a referendum on a proposed EU constitutional treaty to its eventual replacement, the Treaty of Lisbon. New Labour was also responsible for starting to create a domestic culture of conditional EU membership which led to the coalition's EU 'referendums locks', which in turn bridged the

[37] See, eg P Leyland, 'Freedom of Information and the 2009 Parliamentary Expenses Scandal' [2009] *PL* 675.

[38] Letter from the Cabinet Secretary to the Chair of the Justice Select Committee (23 February 2010) https://publications.parliament.uk/pa/cm200910/cmselect/cmjust/396/396we02.htm.

[39] Labour Manifesto 1997 (n 23).

[40] A tradition explored by Trueblood, ch 14 in this volume.

gap to an 'in/out' referendum.[41] Finally, legal analysis of the response to the COVID-19 pandemic was in the first instance primarily framed in terms of human rights questions because the HRA moved the language and conceptual framework of human rights to the centre of the UK constitution.[42]

However, while the New Labour constitution has clearly framed the responses to many major political events since 2010, we can also question the extent to which it had a substantial impact on a number of key strands of political activity. The austerity agenda pursued first by the Coalition government and then by Conservative administrations provides a clear example – this attack on public spending was explicitly framed as a response to New Labour's economic policies, yet the New Labour constitution offered little to obstruct these attempts to contract the state. If one motivation for the New Labour reform programme was to create barriers to a future reshaping of the welfare state following the experience of Thatcherism, then this did not seem to have been achieved. The HRA, for example, provided few obstacles to the radical reduction of welfare benefits, and even where such litigation did succeed it was belated and any constraints on austerity were narrow in effect.[43] While still recognising that the New Labour constitution played a role in shaping the response to austerity,[44] the lack of impact here shows there is a need to recognise the modesty of some of these achievements.

One reason the New Labour constitution provided the background for this series of significant political periods, the majority of which took place under future non-Labour governments, is that the substance of the reform programme has proved to be generally resilient. Whilst the programme originated in the party's general election manifesto, and each of its elements was contested by the Conservative opposition in Parliament, it has nevertheless survived – and largely become stably established during – a long period of Labour being in

[41] For legislation in the New Labour era imposing requirements of approval by Act of Parliament or motions in each House for changes to EU powers, see European Parliamentary Elections Act 2002, s 12 and European Union (Amendment) Act 2008, ss 5–6. For the coalition era referendum locks, see European Union Act 2011, ss 2, 3, 6.

[42] See, eg Joint Committee on Human Rights, *The Government's Response to COVID-19: Human Rights Implications* (21 September 2020, HC 265, HL 125). See generally on this shift, chs 3 (Tyrrell), 4 (Wheatle) and 10 (Masterman) in this volume.

[43] See, eg *R (Reilly) v Secretary of State for Work and Pensions* [2013] UKSC 68 (workfare penalties unlawful but overturned by retrospective legislation); *R (SG) v Secretary of State for Work and Pensions* [2015] UKSC 16 (benefit cap did not unlawfully discriminate against women); *R (Carmichael and others) v Secretary of State for Work and Pensions* [2016] UKSC 58 and *RR v Secretary of State for Work and Pensions* [2019] UKSC 52 (bedroom tax unlawful only in extreme circumstances where spare room needed for carers for those with disabilities); *R (SG) v Secretary of State for Work and Pensions* [2015] UKSC 16 and *R(DA) v Secretary of State for Work and Pensions* [2019] UKSC 21 (benefit cap did not unlawfully discriminate against single mothers); *R (SC, CB and 8 children) v Secretary of State for Work and Pensions* [2021] UKSC 26 (two child limit on child tax credit did not unlawfully discriminate against women, children or children in large families).

[44] On the relationship between law and austerity more generally, see R Knox, 'Against Law-Sterity' (2018) 6 *Salvage* 49.

opposition. The HRA is perhaps the only part of the New Labour constitution which has been routinely treated in overtly partisan fashion.[45] Others, like the existence of the Supreme Court or freedom of information, generally seem to have established themselves as above routine party politics, for now at least. While both have, at different points, been subject to periods of scepticism,[46] for the most part since 2010 they have been relatively stable parts of the structure in which politics happens, rather than matters of ongoing contestation themselves. Where (and for as long as) this has happened, we have the converse of Baker's characterisation of the New Labour project: rather than downgrading the constitution to the status of ordinary party politics, the project succeeded in elevating some issues of partisan controversy above the political fray.

Other elements of the programme have been deepened by governments which might have been expected to be inclined to reverse them. Devolution provides a stark example of this resilience. Originally opposed by the Conservatives, devolution was significantly extended on multiple occasions under both David Cameron, when leading both coalition and majority Conservative governments, and Theresa May.[47] The logic of devolution, as well its substance, has also been embraced by the Conservatives. The English Question is a striking example of how this has been used to their potential advantage: its substance is an old problem for the UK constitution, which significantly predates the New Labour period. But by adopting the logic of the New Labour constitution, the Conservatives were able to recast it as part of the wider narrative of devolution, and take ownership of the problem – in that form – to develop a range of responses, most famously the (now abolished) internal parliamentary process of 'English Votes for English Laws'. The constitutional position of Northern Ireland, now precarious once more after Brexit, is also regularly recast as an issue which is essentially internal to the conceptual framework of devolution. The government of Boris Johnson used this conceptualisation in its attempts to justify a series of potential break points in the EU Withdrawal Agreement which would allow the Northern Ireland Assembly, via a formalised 'devolved consent' mechanism, to vote to overturn the continuing binding effects of many elements of EU law in that part of the UK.[48]

[45] See, eg Conservative Party Manifesto (2015) 60: 'We have stopped prisoners from having the vote, and have deported suspected terrorists such as Abu Qatada, despite all the problems created by Labour's human rights laws.'

[46] See, eg the Independent Commission on Freedom of Information commissioned to review FOI by David Cameron in 2016: https://www.gov.uk/government/publications/independent-commission-on-freedom-of-information-report; 'Supreme Court To Be Overhauled To Curtail Its Constitutional Powers' *Sunday Telegraph* (14 November 2020): https://www.telegraph.co.uk/politics/2020/11/14/britains-supreme-court-faces-overhaul-concerns-us-style-election/.

[47] Under Cameron: Scotland Act 2012; Scotland Act 2016. Under May: Wales Act 2017.

[48] Protocol on Ireland/Northern Ireland, Art 18; UK Government Unilateral Declaration on Consent https://assets.publishing.service.gov.uk/government/uploads/system/uploads/attachment_data/file/840232/Unilateral_Declaration_on_Consent.pdf.

This apparent stability may yet prove fragile. Only now, after the 2019 general election, is the New Labour constitution facing for the first time a period of sustained majority Conservative government. While delivering Brexit has to some extent served as a magnet attracting all constitutional effort, the process of exiting the EU has also created resentments which Boris Johnson's government may come to act on rather than nurse. Reform to judicial review and the role (perhaps even the existence) of the UK Supreme Court may be on the table after the intervention in *Miller (No 2)/Cherry*, which invalidated the Prime Minister's attempted five-week prorogation of Parliament.[49] And while the coronavirus pandemic dominated government attention during 2020 and into 2021, once normality resumes, the Conservatives will have potentially until 2024 to pursue long-standing objectives like reform of human rights law.

Yet, if specific parts of the New Labour programme may now be in jeopardy, some of the broader constitutional shifts which it triggered may still have longer-term impact.

Perhaps the most prominent consequence (or feature) of the programme as a whole is the increased juridification of UK constitutional politics.[50] Matters which were previously tackled through political methods are now often in the purview of the courts.[51] It remains controversial whether this is an inherent substantive feature of the New Labour programme or merely a side effect of the pursuit of other goals, the means to an end. On the one hand, it flows from the drive to decentralise which unites many of the reforms: that decentralising needs policing and the courts naturally fill that role. But while this might be convincing as an analysis of, say, the Supreme Court's jurisdiction over devolution questions, it is far more difficult to see juridification as merely a side effect of, say, making ECHR rights actionable in domestic law through the HRA.

It is likely that at least part of the explanation for the project's resilience is that – to the extent that it is seen as securing a separation or decentralisation of power – then pushback and reversal requires advocating the recentralisation of power in Westminster elites. This might be a hard sell.[52] Here, however, New Labour's juridification remains politically significant: it is more palatable to frame an argument (even in pursuit of identical aims) for the disempowerment of judges than for the empowerment of politicians. This is the primary terrain on which the continuing vulnerability of New Labour's project is likely to manifest itself in the short and medium term.

[49] See, eg The Independent Review of Administrative Law commissioned by the government (CP 407, March 2021), although the Judicial Review and Courts Bill stemming from this review seems unlikely to limit the power of the courts in any major way (and indeed may give the judges greater power in relation to the awarding of quashing remedies).

[50] See, eg D Oliver, *Constitutional Reform in the United Kingdom* (Oxford University Press, 2003).

[51] See in particular chs 3 (Tyrrell), 4 (Wheatle), 6 (McCorkindale), 10 (Masterman), 12 (van Ark) and 15 (Knox) in this volume.

[52] Worthy, ch 8 in this volume, makes a similar argument about freedom of information in particular: 'Dropping FOI would make [Labour] the party of conservatism and secrecy', p 169; see also: Tyrrell, ch 3 in this volume.

In contrast to the juridification of the New Labour reform programme, it might be thought striking that on the surface there was very little countervailing political constitutionalism in the programme. From this perspective, it is possible to critique the ubiquitous transfer of power to the courts across the New Labour programme as having the result that it did not so much put power in the hands of the many as transfer it to a different (and perhaps less accountable) few. Yet, equally, we should not too quickly overlook the submerged political constitutionalism within the New Labour constitution. There was institutional reform to the composition of the House of Lords and to the functioning of the House of Commons, in addition to the new institutions created for the devolved administrations. Regional Development Agencies were a further example of New Labour's experimentation with the institutional organisation of UK's political system.[53]

Key principles of political accountability were also pursued: the Freedom of Information Act 2000 combined legal processes for enforcing information rights with new institutions, most notably the Information Commissioner, to exercise a range of functions, including investigation of complaints and the promotion of more open government. Indeed, until the effective rewriting of the legislation by the UK Supreme Court in *Evans*,[54] the Freedom of Information Act also included an explicit ministerial override power preserving ultimate political discretion regarding disclosure of information. And this preservation of ministerial discretion fitted with a wider philosophy of designing new legal mechanisms with legally limited effects. Two further examples of this tendency are, first, the HRA, designed to give the courts a power to declare legislation incompatible with the ECHR, but not to invalidate it;[55] and second, the devolution Acts, which give primary legislative powers to Scotland, Northern Ireland and (eventually) Wales, but preserve the UK Parliament's continuing right to legislate in all areas,[56] which is instead constrained by constitutional convention.[57]

Nonetheless, it is significant that this is widely viewed as, at best, a secondary strand of the New Labour reform programme. While the political dimensions of the constitution have not been (and indeed cannot be) eliminated,[58] the effect of the New Labour project is often seen as having produced a shift to a 'more legal constitution'.[59] The expansion and increased visibility of constitutional law has

[53] Regional Development Agencies Act 1998; abolished by the Public Bodies Act 2011.

[54] [2015] UKSC 21.

[55] Human Rights Act 1998, s 4.

[56] Scotland Act 1998, s 28(7); Northern Ireland Act 1998, s 5(6); Government of Wales Act 2006, s 107(5).

[57] See A McHarg, 'Reforming the United Kingdom Constitution: Law, Convention, Soft Law' (2008) 71 *MLR* 853.

[58] KD Ewing, 'The Resilience of the Political Constitution' [2013] *German Law Journal* 2111.

[59] See, eg the narrative presented by Taylor, which analyses a range of different reactions to this shift: RB Taylor, 'The Contested Constitution: An Analysis of the Competing Models of British Constitutionalism' [2018] *PL* 500.

two important consequences for the New Labour legacy. First, New Labour's programme of modernisation and rationalisation can be seen as encouraging the false impression that the UK constitution has been depoliticised. Second, the increased prominence of constitutional law – both cumulatively across the sweep of the New Labour programme and in terms of the specific high-profile statutes which have reshaped our political framework – has contributed to a heightened awareness and changed understanding of the constitution.

The constitution that is now most firmly established in the public consciousness is one in the image crafted by New Labour. Labour's reconceptualisation of the constitution as something which is distinct and tangible, and can be deliberately and substantially altered, has influenced other key constitutional actors. As we have seen above, the main political parties have adopted New Labour's reforming preoccupation and distinctive method. We now routinely see – in most manifestos at most general elections – proactive promises for the piecemeal delivery of further constitutional reform. As Gee and Webber put it, 'a reforming spirit has taken hold' of public law, and it has taken hold on timescales which correspond to the creation of the New Labour constitution.[60] The technique promoted by New Labour might seem to be one which would favour non-programmatic change through an accumulation of opportunism, but that does not mean we should accept Baker's position that the constitution is now a policy area like all others. On the contrary, even if the constitution has now been placed more firmly in the political arena, Parliament still treats constitutional legislation differently to other kinds of legislation. After New Labour, constitutional change has gone from being 'what happens'[61] to something which political parties approach as a set piece event.

New Labour's explicit engagement with the constitution also arguably changed the approach of the judiciary. It seems hardly coincidental that the courts' modern 'rediscovery' of constitutional principles occurred in the immediate aftermath of the New Labour reform era. The invention of constitutional statutes as a specific (if questionably coherent) legal category in *Thoburn* took place in the shadow of New Labour's legislative programme, even if it was framed as a response to the challenge of trying to explain the domestic impact of EU law.[62] And the rebirth of common law constitutionalist speculation about limits on parliamentary sovereignty in the (in)famous obiter dicta of Lords Steyn, Hope and Baroness Hale in *Jackson* can equally be seen as a reaction to the New Labour constitution.[63] Lord Steyn described the HRA as creating 'a new legal order', while devolution had 'divided sovereignty'.[64]

[60] G Gee and G Webber, 'A Conservative Disposition and Constitutional Change' (2019) 39 *OJLS* 526, 529.

[61] JAG Griffith, 'The Political Constitution' (1979) 42 *MLR* 1, 19.

[62] [2002] EWHC 195 Admin.

[63] [2005] UKHL 56.

[64] ibid [102].

The need for judicial control over the substance of legislation was required to protect constitutional fundamentals from the dangers of a 'complaisant House of Commons', seemingly a reference to the substantial electoral majorities New Labour won in 1997, 2001 and 2005. Lord Hope and Baroness Hale also connected the enactment of the HRA with a shift in the status of the rule of law. For Lord Hope, 'The rule of law enforced by the courts is the ultimate controlling factor on which our constitution is based', and 'Step by step, gradually but surely', the principle of parliamentary sovereignty was 'being qualified'.[65] For Baroness Hale, the courts 'might even reject' a legislative attempt to subvert the rule of law.[66] In an era in which New Labour revived the constitution as a matter of public debate, the courts capitalised to supplement this new model with ideas of their own creation.

This characterisation of the constitution emerging from the New Labour era also establishes a default direction of travel for future reform. If the New Labour constitution was increasingly overt, ostensibly 'more legal' and with an expanded (and expanding) role for the judiciary, the natural next step would be to enact a codified constitution. This can be presented as representing the completion of New Labour's constitutional reform project. For example, as Bogdanor and Vogenauer argued of the New Labour era in the UK:

> It seems that we may have been undergoing a process, unique in the democratic world, with the exception of the Israeli experience, of transforming an uncodified constitution into a codified one, gradually and piecemeal without any sort of consensus on what the end result should be.[67]

While of course this did not transpire, and is a long way from the agenda of the current Johnson government, it is enough that the New Labour constitution can be interpreted as phase one of a longer codification project. For even if there are deviations along the way, the changes made by New Labour can be viewed as sitting on a continuum of constitutional reform, which culminates in the enactment of a codified text. And regardless of whether this is a realistic or desirable project for a future Labour government, it has the potential to attract the energy of constitutional reformers and to frame any subsequent debate about what would constitute 'radical' reform.[68]

These aspects of New Labour's constitutional legacy interact in interesting ways. New Labour's great achievements may be making us more aware of the constitution, and establishing a method for further constitutional change.

[65] ibid [107], [104].

[66] ibid [159].

[67] V Bogdanor and S Vogenauer, 'Enacting a British Constitution: Some Problems' [2008] *PL* 38, 38–39.

[68] See, eg the work of the House of Commons Political and Constitutional Reform Committee in its inquiry Mapping the Path to Codifying – or not Codifying – the UK's Constitution (2010–2015), which produced a final set of proposals for codification: *A New Magna Carta?* (HC 463, 10 July 2014).

But this method could equally be used for undoing the New Labour constitution. In other words, part of New Labour's legacy of making the constitution a target for planned and deliberate reform is popularising a method for its own reversal by competing political parties. Whether the substance of the New Labour constitution proves to be as resilient as the broader changes in constitutional culture which it has triggered therefore remains to be seen.

Paradoxically, however, if New Labour has reinvigorated our constitutional consciousness in the UK, it may also have embedded a way of thinking about reform which focuses on juridification and codification (or, conversely, resistance to juridification and codification). What is lost (or at least submerged) in this is a richer political debate about the values and effectiveness of the political constitution. The broader New Labour legacy may therefore be to have popularised a potentially vulnerable constitutional model, while constraining our ability to see the variability of constitutionalism and the range of political goals that constitutional reform may be used to pursue. While anything remains possible in theory, given the flexibility of the UK constitution and the role of parliamentary sovereignty within it, attack and defence of New Labour's model may dominate the future of constitutional reform.

Is it possible to break out of this self-reinforcing cycle of greater constitutional consciousness but narrower constitutional horizons? In the final section, we consider the potential future of Labour constitutionalism, which will inevitably be shaped by the legacy of New Labour.

IV. THE FUTURE OF LABOUR CONSTITUTIONALISM

To this point, we have argued that in terms of process, New Labour revived interest in proactive constitutional reform but pursued a generally unsystematic agenda. In terms of substance, we have argued that this programme of reform, while ambitious and far-reaching, lacked a core coherence and was questionably 'Labour' in its content. In terms of the legacy of New Labour's constitution, we have argued that while its specific constitutional model may be in some respects vulnerable, it has established a relatively resilient framework which is likely to define our growing constitutional consciousness for some time to come. Against this backdrop, we turn to consider the future of Labour constitutionalism.

Our analysis of New Labour's constitution generates a number of key questions about the future of constitutional reform. In particular, could a future Labour programme be more coherent, more systematic and more distinctively 'Labour' in its substance? This is not to try to establish an idealised set of reform measures, for that would be inherently contestable in both normative and political terms. Instead, the question for us is what a framework for Labour constitutionalism might now look like, after New Labour.

This is a challenge which flows from the achievements of New Labour, and the distinctive way it put constitutional reform firmly on the political agenda. But it is also a consequence of a deeper tension in left wing constitutional thought. The doubts about the overall coherence and underlying values of the New Labour reform package are not just a result of choices made by the Blair and Brown governments about how to approach constitutional reform and what to prioritise. Rather, the challenge is arguably a more fundamental one, which New Labour managed to avoid as a result of their pragmatic focus: how does any programme of formal constitutional reform align with the Labour Party's key goals of socio-economic redistribution?

The classic Labour response has been to adopt a constitutional philosophy rooted in instrumentalism. On this approach, if the goals of the Labour Party are to achieve profound social and economic change, challenging the unequal distribution of resources, constitutional reform is not an end in itself, but a means to achieve this external political objective. As such, the substance – and indeed the value – of constitutional reform is simply a function of whatever economic or social change it makes possible.[69] The further marginalisation of the House of Lords through the Parliament Act 1949 might be viewed as the archetype of this approach, insofar as it severely restricted the scope for Conservative opposition to Labour's legislative plans in the upper chamber. It is also in this vein that we can understand the anti-juridical focus of Labour's traditional constitutionalism – as Knox argues in his chapter, the central objective was opposing judicial constraints, rather than attempting to cultivate a set of constitutional values.[70]

However, the New Labour era has decisively – and perhaps permanently – changed the premises on which the classic brand of Labour constitutionalism was based. The instrumentalist approach which in effect amounted to 'laissez-faire' constitutionalism has been both displaced and rendered irretrievable. A strategy of socialist minimalism with the respect to the constitution – simply keeping it out of the way, to avoid obstruction of social and economic change – risks ceding the definition of the boundaries of the legal and political system to other actors.[71] In the age of greater constitutional consciousness created by New Labour, if the elected political institutions do not have an explicit theory of what the constitution should be, then other institutions will fill that void. In light of the expanding modern architecture of the common law constitution,[72] this will most likely be the judiciary, but there is no reason other

[69] See KD Ewing, 'Socialism and the Constitution' (2020) 73(1) *Current Legal Problems* 27.

[70] See Knox, ch 15 in this volume.

[71] See M Gordon, 'Parliamentary Sovereignty and Constitutional Futures' in A Bogg, J Rowbottom and AL Young (eds), *The Constitution of Social Democracy* (Hart Publishing, 2020).

[72] See, eg *HS2 Action Alliance v Secretary of State for Transport* [2014] UKSC 3; *Kennedy v Information Commissioner* [2014] UKSC 20; *Pham v Secretary of State for the Home Department* [2015] UKSC 19; *Miller* v *Secretary of State for Exiting the European Union* [2017] UKSC 5; *Miller v Prime Minister* [2019] UKSC 41.

aspiring 'guardians' of the constitution, such as the House of Lords, could not seek to reformulate their role, especially since the unfinished 1999 reforms have given the peers in the upper chamber a restored sense of their own legitimacy.[73] A different challenge is posed by the devolved administrations, but each has an explicit constitutional philosophy driving their ambitions: the notion of popular sovereignty underpins the SNP's campaign for Scottish independence;[74] the Welsh government seeks to enhance its influence through a formalisation of UK intergovernmental machinery;[75] and the position of Northern Ireland is preserved through constitutional accommodation of stark political differences and underpinned by guarantees that any future change in status will be based on popular consent.[76]

As a result, if the third-way constitutionalism of New Labour offered an ambitious but erratic programme of reform, and if there is no way back to the constitutional minimalism of Labour's classic socio-economic instrumentalism, then the question is what might come next. Labour has struggled with this question in the years since 2010. Even under the leadership of Jeremy Corbyn, who sought to mark a decisive break with the Blair and Brown years in many ways, the proposals developed for constitutional reform seemed to be a relatively timid continuation of New Labour's constitutional liberalism.[77] Indeed, the key constitutional idea in the 2019 manifesto was to hold a constitutional convention, which could have been a potentially radical device.[78] However, no details were provided as to the composition, mandate or priorities for such a convention, leaving the clear impression that this proposal was simply a placeholder in the absence of more developed plans. This may be a consequence of an insufficiently reflective approach to reform in the labour movement and on the political left more generally – little fresh attention has been given to overarching questions of constitutional structure or form, and there is no differentiation between reform which fits with a traditional Labour philosophy of the constitution and that which challenges it. Constitutional reform in general is seen as progressive, and therefore viewed as inevitably positive, in broad and sweeping terms.[79]

After New Labour, there is an opportunity and the space for something different. There continue to be major problems with the UK's legal and political system which are ripe to be addressed. New Labour started to deal with a

[73] See, eg M Russell, *The Contemporary House of Lords: Westminster Bicameralism Revived* (Oxford University Press, 2013).

[74] *Scotland's Right to Choose* (2019).

[75] *Reforming Our Union* (2019).

[76] Good Friday Agreement (1998); Northern Ireland Act 1998, s 1.

[77] See KD Ewing, 'Jeremy Corbyn and the Law of Social Democracy' (2017) 28 *King's Law Journal* 343.

[78] *It's Time for Real Change* (Labour Party, 2019) 81.

[79] eg SP Griffin, 'Re-making the British State: For the Many, Not the Few' (Red Party Collective, 2021) https://redpapercollective.net/?p=22. This report was commissioned by the Labour Party under the leadership of Jeremy Corbyn, and argues for 'progressive federalism' but within the structures of a broadly standard liberal codified constitution.

number of problematic anomalies (such as the House of Lords, both in terms of its hereditary composition and its continuing judicial role), and supplemented the core constitution with significant new institutions (especially in the devolution settlement) and potential mechanisms of accountability (the HRA and the Freedom of Information Act). Yet it is equally clear that to move beyond both socio-economic instrumentalism and New Labour's piecemeal liberalism, there is a need for a framework for Labour constitutionalism which can help to determine the priorities, processes and principles of a future reform programme.

In beginning to outline a potential framework for Labour constitutionalism here, we are not purporting to offer an ideal or definitive model. Instead, our aim is to map out the kind of approach to constitutional reform which could represent an advance on the classic minimalism of the past, in the context of the legacy of New Labour. This is not a precise prescription, but an argument for a reorientation which focuses us more directly on the values, means and aims of a future programme of left-wing constitutional reform.

First, in terms of 'values', we might expect a programme of Labour constitutionalism to prioritise democracy, equality and accountability. These are clearly abstract ideas which could entail a variety of different things in practice. But with respect to democracy, there are plenty of non-democratic or insufficiently democratic institutional arrangements in the UK which deserve attention – this might obviously include completing Lords reform and returning to electoral reform for the Commons (especially in an era when Labour must find a majority under the first-past-the-post voting system without being able to rely on a swathe of Scottish seats that are now held by the SNP[80]). Abolition of the monarchy is (perhaps unfortunately) not likely to be sufficiently popular, but reform of the powers wielded by or in the name of the Queen through full statutory codification of the royal prerogative could at least remove lingering concerns about potential royal involvement or influence, while providing an opportunity for parliamentary redefinition of the scope of this authority. The role of direct democratic mechanisms in the constitution – whether referendums or popular initiatives – could also be evaluated. With respect to equality, in an age of division and alienation, it would be important to try to give ordinary citizens greater influence over and access to power, while making sure those in power reflect the people they serve. This could involve institutionalisation of citizens' assemblies into decision-making processes and efforts to set binding targets for equal representation in key institutions like the senior judiciary and the civil service.[81] With respect to accountability, it would be important to consider both legal and political mechanisms. This would surely include restoring access to the justice

[80] See, eg J Curtice, 'Labour's Post-Brexit Electoral Strategy' (2021) 27 *IPPR Progressive Review* 414.

[81] See, eg the recommendations of a Labour review of judicial appointments under Ed Miliband: https://www.theguardian.com/law/2014/nov/06/judge-quota-system-recommended-to-labour-party.

system through proper funding of legal advice to ensure that the rights are real rather than hypothetical, and establishing more authoritative political processes for ensuring that standards of conduct in public life – including but not exclusively focused on government ministers – could be independently and robustly enforced.

Second, in terms of 'means', a future programme of Labour constitutionalism might be expected to focus on substantive institutional change rather than formal rationalisation of the status quo. The purpose of such a constitutional project would be to genuinely alter the existing legal and political system, instead of simply trying to clarify what is currently uncertain or reshuffle power among the existing branches of government. In addition to supporting the pursuit of the kinds of reform mentioned above, the key consequence of such an approach would be to recognise that codification of the constitution would be at best a distraction and at worst an exercise which simply served to entrench a flawed status quo. Of course, some Labour figures have treated the adoption of a codified constitution as a vehicle for implementing a body of radical changes through a single act.[82] Yet the procedural challenges of introducing a 'written' constitution, and the likely need for some degree of consensus to underpin a single, definitive constitutional text, would be major barriers to the successful completion of such a process. And even if achieved, no matter how carefully such a constitution was drafted, the consequences would inevitably be an expanded role for the judiciary and greater constraint of the scope for political action, which is inconsistent with the need for future Labour governments to have the capacity to deliver policies which bring about far-reaching social and economic change. This is not to say that any formalisation is undesirable, if it would enhance the effective operation of existing institutional relationships – the UK's intergovernmental decision-making architecture being an obvious target for statutory reinforcement. But this narrower type of formalisation should be aimed at facilitating substantive change, rather than the pursuit of formalising for its own sake.

Third, in terms of 'aims', we should expect Labour constitutionalism to be focused on redistributing political power as well as economic and social power. In part, this should prompt attempts to empower and engage citizens and representative collective organisations (most obviously trade unions),[83] rather than settling for clarifying the relationships between the traditional triumvirate of legislature, executive and judiciary. In addition to thinking about how institutions composed of ordinary citizens might be embedded in political decision-making (perhaps using random selection and policy focused citizens' juries), it would also be crucial to consider the current uneven distribution

[82] See, eg T Benn and A Hood, *Common Sense: A New Constitution for Britain* (Hutchinson, 1993).

[83] On which see Knox, ch 15 in this volume.

of power and resources between different levels of local and national government. This might involve better protection for the autonomy of the existing devolved institutions, enhanced powers and funding for local government, or a more consistent and more democratic approach to regional representation within England. It may also be important to think about where and how disempowerment may be required, including through reform to the funding of political parties, election campaigns and lobbying.[84] Future redistribution of political power ought to be more sceptical of juridification, more reflective about the characteristics of the judiciary, and more enthusiastic about other potential beneficiaries. In the event that the common law becomes a renewed barrier to social and economic change, it might become important to give consideration to substantive constraints on judicial authority,[85] or to institutional reconstitution of the process for appointing the judiciary.[86]

Even considered in outline only, this would be an immensely ambitious package of constitutional change, and there would no doubt be many obstacles to delivering it. There would also be significant challenges compared to 1997 in even conceiving of a UK-wide constitutional reform programme for Labour, given that the Labour Party in Scotland and in Wales is increasingly diverging from UK Labour, and the party does not contest elections in Northern Ireland. But this growing complexity reinforces the need for a clear central constitutional platform which has the potential to reinforce Labour priorities at the UK level, including by strengthening the position of the democratic devolved institutions.

Our crucial objective here is not to define a complete programme of future constitutional reform, but to give an indication of the kind of overarching package that left-wing values, means and aims might inspire. A clearer conception of the future of Labour constitutional reform requires definition of the idea of Labour constitutionalism. This must go beyond constitutional minimalism, because the New Labour constitution has become an explicit construct, rather than an implicit tool. And while any future reform project will be developed in the shadow of what was done by New Labour, it must also push beyond that, and be based on a more systematic framework which explains, organises and justifies the priorities which have been selected. Even if this repoliticisation of constitutionalism generates disagreement about the specific values, means and aims of constitutional reform which we have identified in this chapter, greater clarity and consistency about these three things would be essential to surpass the New Labour constitution.

[84] See, eg J Rowbottom, *Democracy Distorted: Wealth, Influence and Democratic Politics* (Cambridge University Press, 2010); KD Ewing, J Rowbottom, and JC Tham, *The Funding of Political Parties: Where Now?* (Routledge, 2012).

[85] See, eg clause 3 in the Dissolution and Calling of Parliaments Bill, designed to insulate an important part of the democratic political process from legal evaluation.

[86] See, eg Ewing, 'Socialism and the Constitution' (2020) 57.

V. CONCLUSION

The modern UK constitution has been, and for now remains, the New Labour constitution. In the 13 years between 1997 and 2010, successive New Labour governments changed our approach to constitutional reform, and the substance of many aspects of the constitution. Many components of this settlement have proven resilient, although the shift in attitude to constitutional reform heralded by New Labour means that a number of them remain vulnerable, as alternative governments continue to pursue their own proactive programmes of reform in response. So far, deviation from the New Labour settlement has been more discussed than actually implemented. However, in the aftermath of Brexit, some of the foundations of the New Labour constitution – devolution, the HRA, the Supreme Court and freedom of information – may be the subject of further radical change in the years ahead.

However, the legacy of the New Labour era as a defining period of UK constitutional change does not entirely depend on the longevity of its substantive foundations. New Labour opened up the UK constitution as a target for deliberate and extensive legal and political reform. In so doing, 'the constitution' has become a material part of our politics, rather than an unseen tool to be used to deliver (or fail to deliver) policy goals. The New Labour era has changed our consciousness of the constitution, and the practice of key constitutional actors such as political parties and the courts, while also providing a framework which will shape debates about future reform.

The extent to which this was a distinctively 'Labour' achievement remains open to question. The juridification at the heart of New Labour's project was a clear departure from past socialist constitutional instrumentalism, which sought to sideline rather than embrace the judiciary. The absence of a systematic approach to reform, or a clear principled rationale for the New Labour programme, also means that it can be seen as a liberal modernising project closely connected with the politics of the third way. If this third-way constitutionalism contributed (at least in part) to a depoliticisation of constitutional reform, then we might expect a reaction which repoliticises the constitution in the present and the future.

We have tried to sketch out what this legacy might mean for the definition of a future Labour programme of reform. The framework of values, means and aims of constitutional reform we have outlined is designed not to provide a prescriptive programme, but to show some of the key considerations in taking the next steps beyond the New Labour constitution. After the New Labour era, there can be no return to a more traditional Labour philosophy of constitutional change: instead, the future challenge is to develop a more substantive theory of Labour constitutionalism, and to use this to create a radical and coherent package of reforms to address the continuing deficiencies in the UK's legal and political system.

Index

www.ingramcontent.com/pod-product-compliance
Ingram Content Group UK Ltd.
Pitfield, Milton Keynes, MK11 3LW, UK
UKHW020906190926
475560UK00010B/305

9 781509 924646